Where Have All the Flowers Gone
A Singalong Memoir

Where Have all the Flowers Gone
A Singalong Memoir

by PETE SEEGER

1st Edition Edited by Peter Blood

Revised Edition, 2009
Edited by Michael Miller
& Sarah A. Elisabeth

A SingOut! Publication

IN ASSOCIATION WITH W. W. NORTON & COMPANY
NEW YORK • LONDON

Editors: **Peter Blood** (1st & 2nd ed.), **Michael Miller & Sarah A. Elisabeth** (2nd ed.)
Art Director: **Kristen P. Morgan** (1st ed.), **Ed Courrier** (2nd ed.)
Executive Director: **Mark D. Moss**
Proofreading: **Scott Atkinson, Mark D. Moss, Blaine Waide**
Text layout, music typesetting: **John Roberts**
Cover illustration: **Eric von Schmidt**
Interior line drawings: **Pete Seeger** (unless otherwise noted)
Bibliography, Discography, and Indexes: **Peter Blood**

ISBN: 978-0-393-33861-4

Library of Congress Cataloging-in-Publication Data

Seeger, Pete, 1919-
  Where have all the flowers gone : a singalong memoir / by Pete Seeger. — Rev. ed.
      p. cm.
  "A Sing Out! Publication."
  Includes bibliographical references and index.
  ISBN 978-0-393-33861-4 (pbk.)
  1. Seeger, Pete, 1919- 2. Folk singers—United States—Biography.
I. Title.
  ML420.S445A3 2009
  782.42162'130092—dc22
  [B]
                              2009035881

Sing Out! Publications / Bethlehem, PA
www.singout.org

Distributed by
W. W. Norton & Company
500 Fifth Avenue, New York, NY 10110
www.wwnorton.com

2 3 4 5 6 7 8 9 0

To Toshi

Acknowledgments

*"I have
drunk
from wells
I did not
dig,
been
warmed
by fires
I did
not build"* *

First, a big hooray for Ed Courrier, art director of *Sing Out!* magazine, who sees this revised edition to press and makes it all look pretty. Next, since technology may save the human race if it doesn't wipe us out first, let's thank printers, papermakers, truckers and salespersons that this book is now in your hands.

It was first put together in the early 1990s, reprinted five years later with only a few typos corrected. This edition has cut out some songs of only academic interest and cut down some music which few can read. And anyway, hardworking Jim Capaldi has put a lot of it on his Web site (<www.peteseeger.net>), which I never see but am told will be handy in years to come. This edition also adds a few words and melodies that have come to me in the last fifteen years – see the Postscript, p. 262.

But the writing and rewriting of the book could never have been done without the help of many others, principally Peter Blood, editor of the first edition in 1993. Then many others: Eric Nemeyer, Scott Atkinson and Mark Moss of *Sing Out!* And typists: Linda Beatty, Andra Sramek, Debbie Schwartz. Original page layouts by Kristen P. Morgan. Proofreader Jackie Alper.

For this revised 2009 edition, I had the indispensable help of Michael Miller, who found the time to come up to our mountainside to help hammer these pages into shape. This edition also has a better index and discography. Thanks, Peter Blood! Thanks, to the late Harold Leventhal, for urging me in 1988 to put out a book of "my own songs." And in the last two years, talented writer and musician Sarah Elisabeth worked with me to finish the job.

For music advice, as well as music computing, I was lucky to get the help of singer John Roberts through long years of rewriting. See John's picture on p. 241.

Thanks to songwriters and publishers who allowed me to reprint copyrighted songs. Thanks to unknown thousands of musicians and poets whose work I have tried to build on.

For over half a century I've worked with two music publishers, good friends of each other. Now younger generations are taking over the businesses. If anyone ever needs permission to record or reprint any of my songs, here's where to write:

TRO, 266 W. 37th St., New York, NY 10018; <info@songways.com>.

Sanga Music Group, c/o The Royalty Network, 224 W. 30th St., Suite 1007, New York, NY 10107; <www.roynet.com>.

Likewise, I hope anyone who translates any of my songs will send copies to them. Or if they want to find out what translations already exist, they can easily do it by e-mail to the publishers. See page 15 and the above computer links.

Thanks to artists and photographers, especially Len Munnik, Bülbül, Eunice Militante, Alexandro Stuart, Ashley James and Ezio Peterson.

Thanks to the archives of *The Peoples Weekly World* and The Fellowship of Reconciliation for help in locating pictures, also Gene Shay, Joe Hickerson, Harold Leventhal, Joy Graeme, Judy Bell, and Toshi Seeger for locating many things.

Thanks to friends on several continents who took the trouble to read earlier drafts and make suggestions:

Rick Abrams	Francisco da Costa	Reuben Musgrave	Steve Sedberry
Greg Artzner	Bill Goodman	Lillebjørn Nilsen	Rod Sinclair
Antoon Aukes	Joy Graeme	Shari Nilsen	Michael Skuppin
Judy Bell	Fred Hellerman	Ruth Pelham	Joe Stead
Bob Bossin	Greg Landau	Vladimir Pozner	Dario Toccaceli
Oscar Brand	Terry Leonino	Gretchen Reed	Kan Yazawa
Geoff Brown	Harold Leventhal	Larry Richmond	
Suman Chatterjee	Bob Lumer	Will Schmid	

I couldn't take everyone's advice, but I took a lot of it. The book is better, thanks to you all. But I send it to the printer now with misgivings. Every project I've ever worked on (songs, houses, boats, marriage, organizations) needed changes and amendments. What if a few months from now it's obvious I made a big mistake?

But right now I don't want to make the mistake of delaying longer. Or the mistake of staying silent. Ready or not, here 'tis.

* **Thanks,**
Harvard Magazine

Table of Contents

Introduction to the 2009 Edition 8

Chapter 1: *All Mixed Up* 11

Chapter 2: *If I Had a Hammer* – *Politics, Unions, 1939-1950* 17

Chapter 3: *Abiyoyo* – *Kids, Stories* 45

Chapter 4: *Kisses Sweeter than Wine* – *Love Songs and Some Music without Words* 63

Chapter 5: *Bells of Rhymney* – *New Tunes to Others' Words* 85

Chapter 6: *Guantanamera* – *Translations Pro and Con, New Words to Others' Tunes* 117

Chapter 7: *Waist Deep in the Big Muddy* – *The Vietnam War* 147

Chapter 8: *Turn, Turn, Turn* – *Songs from the Great Old Book* 171

Chapter 9: *Sailing Down My Golden River* – *Think Globally, Sing Locally* 201

Chapter 10: *Well May the World Go* 227

Extroduction 261

Postscript 262

Music Notation Is a Kind of Shorthand – *An Appendix* 284

    Tablature 288

    Dropped D Tuning 289

Bibliography 290

Discography 291

Index: *Songs, First Lines, Persons, Subjects, Illustrations* 300

Cover Illustration Key 313

Introduction to the 2009 Edition

I was about 11 years old when I read in a newspaper an interview with the English writer H.G. Wells. Says he, "For human society it's a race between education and oblivion." I think he was right, but how to get the education? They say the best teacher is experience. But it can be expensive. An old joke: Education is when you learn to read the fine print. Experience is what you get when you don't read the fine print.

In my own experience, many of the most important gains for the human race have been accompanied by songs. The early union movement. The civil rights movement of the 1950s and 1960s. Getting out of Vietnam. The women's movement of the 1970s and 1980s. Throughout history it has been true. In spite of "The Establishment."

Plato is supposed to have said, "It's very dangerous to allow the wrong kind of music in the Republic." And an Arab proverb says, "When the king puts the poet on his payroll, he cuts off the tongue of the poet." I think this whenever I get a job on TV.

For years I've been able to make a living mainly singing for kids in schools and colleges, while I've sung for free for picket lines or demonstrations or clean-the-river parties. Usually I've sung songs put together by other people, past or present, but increasingly I tried to put together words and melodies worth singing.

Of course, for every ten ideas I get, I manage to get one song worth singing once. And for every ten songs worth singing once I get one song worth trying to pass on to others. For many of the songs in this book I found new words to fit an old melody, or found a new melody for some old words. For some songs I was just a matchmaker, bringing an old melody together with someone else's words. Sometimes I made up new words and melody but used old chord patterns. So this is another "How to" book, like others I've written. Or perhaps largely a "How not to" book.

I advise you to skim through it first, ignoring whole sections if you like. But if you come to a melody or words you like, take the time to get acquainted. And keep in mind that what's a good song for one place and time is not right for another place and time. You're the one to decide.

Let's get the world singing. John Philip Sousa* asked in 1910, "What will happen to the American voice now that the phonograph has been invented?" To which I would add: How many mothers will sing lullabies to their children now that the TV has been invented?

*The bandleader, who wrote "The Stars and Stripes Forever," also sung as "Be Kind to Your Web-footed Friends"

This book was first published in 1993. For years I was depressed about the many mistakes in that edition. But as I got older and my brain, as well as my fingers, couldn't work so well, I had to admit that now, at age 90, I couldn't rewrite it the way I might wish. But with help I've managed to correct hundreds of small errors and a half-dozen big ones. There's also a new "Postscript" with a few songs put together in the last 15 years.

The biggest change in the new edition has been to accompany it with a CD containing 267 MP3 files. At the touch of a button you can hear, more or less, the beginning of every song. Even so, you may want to check out pp. 284-289. To be able to pick a tune off a page is a handy thing. If you want to listen to the whole song, check the discography that begins on p. 291. There are lots of song words and other information on Jim Capaldi's Web site: <www.peteseeger.net>.

Not in the book are hundreds of songs I attempted and then discarded. Nor hundreds of good songs I've sung which I've learned from other people. Songs like:

- "House of the Rising Sun," "Sweet Roseanne," "Long John," "Last Month of the Year" — three of the many, many songs taught me by Alan Lomax.
- "Deportee," "Union Maid," "Reuben James" — three of the many songs given us by Woody Guthrie.
- "Sylvie," "Midnight Special," "Goodnight Irene," "Poor Howard" — three of the many songs learned from Huddie Ledbetter, better known as Lead Belly.
- "Amazing Grace," "Follow the Drinking Gourd," learned from Lee Hays.
- "Go Down Old Hannah," which I learned when, with Toshi and John Lomax Jr., we recorded Andrew B. Crane at Retrieve State Farm, Texas, in 1950.
- "She'll Be Coming 'Round the Mountain, Toot Toot!" — learned from David Johnson and "Let's Go on a Bear Hunt" learned from Alvin Poussaint.
- "Cristo Ya Nacio," the great Christmas song by Carlos Mejia Godoy of Nicaragua. "De Colores," an old Spanish folk song now part of "Liberation theology" throughout Latin America.

As the world crisis deepens, many are pessimistic: the rich are still getting richer; billions of people are in terrible poverty; oceans are rising; precious resources are getting gobbled up; populations still exploding. When will the human race straighten up and fly right?

God only knows what the future will be. But I find myself getting a little more optimistic. Why? Because at last people worldwide are realizing that unless there is some sort of world peace, there'll be no world at all. We've had a lot of narrow escapes already. U.S. General Curtis LeMay tried his best to start WWIII. Eisenhower's people thwarted him in 1954. Kennedy stopped him in 1962. But Murphy's Law says that if an accident can happen, sooner or later it will. In the USSR in 1984, Col. Stanislav Petrov did not press a nuclear button when computers mistakenly lit up. Now there are chemical and biological weapons that could wipe us all off the face of the earth. Murphy's Law says that "If anything can go wrong, sooner or later, it will."

But yes, I feel, in an upside-down way, a little more optimistic. Why? Because everywhere in our country, and throughout the world, there are more and more good little things happening. Little organizations. Little political groups, little religious groups, little scientific groups, little cultural groups. Little groups, like the Hudson River Sloop Clearwater (see Chapter 9, pp. 201-225), which are partly scientific, partly political, partly cultural. And all these little organizations realize that they have to reach out and co-exist in some way.

Songs can help. That's why this book has been put together. Sad songs, funny songs, old songs, new songs. Sing them in any key convenient for you, high or low. I confess that for years I wrote songs down in tenors' keys. Now I find that many write in keys for altos, with ledger lines above instead of below the staff. I've tried hard to put down melodies, tempos, to get the songs written as accurately as possible.

Now, as I pencil these lines, close to age 90, in bed with my foot up in the air in a sling, I know I'm lucky to be alive. Lucky that Sing Out Corporation (the non-profit publisher of this book and *Sing Out!* magazine) is alive and kicking. And hoping that this book can be part of the worldwide effort to bring this world together, as we learn the art and science of human relationships (see FDR, p. 283).

Then, someday the great art and science of war and military weaponry will be something our greatgrand-children's children will read about, like cannibalism.

As Woody Guthrie said in his first (mimeographed) songbook: "This songbook got an ironclad copyright, number 586139772405318962 and anyone caught singing one of these songs will be ... a good friend of mine 'cause that's why I wrote it."

And why I wrote this for you.

old Pete

Lifelong teacher Peter Blood agreed back in 1990 to be the editor of this book. With his wife, Annie Patterson, he was also the editor of the million-seller songbook *Rise Up Singing*. Over three years we worked and sometimes wrestled together on a host of issues from the organization of the book to what to leave in and what to leave out and even the best titles for several songs. He also created the book's bibliography, discography and index and updated all three for this edition.

In 2004 I found my plans to put out an enlarged and revised edition of the book had bogged down. Fortunately, I met Michael Miller, news editor and writer with thirty years of experience, and also a guitar picker who had learned indirectly through me. He took on the job of preparing this edition for the press. The job was three-quarters finished when his full-time employer, the Reuters news agency, assigned him to Tokyo! Once again I bogged down.

In 2006 I was able to get editorial help from Sarah A. Elisabeth, a trained writer and musician, actress (and herbalist as well) to take over the job of seeing this book finally get to press, including preparing the recordings that accompany the book. The job was not made easier by my continually changing my mind, adding this, subtracting that.

Also, this book was finished thanks to the skilled work of musician David Bernz, who also recorded and gathered the audio files on the data CD. His father Harold helped me build my log cabin, and Dave grew up as a next-door neighbor to Lee Hays. Now he's put together a great quartet which puts on a traveling show: "The Work o' the Weavers."

Now I say to all four of you: BLESS YOU ALL!!!

Theme from "The Goofing-Off Suite"

A01

In my family, I got a favored role. If I was lying on the bed playing the banjo or guitar while there was lots of other work to be done, my family said, "Pop's practicing." So it was that, in 1956, Folkways issued an LP called *The Goofing-Off Suite*. This melody and its accompaniment are so simple that it seems presumptuous to call it a song. Yet it lingers in the memory. I start this book with it.

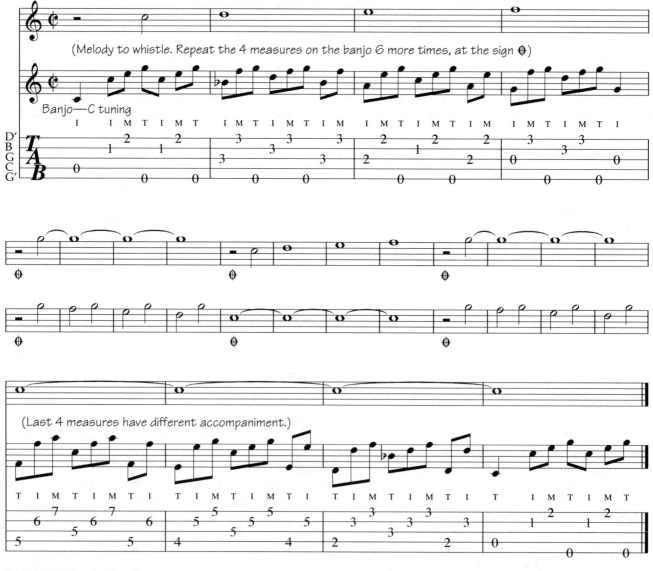

Originally titled "Opening Theme"
By Pete Seeger (1955)
© 1959 (renewed) by Sanga Music Inc.

I've never been satisfied with any words I put to this simple tune, but this 1995 attempt sticks with me:

Some day you and I ....
Will join earth and sky ....
If loved ones here still carry on ....
Then somehow we're not wholly gone ....

Chapter 1: *All Mixed Up*

This book tells the story of one person's attempts, over a long lifetime, to put together new songs. Sometimes changing old songs slightly, adding new words to old melodies, or new melodies to old words. Combining traditions from many lands. "Something old, something new, something borrowed and something blue," like the bride's wedding dress. If you're looking for songs, skip ahead. Ignore the personal chit-chat between the songs. But if you're curious about the life of this musician in 20th Century America, here goes.

I was born in 1919 in New York City. On both sides of my family, I come from people used to putting pen to paper. Letters, diaries, sermons, journalism, occasionally poems or books. Most of my forebears were old New England, but I had a German great-great-grandfather, a Dutch great-great-grandmother, an Irish great-grandmother, a French great-grandfather – doctors, small businessmen, teachers, male and female. Long live Romeo and Juliet.

My mother was a good violinist.[1] My father was head of the music department at the University of California, Berkeley. But, he got radicalized by some fellow professors. In 1918 he was making speeches against imperialist war and got fired. Back east he got the great idea to take the music of Bach and Beethoven out to the countryside. He built one of America's first automobile trailers in his parents' barn in upstate New York. It looked more like a covered wagon, with a canvas top and four solid rubber tires, pulled by a Model T Ford. It was to be kind of a one-family Chautauqua tour.

But, roads in 1921 were mostly unpaved. The Tin Lizzie pulled the trailer at an average speed of 20 to 25 miles an hour. My mother had to wash my diapers in an iron pot over an open fire. She finally said, "Charlie, this is not going to work." They returned to New York and got jobs teaching at the Institute of Musical Art (now Juilliard). It was a world of high ideals, long training, great discipline. But, early in life I learned that rules were made to be broken. Henry Cowell, the modern composer, was a family friend. When I was six, I remember him playing the piano with his fists.

My mother had hoped that one of her children would play the violin. She bought miniature fiddles

MY MOTHER, CONSTANCE

for my two older brothers. They rebelled. When I came along my father said, "Oh, let Peter enjoy himself." But she left musical instruments all around the house. I remember having fun at age four or five making a racket on Autoharp, pennywhistle, marimba, a pull-push accordion, a piano, a pump organ. All by ear.

At age eight I was given a ukulele. Started picking out chords, learning their names. At boarding school I learned popular tunes of the day. Silly words but clever rhymes. Plunk, plunk. My father was researching some of the few collections of folk music available in those days. I learned from him that there were often different versions of the same song. People changed words, melody, made up new verses. This was an important lesson: you can choose the version of the song you want to sing.

[1]Constance DeClyvver Edson (1886-1975) was ⅜ English descent, ¼ French, ¼ Irish, ⅛ Dutch. My father, Charles Louis Seeger (1886-1978), was ⅛ German and the rest English settlers in Massachusetts. So far as I know. One never knows what went on between the sheets. We're all distant cousins, all 7+ billion of us. A grandfather and a great-grandmother played piano, another could rattle the bones, another loved to sing and dance, into her 70s.

© The New York Times

THIS PHOTO FROM 1921 WAS TAKEN ON THE STREETS OF WASHINGTON, D.C. THAT'S ME HOLDING MY MOTHER'S HAND, AND MY BROTHERS CHARLES AND JOHN STANDING ON THE RUNNING BOARD OF THE MODEL T WITH MY FATHER.

Age 17, in Washington, D.C., I met the folk song collector Alan Lomax, who showed me thousands of songs I never knew my country had. Through Alan, I also met Lead Belly, Aunt Molly Jackson, Jim Garland and Sarah Ogan, all southern singers and makers of songs, who turned my teen-age mind around, politically as well as musically. I gave up ambitions to be a journalist.

And at age 20, I met Woody Guthrie, the most prolific songwriter of them all. He, too, used a standard technique of putting new words to old tunes (see p. 85). One can make up a new song by changing around an old song. Who cares if it is not completely original? The aim in this world is to do a good job, not to try and prove how original one can be. I had long been acquainted with the jazz technique of taking over a pop melody and changing it a bit. So when I heard Woody sing Jimmie Rodgers' yodeling blues "T for Texas," just having registered for the draft (October 1940) it inspired me to put together this "new" song:

C for Conscription

A02

Well it's C_____ for Con-
scription,_____ C for Cap-i-tol Hill._____
(yodel)
C for Conscription, C for Cap-i-tol Hill,_____
(falsetto) hey, hey, hey._____ And it's C for the
Congress that passed that goddam bill. Yodel-
lay-ee Yeow! hoo, hoo, hoo,_ hoo._____

Words by Pete Seeger (1940) Music adapted from a traditional blues
© 1993 by Stormking Music Inc.

Two years later I was willingly in uniform for three and a half years, helping to defeat the "Axis powers," Germany, Italy and Japan. Occasionally these days, I find myself singing peace songs and soldier songs side by side.

For 60 years I was able to make a living standing on a platform, with a microphone to help, and for an hour or two, exploring a wide range of old songs and new songs, sometimes circling around a subject. "The truth is a rabbit in a bramble patch. One can rarely put one's hand upon it. One can only circle around and point, saying 'It's somewhere in there.'" (CLS)[2]

I once sang more stories of long ago and far away. Within recent decades I've sung more stories of far away and not so much of long ago. And in recent times, one of the main purposes of my own singing is to persuade other people to sing together. It's fun. It is fun to learn how to harmonize. It is fun to learn how to play with the rhythm.

In a program of 20 or 30 songs or more, I'll usually find myself singing at least one or two that I've helped to put together. I've rarely tried to do a whole program out of just songs that I've helped compose. More often some other songwriter or some old song can carry the program forward better.

Nevertheless, in this particular volume I decided to explore my own experiments. Originally I wanted to call the book *The Songwriter As a Joiner.*

This was partly a pun, because through my life at various times I've joined others in some kind of an organization, consciously or unconsciously, reluctant or enthusiastic: family, school, choir, performing group, student union, Communist Party, U.S. Army, marriage, *Sing Out!* magazine, Sloop *Clearwater*, musicians union, Unitarian Universalist church, volunteer fire department, veterans' organization, etc.

But also I was thinking of Beethoven, who once said, "I am a joiner," referring to a cabinetmaker who joins and fits pieces of wood together.

Speaking of Beethoven, my father once spent an evening discussing with other musicologists how much of a Beethoven symphony was original Beethoven, and how much was inherited from tradition and from other composers. At first it seemed that it might be 50/50.

But as they talked, they recognized that Beethoven used major and minor scales invented centuries earlier and the symphonic form developed by Haydn and Mozart. He used musical instruments from many parts of the world. They concluded that about 10 percent of a Beethoven symphony could be said to be original Beethoven. About 90% was tradition, or inherited from other composers.

MY FATHER, CHARLES

Photo by Daniel Seeger

[2]Throughout this volume, I'll try to give credit where credit is due. All my life I've quoted my musicologist father (above), so if you see (CLS), you will know it refers to something he said or wrote.

WOODY GUTHRIE & LEAD BELLY
Photo by Stephen Deutch

USA National Archives

ALAN LOMAX IN 1941.

AUNT MOLLY JACKSON (above), HER YOUNG
HALF-SISTER SARAH OGAN (right) AND BROTHER
JIM GARLAND (far right). THEY ALL WROTE SONGS
DURING THE COAL MINERS' STRIKE, 1932. THEN
THEY CAME TO NYC.

JIM GARLAND WROTE
"THE DEATH OF
HARRY SIMMS" AND
"I DON'T WANT YOUR
MILLIONS MISTER."

Of course, Beethoven was able to put together great music no one else had been able to put together before or since. So, we don't belittle his genius any more than we belittle Shakespeare for getting plots for his plays from old sources.

At one time I had hoped to have drawings, sketches of the people who had helped put together these songs: a sketch of Lee Hays, who wrote the words of "If I Had a Hammer." A sketch of Peter, Paul & Mary, who changed my melody of that song (and only then did it "take off"). A sketch of some 19th Century Don Cossack soldiers singing an old Russian song, "Koloda Duda," whose verses inspired "Where Have All the Flowers Gone" (see pp.166-169). A picture of the women and men in a congregation in a black church in the 1870s or the 1880s for the song "Jacob's Ladder." A picture of some tough, frowning intellectual. Bearded, sandaled, with a traditional Hebrew robe. That would be Ecclesiastes (in Hebrew, Koheleth), who wrote most of the words of "Turn, Turn, Turn" around the year 252 B.C.E.

Such pictures were too ambitious an idea. Eric von Schmidt put most of 'em on the cover. Besides, how could we picture all the numberless, nameless people who invented the harmony, rhythms, scales which we use? Some of these folks might have lived within the last few hundred years, but most of them lived *ages* ago. Likewise, how would we picture the

people on several different continents who put together the instruments I play and the variety of languages I speak and write in? Impossible.

Thousands of years ago our ancestors, wherever they lived on this earth, knew only to trust their own tribe, and struggle to the death against any other tribe entering their hunting grounds. Then, clever folks learned how to plant seeds and use symbols, language, numbers. They learned how to use boats, horses, wheels. Now we've spread over all the earth, and find ourselves jammed in cities, competing for crumbs from the rich man's table.

My guess is that if there's a human race still here in a hundred years it will be because we've learned to value Survival over $uccess, to live and learn, to grin and bear it. We'll use our new tools of communication to reach out to our near or distant cousins, hard-working folks in every single corner of this globe. A worldwide search for justice.

In trying to find ways we can work together, we'll use sports, arts, humor of many kinds. I've tried to combine old, old songs with brand new ones. Tried singing in different languages. Tried working with little kids, and with old folks. And above all urged folks to participate, in politics, in music, in all life.

For example, on the next page you'll find a song put together in 1960. I swiped a Caribbean melody and a Caribbean beat. See what you can make of it.

All Mixed Up

A03...

1. You know, this language that we speak
   Is part <u>German</u>, part Latin, and part Greek,
   With some <u>Celtic</u> and Arabic and Scandinavian*
     all in the heap,
   — Well amended by the people in the street.
   <u>Choc</u>taw gave us the word "okay," **
   "Vam<u>oose</u>" is a word from Mexico way,
   And <u>all</u> of this is a hint, I suspect,
   — Of what comes next: I think that this

CHORUS (AFTER EACH VERSE EXCEPT VERSE 3):
I think that this whole world
Soon, mama, my whole wide world
Soon, mama, my whole world,
Soon gonna be get mixed up.
Soon, mama, my whole world
Soon, mama, my whole wide world ... **(etc.)**

2. I like <u>Polish</u> sausage, I like Spanish rice
   — Pizza pie is also nice
   <u>Corn</u> and beans from the Indians here
   <u>Washed</u> down by some German beer
   <u>Marco</u> Polo traveled by camel and pony
   — Brought to Italy the first macaroni
   And <u>you</u> and I, as well as we're able
   — Put it all on the table.
   I think that this *** **(chorus)**

3. There <u>were</u> no redheaded Irishmen
   Before the <u>Vikings</u> landed in Ireland.
   <u>How</u> many Romans had dark curly hair
   Bef<u>ore</u> they brought slaves from Africa?
   No <u>race</u> on earth is completely pure;
   Nor is <u>any</u> one's mind and that's for sure.
   The <u>winds</u> mix the dust of every land,
   And <u>so</u> will woman and man. *** **(no chorus)**

4. Oh, <u>this</u> doesn't mean we will all be the same.
   We'll have <u>different</u> faces and different names.
   <u>Long</u> live many different kinds of races
   And <u>difference</u> of opinion; that makes horse races.
   Just re<u>member</u> The Rule About Rules, brother:
   "What's <u>right</u> with one is wrong with another."
   <u>And</u> take a tip from La Belle France
   — "Vive la difference."
   I think that this **** **(chorus)**

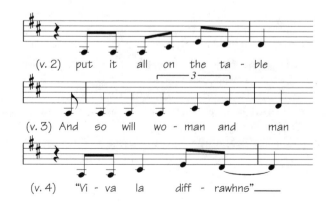

Words by Pete Seeger (1960), tune from Louise Bennett
© 1965 (renewed) by Stormking Music Inc.

* This irregularity, a 6/4 measure, is only in the first verse.
  The rest of the verses hold to ¢ time.
** Still argued about. See p. 88.
*** See variant melodies for the last line of verses 2, 3, 4.
**** Repeat chorus: "Soon Mama my whole world" after verse 4.

Although I put this song together in 1960, only within the last few years did I realize how effective it could be as an audience sing-a-long. After the first verse and first chorus I simply say the words clearly: "Soon, mama, my whole world. Soon, mama, my whole wide world. Soon, mama, my whole world. Soon gonna be get mixed up." Then, with arm gestures I encourage the crowd to sing, making sure they get the crisp effect of the ungrammatical syllables at the end.

After the second verse's chorus I'll call out "Sing it again!" right while the crowd is singing those last four syllables. Then to give a little relief from all this talking and teaching and singing, I'll whistle a verse, improvising as well as I can. It's a fun rhythm. Now, the third and fourth verses come, with not a second's pause before starting the fourth verse. And at the end it's good to even repeat the chorus a second or third time, ending abruptly. You'll be rewarded with a moment of dead silence after the word "up."

Guitarists may like to try playing this chorus. For an explanation of TAB (tablature), see pp. 288-289. If you can't read music, listen to track **A...3** on the CDs accompanying this book.

Where did I get this tune and rhythm from? In 1932, I first got bitten by the Caribbean music bug. "The Peanut Vendor" from Cuba was on all the airwaves. Seventy-odd years later I'm still captivated by the rhythms, the agile melodies. In 1991 I discovered that it was Louise Bennett, Jamaican folklorist, who in 1952 sang me a song which is almost identical to this melody: "Woman Tawry Lang."

Maybe Americans have found it easier to latch on to new traditions because we are uprooted people, and have few deep roots. But as compensation, we've often developed the ability to put down new roots very quickly.

If I'm encouraging people to mix things up, what happens to the International Copyright Law?

First, consider the overall picture:

"Judge the musicality of a nation not by the presence of virtuosos, but by the general level of the population which knows how to make music." (CLS) This quote from my father is roughly the equivalent of what was said by the African-American scholar, W.E.B. Du Bois, "I would judge the wealth of a nation not by the presence of millionaires but by the absence of poverty."

I think they're both right, yet our technology and our economic system seem to produce the present bad situation: millions of people feel themselves poor and powerless; millions feel that music is something to be made only by experts. I have spent a life "borrowing" others' ideas. I really can't object if people borrow some of mine. I am glad if someone can improve my song (see pp. 38, 173).

If people simply want to sing my songs their own way I usually say hooray. Bernice Reagon heard me sing "Oh, Had I a Golden Thread" with a fast banjo accompaniment. I heard her sing it unaccompanied with a changed melody (see p. 67).

When I complimented her on her new melody, she said in surprise, "I didn't know I had made up a new melody. I was just singing it more or less as I could remember you singing it."

Eva Cassidy changed it more. That's "the folk process" (CLS) – my father invented the phrase.

However, I'm grateful to the International Copyright Convention (CISAC) rules. There are commercial type folks who would love to make new words to these songs and use them as singing commercials, were they not stopped by the copyright law. Even so, some songs have been nearly massacred by pop translators. In Italy there was a hit record, "If I had a hammer, I'd hit you on the head/Because you stole my man, you so-and-so." And in France it took the young political radicals to force a publisher to withdraw a version of "Guantanamera," which had the usual "Baby, I love you" lyrics. They said to the publisher, "You cannot do that to José Marti's great international poetry."

Here's a possible compromise. I hope that people will try and improve my songs, but if they're going to go ahead and make recordings to sell, or make some other commercial use of one of my songs, I hope they'll write me and give me a chance to say yes or no. I've done this numerous times already with the children's story "Abiyoyo." Over the last 30 years, dozens of people have made slightly different versions of the story. But one person made such big changes, I suggested that she retitle it almost anything singable, perhaps, "Amiyaya," so that there wouldn't be any confusion in people's minds.

In general, one can say: go ahead, improvise. Add or subtract words, music – as long as you're doing it non-commercially. But if you're doing your changed version on network TV or recording it for sale – get permission first. Admittedly, in between is a large gray area – which keeps lawyers in business.

So sing, change. Add to. Subtract.

But beware multiplying. If you record and start making hundreds of copies, watch out. Write a letter first. Get permission.

Not all multiplying is commercial. If you want to teach any of the songs in this book to your family or friends or to a choir, I SAY MAKE PHOTOCOPIES. ENLARGE THE COPY OF THE SONG SO IT'S EASIER TO READ. RE-PASTE IT SO IT FITS THE PAGE BETTER. LONG LIVE COPYING MACHINES!

It all boils down to what I would most like to do as a musician. Put songs on people's lips instead of just in their ears.

While I don't wish my publishers ill – (I'm a lucky songwriter to be working with several honest and hard-working publishers) – my main hope in putting together this book is that I can encourage other singers and songwriters in various places and times to write songs. To adapt and rewrite other songs. To use songs not to get rich or famous, but to help this world survive. I wish I could live long enough to see more people singing again, either solo or in groups. For recreation. For reverence. For learning and laughter. For struggle. For hope, for understanding.

I know I won't live that long, but if this world survives, I believe that modern industrialized people will learn to sing again.

A word about the term "folk song." It was invented by European scholars in the mid-19th Century to mean the music of the peasant class, ancient and anonymous. In the U.S.A., it was used by people like John Lomax who collected songs of cowboys and lumberjacks, coal miners and prisoners on Southern chain gangs. Along came balladmaker Woody Guthrie and a string of people following him, and all of us get called "folk singers" if we are professionally singing for a living using an acoustic guitar.

By this new definition, a grandmother in a rocking chair singing a 400-year-old song to a baby in her lap is not a folk singer because she's not on a platform with a guitar in her hand and a microphone in front of her. She's just an old woman singing an old song.

By this definition a black man singing a 100-year-old traditional blues is not a folk singer if he's using an electric guitar to answer vocal phrases, as in so much African-American music. Likewise the call-and-response singing in tens of thousands of black churches, in the south and north, is not thought of as folk music. Nor the songs in hundreds of different languages still sung by people who have recently landed on these shores or whose ancestors lived here long before Columbus. Though their songs are ancient and anonymous. And they are folks, too.

No, according to the pop definition, to be a "folk singer" you have to be a (white) person on stage with an acoustic guitar singing a song in English. A song you just made up. That's a folk song.

A silly misuse of the term "folk music." I use the phrase as little as possible now. Call me a river singer.

If you can't read music, this volume alone will probably be of limited use. But if you have the CD that is made to accompany it, I hope you can get a good enough idea of the song to decide what you think of it, or what to tell someone else about it. The CD includes at least the first verse and chorus of every song. Look at the small black rectangle next to the title of every song. In it will be the capital letter (A, B or C) for the CD, and the number of the track – as you've seen earlier in this chapter. To get the CD, visit Sing Out! on the Web at <www.singout.org> or contact them at P.O. Box 5460, Bethlehem, PA 18015, or 1-888-SING-OUT.

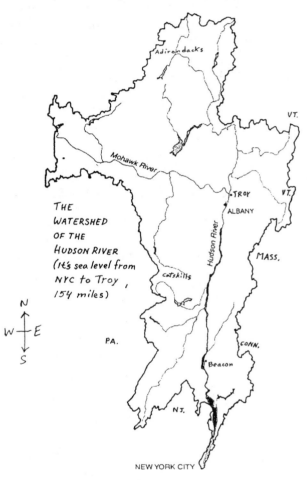

THE WATERSHED OF THE HUDSON RIVER (It's sea level from NYC to Troy, 154 miles)

For some songs, commercial recordings are still available – see the discography. In any case, remember that each singer has to make up her/his mind how to fit the words to the melody, and in what key to sing it. How fast or slow. With drums or a cappella.

Now that you've got the general idea of what this book is about, I'll ramble on. In general, my advice to a reader is to skim quickly through the book to see what its scope is, then turn back to some song you might like to get better acquainted with. Spend a little time with it.

Some chapters are roughly chronological. Other chapters group the songs in other ways. But, putting songs in categories is like trying to categorize people. One can be fooled.

Chapter 2: *If I Had a Hammer –*
Politics, Unions, 1939-1950

> "Mr. Vallee, if you can record a song which will make the American people forget the depression, I'll give you a medal."
>
> — *President Herbert Hoover, in 1930,*
> *to pop singer Rudy Vallee*

I dropped out of college in 1938, aged 19. Got too interested in politics. Let my marks slip. Lost my scholarship. Family finances too low.

I'd run school newspapers for six years in boarding schools, so I looked for a job as a reporter on a newspaper. No luck. Studied watercolor painting for a short while. Spent a summer bicycling, camping, painting watercolor pictures of farmers' houses in return for food.

In the winter of 1939, I was a member of a young artists group in New York City. It was a branch of the Young Communist League. We met weekly, 25 to 50 of us, in a loft near 14th Street. Come spring I helped build a set of puppets. Come summer I joined three others giving puppet shows in the small towns of upstate New York. In August 20,000 dairy farmers went on strike against Bordens and Sheffields, the big companies that dictated the price of milk. Farmers were getting 2¢ a quart ($1 for a 48-qt. can), when milk was selling for 10-12¢ a quart in stores.

Our puppet show went from strike meeting to strike meeting. I played the part of a cow who tells the farmer he's foolish not to get together with other farmers to demand a decent return for their labor. Between acts I sang "The Farmer Is the Man That Feeds Them All" in front of the stage. And it wasn't hard to change the 1920 cotton farmers' song, "Seven Cent Cotton and Forty Cent Meat, How in the World Can a Poor Man Eat," to sing it to dairy farmers as "One Dollar Milk and 40 Cent Meat." I also changed "Pretty Polly," a Kentucky ballad about seduction and murder, into "Mister Farmer," telling how they were seduced and cheated by the big-money boys.

Writing songs was a heady experience. The folk process was working for me. In the fall I was persuaded by Alan Lomax to quit looking for a job on a newspaper and come to Washington to help him go through stacks of old country music records looking for interesting songs. In the 1920s the country music business was just getting started. Singers came out of the hills singing old English ballads and hard times blues.

And in February 1940 Woody Guthrie hitched from California to the New York Island, and my life was never the same again.

Woody must have liked my banjo picking, because everything else about me must have seemed pretty strange to him. I didn't drink or smoke or chase girls. He said to someone, "That Seeger guy is the youngest man I ever knew."

Alan Lomax had spent five years putting together a great collection of protest songs collected from farmers, coal miners, textile workers, etc. – men and women mainly in the southern and western states. He gave us a big stack of disks and paper and said, "Why don't you two finish working all this into a book?" I transcribed tunes and words; Woody wrote introductions; friends in New York, Elizabeth Higgins and sculptor Harold Ambellan, let us camp in their studio. Elizabeth saved a carbon copy of the manuscript, *Hard Hitting Songs for Hard Hit People* (I suggested the name). Thanks to her saving a copy, it finally did get published in 1966; but in 1940, no luck. In June, Woody let me tag along with him to visit his wife Mary and their three little kids in the Texas panhandle. Along the way I found I could make up a new tune if someone else did the words.

Here's Woody's introduction to the song, "66 Highway Blues":

> You built that highway and they can put you in jail for thumbing a ride on it. You built that railroad and they boot you off, shake you down, search your pockets and make you spend your last red cent to buy a ticket into the next town. Then the watchmen and cops in the town shove you out. They get you all rounded up like a herd of sheep heading for the sledge hammer and drive you off down the road saying, "Take warning, boys, and don't ever show yourself in this town again..."

In McAlester, Okla., in Haileyville, Okla., in Amarillo, Texas, in Deming, Tucson, Phoenix, Yuma, Needles, Los Angeles, Frisco, Tracy, Bakersfield, almost everywhere you can think of, they chase you off the trains and make you hit the highway. Sometimes a hundred or more of you, sometimes fifty or sixty out of a single box car. That means walk. Root, hog, or die.

I had part of this tune in my head, but couldn't get no front end for it. Pete fixed that up. He furnished the engine, and me the cars, and then we loaded in the words and we whistled out of the yards from New York City to Oklahoma City, and when we got there we took down our banjo and git-fiddle and chugged her off just like you see here. She's a high roller, an easy rider, a flat wheel bouncer and a tight brake baby with a whiskey driver.

66 Highway Blues

A04

Words by Woody Guthrie   Music by Pete Seeger (1940)
© 1966 by Stormking Music Inc.

1. There is a highway from coast to the coast,
   New York to Los Angeles.
   I'm a-goin' down that road with troubles on my mind
   I got them 66 Highway blues.

2. Every old town that I ramble 'round,
   Down that lonesome road,
   The police in yo' town they shove me around,
   I got them 66 Highway blues.

3. Makes me no difference wherever I ramble,
   Lord, wherever I go,
   I don't wanna be pushed around by th' police in
     yo' town,
   I got them 66 Highway blues.

4. Been on this road for a mighty long time,
   Ten million men like me,
   You drive us from yo' town, we ramble around,
   And got them 66 Highway blues.

5. Sometimes I think I'll blow down a cop,
   Lord, you treat me so mean,
   I done lost my gal, I ain't got a dime,
   I got them 66 Highway blues.

6. Sometimes I think I'll get me a gun,
   Thirty eight or big forty fo',
   But a number for a name and a big 99,
   Is worse than 66 Highway blues.

7. I'm gonna start me a hungry man's union,
   Ain'ta gonna charge no dues,
   Gonna march down that road to the
     Wall Street walls
   A-singin' those 66 Highway blues.

Highlander Folk School

WOODY AND PETE AT THE HIGHLANDER FOLK SCHOOL, 1940

Later in 1940 I cut out on my own to continue my education, hitchhiking and riding freights. Woody taught me half a dozen well-known commercial country songs worth a quarter in any Western bar.

"Pete, you go into a bar with your banjo on your back and buy you a nickel beer. Sip it real slow. Sooner or later someone will say, 'Kid, can you play that thing?'

"Don't be too eager. Say, 'Maybe. A little.' Keep sipping your beer. Finally someone will say, 'Kid, I got a quarter for you if you'll pick us a tune.' *Now* you swing it around and play something."

I worked my way to Butte, Montana, back to Chicago, then down to Alabama, visiting the family of Joe Gelders, heroic left-wing professor. On October 16th, I registered for the draft in Scottsboro, Alabama. Visited the Harlan County, Kentucky, coal country. Visited a construction camp in north Florida, textile towns in North Carolina. Back north, decided to hitchhike through my old homeland of New England. It was December. Almost froze. Back to New York. Heard about a man named Lee Hays

AMERICAN YOUTH CONGRESS RALLY AT THE WHITE HOUSE, 1940

who was also trying to get a book of union songs published. It seemed sensible to get together. I knocked on his door, met his roommate, Mill Lampell, too. A few weeks later the three of us were singing for left-wing fundraising parties around the Five Boroughs. "The Subway Circuit," we called it. By February we knew we had to choose us a name. I read aloud to Lee from Woody's introductions to *Hard Hitting Songs* and came across the word "Almanac."

"Hold on," said Lee. "Back where I come from, a family had two books. The Bible, to help 'em to the next world. The Almanac, to help 'em through the present world. We've got an Almanac. Of course, most Congressmen can't read it."

We became the Almanac Singers.

These were the days of Hitler's aerial blitz of Britain, the Russian invasion of Finland. A large section of the American (and English and French) establishment was still hoping to sic Hitler on Russia,* the way they'd stopped "dangerous leftism" in Spain by helping General Franco. Harry Truman (then in Congress, ten years later U.S. president) is supposed to have said that we should try to get Hitler and Stalin fighting each other. Then they'd both be so weak they'd not cause any trouble for us. Conservative Republicans spoke at "America First" rallies.

A large section of the left remembered World War I and didn't want to help the old imperialist Churchill.

*In August '39, Stalin pulled the rug out from under them; he said in effect: "You want to sic him on me? I'll sic him on you." And signed a non-aggression pact with Germany.

Woody had written a song about the American Youth Congress going to Washington in February, 1940.

I persuaded Woody to put the song, "Why Do You Stand There in the Rain?" in the book *Hard Hitting Songs*. This is his introduction for it:

A few days before the 6,000 members of the American Youth Congress took their trip to Washington to ask the President for jobs and peace, I hoboed in from Galveston, Texas, up to the Missouri line. Rode to Pittsburgh, then hit the road a-walking again from Pittsburgh to New York in the snow.

It was snowing all of the way from Texas. Mississippi River was froze up worse than a Montana Well Digger; the Susquehannah River was six foot of solid ice, wind a-blowin' like a Republican promise, and colder'n a Wall Street kiss. But I got to town.

I hadn't been here but a couple or three days till I picked up a noise-paper and it said there that the 6,000 had been over to call on Roosevelt at his Whitehouse – and he called their trip and their stuff that they stood for 'twaddle.' It come up a big soaking rain and he made the kids a 30-minute speech in it.

Wrote up this little song about it. Ain't nothing fancy about it. Lots of better ones in this book made up by folks that was fightin' and dyin' on picket lines, but – anyhow, would like to dedicate this song to them 6,000 kids, and about 130 million others in this country that got soaked the same day.

Why Do You Stand There in the Rain?

A05

VERSE

E
1. It was rain-ing might-y hard on that

A
old Cap-i-tol yard, When the

B7
young folks gath-ered at the White House

E
gate, And the Pres-i-dent raised his

A
head and to the young folks said: Tell me

B7   E
why do you stand there in the rain?

A   E
Why do you stand there in the rain?

CHORUS

B7*   B7*
Why do you stand there in the rain?

E
These are strange car-ry-in's on, on the

A
White House Cap-i-tol lawn, Tell me

B7   E
why do you stand there in the rain?

*Woody hated to use fancy chords, and used B⁷ here, though most of us would use F#⁷ because of the A# in the melody in the next measure.

1. It was raining mighty hard in that old capitol yard,
   When the young folks gathered at the
       White House gate,
   And the president raised his head and to the
       young folk said:
   Tell me, why do you stand there in the rain?

CHORUS (AFTER EACH VERSE):
Why do you stand there in the rain?
Why do you stand there in the rain?
These are strange carryin's on
On the White House Capitol lawn,
Tell me, why do you stand there in the rain?

2. My dear children don't you know that unless by
       law you go,
   That your journey here must all be walked in vain.
   You gotta make your resolution by the
       U.S. Constitution,
   Then you won't get left a-standing in the rain.

3. Well they tell me they've got lands where they
       will not let you stand
   In the rain and ask for jobs upon the lawn,
   Thank God, in the U.S.A. you can stand there
       every day,
   But I would not guarantee they'd take you on.

4. Then, the President's voice did ring, why, this is
       the silliest thing
   I have heard in all my 58 years of life
   But it all just stands to reason as he passes
       another season
   He'll be smarter by the time he's 59.

5. Now, before this storm could break, Mr. John L.
       Lewis spake,
   And he said you asked for jobs; what did you get?
   A kid of seventeen, he was pretty smart, it seemed,
   Said we went there for a job, but we got wet.

6. Now, the guns in Europe roar as they have
       so oft before
   And the warlords play the same old game again,
   While they butcher and they kill, Uncle Sam
       foots the bill
   With his own dear children standing in the rain.

Words & music by Woody Guthrie (1940)
© 1966 Stormking Music Inc.

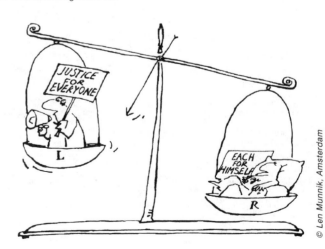

© Len Munnik, Amsterdam

Lee and Mill heard me sing a North Carolina ditty, "The Young Man Who Wouldn't Hoe Corn,"

I'll sing you a song and it's not very long
It's about a young man who wouldn't hoe corn
The reason why I cannot tell,
This young man was always well.

Soon Mill made up a new song using the same tune. Short. Effective. I still get requests for it. It should be sung deadpan, ending abruptly. Lee always marvelled at the dead silence that followed me singing it. The deadly serious ending, after the cheerful plunk, plunk of the banjo.

Strange Death of John Doe

Words by Lee Hays, Pete Seeger & Millard Lampell (1941)
Music: traditional ("The Young Man Who Wouldn't Hoe Corn")
© 1950 (renewed) by Stormking Music Inc.

1. I'll sing you a song and it's not very long.
   It's about a young man who never did wrong;
   Suddenly he died one day.
   The reason why, No one would say.

2. He was tall and long and his arms were strong,
   And this is the strange part of my song;
   He was always well from foot to head,
   And then one day they found him dead.

3. They found him dead so I've been told,
   His eyes were closed, his heart was cold;
   Only one clue to how he died —
   A bayonet sticking in his side.

LEE HAYS & PETE SEEGER, N.Y.C., 1946

Mill Lampell and Lee wrote a far nastier song. We Almanacs were singing it all over New York in 1940, for left-wing gatherings. This is just the chorus:

Ballad of October 16th

Words & music by Millard Lampell & Lee Hays (1940)
© 1993 by Stormking Music Inc.

Lee said to me, "If we made up some more peace songs, we'd have enough to get a record album out." He and I spent an evening at the home of Helen Simon, and in four short hours wrote four songs. Here's one (new melody, too):

Plow Under

Words & music by Lee Hays & Pete Seeger (1941)
© 1993 by Stormking Music Inc.

In 1990 Helen wrote me from Los Angeles: "You're really undertaking quite a task: tracing the transition from 'Plow Under' to 'Reuben James' etc. I remain convinced that it *was* a phony war at the outset. However we lefties weren't hep enough to note how it had changed when popular resistance to the German onslaught began in Yugoslavia ... before the invasion of the USSR."

In April a house party in Greenwich Village raised $300 (equivalent of $4,000 in 2005) and the album *Songs for John Doe* came out a month later on a little independent label. Josh White helped us make it. I'd knocked on his door, and on 24 hours' notice he contributed his voice and guitar. The album, three 78 rpm shellac discs, was distributed by left-wing bookstores across the country. The poet Archibald MacLeish, Librarian of Congress, played it for Roosevelt. "Can't we forbid this?" says the President (I later heard). "Not unless you want to ignore the First Amendment," says MacLeish.

"Well, only a few left-wingers will ever hear it," said Roosevelt, and he was right. But for history's sake, here are the words of another song. Tune of the fast banjo tune "Ida Red."

Franklin D... A09

Franklin D., listen to me
You ain't gonna send me 'cross the sea
   'Cross the sea, 'cross the sea
   You ain't gonna send me across the sea

Lafayette, we are here
We're gonna stay right over here
   Over here, over here
   We're gonna stay right over here

J.P. Morgan's big and plump
Eighty-four inches 'round the rump
   'Round the rump, 'round the rump
   Eighty-four inches 'round the rump

Marcantonio* is the best
But I wouldn't give a nickel for all the rest
   All the rest, all the rest.
   I wouldn't give a nickel for all the rest

(And there were more deathless verses)

Words by Millard Lampell, Lee Hays & Pete Seeger (1941)
Music: traditional banjo tune ("Ida Red")
© 1993 by Stormking Music Inc.

*U.S. Congressman from Manhattan, NYC.

Should I apologize for all this? I think so. How *should* Hitler have been stopped? Litvinov, the Soviet delegate to the League of Nations, in '36 proposed a worldwide quarantine on all aggressors (Japan in Manchuria, Italy in Ethiopia), but got no takers. For more on those times check out pacifist Dave Dellinger's book *From Yale to Jail*. At any rate, today I'll apologize for a number of things, such as thinking that Stalin was simply a "hard driver" and not a supremely cruel misleader. I guess anyone who calls himself or herself a Christian should be prepared to apologize for the Inquisition, the burning of heretics by Protestants, the slaughter of Jews and Muslims by Crusaders. White people in the U.S.A. could consider apologizing for stealing land from Native Americans and enslaving Africans. Europeans could apologize for worldwide conquests, Mongolians for Genghis Khan. And supporters of Roosevelt could apologize for his support of Somoza, of Southern white Democrats, of Franco's Spain, for putting Japanese-Americans in concentration camps. Who should my granddaughter Moraya apologize to? She's part African, part European, part Chinese, part Japanese, part Native American.

Let's look ahead.

The Almanacs one month later recorded six union songs and called the album *Talking Union*. In the mid-fifties Folkways Records reissued it; it's still available and used 50 years later. Here's the title song, a 1941 rap!

Talking Union

If you want high-er wag-es, let me tell you what to do: You got to talk to the work-ers in the shop with you;— You got to build you a un-ion, got to make it strong, But if you all stick to-geth-er, folks, 'twon't be long,— You get short-er hours,— Bet-ter work-ing con-di-tions. Va-ca-tions with pay,— Take your kids to the sea-shore.

Words by Millard Lampell, Lee Hays & Pete Seeger (1941)
Music: traditional ("talking blues")
© 1947 (renewed) by Stormking Music Inc.

If you want higher wages, let me tell you what to do;
You got to talk to the workers in the shop with you;
You got to build you a union, got to make it strong,
But if you all stick together, now, 'twont be long.
    You get shorter hours,
    Better working conditions.
    Vacations with pay,
    Take the kids to the seashore.

It ain't quite this simple, so I better explain
Just why you got to ride on the union train;
'Cause if you wait for the boss to raise your pay,
We'll all be waiting till Judgement Day;
    We'll all be buried – gone to Heaven –
    Saint Peter'll be the straw boss then.

Now, you know you're underpaid, but the boss says you ain't;
He speeds up the work till you're 'bout to faint,
You may be down and out, but you ain't beaten,
Pass out a leaflet and call a meetin' –
    Talk it over – speak your mind –
    Decide to do something about it.

'Course, the boss may persuade some poor damn fool
To go to your meeting and act like a stool;
But you can always tell a stool, though – that's a fact;
He's got a rotten streak a-running down his back;
    He doesn't have to stool – he makes a good living
    On what he takes out of blind men's cups.

You got a union now; you're sitting pretty;
Put some people on the steering committee.
The boss won't listen when just one squawks,
But he's got to listen when the union talks.
    He better –
    He'll be mighty lonely one of these days.

Suppose he's workin' you so hard it's just outrageous,
He's paying you all starvation wages;
You go to the boss, and the boss would yell,
"Before I raise your pay I'd see you all in Hell."
Well, he's puffing a big see-gar and feeling mighty slick,
He thinks he's got your union licked.
He looks out the window, and what does he see
But a thousand pickets, and they all agree
    He's a bastard – unfair – slave driver –
    Bet he beats his own wife.

Now, folks, you've come to the hardest time;
The boss will try to bust your picket line.
He'll call out the police, the National Guard;
They'll tell you it's a crime to have a union card.
They'll raid your meeting, hit you on the head.
Call every one of you a doggone Red –
    Unpatriotic – Moscow agents –
    Bomb throwers, even the kids.

But out in Detroit here's what they found,
And out in Frisco here's what they found,
And out in Pittsburgh here's what they found,
And down in Bethlehem here's what they found,
That if you don't let Red-baiting break you up,
If you don't let stool pigeons break you up,
If you don't let vigilantes break you up,
And if you don't let race hatred break you up –
    You'll win – What I mean –
    Take it easy – but take it.

A11

Mill and Lee wrote most of those verses, with a little help from me. Then for a couple weeks we were stymied. Sitting on the roof one spring day, I got inspired to write the last ten lines. (In the 1980s I cleaned up this song. I once assumed that I was singing to an all-male work force. As printed here, it's less sexist than it used to be.)

The "talking blues" verse form we'd learned from Woody. In some ways it's a better form than the sonnet. Vern Partlow wrote "Talking Atom." Woody's "Talking Dustbowl" is a classic. He learned the talking blues from records of Robert Land, who did the "original" verses on the Grand Ole Opry. And of course Land must have got the form from African-Americans. Who? Where? Here's some of Land's verses.

If you want to go to heaven let me tell you what to do.
Got to grease your feet in a little mutton stew.
Slide out of the devil's hand.
Ooze over to the promised land.
　　Take it easy —
　　Go greasy.

Ain't no use me working so hard.
I got a gal in the rich folks' yard.
They kill a chicken — she sends me the head.
Thinks I'm working, I'm a-laying up in bed.
　　Dreaming about her —
　　And three other women.

Down in the hen house on my knees,
I thought I heard a chicken sneeze.
It was only the rooster saying his prayers,
Giving out thanks to the hens upstairs.
　　Rooster preaching —
　　Hens a-singing —
　　Little young pullets doing the best they could.

Authors unknown
Traditional African-American

Whereas modern rap songs can have a whole electric band to accompany them, the "talking blues" of 60 years ago used just a guitar, or in my case a banjo. I'd use it to decorate the space between some of the verses.

HARRY BRIDGES

The 78 rpm album *Talking Union* turned out so well that a month later the Almanacs were asked by the Harry Bridges Defense Committee to compose a song and record it. (Harry Bridges was a West Coast union leader.) In a few hours Millard Lampell and Lee Hays, again with a little help from me, got the job done. Six weeks later, after Woody joined us, we sang it in the San Francisco longshoreman's union hall, with Bridges present, and got a standing ovation. The melody is what

I call "the great American folk tune," since it's been used for so many different songs. It was originally Irish.

The Ballad of Harry Bridges

VERSE

1. Let me tell you of a sail-or, Har-ry
2. There was only a comp'-ny un-ion, the

Bridg-es is his name, An hon-est un-ion
boss-es had their way. A work-er had to

lead-er who the boss-es tried to
stand in line for a lous-y dollar a

frame, He left home in Aus-tral-ia, to
day. When up spoke Har-ry Bridg-es: Us

sail the seas a - round, He sailed a-cross the
work-ers got to get wise. Our wives and kids will

o - cean to land in Fris-co town.
starve to death if we don't get or-gan - ized.

CHORUS

Oh, the F. B. I. is wor-ried, the boss-es they are

scared, They can't de-port six mil-lion men they

know._____ And we're not going to let them send

Har-ry o-ver the seas, We'll fight for Har-ry

Bridg-es and build the C. I. O._____

Words by Lee Hays, Millard Lampell & Pete Seeger (1941)
Music: traditional ("The Great American Folk Melody")
© 1966 by Stormking Music Inc.

1. Let me tell you of a sailor, Harry Bridges is his name,
An honest union leader who the bosses tried to frame,
He left home in Australia, to sail the seas around,
He sailed across the ocean to land in Frisco town.

2. There was only a company union, the bosses had
their way.
A worker had to stand in line for a lousy dollar a day.
When up spoke Harry Bridges, "Us workers got to
get wise.
Our wives and kids will starve to death if we don't
get organized."

CHORUS (AFTER MOST OR ALL VERSES):
Oh, the FBI is worried, the bosses they are scared
They can't deport six million men they know.
And we're not going to let them send Harry over the seas.
We'll fight for Harry Bridges and build the CIO.

3. They built a big bonfire by the Matson Line that night.
They threw their fink books in it and they said we're
going to fight.
You've got to pay a living wage or we're going to take
a walk.
They told it to the bosses but the bosses wouldn't talk.

4. They said there's only one way left to get that
contract signed.
And all around the waterfront they threw their
picket line.
They called it Bloody Thursday, the fifth day of July,
Four hundred men were wounded and two were left
to die.

5. Now that was seven years ago and in the time since then
Harry's organized thousands more and made them
union men.
"We must try to bribe him," the shipping bosses said,
"And if he won't accept the bribe, we'll say that he's
a red."

6. The bosses brought a trial to deport him over the seas,
But the judge said, "He's an honest man, I got to set
him free,"
Then they brought another trial to frame him if they can.
But right by Harry Bridges stands every working man.

Gary Huck, United Electrical Workers/ Huck-Conopacki

In June '41 Woody quit his job writing songs for the Bonneville Power Administration ("Roll On, Columbia" and lots more) and hitchhiked east. I think he arrived about a day or two after Hitler invaded the USSR. He walked in the door of the Almanac House (a small loft in the East Village) and with a wry grin said, "Well, I guess we won't be singing any more peace songs for a while."

I said, "You mean I have to support Churchill?"

"Why, Churchill said, 'All support to the gallant Soviet allies!'"

"Is this the same guy who said 20 years ago, 'We must strangle the Bolshevik infant in its cradle!'?"

"Yep. Churchill's changed. We got to."

Woody was right. Anti-communists ridiculed our "great flip flop." The Almanacs sang union songs to the West Coast and back, and then made up a string of win-the-war ballads which were recorded soon after Pearl Harbor. Woody's "Reuben James" was the most longlasting of these songs.

Reuben James
(The Sinking of the Reuben James)

1. Have you heard of a ship called the good Reuben James
   Manned by hard fighting men both of honor and fame.
   She flew the stars and stripes of the land of the free,
   But now she's in her grave at the bottom of the sea.

CHORUS (AFTER EACH VERSE):
Tell me what were their names?
Tell me what were their names?
Did you have a friend on the good Reuben James?
Tell me what were their names?
Tell me what were their names?
Did you have a friend on the good Reuben James?

2. It was there in the dark of that uncertain night,
   That we watched for the U-boat and waited for a fight;
   Then a whine and a rock and a great explosion roared,
   And they laid the Reuben James on the cold ocean floor.

3. One hundred men went down in that dark watery grave;
   When that good ship went down only forty-four were saved.
   'Twas the last day of October that we saved the forty-four
   From the cold icy waters off that cold Iceland shore.

4. Now tonight there are lights in our country so bright
   In the farms and in the cities they are telling of this fight,
   And now our mighty battleships will steam the bounding main,
   And remember the name of the good Reuben James.

(Guitarists: Capo up if you want, and use G chords. Tenors can ring out fine in the key of C.)

See p. 86 for details on how Woody put this song together. In the 1950s, Fred Hellerman of the Weavers made a good new verse.

5. Now many years have passed since those brave men
        are gone
    And those cold icy waters are still and they're calm.
    Now many years have passed but I still wonder why.
    The worst of men must fight and the best of men
        must die.

I stopped singing "Talking Union." Made up a new talking blues. Sang it through World War II, in Southern training camps and in the Western Pacific. The Communist Party had influence in the labor movement then, and pushed it to a no-strike pledge for the duration.

Dear Mr. President

Dear Mr. President, I set me down,
To send you greetings from my home town,
And send you best wishes from all the friends I know
In Texas, Alabama, Ohio,
    And affiliated places. Brooklyn – Mississippi –

I'm an ordinary guy, worked most of my life,
Sometime I'll settle down with my kids and wife,
And I like to see a movie or take a little drink.
I like being free to say what I think,
    Sort of runs in the family –
    My grandpa crossed the ocean for the same reason.

Now I hate Hitler and I can tell you why,
He's caused lots of good folks to suffer and die.
He's got a way of shoving folks around,
I figure it's about time we slapped him down,
    Give him a dose of his own medicine –
    Lead poisoning.

Now Mr. President, we haven't always agreed in the past,
    I know,
But that ain't at all important, now,
What is important is what we got to do,
We got to lick Mr. Hitler, and until we do,
    Other things can wait –
    In other words, first we got a skunk to skin.

War means overtime and higher prices,
But we're all willing to make sacrifices,
Hell, I'd even stop fighting with my mother-in-law,
'Cause we need her too, to win the war –
    Old battle axe.

Now as I think of our great land,
Of the cities and towns and farming land,
There's so many good people working every day,
I know it ain't perfect but it will be some day,
    Just give us a little time –

This is the reason that I want to fight,
Not because everything's perfect or everything's right.
    No. it's just the opposite – I'm fighting because
I want a better America with better laws,
And better homes and jobs and schools,
And no more Jim Crow and no more rules,
    Like you can't ride on this train 'cause you're a Negro –
    You can't live here 'cause you're a Jew –
    You can't work here 'cause you're a union man –

There's a line keeps running through my head,
I think it was something Joe Louis* once said,
    Said, "There's lots of things wrong –
    But Hitler won't help 'em."

Now Mr. President, you're commander-in-chief of our
    armed forces,
Ships and planes, and the tanks and horses.
I guess you know best just where I can fight,
All I want to be is situated right –
    To do the most damage.

I never was one to try and shirk,
And let the other fellow do all the work,
So when the time comes, I'll be on hand,
And make good use of these two hands.
    Quit playing this banjo around with the boys,
    And exchange it for something that makes more noise.
So Mr. President

We got this one big job to do,
That's lick Mr. Hitler and when we're through,
Let no one else ever take his place,
To trample down the human race.
    So what I want is you to give me a gun –
    So we can hurry up and get the job done.

Words by Pete Seeger (1942) Tune: traditional ("talking blues")
© 1993 by Stormking Music Inc.

*World heavyweight boxing champion; African-American.

And we Almanacs even (briefly) got on the air with new words to "Old Joe Clark," the old fiddle tune.

Round and Round Hitler's Grave

1. I wish I had a bushel,
    I wish I had a peck,
    I wish I had a rope to tie
    Around old Hitler's neck.

CHORUS (AFTER EACH VERSE):
Hey! Round and round Hitler's grave,
Round and round we go.
Gonna lay that poor boy down.
He won't get up no more.

2. Mussolini won't last long
    Tell you the reason why
    We're a-gonna salt his beef
    And hang it up to dry.

3. I'm a-going to Berlin
    To Mister Hitler's town
    I'm gonna take my forty-four
    And blow his playhouse down.

4. The German Army general staff
    I guess they missed connections.
    They went a hundred miles a day
    But in the wrong direction.

5. Hitler went to Russia
    In search of Russian oil,
    But the only oil he'll find there
    Is a pot in which he'll boil.

6. Mister Hitler's traveling mighty fast
    But he's on a single track,
    He started down that Moscow road
    But now he's coming back.

We got to sing the song January '42, on a nationwide CBS broadcast, "This Is War." But the next day a headline in a major New York newspaper said "Commie Singers Try To Infiltrate Radio," and that was the last job we got.

We did make a record album (three 78 RPM discs), but they didn't sell outside left circles. "Reuben James," "Dear Mr. President," "Belt Line Girl" (by Sis Cunningham, who had joined the Almanacs in October) and the song "Deliver the Goods," which Oscar Brand still sings, with more peaceful words.

Deliver the Goods

all work be-hind the sol-dier and the

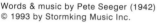

sail-or, We're work-ing in the cit-y and we're

work-ing in the woods, And we'll all work to-

geth-er to de-liv-er the goods.

Words & music by Pete Seeger (1942)
© 1993 by Stormking Music Inc.

CHORUS (AFTER EACH VERSE):
The butcher, the baker, the tinker and the tailor,
We'll all work behind the soldier and sailor,
We're working in the cities, we're working in the woods,
And we'll all work together to deliver the goods.

1. It's gonna take everybody to win this war,
    The butcher and the baker and the clerk in the store,
    The guys who sail the ships and the guys who run
      the trains,
    And the farmer raising wheat upon the
      Kansas plains.

2. I got a new job and I'm working overtime,
    Turning out tanks on the assembly line,
    Got to crank up the factories like the president said,
    Damn the torpedoes, full speed ahead.

3. I bet this tank will look mighty fine,
    Punching holes in Mr. Hitler's line,
    And if Adolf wakes up after the raid,
    He'll find every piece of shrapnel says "Union made."

4. From New York City to 'Frisco Bay,
    We're speeding up production every day,
    And every time a wheel goes 'round,
    It carries Mr. Hitler to the burying ground.

5. Now me and my boss we never did agree,
    If a thing helped him, then it didn't help me,
    But when a burglar tries to bust into your house,
    You stop fighting with the landlord and throw
      him out.

THE ALMANAC SINGERS, GREENWICH VILLAGE, JANUARY, 1942
WOODY GUTHRIE, MILLARD LAMPELL, BESS HAWES, PETE SEEGER, ARTHUR STERN, SIS CUNNINGHAM

Of course, life was not all "politics." Lots of dancing, eating, joking, loving. Once, after a session accompanying Woody playing some popular Mexican folk songs, I tried to play a blues. It came out sounding Mexican. It's not truly Mexican nor truly a blues. Woody tried making up words, but nothing stuck. It is still a tune wanting lyrics. I titled it "Mexican Blues." Leaf past these two pages if you are not a guitar picker.

Mexican Blues

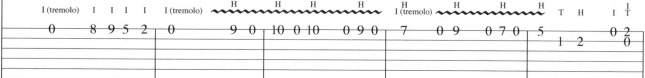

By Pete Seeger (1941)
© 1959 (renewed) by Sanga Music Inc.

* The tremolo here is played by the right index finger, bringing it back and forth lightly over the top strings. See p. 122.

PETE SEEGER & ELEANOR ROOSEVELT
AT A SERVICEMEN'S CLUB IN WASHINGTON, D.C., 1944

I was drafted in July '42. At Keesler Field, Mississippi, learning the hydraulic system of the B-24 bomber, I used "Lincoln and Liberty Too" (a 4/4 version of "Rosin the Beau") to make a song for my fellow mechanics.

Aircraft Mechanic Song

A17

You have heard of the pi-lot so dar-ing, As he grace-ful-ly floats through the air. But with-out all the boys in the hang-ar He would-n't be fly-ing up there.

The complete song is available from Stormking Music.

Words by Pete Seeger (1942)
Music: traditional ("Lincoln & Liberty Too")
© 1993 by Stormking Music Inc.

But, I'm ashamed to say, I wrote hardly any songs the next three years in service. Except a nasty ditty about officers, predicting their postwar demotion: "He'll go back to selling shoes." Unfair. To shoe salesmen.

I stayed at Keesler Field an extra six months because Military Intelligence got to investigating my left-wing opinions, first opening my mail, then later calling me in for questioning. But finally in '44 I was permitted to go overseas as a musician. I ended up in charge of hospital entertainment on the island of Saipan, north of Guam, Western Pacific. I was still a private. At staff headquarters we called ourselves the "Chairborne Infantry," "Paragraph Troops." I tell people I was in the U.S. Army for three and a half years in WWII — but what did I mainly do to beat the fascists? Play the banjo.

Before I went overseas though, the main event for me in 1943 was getting married to Toshi-Aline Ohta, age 21. We'd met a few years earlier in New York when square dancing, found we had much in common. Her parents were both extraordinary people. We were all very close. Her mother, descended from old Virginny (slave owners), had declared her independence from that racist part of her tradition, moved to Greenwich Village, married a Japanese who was in political exile, as militarists were taking over his homeland. He did important and dangerous work for the U.S. Army in WWII.

On my first furlough Toshi and I made it legal. Daily letters flew back and forth between us for three and a half years. Hooray for the U.S. Army postal system.

In '45 the war ended. Lee Hays and I corresponded. "After the war we'll need an organization for people like us to keep in touch — a newsletter. New songs. Old songs. Songs to support the United Nations, to support labor, to oppose racists." FDR was dead. We'd oppose the reactionaries who'd repeal the New Deal.

I was mustered out December '45. In January '46 the first copies of the *People's Songs* bulletin came off the mimeograph machine. I found myself trying to be an organizer as well as a singer.

But the Cold War took over. Most unions kicked out us "reds." We suffered one defeat after another. Nevertheless, some fine songs were first published by our 16-page *People's Songs*. In 1948 we printed a song, "We Will Overcome."

Where did the song come from? In 1909, the *United Mine Workers' Journal* printed a letter from a bi-racial local in Alabama that told how the state's "tyrant governor" shut down an organizing drive. "That was one of the saddest times that the miner ever experienced in the state of Alabama," the letter said. "The Empire local met every day, 351 strong – open air exercises, with prayer – and that good old song was sung at every meeting, 'We Will Overcome Some Day.' " *

*Thanks to Daniel Letwin of Pennsylvania State University, who found this reference while researching for his book *The Challenge of Interracial Unionism: Alabama Coal Miners, 1878-1921* (University of North Carolina Press, 1998).

It seems most likely that the song we know now started in the late 19th Century when some union member put union verses to an old spiritual. The latter is still sung.

I'll Be All Right

Traditional African-American gospel hymn

In January 1946, some 300 workers – black women, mostly – were on strike at the American Tobacco factory in Charleston, South Carolina. Some recall one of the strikers, Lucille Simmons, leading the song on the picket line very, very slowly, "long meter" style, so the harmony could develop, with high and low voices. "We . . . will . . . o . . . ver . . . co . . . me."

That year some of the strikers visited a small labor school in Tennessee, the Highlander Folk School. Zilphia Horton, the music director (her husband Myles started the school), had a good alto voice. "We Will Overcome" became her favorite song. In 1947 in New York she taught it to me, and the next year I printed it in our little newsletter *People's Songs* (circulation 2,000).

Sometime during the '50s "We Will Overcome" became "We Shall Overcome." No one is certain who changed "will" to "shall." It could have been me, but it might have been Septima Clarke, the director of education at Highlander. She always preferred "shall," since it opens up the voice and sings better.

Zilphia died in 1956. In August '57 Myles wrote me: "We're having a 25th anniversary of our school in August. Would you come down and help lead some singing?"

About 75 people were in the main room at Highlander, an old farmhouse. Present were two young black preachers who had just led a successful bus boycott in Montgomery, Alabama, the Rev. Martin Luther King and the Rev. Ralph Abernathy. Anne Braden drove King up to Kentucky the next day, and she remembers him in the back seat saying, "We Shall Overcome — that song really sticks with you, doesn't it?"

But the person who really got the civil rights movement singing it was Guy Carawan. His parents were from North Carolina, but he was raised in California, where he and his friend Frank Hamilton heard the song from Zilphia when she was in Los Angeles on a fundraising tour. Frank had been learning gospel music at a local black church where they used 12/8 time for some slow songs — that is, each of the four beats was divided into three short beats. This is an important rhythmic change. It's the same rhythm I use for the old spiritual "Jacob's Ladder" (see p. 198).

Guy started working at Highlander full-time as music director in 1959. In 1960 he organized a weekend workshop, "Singing in the Movement," for 70 young people from all over the South. The hit song of the weekend was "We Shall Overcome."

Six weeks later Guy was in Raleigh, North Carolina, for the founding convention of the Student Nonviolent Coordinating Committee, or SNCC (pronounced "snick"). Somebody hollered, "Guy! Teach us

'We Shall Overcome.'" They started the tradition of everyone crossing arms in front of them and grasping the hands of the persons at right and left, swaying slowly from side to side, shoulders touching, while singing.

A month later the song was all across the South. In '63 I recorded it at a Carnegie Hall concert. Within a few years it was known worldwide. In 1994, in a small village near Calcutta, India, a man and his daughter sang it to me in Bengali.

My manager and publisher, Harold Leventhal, said, "Pete, if you don't copyright this song, some Hollywood character will. He'll put new lyrics to it like, 'Baby, let's you and me overcome tonight.'" So Guy, Frank and I allowed our names to be used, but we set up the "We Shall Overcome Fund," chaired by Dr. Bernice Johnson Reagon. All royalties from any recording of the song go to this nonprofit fund, which distributes the funds "for black music in the South."

And here we are still making up new verses to it. After the 9/11 attacks people reached out to each other's hands and sang it. Here are just some of the many verses added. I made up verses 12 and 13.

TOP ROW:
ZILPHIA HORTON;
FRANK HAMILTON;
GUY CARAWAN;

BOTTOM ROW:
THE NASHVILLE QUARTET:
SAMUEL COLLIER,
JOSEPH CARTER, BERNARD LAFAYETTE, JAMES BEVEL; AND THE MONTGOMERY TRIO:
MINNIE HENDRICK, MARY ETHEL DOZIER, GLADYS BURNETTE CARTER

Photo by Robert Reiser

(LEFT) DR. BERNICE JOHNSON REAGON. (ABOVE) DR. MARTIN LUTHER KING JR., PETE SEEGER, CHARIS HORTON (ZILPHIA'S DAUGHTER), ROSA PARKS, REV. RALPH ABERNATHY, AT HIGHLANDER, 1957

We Shall Overcome `A19...`

Slow, steady beat ♩ = 80

1. We shall o-ver-come,___ We shall o-ver-come,___ We shall o-ver-come some day.___ Oh,___ deep in my heart, (I know that) I do be-lieve, (Ohh)___ We shall o-ver-come some day.___

(Basses) (Basses)

NOTE: I accompany it in 12/8 time:

Musical & lyrical adaptation by Zilphia Horton, Frank Hamilton, Guy Carawan & Pete Seeger. Inspired by African-American gospel singing, members of the Food & Tobacco Workers Union, Charleston, SC, and the southern Civil Rights Movement. TRO - © 1960 (renewed) & 1963 (renewed) Ludlow Music, Inc., New York, NY. All royalties derived from this composition are being contributed to the We Shall Overcome Fund and the Freedom Movement under the trusteeship of the writers.

We shall overcome, we shall overcome,
We shall overcome someday.
Deep in my heart, I do believe
We shall overcome someday.

1. We shall live in peace,
   We shall live in peace,
   We shall live in peace someday.
   Oh, deep in my heart, I do believe
   We shall overcome someday.

2. We shall all be free, (3x)
   Oh, deep in my heart, I do believe
   We shall overcome someday.

3. We are not afraid ... (TODAY!)   `A...19`
4. We shall be like "Him" ...
5. We shall stand together ... (NOW!)
6. We shall work together ... (NOW!)
7. The Lord will see us through ...
8. We shall end Jim Crow ...
9. The truth will set us free ...
10. Black and white together ... (NOW!)
11. Love will see us through ...
12. We'll walk hand in hand ...
13. The whole wide world around ...
14. We shall overcome ...

Now it's been sung around the world in Europe, Asia, Africa, Latin America (where it's sometimes sung "Todos venceremos").

SEPTIMA CLARKE & ROSA PARKS

Step By Step

Step by step the long-est march can be won, can be won. Man-y stones can form an arch, sin-gly none, sin-gly none. And by un-ion what we will can— be ac-com-plished still. Drops of wa-ter turn a mill, sin-gly none, sin-gly none.

Words: author unknown. From the preamble to the constitution of the American Mineworkers Association (1863)
Music arranged & adapted by Waldemar Hills & Pete Seeger (1948)
from the traditional Irish song "The Praties They Grow Small"
© 1991 by Sanga Music Inc.

Incidentally, not everyone has been enthusiastic about the song. Lillian Hellman once scornfully remarked to me, "Overcome *someday? Someday?*" But Bernice Reagon, when I told her this, replied, "If we said 'next week,' what would we sing the week after next?"

Toshi and I were on the Selma to Montgomery march in '65, and by then some had found a new way to add to the song. Right after it was sung, someone would shout "What do we want?" and everyone within earshot would shout "FREEDOM!" – "When do we want it?" – "NOW!" It was a good answer to Lillian Hellman's criticism.

★ ★ ★

Waldemar Hille, editing the *People's Songs* bulletin in 1948, once showed me two short verses he found when researching U.S. labor history.

> Step by step the longest march
> Can be won, can be won.
> Many stones can form an arch,
> Singly none, singly none,
> And by union, what we will
> Can be accomplished still
> Drops of water turn a mill
> Singly none, singly none.

It was printed in the preamble to the constitution of an 1860 Pennsylvania coal miners' union. Says Wally, "Good verse." Says I, "What's the tune?"

"I don't know," says Wally, "I suppose some old Irish tune might fit it. Like the song from the Irish famine of the 1840s. 'The Praties They Grow Small.'"

"Let's try it," says I. It fit. And has been sung to that melody ever since.

Years later Paloma Maruga and Sylvia Arana have carried the song a step further. Long live bilingualism!

> Paso a paso ellargo andar
> Terminará, terminará
> Piedra más piedra un areo son
> Solas no, solos no
> Uno más uno Todos unidos
> Todo podemos lograr
> Gotas de agua un molino son
> Solas no, solos no

Translated by Paloma Maruga & Sylvia Arana

People's Songs (Inc. non-profit), put on some inspiring hootenannies, had branches out west, helped put on a great singing presidential campaign for Henry Wallace (who lost disastrously). But we went broke in February '49. In December 1948 Lee Hays, Ronnie Gilbert, Fred Hellerman, and I had started a singing group. After four months we picked a name: the Weavers. One of our first records, in October, was a 78 rpm single, a ballad recounting the Ku Klux Klan-organized attack on an outdoor concert by Paul Robeson in Peekskill, New York, in September '49. I wanted our new group to sing there but was turned down. Instead I sang two or three songs as an opener. Our car had every window broken by stone throwers as police looked on.

Hold the Line

1. Let me tell you the story of a line that was held,
   And many brave men and women whose courage we
      know well,
   How we held the line at Peekskill on that long
      September day!
   We will hold the line forever till the people have
      their way.

CHORUS (AFTER EACH VERSE):
Hold the line!
Hold the line!
As we held the line at Peekskill
We will hold it everywhere.
Hold the line!
Hold the line!
We will hold the line forever
Till there's freedom ev'rywhere.

2. There was music, there was singing, people listened
      everywhere;
   The people they were smiling, so happy to be there—
   While on the road behind us, the fascists
      waited there,
   Their curses could not drown out the music in
      the air.

3. The grounds were all surrounded by a band of
      gallant men,
   Shoulder to shoulder, no fascist could get in,
   The music of the people was heard for miles around,
   Well guarded by the workers, their courage made us
      proud.

A21

4. When the music all was over, we started to go home,
   We did not know the trouble and the pain that was
      to come,
   We got into our buses and drove out through
      the gate,
   And saw the gangster police, their faces filled
      with hate.

5. Then without any warning the rocks began to come,
   The cops and troopers laughed to see the damage
      that was done,
   They ran us through a gauntlet, to their
      everlasting shame,
   And the cowards there attacked us, damnation to
      their name.

6. All across the nation the people heard the tale,
   And marvelled at the concert, and knew we
      had not failed,
   We shed our blood at Peekskill, and suffered many
      a pain,
   But we stood up to the fascists and they'll live to
      know the shame!

Words by Lee Hays Music by Pete Seeger (1949)
© 1959 (renewed) by Sanga Music Inc.

★ ★ ★

In the Weavers, as in the Almanacs, my main contribution was as an accompanist, a singer, an arranger. A finder of songs more than a writer of songs. But Lee kept writing lyrics and asking me to try and find melodies for them.

THE WEAVERS, 1949

Tomorrow is a Highway

A22

Moderately

To - mor-row__ is a__ high-way__ broad and
fair_____ And we____ are the
man-y who'll trav-el____ there._____ To -
mor-row__ is a__ high-way__ broad and
fair, And we__ are the work-ers who'll build it__
there; And we____ will build it there.

Words by Lee Hays   Music by Pete Seeger (1949)
TRO - © 1950 (renewed) Folkways Music Publishers, Inc., New York, NY.
Used by permission.

1. Tomorrow is a highway broad and fair,
   And we are the many who'll travel there.
   Tomorrow is a highway broad and fair,
   And we are the workers who'll build it there;
   And we will build it there.

2. Come, let us build a way for all mankind.
   A way to leave this evil year behind,
   To travel onward to a better year
   Where love is, and there will be no fear,
   Where love is, and no fear.

3. Now is the shadowed year when evil men,
   When men of evil thunder war again.
   Shall tyrants once again be free to tread,
   Above our most brave and honored dead?
   Our brave and honored dead.

4. O, comrades, come and travel on with me,
   We'll go to our new year of liberty.
   Come, walk upright, along the people's way,
   From darkness, unto the people's day.
   From dark, to sunlit day.

5. Tomorrow is a highway broad and fair
   And hate and greed shall never travel there
   But only they who've learned the peaceful way
   Of brotherhood, to greet the coming day.
   We hail the coming day.

THIRTY YEARS LATER:

Drawing by Mike Sherker

THE WEAVERS, 1980

★ ★ ★

In January '49, we wrought better than we thought. "The Hammer Song" was printed on the cover of the very first issue of *Sing Out!* magazine, the successor to *People's Songs.* Turn the page.

"If I Had a Hammer"
Words by Lee Hays   Music by Pete Seeger (1949)
TRO - © 1958 (renewed) & 1962 (renewed)
Ludlow Music, Inc., New York, NY.

Us Weavers recorded it this way in the fall of '49, for a microscopic label, Charter Records. Lee Hays used to say, "It was a collector's item — nobody but collectors ever bought it." A year later, when the Weavers were temporarily "on the charts," our then-manager Pete Kameron wouldn't let us perform it. ("I'm trying to cool down the blacklisters; that song would encourage them.") But nine years later three young friends formed a trio, Peter, Paul and Mary, and had a surprise hit with the song. Their re-arrangement, which swept the world, is on pp. 40–41. And others, like Sam Cooke, have made inspiring recordings of the song. (See p. 41.)

PETER YARROW, NOEL PAUL STOOKEY, MARY TRAVERS

It was a young radical activist, Libby Gisser, in 1952, who insisted on singing "my brothers and my sisters" instead of "all of my brothers." Lee resisted the change at first. "It doesn't ripple off the tongue as well. How about 'all of my siblings?'" He finally gave in. It was sung in Europe and elsewhere in the '50s, sometimes with variant melodies, sometimes with added verses, "If I Had a Drum; If I Had a Trumpet," etc.

Victor Jara, the great protest singer of Chile, made up a version in Spanish.

1. Si tuviera un martillo
    Golpearía en la mañana
    Golpearía en la noche
    Por todo el país.
CHORUS (AFTER EACH VERSE):
Alerta_el pelligro
Debemos unirnos
Para defender la paz.

2. Si tuviera una campana
    Tocaría en la mañana
    Tocaría en la noche
    Por todo el país.

3. Si tuviera una canción
    Cantaría en la mañana
    Cantaría en la noche
    Por todo el país.

4. Ahora tengo un martillo
    Y tengo una campana
    Y tengo una canción que cantar
    Por todo el país.
    Martillo de justicia
    Campana de libertad
    Y una canción de paz.

El Martillito

`A24`

VERSE
1. Si tu-vie-ra_un mar-ti-llo

Gol-pea-rí-a_en la ma-ña-na

Gol-pea-rí-a_en la no-che

CHORUS
Por to-do_el pa-ís. A-ler-ta_al pel-

i-gro De-be-mos u-nir-nos

Pa-ra de-fen-der La paz.

"WE GAVE HIM A HAMMER. HE HAMMERS IN THE MORNING, HE HAMMERS IN THE EVENING ALL OVER THIS LAND!"

For the last 35 years I've sung a composite version (see p. 42). Nowadays, I'm mostly a songleader shouting the words, with the crowd doing the singing. But I found chords and a bass line I really like; I play it in Dropped D tuning, but my 12-string guitar is tuned low, so it comes out sounding in C.

When I get a crowd singing, I sometimes joke that one can sing the melody as I wrote it, or as various others have changed it, all at the same time. Somehow they all harmonize with each other.

There's a good moral here, for the world.

If I Had a Hammer
(as sung by Peter, Paul and Mary)

A25

Words by Lee Hays Music by Pete Seeger (1949)
TRO - © 1958 (renewed) & 1962 (renewed) Ludlow Music, Inc., New York, NY.

1. If I had a hammer,
    I'd hammer in the mornin',
    I'd hammer in the evenin',
      All over this land.
    I'd hammer out danger,
    I'd hammer out a warning,
    I'd hammer out love between
    My brothers and my sisters,
      All over this land.

2. If I had a bell,
    I'd ring it in the mornin',
    I'd ring it in the evenin',
      All over this land.
    I'd ring out danger,
    I'd ring out a warning,
    I'd ring out love between
    My brothers and my sisters,
      All over this land.

3. If I
    had a
    song…
    (etc.)

4. Well, I got a hammer,
    And I got a bell
    And I got a song—to—sing
      All over this land
    It's the hammer of justice,
    It's the bell of freedom,
    It's the song about love between
    My brothers and my sisters,
      All over this land.

On the record *Sam Cooke at the Copa* you can hear his high F♯ note. He sang in E, not A.

Sam Cooke at the Copa (1964) © 2003 ABKCO Music & Records,Inc.,1700 Broadway, New York, NY.

If I Had a Hammer
(A Songleader's Version)

A27

Words by Lee Hays   Music by Pete Seeger (1949 & on)
TRO - © 1958 (renewed), 1962 (renewed) & 1993 Ludlow Music, Inc., New York, NY.

Life changes a little at a time. Only two words changed in the next lyric.

Back in the late '30s a wonderful Communist humorist and writer named Mike Quin wrote three short verses titled "How Much for Spain?" as a collection speech for medical aid to Spain. The elected government there had been attacked by General Francisco Franco and was desperately trying to survive. Corporations in the USA were trying to help Franco. After all, he was fighting Communism, wasn't he? I've found that Mike's poem is still one of the best collection speeches anyone could make. I've only changed two words from Mike's original.

MIKE QUIN WITH WIFE MARY & SON COLIN

The Long Collection Speech
(original title, "How Much for Spain?")

The long collection speech is done
And now the felt hat goes
From hand to hand its hopeful way
Along the restless rows.

In purse and pocket finger feel
And count the coins by touch.
Minds ponder what they can afford
And hesitate: How much?

In that brief jostled moment
When the battered hat arrives
Try, friends,* to remember that
Some folks* put in their lives.

By Mike Quin (1937), adapted by Pete Seeger (1947)
© Mike Quin. Used by permission.

*Originally "brothers" and "men."

In November of '49 the Weavers made up some campaign songs attempting to elect Vito Marcantonio mayor of New York City and re-elect African-American Communist Ben Davis to the City Council. Both lost, but for years Lee Hays and I used to laugh to think that one of the most rhythmically successful verses we ever put together was

sung only once. At a Madison Square Garden rally. The basic tune was "New York City," a blues stomp Lead Belly had put together in 1935. It had been a favorite of the Almanac Singers. We liked to improvise verses.

Here We Are in Madison Square

Here we are__ in Mad-i-son Square,
Da - vis for Coun - cil, Marc - an -
to - ni - o for May-or, in New York Cit - y,
(New York Cit - y), in New York Cit - y,
(New York Cit - y), In New York Cit - y, you
real - ly got to know your line.__

Words by Ronnie Gilbert, Lee Hays, Fred Hellerman & Pete Seeger (1949)
Music adapted from the song "New York City" by Huddie Ledbetter
TRO - © 1992 & 1993 Folkways Music Publishers, Inc., New York, NY.
Used by permission.

In December '49 four of us, the Weavers, were about to go our separate ways. We wanted to sing for working folks, for the left-wing types. But McCarthyism was coming in. We had no offers of jobs from unions.

As a last resort (fate worse than death) we took a job in a tiny Greenwich Village nightclub, the Village Vanguard. Microscopic pay. There, lightning struck, as it occasionally does in the music business. The well-known band leader, Gordon Jenkins, fell in love with our work, got us a Decca recording contract.

For me the Village Vanguard was an education. Into it came a wider range of folks than I'd expected, including Hillel and Aviva, two young Israeli musicians fascinated by us mixed-up Americans singing songs in Yiddish and Hebrew ("Tzena Tzena").

Hillel (later his name was Ilka Raveh) taught me to make and play the open-ended reed flute called "chalil" in Hebrew and "nai" in Arabic. He learned from Arab shepherds how to play it, and he got an incredible soft tone from it. A Bedouin friend listening to him once, said "That's not music. That's talking to God."

For Ilka and his Arab friend I made up a melody I put at the end of this book, p. 260. I call it "How Soon?" As I play it, I wonder how long before peace comes to that region. And to our world. As it must, sooner or later. With or without people.

Chapter 3: *Abiyoyo – Kids, Stories*

In 1939 I was still looking for a job on a newspaper and not getting one. My father's younger sister Elizabeth, a schoolteacher, phoned me. "Peter, could you come sing some of your songs for my class? I can get five dollars for you." It seemed like stealing. Many jobs then only paid 25 or 50 cents an hour. But soon I was singing for some other schools, and then in summer camps for children – "Skip to My Lou," "John Henry." Kids! They make life worth living.

After *People's Songs* folded in February '49, Lee Hays and I (and Fred Hellerman and Ronnie Gilbert) tried to start a new quartet, the Weavers. But jobs were few and far between. In June '49 by a great stroke of luck, Toshi and I were fortunate to find a few acres for sale on a wooded mountainside overlooking the Hudson, 60 miles north of the Big City. Only $100 an acre!

For two summers Toshi cooked over an open fire, helped me build a log cabin. The third summer we moved in permanently. For two winters I toured with the Weavers, then as the blacklist put us out of business, we took a sabbatical in '52. Lee said it turned into a Mondical and a Tuesdical. I started teaching in a small "alternative" school in New York City one day a week, and on the weekend picked up a few dollars singing somewhere.

The so-called "folk music scene" hardly existed at the time, but it was building. *People's Songs* had folded in '49 but with an "Interim Newsletter" I kept a few of us in touch. *Sing Out!* magazine started up in 1950.

Moses Asch had me record one album after another for his tiny company, Folkways. It encouraged me to explore a variety of old traditions and to experiment with songwriting as well.

Our kids were little then. I'm certainly not the first versifier inspired by small children. Most of the songs or stories in this chapter would not have been put together without the existence of three small people now all grown up, with kids of their own. Danny, Mika, Tinya. They taught me so much. I'm still learning from their mother.

The Clearwater[1] knows Toshi Seeger as an ace organizer. After having to organize me for 66 years, no wonder. But she's the wisest person I know: Perspicacious. Peppery. A Paradigm with Pots and Pans.[2] Calling Toshi a good cook is like calling Louis Armstrong a good trumpet player. And we are both proud to be parents of those three.

Crawly Creepy Little Mousie

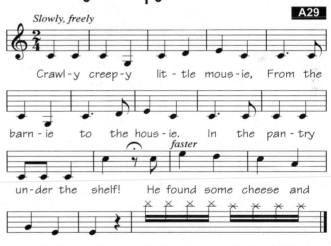

Slowly, freely

Crawl-y creep-y lit-tle mous-ie, From the barn-ie to the hous-ie. In the pan-try un-der the shelf! *faster* He found some cheese and helped him-self. Nib-ble Nib-ble Nib-ble Nib-ble!

Words traditional (nursery rhyme)
Music adapted & arranged by Pete Seeger (1959) based on the song "Doodle Dandy" collected, adapted & arranged by Frank Warner
TRO - © Copyright 1971, 1984 & 1993 Melody Trails, Inc., New York, NY.

There's no accompaniment to this song. You sit a baby or small child in your lap. Start your fingers walking up their leg, arm, or back, always ending tickling under the chin.

I read the words, an old Scottish or English nursery game, in a book. Put a tune to it. Only 30(!) years later did I realize that I swiped the tune from a marching song of 1776, which I heard Frank Warner sing:

[1] See Chapter 9.
[2] See "A Little a' This 'n' That" on p. 256. I'm good at washing 'em.

Doodle Dandy `A30`

Doodle doodle doodle Dandy, Cornstalk rum and-a
home-made brandy, Indian pudding and pumpkin pie,
That will make the Yan-kees fly! (banjo)

Traditional song (U.S., 1783) Collected, adapted & arranged by Frank Warner
TRO – © Copyright 1971 & 1984 Melody Trails, Inc., New York, NY.
From *Traditional American Folk Songs from the Anne & Frank Warner Collection*,
Syracuse University Press, 1984.

Here are some 2002 words for the same melody:

Crawly Creepy Little Viney

Crawly creepy little viney
'Round the tree goes twisty twiney
But 'long comes Grandpa with his shears
Snip! He's cutting short your years.

> "Not so fast," says little viney
> "You think you've stopped my twisty twiney,
> But you just cut me near the top.
> Down below my roots don't stop."

Ah! Through life it's all a struggle,
Enough to make your mind go buggle
But if we can laugh and make up rhymes
We might live a longer time.

In the early 1920s, my father was at a low point in his life. Fired as a professor for making speeches against imperialistic war. Tried to take "good music" out to people in small towns, with his family living in a home-made trailer pulled by a Model T Ford (see p. 11 and p. 282). Failed. Marriage breaking up. He decided he might as well enjoy his children while they were still children. All summer, every summer for ten years we camped out in a barn 200 feet from his parents' comfortable home. In our barn no telephone, no electricity, no plumbing. One summer we all made model boats, another summer model airplanes. On trips to the beach and back, my brother John and I would harmonize all the way.

And at night my father would improvise bedtime stories for me, which I found hilarious[3]. Twenty-five years later I tried to recollect some of them for my own children. This one ended getting on record and in print. The song was well-known early in this century as "May Irwin's[4] Frog Song" and had verses. Here I start and end with whistling. Accompaniment is handy but not necessary.

[3]Oscar Brand just told me that May Irwin also wrote "Take Me Out to the Ball Game."
[4]See Bibliography: *Pete Seeger's Storytelling Book.*

The Foolish Frog `A31`

(Start by whistling the tune below. Some sparkling banjo notes can fill in the 7th measure.)

There was once a farmer, walking down the road, whistling a tune to himself. He said, "Dog-gone, I wish I had some words to that song. But all I've got is the melody."

Just then he came to a little bridge. He leaned on the railing, looking down at the brook. There was a big old bullfrog, hopping from bank to bank. (SOUND EFFECTS). Well, the bullfrog looked up, and saw the farmer, and decided to show off. He took an extra special big hop.

Z-z-z-z-z-ztt! He landed, splash! in the mud, and got himself all dirty. The farmer laughed and laughed and started singing:

`A32`

Way down south in the yank-e-ty yank
bull-frog jumped from bank to bank Just because he'd no-thing bet-ter for to do
He stubbed his toe and fell in the wa-ter. You could
hear him hol-ler for a mile and a quar-ter, Just because he'd no-thing bet-ter for to do!

Now, the farmer went walking down the road, feeling mighty proud of himself for making up a song. He went down to the corner store, bought himself some groceries, and a pair of work gloves, and a plug of chewing tobacco, and said:

"Oh, before I go, I have to sing you my new song."

"Go on home," says the storekeeper. "I'm busy here. See all these customers."

"I won't pay you my money unless you let me sing my song!"

"Well, sing it and get it over with," says the storekeeper.

The farmer started singing, and the man in the store cried out, "That's a wo-o-onderful song. Gather 'round everybody, we'll have a party!" And he passed around the free strawberry pop and the free soda crackers, and everybody was stamping on the floor.

Meanwhile, ... all the wives and children back home were sitting down to supper, and — where's father? The mothers said, "Children, you better run down to the corner store and fetch your old man. He's probably down there wasting his time as usual."

So all the children run down the road. They run inside the corner store. You know, they heard that music, they forgot about coming home. The children started singing. (THE SONG IS REPEATED IN A HIGH VOICE). And they were passing around the free strawberry pop and stamping on the floor...

In every farmhouse it was the same situation. The mothers said, "Do they expect us to work all day and nobody show up?" They started down the road waving their frying pans. Well, they get near, and hear that music, and they forget about being mad. They drop the frying pans in the gutter, walk in the store, and the mothers start singing! "Way down south in the yankety-yank, a bullfrog jumped from bank to bank..." And they were passing around the free strawberry pop and the free soda crackers, and everybody was stamping on the floor!

Meanwhile, ... out in the barns, all the cows started talking. "Where is everybody? We're supposed to be milked; it's getting mighty uncomfortable!" The cows left their stalls: wobbled out of the barn and down the road right into the corner store. The cows started singing: "Moo, moo, moo, moo. Moo, moo, moo, moo. Moo-moo, moo-moo, moo-moo, mooooo." And the cows' tails were swishing out the windows, and they were stamping on the floor, and drinking the free strawberry pop and eating the free soda crackers.

Out in the barnyard all the chickens said, "Where is everybody? We're supposed to be fed; we're getting hungry." The chickens hopped over the fence, hopped down the road, hopped into the store. The chickens started. (CHICKEN IMITATION) — P'k, P'k, P'k. And the chickens were stamping on the floor and drinking the free strawberry ...

Meanwhile, ... all the barns started talking to each other. "We feel mighty empty," they said, "without any cows, or any chickens. I guess we'll have to go find them." So the barns picked themselves off their foundations, galumped down the road, and s-q-u-e-e-z-e-d themselves into that corner store, believe it or not. Did you ever hear a rusty hinge on a barn door? That's the way the barns sang:

"Eeeeeee, eeeeee, errrrrrrrrrrrrrrrrrrr."

Out in the fields, all the grass says: "Where is everybody? The cows are supposed to come and eat us. I guess we'll have to go find them." The grass picked itself up and swished off down the road, and swished right into the store, and the grass started:

"Whsh-whsh-sh-sh-sh. Sh-sh-sh-sh-sh-shhh. Sh-sh-sh-sh-sh-sh-sh-shhhhh."

Of course, when the grass was gone, the fields were gone. The brook said: "I don't have any banks to flow between." The brook bubbled down the road. It bubbled right into the corner store.

"Bublbublbublbublbublbublbublbublbublbublbublbub!" (YOUR TONGUE FLAPS PAST YOUR UPPER LIP).

The brook was bubbling up and down the stairway! The grass was growing out the chimney! Feathers flying through the air! Cows' tails swishing out the windows! Everybody stamping on the floor and drinking the FREE strawberry pop and eating the FREE soda crackers!

Meanwhile, there's the bullfrog in mid-air.

He looks down. There's nothing underneath him. He looks over. There's no bank to land on. (FROG VOICE) "Where am I?" And he starts hopping down the road. The road rolled itself up behind him like a roll of toilet paper. (BANJO MAKES SOUND OF HOPPING).

"Hey, what's that racket down at the corner store?" says the frog.

"Why...They're singing! They're singing about ME!" And he was so proud he puffed himself up with pride!

And he puffed, and he puffed, and he POOM!!!

He exploded. Cows, barns, chickens, houses, farmers, wives, children — the whole corner store went up in the air. And then everybody floated down. They landed right where they were supposed to have been the whole time. Sat down eating supper feeling kind of foolish for themselves.

Next day they went out to find the frog. They looked high, they looked low. Strawberry pop bottles and soda crackers in all directions. But no frog. So all there is left of the frog is the song. We might as well sing 'er once again.

(SING TUNE THROUGH)

Can you whistle?

(WHISTLE IT THROUGH, FOR AN ENDING)

Song by May Irwin (19th c.), adapted by Pete Seeger
Story by Charles Seeger (1924) & Pete Seeger
© 1955 (renewed) by Stormking Music Inc.

Sweepy, Sweepy, Sweepy

A33

VERSE 1 ONLY

1. Sweep-y sweep-y sweep-y, Sweep-y sweep-y sweep-y, Sweep-y sweep-y sweep-y, Sweep-ing up the floor. Sweep-y sweep-y sweep-y, Sweep-y sweep-y sweep-y, Sweep-y sweep-y sweep-y, till there ain't no more.

VERSES 2–9

2. Dust-y dust-y dust-y, Dust-y dust-y dust-y, Dust-y dust-y dust-y, dust-ing up the shelf. Dust-y dust-y dust-y, Dust-y dust-y dust-y dust-y, Do-ing it my-self.

Words & music by Pete Seeger & Mika Salter Seeger (1954)
TRO – © 1957 (renewed) & 1965 (renewed) Ludlow Music, Inc., New York, NY.

Mika was age seven or eight, I think. We were in the middle of a big house cleaning. Neither of us can remember who made up what verses.

1. Sweepy, sweepy, sweepy
Sweepy, sweepy, sweepy
Sweepy, sweepy, sweepy
Sweepin' up the floor
Sweepy, sweepy, sweepy
Sweepy, sweepy, sweepy
Sweepy, sweepy, sweepy
'Til there ain't no more!

2. Dusty, dusty, dusty (3x)
Dustin' up the shelf
Dusty, dusty, dusty (3x)
Doin' it my self!

3. Putty, putty, putty (3x)
Puttin' things away
Putty, putty, putty (3x)
Then go out and play!

4. Moppy, moppy, moppy (3x)
Moppin' up the room
Moppy, moppy, moppy (3x)
Foom! Foom! Foom!

5. Cleany, cleany, cleany (3x)
Clean the window panes
Cleany, cleany, cleany (3x)
'Til you see through again!

6. Throwy, throwy, throwy (3x)
Throwin' things away
Throwy, throwy, throwy (3x)
Far away!

7. Makey, makey, makey (3x)
Makin' up the bed
Makey, makey, makey (3x)
That's what I said!

8. Shakey, shakey, shakey (3x)
Shakin' out the sheet
Shakey, shakey, shakey (3x)
'Til the two ends meet!

9. Washy, washy, washy (3x)
Washin' up the dishes
Washy, washy, washy (3x)
And the soap suds squishes!

REPEAT FIRST VERSE

Keep Away
from the wisdom which doesn't cry
the philosophy which doesn't laugh
and the greatness which doesn't bow
before children.

— Khalil Gibran

DANNY & MIKA SEEGER, 1953

1. I wonder, I wonder, I wonder
   What Tinya* can possibly do?
   I wonder, I wonder, I wonder
   What Tinya can possibly do?

2. She can play with her blocks,
   Or go throw some rocks,
   Or climb a tree and look at the view.
   I wonder, I wonder, I wonder
   What Tinya can possibly do

3. I see someone's hand,
   I see someone's hair,
   I hear someone go peek-a-boo.
   I wonder, I wonder, I wonder
   What Tinya can possibly do.

4. She crawls on the floor,
   She looks 'round the door,
   She's tryin' to wear my shoe.
   I wonder, I wonder, I wonder
   What Tinya can possibly do.

5. I see someone's hair,
   I see someone's toe,
   But I can't guess possibly who.
   I wonder, I wonder, I wonder
   What Tinya can possibly do.

REPEAT FIRST VERSE

*Of course you put into a song the name of the child you are singing it to. My stepmother, Ruth Crawford Seeger, gave me the idea to do this when she put out the book *American Folksongs for Children* in 1949.

I Wonder, I Wonder, I Wonder

CHORUS

I won-der, I won-der, I won-der
what Tin-ya* can pos-si-bly do?
I won-der, I won-der, I won-der
what Tin-ya can pos-si-bly do?

VERSE

1. She can play with her blocks, or go throw some
rocks, or climb a tree and look at the view.
I won-der, I won-der, I won-der
what Tin-ya can pos-si-bly do?

Words & music by Pete Seeger (1956)
© 1970 by Stormking Music Inc.

TINYA SEEGER, 1956

Photo by Toshi Seeger

CHINA, 1972

To Everyone in All the World

A35

To ev-'ry-one in all the world I reach my hand, I shake their hand. To ev-'ry-one in all the world I shake my hand like this. All, all to-geth-er, the whole wide world a-round. I may not know your lin-go, but I can say, By jin-go, No mat-ter where you live, we can shake hands.

Words & music by Pete Seeger (1956)
© 1990 by Stormking Music Inc.

This French translation is by Raffi, who has spread the song across Canada. Thank you, Raffi!

A36

A tous et chacun dans le monde
Je tends la main, j'leur donne la main.
A tous et chacun dans le monde
Je donne la main comme ça.

Tous, tous ensemble,
Au monde entier je chante.
C'est très facile entre humains,
Avec une poignée de main,
N'importe où dans le monde,
On peut s'en tendre.

Alisa and Umberto Mariani rounded up translations into Russian, Korean, Spanish and Italian.

Now's a good time to thank folklorist Alan Lomax for not only teaching me, but teaching the USA a lot of its best music. The 20th Century revival of interest in "American Folk Music" is due more to the work of this man than any other person. His father, John Lomax, started collecting cowboy songs in the year 1900. Most folklore collectors tend to dig up bones from one graveyard and bury them in another (in libraries). But old John wanted to make a nation aware of its own great songs. He got President Theodore Roosevelt to write an introduction for his book *Cowboy Songs* in 1908. Other collections followed.

THREE GENERATIONS OF JOHN A. LOMAXES, 1940s

John A. Lomax Papers, Ctr. for Am. Hist., UT Austin, TX

In the mid-1930s, his son Alan was put in charge of the Archives of Folk Song at the Library of Congress, and in a few short years of energetic work accomplished what others might have taken a lifetime to do. I and others picked up the songs Alan taught us and made a living singing them ever since. Many tunes we take for granted today, like "House of the Rising Sun" and "Home On the Range," would not be known today had they not been collected and published by his father, John A. Lomax, or by him.

The inspiration for the next song was an African-American children's song, "Little Bird Fly Through My Window," which the Lomaxes collected. The irregular 5/4 measure is part of its charm.

Little Girl See Through My Window

Lit-tle girl, lit-tle girl, see
through my win-dow. Lit-tle girl, lit-tle girl, see
through my win-dow. Lit-tle girl, lit-tle girl, see
through my win-dow. See what you can see.

1. I see the ships and the air-y-o-plane, I
see the cars and choo-choo trains a-
round the ring-o world-o.___

Words by Pete Seeger (1956)
Tune: "Little Bird, Go Through My Window"
collected, adapted & arranged by John A. & Alan Lomax
Additional words by Terry Leonino and Greg Artzner
TRO – © 1941 (renewed) & 1970 Ludlow Music, Inc. & Stormking Music Inc. NY, NY.

CHORUS:
Little girl, little girl,
See through my window.
Little girl, little girl,
See through my window.
Little girl, little girl,
See through my window.
See what you can see.

1. I <u>see</u> the ships and the <u>airy</u>-o-planes,
I <u>see</u> the cars and the <u>choo</u> choo trains
A<u>round</u> the ring-o <u>world</u>-o.*

2. I <u>see</u> the rich, I <u>see</u> the poor
I <u>see</u> millions, <u>millions</u> more
Around the ring-o world-o.

3. I <u>see</u> the clever, I <u>see</u> the smart,
I <u>see</u> the folks who <u>have</u> no heart
Around the ring-o world-o.

4. I <u>see</u> a world where <u>them</u> and me
Can <u>dwell</u> in sweet se<u>reni</u>ty
Around the ring-o world-o.

5. I <u>see</u> the chains and the <u>prisons</u> too,
I <u>see</u> the hammers to <u>break</u> 'em through
Around the ring-o world-o.

6. I <u>see</u> the waters <u>and</u> the lands
Just <u>waiting</u> for a <u>helping</u> hand
Around the ring-o world-o.

*You can sing each verse twice so your audience can join in.

Terry Leonino and Greg Artzner, who sing under the name "Magpie," made up a raft of new verses in the 1980s. They started where I left off.

CHORUS:
Little bird, little bird
Fly through my window, (REPEAT 3 TIMES)
See what you can see.

I see the rivers, lakes and streams
Teeming with life and flowing clean
Around the ring-o world, O.

I see the people everywhere
All healing water, land and air

I see recycling and such
So we don't have to waste so much

I see the wolf and grizzly bear,
The circling eagle in the air

I see the forests growing tall
Provide for creatures great and small

I see mountains no longer mined
Respected by all humankind

I see the people of all lands
All reaching out and joining hands

SINCE THIS BOOK WAS FIRST PUBLISHED, TOSHI AND I HAVE TWO NEW GRANDDAUGHTERS: PENNY ALINE BOSSOM-SEEGER (BORN MAY 17, 1995) AND ISABELLE LONG BOSSOM-SEEGER (BORN MAY 17, 2000)!

One Grain of Sand

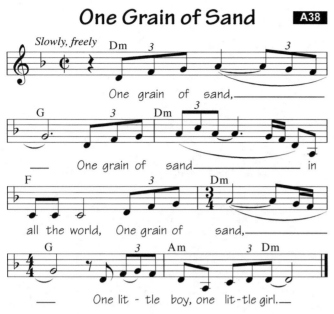

Words & music by Pete Seeger (1955)
TRO – © 1957 (renewed) & 1965 (renewed) Ludlow Music, Inc., New York, NY.

1. One grain of sand,
   One grain of sand, in all the world,
   One grain of sand,
   One little boy, one little girl.

2. One grain of sand,
   One lonely star up in the blue,*
   One grain of sand,
   One little me, one little you.

3. One grain of sand,
   One drop of water in the sea,
   One grain of sand,
   One little you, one little me.

4. One grain of sand,
   One leaf of grass upon a plain,
   One grain of sand,
   I'll sing it now again and again, again
   And again, again and again.**

5. One grain of sand,
   One grain of sand in all the world,
   One grain of sand,
   One little boy, one little girl.

6. One grain of sand,
   One grain of sand is all my joy,
   One grain of sand,
   One little girl, one little boy.

7. One grain of sand,
   One lonely star up in the sky,
   One grain of sand,
   One little you, one little I.

8. The sun will rise,
   The sun will rise and then go down,
   The sun will rise,
   One little world goes round and round and round
   And round, and round and round and round
     and round.***

9. So close your eyes,
   So close your eyes and go to sleep,
   So close your eyes,
   One little smile, one little weep.

10. One grain of sand,
    One grain of sand on an endless shore
    One grain of sand,
    One little life, who'd ask for more.

11. One grain of sand.
    One drop of water in the sea,
    One grain of sand,
    One little you, one little me.

12. One grain of sand,
    One grain of sand is all my own,
    One grain of sand,
    One grain of sand is home sweet home.

13. So go to sleep,
    So go to sleep by the endless sea,
    So go to sleep,
    I'll hold you close, so close to me.

REPEAT FIRST VERSE

* Verse 2

** Verse 3 similar to Verse 9 below

*** Verse 9

This can be a long song. It all depends how sleepy the baby is. But you know, some of my most successful singing has been when 100 percent of my audience goes sound asleep.

Linda Wingerter made a beautiful children's book of this song, illustrated with her paintings of families sleeping and waking all over the world. It's called *One Grain of Sand: A Lullaby* and was published by Megan Tingley Publishing in 2003.

Sweet-a-Little Baby

CHORUS

Sweet - a lit - tle ba - by,
sweet-a lit - tle ba - by, sweet-a lit - tle
ba - by, be - longs___ to eve - ry - bod - y.
Sweet-a lit - tle ba - by, sweet-a lit - tle
ba - by mine._____

VERSE

1. Sum - mer is a - com - ing and the
win - ter is gone.___ Spring - time's a -
flower - ing all day long.___
Hm_____

Words & music by Pete Seeger (1955)
TRO - © 1957 (renewed) & 1965 (renewed) Ludlow Music, Inc., New York, NY.

CHORUS (AFTER EACH VERSE):
Sweet-a little baby, sweet-a little baby,
Sweet-a little baby belongs to ev'rybody!
Sweet-a little baby, sweet-a little baby mine.

1. Summer is a-comin' and the winter is gone.
   Springtime's a-flowerin' all day long.
   Summer is a-comin' and the winter is gone,
   Springtime's a-flowerin' all day long. Hm—

2. She's got a sister and a brother, too,
   And someday she'll be a big girl, too.
   She's got a sister and a brother, too,
   And some day she'll be a big girl, too. Hm—

3. She's got a mama and a papa so tall,
   Her mama's so pretty and that ain't all.
   She's got a mama and a papa so tall,
   Her mama's so pretty and that ain't all. Hm—

4. Winter is a-comin' and the north wind blows,
   And everybody in the house gets sniffles in
     their nose.
   Winter is a-comin' and the north wind blows,
   And everybody in the house gets sniffles in their
     nose. Hm—

5. She's got two bright eyes and a snub, snub nose,
   And where she got 'em Lord only knows.
   She's got two bright eyes and a snub, snub nose,
   And where she got 'em Lord only knows. Hm—

6. She's getting sleepy, now, close your eyes,
   Now don't I wish you'd stay this size.
   She's getting sleepy, now, close your eyes,
   Now don't I wish you'd stay this size. Hm—

Photo by Diana Davies

MOSES ASCH

Most of these children's songs here just popped out when I was playing with my kids back in the 1950s. At the time I could wander into the office of Moe Asch (Folkways Records) almost any time, on little or no notice. He'd prop up a mic in front of me, and I'd sing the latest songs I'd learned or made up. A half hour later I'd be on my way. A few months later he might have included some of the songs in a new Folkways LP he was showing school teachers at some educational convention. The sales of these records were very small by any commercial standard. Hardly a single record store bothered to carry Folkways. But little by little we all grew and learned.

Where's My Pajamas

1. Where's my pa - ja - mas? Where's my pa-

ja - mas? Where's my pa - ja - mas? She

hol - lered 'round the room, Hey! Where's my pa-

ja - mas? Where's my pa - ja - mas?

Where's my pa - ja - mas? A - round the room!

Words & music by Pete Seeger (1957)
© 1985 by Stormking Music Inc.

1. Where's my pajamas? (3x)
   She hollered 'round the room, Hey!
   Where's my pajamas? (3x)
   Around the room.

2. Where's my pillow? (3x)
   She hollered 'round the room, Hey!
   Where's my pillow? (3x)
   Around the room.

3. Where's my blanket? (3x)
   She hollered 'round the room...etc.

4. Where's my Teddy? (3x)
   She hollered 'round the room...etc.

5. Where's my kisses? (3x)
   She hollered 'round the room...etc.

All these songs don't mean I was a particularly good father. Half the time I was away singing some place. One year Toshi counted the days I was home: 90 out of the year's 365. That might have been the year after I was sentenced to jail for a year, for not cooperating with the House Committee on Un-American Activities. We accepted almost every job offered, on the assumption that most of them would be cancelled. But none of them were. The Court of Appeals acquitted me. It was a horrendously busy year. Toshi said, "Never again. Next time no appeal. Let him go to jail."

As for me, I'll never sing these songs without seeing in my mind's eye certain little children. Something good that has happened can never be made to unhappen. And never is a long time.

Now there are grandchildren.

TINYA SEEGER WITH SON KITAMA, 1981

Little Fat Baby

Some-day you'll be a-ble to walk.

Some-day you'll be a - ble to talk.

No more will you poop in your pants.

You'll be a - ble to sing and dance.

And_ then, oh_ then, oh_ then, oh_ then,___

I'll wish I had that lit-tle fat ba - by

in my arms a - gainnn._____

Words & music by Pete Seeger (1982)   © 1993 by Sanga Music Inc.

TAO RODRIGUEZ & CASSIE SEEGER WITH THEIR GRANDFATHER, 1974

You'll Sing to Me Too

Words & music by Pete Seeger (1973) © 1993 by Sanga Music Inc.

1. I don't know where I'll go
    But we're here, and we're near
    So I'll sing to you and someday you'll sing to me too.
CHORUS:
I will sing to you, I will sing to you
I will sing to you and someday you'll sing to me too.

2. We don't know where we'll go
    But we're here, and we're near
    So I'll sing to you and someday you'll sing to me too.

3. I don't know, where I'll go
    But we're here and we're near
    So I'll sing to you and someday you'll sing to me too.

LAST CHORUS:
You'll sing to me too, You'll sing to me too.
I will sing to you and someday you'll sing to me too.

And we do sing together.

TAO & PETE, NEW YORK CITY, 1992

Hey, do you know someone who's had to hire a moving van when they move? Here's a chorus for them. It goes to the well-known song "So hoist up the John B. sails, see how the mainsail sets." I made the words up in 1949 when we moved our small family 60 miles upstate from New York City and my wife's parents got jobs as caretakers of a nearby children's camp.

Load Up the Moving Van

So load up the moving van,
Here comes the moving man,
Leave New York City far behind.
Goodbye, goodbye,
Goodbye, goodbye,
Leave Greenwich Village
A long way behind.

I can't remember any verses, except one that started:

Oh, grandma she got drunk
After packing all the trunks . . .

Toshi's mother was deeply religious in her own way, but also had a fine sense of humor and put up with my diabolical materialism.

If I'm singing for kids, at a school or a camp, I'll stick to surefire songs: "Skip to My Lou," "She'll Be Comin' Round the Mountain," ("Toot Toot" in falsetto) "The Old Lady That Swallowed a Fly" and Larry Penn's "I'm a Little Cookie." And for real toddlers, "Eensy Weensy Spider" and "The Wheels On the Bus Go 'Round and 'Round." Ten-year-olds love "Green and Yeller." I still like to lead "Let's Go On a Bear Hunt." Oh, and "The Green Grass Grows All Around."

If I can find colored chalk and an easel, I'll sing "I Had a Rooster." I've forgotten where I learned it — maybe from Alan Lomax or from my stepmother Ruth, who put together three wonderful collections — *American Folk Songs for Children, Animal Folk Songs*, and *American Folk Songs for Christmas* — before she was cut down by cancer at age 51. If the books are temporarily out of print when you read this, go to a library.

I Had a Rooster

A44
A45
A46

1. I had a rooster and the rooster pleased me. I
2. I had a cat__ and the cat pleased me. I
3. I had a pig__ and the pig pleased me. I
4. I had a cow__ and the cow pleased me. I
5. I had a ba-by and the ba-by pleased me. I

fed__ my rooster on a green ber-ry tree, the
fed__ my cat__ on a green ber-ry tree, the (to C)
fed__ my pig__ on a green ber-ry tree, the (to D)
fed__ my cow__ on a green ber-ry tree, the (to E)
fed__ my ba-by on a green ber-ry tree, the (to F)

(B) lit-tle rooster goes cock-a-doodle-doo de

doodle-dy doodle-dy doodle-dy doo.

(C) lit-tle cat__ goes "Meow! Meow!" the to B

(D) lit-tle pig goes__ "Oink, oink, oink," the to C

(E) lit-tle cow__ goes "Moo! Moo!" the to D

(F) lit-tle ba-by goes "Wah! Wah!" the to E

Now you, dear reader of this page, may never have tried to draw a picture. But just as some who have never danced can learn a dance step, or some who have never cooked can follow a recipe, now I'm urging you to learn how to draw a few simple pictures. It's fun!

If you've got a good gang of kids in front, don't just sing the song – draw pictures. Use different colored chalk or pastels – red for the rooster, black for the cat, pink for the pig, purple for the cow, blue and light brown for the baby. For a small crowd, felt-tip pens are OK, but with a big crowd you'll need a big pad – maybe even a long Japanese brush with paint, ink or dye. Or soft pastels.

When I'm singing in a school I'd draw a picture for each verse of the song – four or five pictures if short of time, seven or eight if there was enough room. I ask a small kid to hold up the picture of the rooster (first verse) at my left. The next picture (a cat) is given to a kid who stands nearer me on my left. The next picture is held on my right, the next further to my right, and so on. The crowd makes appropriate sounds, and it's a fun song as they try to guess what I'm drawing.

I've given you the song. Now here's a stroke-by-stroke description of how I do it. I've done it in Carnegie Hall as well as for kindergarten classes.

"Before the next song I have to draw you a picture of what we're going to be singing about. See if you can guess what I'm drawing."

"What is it?" I add a line.

"Now do you recognize it?" I draw three tailfeathers.

Now most recognize what it is. *"A rooster!"* I quickly finish it off.

I tear off the single big sheet of paper. **"Does some kid want to hold this up while I sing the song?"** It sometimes takes a few seconds before one child is bold enough to come forward, but I have him or her hold the picture, and we sing verse 1.

"We need another picture for the next verse."

"What is it?" "What is it?"

The kids are shouting, *"A cat, a cat!"*

"That's right." I quickly add eyes, nose and whiskers and give the drawing to another kid.

"How does a cat sound?" *"Meow, meow!"* They all do it with me. **"Let's all sing the song."** And we sing verse 2. There are now two kids on stage with me. I point to each picture when we all go *"Meow"* and end with *"the little rooster goes cockadoodle doo, de doodledy doodledy doodledy doo."*

"Now we need another picture."

"What is it?"

"What is it?"

"A pig, a pig!"

"How does a pig sound?" I make the sounds: **"Oink oink oink,"** and now we often have a problem — there are more kids who want to hold a picture. Sometimes two little kids can hold one big picture. Point to each picture at the appropriate time as we all sing.

"Next verse! What's this?" I start by drawing the tail of the cow.

A questioning glance at the audience

"No guesses?"

"A cow!" someone shouts. **"Yes, it's the south end of a cow headed north."**

I add the udder, teats and head.

"How does a cow go?" Lowest tone of voice: **"Mooo, mooo! Let's sing it!"**

The whole crowd is now singing the song all the way through with me. If I'm in a small classroom I need no mike as I walk behind the row of kids holding pictures, but if I'm in a big hall I might use a lavalier mike with a radio transmitter in my belt or back pocket. I can be heard as I lead the song while walking across the stage.

"One more verse!" Start with light blue for the baby's diapers. Pause. Look at my audience.

"What is it?" Use light brown to add the baby's legs.

"What is it?" Add the baby's body and nipples.

By now they're all shouting, *"A baby, a baby!"*

Quickly I add the head, then the open mouth, the nose and lastly the two teardrops.

"How does a baby sound?" All join in: *"WAH, WAH!"*

"OK, we need two people to hold this picture." The picture is wider than it is tall. I walk to my right, to give the picture to two or more kids, and now they sing from left to right the appropriate sounds for each picture. As the song ends I say, **"Kids, you can take the pictures home with you."** (I'm proud of my minimalist sketches.)

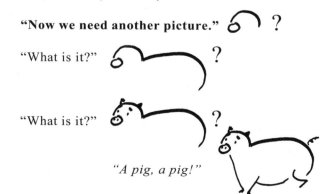

Hush Little Baby
(The Hambone Lesson)

Many know these words sung slowly as a lullaby, but I've found it a great game song when speeded up. The songleader does not sing the last word, the one that rhymes each couplet. The listeners, two — or two thousand — do that.

I first demonstrate a simplified version of what many black children know as "the Hambone." This is the "accompaniment." No banjo, no guitar. I learned it from Sonny Terry's nephew, J.C. Burris. Who knows? The idea could have started off in Africa thousands of years ago.

The songleader either sits or goes into a slight crouch. Feet pat two times each measure, while hands pat eight times to each measure. Later, when the hands accentuate every third pat (see accents P over the music), the feet help keep it all together — the "basic beat."

Left and right hands alternate. Rock-steady tempo throughout.

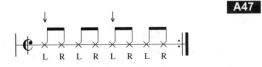

The arrows above the notes show the conventional downbeats emphasized by the voice. In the column at right you'll see all sorts of syncopated off beats emphasized when you pat on the back of your hands, your chest, etc. — it's not something you can learn in a few minutes.

The above rhythm, hopefully picked up by others learning from you, continues while you talk:

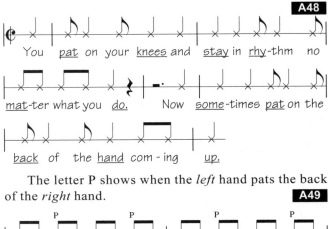

The letter P shows when the *left* hand pats the back of the *right* hand.

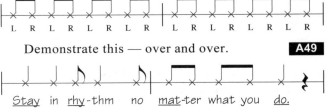

Demonstrate this — over and over.

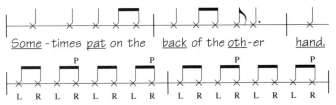

When they have hand clapping, feet tapping, give them a variation.

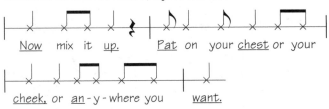

Note the accents showing when the right hand pats the back of the left hand, up in the air.

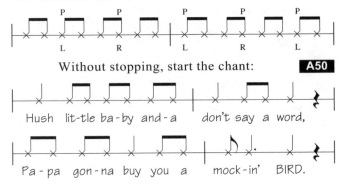

Only a few will be able to keep up with you, but it's fun to try. Whether you pat on the backs of of your hands, or your chest or cheeks, these accented beats are now sounding every *third* eighth note. Keep your feet patting the basic 4/4 time or you'll be confused yourself. Your hands emphasize every *third* eighth note, so only the first two measures look like this:

Without stopping, start the chant:

The capitalized word at the end of every other line is supposed to be said by the listeners, not the songleader. The rhyme usually cues them in, even if they never heard the chant before.

Sometimes I either point at the listener(s), or cup an ear to indicate that they are supposed to call out rhyming words.

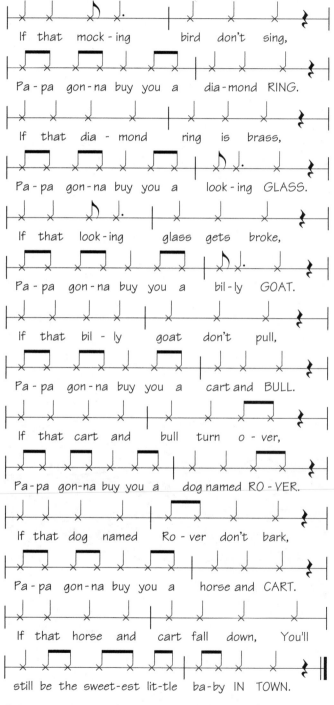

Collected, adapted & arranged by John A. Lomax & Alan Lomax
New musical arrangement by Pete Seeger (1993)
TRO - © 1941 (renewed) & 1993 Ludlow Music, Inc. & Melody Trails, Inc.,
New York, NY.

And you end it abruptly. By now everyone gets the word "TOWN."

A Five-Part Handslap

Well, you've just seen how in the middle of a fast 4/4 time you can emphasize every third slap. Here's how you can emphasize every *fifth* slap while still in 4/4 time. I was only nine years old when I invented this. At various times in my life I remembered the "skill" but never knew what to do with it. So now I hand it on to you to waste your time with. I never saw anyone else do it.

1. Right hand slaps the side of the right leg coming *up*.
2. Left hand slaps the side of the left leg coming *up*.
3. The fingers of the right hand slap the palm of the left hand, *as the two hands pass each other* in front of you, right hand going down, left hand going up.
4. Right hand slaps the top of the right leg going *down*.
5. Left hand slaps the top of the left leg going *down*.

Try the pattern below over and over slowly. "T" stands for toes or heels tapping on the first and third beat of every measure. "S" stands for "slap."

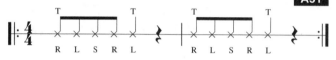

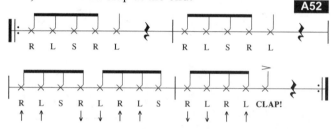

Do it slowly at first. Gradually speed up. Keep your feet tapping, twice every measure. When you can do this over and over, speed up. Try extending the pattern like this, with a handclap at the end.

You've started learning this sitting down. Now try standing in a slight crouch. What was the top of your leg is now the front of your leg. Tap toe or tap with heel. Your whole body is moving. Slow at first, then faster and faster. Then extend the pattern. It helps at first to count.

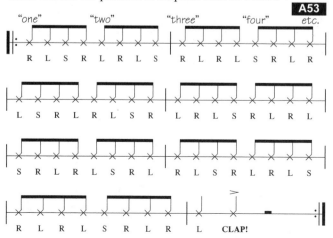

You're on your own from now on. Keep the beats regular. You'll gradually learn to keep it all smooth. Get the skill into your hands and out of your head.

★ ★ ★

In a book of African folk tunes notated by J.N. Maselwa and Rev. H.C.N. Smith, published (with no copyright of any sort) by St. Matthew's, a missionary college in South Africa, I came across a lullaby. A footnote explained that it was sung as part of a story about a monster called Abiyoyo. "The parents get the giant dancing, and when it falls down in a fit, it is dispatched by the parents." From that hint, I improvised a new story for my own children, not realizing at the time how closely the symbolism hit home.

They wanted to hear the story the next night. And the next. I tried telling it to other kids at a summer camp, and acting it out more. Little did I know I'd tell the story, and sing the song, a thousand times in the next half century. Here's the story:

Abiyoyo

A54...

(START BY SINGING THE SONG.)

Lo-o-ong time ago there was a little boy, who played a ukulele. He'd go around town: plonk! plonk! plonk! The grownups would say:

"Take that thing out of here." (KICKING MOTION)

Not only that. The boy's father would get in trouble. The father was a magician. He had a magic wand. He could go Zoop! and make things disappear. But the father was a practical joker. He'd come up to someone doing a hard job of work — (MAKE MOTIONS OF SAWING WITH A HANDSAW) zzt, zzt, zzt. Up comes the father: Zoop! The saw would disappear. He'd come up to someone just about to drink a nice glass of...something. Zoop! The glass would disappear. He'd

come up to someone just about to sit down after a hard day's work, and zoop! no chair.

People got tired of this. They said to the father: "You get out of here. Take your magic wand and your practical jokes and you and your son..." (POINT TO THE SIDE. MAKE MOTION OF KICKING.)

The boy and his father were ostracized. That means, they made 'em live on the outskirts of town. (BANJO STARTS A LOW, MENACING STRUM ON THE LOWEST STRING)

Now, in this town they used to tell stories. The old people used to tell stories about the monsters and giants that lived in the old days! They used to tell a story about Abiyoyo. They said he was as tall as a tree, and could eat...people...up. Of course, nobody believed it, but they told the stories anyway.

But one day, one day, the sun rose, blood red over the hill. And the first people that got up and looked out of their window — they saw a great big shadow in front of the sun. And they could feel the whole ground shake.

(STOMP, STOMP.)

Women screamed. (AUDIENCE RESPONSE) Strong men fainted. (UUGH). Run for your lives! (PATTER, PATTER) Abiyoyo's coming!

Down through the fields he came. He came to the sheep pasture and grabs a whole sheep. Yeowp! He eats it down in one bite. He comes to the cow pasture. Yuhk!

Just then the boy and his father woke up. I think they'd been up late the night before at a party. The boy rubbed his eyes.

"Hey, Pa, what's coming over the fields?"

CLEARWATER FESTIVAL, 1981

Photo by Charles Porter

"Oh, son. It's Abiyoyo. Oh, if only I could get him to lie down. I could make him disappear."

The boy said, "Come with me, father." He grabbed his father by one hand. The father grabbed the magic wand, and the boy grabbed his ukulele. Over the fields they went, right up to where Abiyoyo was.

People screamed "Don't go near him! He'll eat you alive!"

There was Abiyoyo (ARMS OUTSTRETCHED). *He had long fingernails, 'cause he never cut 'em. He had slobbery teeth, 'cause he never brushed them. Matted hair, 'cause he never combed it. Stinking feet, 'cause he never washed them. He was just about to come down with his claws, when the boy whipped out his ukulele.*

(SINGING:)   **A...54**
Abiyoyo, Abiyoyo
Abiyoyo, Abiyoyo
Abiyoyo, yo yoyo yo yoyo
Abiyoyo, yo yoyo yo yoyo...

Well, the giant had never heard a song about himself before; a foolish grin spread across his face. He started to dance.

ABIYOYO, ABIYOYO,

The boy went faster (DANCE AROUND).

ABIYOYO, YO YOYO, YO YOYO
ABIYOYO, YO YOYO...

The giant got out of breath. He staggered. He fell down flat on the ground.

Zoop, zoop! (POINT DOWN).

People looked out of their windows. "Abiyoyo disappeared!" They ran across the fields, lifted the boy and his father up on their shoulders.

"Come on back to town. Bring your damn ukulele." And they all sang:

Abiyoyo, Abiyoyo
Abiyoyo, Abiyoyo
Abiyoyo, yo yoyo yo yoyo
Abiyoyo, yo yoyo yo yoyo.

Story by Pete Seeger (1952) Song: traditional Xhosa lullaby
© 1963 (renewed) Sanga Music Inc. 50% of all royalties go through the Ubuntu Fund directly to South Africa.

The folk process in summer camps has produced new versions of it. I urge any parent reading this to try telling stories by ear instead of always relying on the printed page. After retelling the old favorites, reshape stories from anywhere and everywhere (movies, novels, the Bible, TV shows, anecdotes and riddles). Before long you'll be making up brand new stories. How? Start thinking, "What would happen *if...?*"

Hey, if like me, you start getting paid for telling this story, and you'd like to get some money to the Xhosa people (it's a Xhosa lullaby), get in touch with the Ubuntu Education Fund (<www.ubuntufund.org>). They are raising money for scholarships and libraries in the southeastern part of South Africa where Xhosa people live, near Durban and Port Elizabeth. The word "ubuntu" means "share" in the Xhosa language. In 2001, I got together with the two main publishers I've worked with, and we drew up the following statement:

The Campaign for Public Domain Reform

Songs have been written all over the world which have fallen into public domain. These songs continue to be used by contemporary recording artists and record companies as sources of inspiration for new songs. In these cases, the new copyrights and recording masters owe a monetary debt to the original sources.

It is our quest to recognize and honor the original sources of lyric and/or music content which have been and continue to be included in contemporary music.

We propose that a share of mechanical, print and performing royalties from such new works be sent to the "public domain commission" in the country of origin. Such commission will determine where the funds can be used.

This income will serve the cultures and countries which have helped inspire us. The idea is catching on. Contact the WIPO office in Geneva, Switzerland.

In November 2004 we held a day-long conference on this issue called "Music, the Public Domain and the Cultural Commons." It was an unusual mix of songwriters, performers, publishers, agents, record producers, anthropologists, music historians, cultural activists, entertainment lawyers and club owners, along with some people from Africa and other continents.

We also examined the sharing of songs *not* in the public domain, the impact of new technologies on music distribution, expanding intellectual property law, "people's law," the Internet and the "cultural commons." Several generations of diverse musicians discussed the problems of music and money and grappled with the thorny problem of the difference between appreciation and exploitation. Without the hassle of changing international copyright laws, we agreed that lots of things could be done. For more information on the conference and follow-up events go to <www.cipa-apex.org>.

About age nine I discovered a great song to sing while on a swing — the length of the chain or ropes holding the seat should be no longer than six or seven feet or the song goes too slow. The underlined words should be sung when leaning back and trying to make your toes touch the clouds.

Oh, How He Lied A55

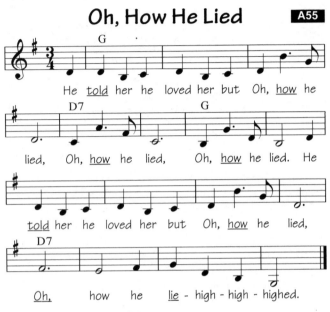

Author unkwnown (19th C. U.S.A.)

1. He <u>told</u> her he loved her, but
   Oh <u>how</u> he lied, oh <u>how</u> he lied, oh <u>how</u> he lied.
   He <u>told</u> her he loved her, but oh <u>how</u> he lied,
   <u>Oh</u> how he <u>lie</u>-high-high-highed.

2. They <u>were</u> to be married, but
   She <u>up</u> and died, she <u>up</u> and died, she <u>up</u> and died.
   They <u>were</u> to be married, but she <u>up</u> and died.
   <u>She</u>-up-and-<u>die</u>-high-high-highed.

3. He <u>went</u> to the fun-er-al but
   Just <u>for</u> the ride (3x)
   He <u>went</u> to the fun-er-al but just <u>for</u> the ride,
   <u>Just</u>-for-the-<u>ri</u>-high-high-highed.

4. <u>She</u> went to heaven and
   <u>Flip-flop</u> she flied (3x)
   <u>She</u> went to heaven and flip-<u>flop</u> she flied,
   Flip-flop she <u>fly</u>-high-high-highed.

5. <u>He</u> went the other way and
   <u>Frizzled</u> and fried (3x)
   <u>He</u> went the other way and <u>frizzled</u> and fried,
   Frizzled and <u>fry</u>-high-high-highed.

And now I'm reminded that one of the best children's songs of all time (probably made up by kids) is "She'll Be Coming 'Round the Mountain When She Comes (Toot Toot)." Each verse has a different action to go with it, and the last line is "cumulative" with the last line of previous verses. The order of the verses I like best is:

2. She'll be driving six white horses... (whoa back)
3. And we'll all go out to meet her... (Hi babe)
4. We will all have chicken and dumplings... (yum yum)
5. She will have to sleep with Grandma... (snore-wheeze)
6. She'll be wearing red pajamas.. (scratch scratch)

Now, I realize that many songwriting friends regularly write songs with children in schools. Sandy Byer in *Sing Out!* magazine (v. 36, #1) wrote it up in detail.

For young children you might want to begin with zipper songs.[4] "The More We Get Together" as done by Ella Jenkins is an example of a zipper song. You can ask the children what else they can do besides "get together."…

You could expand this process by using zipper songs that require a longer response. A song like "Aiken Drum" is a good example. Students can make up phrases like, "and his hair was made of spaghetti," or "his hands were made of pizza," or "his ears were made of lettuce," etc.…

When working with one class at a time, some performers and teachers like to use written templates to include all the students. Rosalie Sorrels' song, "I'm Gonna Tell" seems to be a popular choice:

> I'm gonna tell, I'm gonna tell
> I'm gonna holler and I'm gonna yell
> I'm gonna tell Mama 'bout everything you do,
> I'm gonna tell on you.

The students are each given a page on which is written:

> "I'm gonna tell _____,
> I'm gonna tell _____,
> I'm gonna tell _____,
> I'm gonna tell on you."

The students then write in their suggestions, making sure that the first two lines rhyme and that the last word of the third line rhymes with "you." For example, "I'm gonna tell that you hit me on the head, I'm gonna tell that you threw up in bed, I'm gonna tell why our cat is now blue, I'm gonna tell on you." Then the class can sing back all the verses they made up.

Sandy suggested people contact the Children's Music Network, P.O. Box 1341, Evanston, IL 60204-1341, phone 1-847-733-8003, <www.cmnonline.org>. Writes Sandy: "Most performers agree that in group songwriting one needs to choose… a topic." Bob Reid of Santa Cruz, Calif., says, "Everyone should come away with a sense that songwriting is fun and easy, not boring and difficult." (Bob made up the song "Water," now the theme song of the UN year of fresh water.)

---

[4]Lee Hays gave the name "zipper song" to any song that could get a new verse by zipping in one new word.

Chapter 4: *Kisses Sweeter than Wine –*
Love Songs and Some Music without Words

Love songs? In much of 18th and 19th Century rural America there were two kinds of music: church music and "love songs," which meant sinful songs. All the old English ballads were called "love songs." But once I put out an LP record *Love Songs for Friends and Foes* claiming that most of the songs I sing are love songs — love of home, family, country, world, etc. In this chapter my definition is (only) a bit restricted.

In the mid-1950s I was blacklisted from radio and TV work and "night club" work. But across the river from where I live, in the foothills of the Catskills, were some resorts which didn't think much of the blacklist; and every summer I'd get a few weekend jobs where I could sing my brand of old American folk songs, union songs, peace songs and songs from other countries.

Driving home late at night over the Shawangunk Mountains and rolling farmland I found myself putting new words to a simple but great old Irish air. It was once a love song, but I knew it best with words from the 1916 Easter Rebellion — the last line went

> "…And Britannia's sons
> With their long range guns
> Sailed…in…through the foggy dew…"

Over the Hills

A56

Freely. Best sung unaccompanied

O-ver the hills I_ went one day, a-
dream-ing of my-self and you, And the
spring-time of years since first we met and_
all_ that_ we've been through. May I
not with de-light still_ dream of the years of the

"HE'S OUT FIGHTING FOR OPPRESSED PEOPLES."

sum - mer and fall_ to be? And the
man-y man-y ver - ses_ still to be sung in the
bal - lad of you and me.

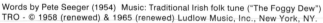

Words by Pete Seeger (1954) Music: Traditional Irish folk tune ("The Foggy Dew")
TRO - © 1958 (renewed) & 1965 (renewed) Ludlow Music, Inc., New York, NY.

A love song I've sung more often is "Kisses Sweeter Than Wine." Interesting story behind it. Lead Belly (Huddie Ledbetter) was living in New York in the 1940s. (For more about this extraordinary man and musician, see *The Life and Legend of Leadbelly* by Charles Wolfe and Kip Lornell, Harper Collins Publishers.) Once at a Greenwich Village party Lead Belly heard an Irish artist, Sam Kennedy, singing a lonesome old Irish song, "Drimmin Down ."

> A sorrowful ditty I'll tell ye right now,
> Of an old man that had but one cow.
> He took her to the field to be fed,
> And all of a sudden poor Drimmer dropped dead,
> Oh — mush-a sweeter than thou.*

Traditional (Irish)

*I don't know what it means, either.

Lead Belly liked the tune, but he wanted to sing it his own way. Some time later, at another crowded Greenwich Village party, he took Sam Kennedy aside into the bathroom, the only quiet place they could find. He said, "Sam, I'd like to sing your song, but I'm changing it a little, and I wonder if it is O.K. with you." Sam was very polite. He said, "Lead Belly, it's an old, old song. Everybody's got a right to sing it the way they want to. You sing it your way; I'll sing it my way." Lead Belly had added rhythm. Also garbled the words.

Once, I was humming through the melody as Lead Belly sang it. I was intrigued by the unusual chords Lead Belly used to accompany it. He'd played A major 7th chords, but sang it in A minor.

But I couldn't remember his words. I found myself singing, "Oh-oh, kisses sweeter than wine."

I knew it was a good idea for a chorus, but I wasn't skilled enough to figure what the heck to do with the rest of the song. I jotted the idea on a scrap of paper and dropped it in a file labeled "song ideas 1949."

It's a year later. Us four Weavers (Lee, Ronnie, Fred and me) found ourselves in a most unexpected situation. Thanks to the enthusiasm of bandleader Gordon Jenkins, we'd recorded one of the songs of Lead Belly, who'd died penniless the year before.

"Goodnight Irene" sold more records than any other pop song since WWII. In the summer of 1950 you couldn't escape it. A waltz yet! In a roadside diner we heard someone say, "Turn that jukebox off! I've heard that song 50 times this week."

And the Weavers found ourselves on tour going from one expensive nightspot to another — the Thunderbird Hotel in Las Vegas, Ciro's in Hollywood. In Houston's Shamrock Hotel we were sitting around a swimming pool contemplating a letter from our manager, "Decca Records wants to record some new songs. Please start rehearsing them."

Lee says, "Pete, get out your folder of song ideas; let's go through them, see if there's something we can work on."

I'm humming this idea and that as I leaf through scraps of paper. I come to this. Lee said, "Hold on, let me try it."

Next morning he came back with about six or seven verses. As I remember we pared them down to five. Sometimes I only sing four verses and get away with it. It was a mild seller back in 1950 — a much better seller a few years later when pop singer Jimmie Rodgers did it. But what makes me really happy is that it has become a standard with many people. The songwriter as a matchmaker!

Now, who should we credit on this song? The Irish, certainly. Sam Kennedy, who taught it to us. Lead Belly, for adding rhythm and blues chords. Me, for two new words for the refrain. Lee, who wrote seven verses. Fred and Ronnie for paring them down to five. Who cares? I know the song publisher, The Richmond Organization (TRO), cares. I guess folks whom TRO allows to reprint the song, care about this, too. I think some money should go to Ireland, to the public domain committee. (See p. 61, the Campaign for Public Domain Reform.)

Kisses Sweeter than Wine

Words by Ronnie Gilbert, Lee Hays, Fred Hellerman & Pete Seeger (1950)
Music by Huddie Ledbetter
TRO - © 1951 (renewed) & 1958 (renewed) Folkways Music Publishers, Inc., NY, NY.

1. When I was a young man* and never been kissed
   I got to thinking over what I had missed.
   I got me a girl, I kissed her and then,
   Oh Lord, I kissed her again.

CHORUS (AFTER EACH VERSE):
Oh, kisses sweeter than wine,
Oh, kisses sweeter than wine.

2. He asked me to marry and be his sweet wife,
   And we would be so happy all of our life,
   He begged and he pleaded like a natural man,
     and then,
   Oh Lord, I gave him my hand.

3. I worked mighty hard and so did my wife,
   Workin' hand in hand, to make a good life.
   With corn in the field and wheat in the bin, I was,
   Oh Lord, the father of twins.

*Adjust words throughout depending if the verses are sung by a man or woman.

4. Our children numbered just about four,
   They all had sweethearts a-knockin' at the door.
   They all got married and they didn't hesitate; I was,
   Oh Lord, the grandfather of eight.

5. Now we are old, gettin' ready to go,
   We get to thinkin' what happened a long time ago.
   Had a lot of kids, trouble and pain, but,
   Oh Lord, we'd do it again.

When I sang this song at the wedding of Dave Bernz and Mai Jacobs (she's Walter Lowenfels' granddaughter), I got the crowd to sing the chorus over and over. They sang better each time. I'd call out:

"Oh, sing it again" (chorus)
"Let's hear just the women" (chorus)
"Let's hear just the men" (chorus)
"How about just the grandparents" (chorus)
"Hey, let's sing it for all the great-grandparents, they live in our memory, hey, for *all* the ancestors" (chorus)
Pause (chorus)

"Let's sing it for all those who never had any children but who left us things we use: the word-makers, the picture makers, the inventors of things and recipes, the bridgemakers, the liberators, the peacemakers." (chorus)
Pause (chorus)

"One more time. For all the generations to come."

Oh__ oo__ kisses sweeter than wine.
Oh__ oo__ kisses__ sweeter__ than wine......

Four children? Eight grandchildren? This is certainly the most subversive song I've ever sung. Subversive to a stable world, certainly. Use a little arithmetic:

We each had 2 parents, 4 grandparents, 8 great-grandparents. Unless someone married a 1st cousin or 2nd cousin. Right? So 10 generations ago, say 330 years, each of us had 1,024 ancestors somewhere in the world. Or slightly less, because almost certainly now there's been some coupling between distant cousins.

Go back a mere 1,330 years and we each could have had over 1,000,000,000,000 (one thousand billion) ancestors except that we're sure there were less than one billion people on earth at that time.

So most of us 6+ billion (in 2006) humans on Earth are distant cousins of each other, if you go back enough thousands of years, before our omnivorous ancestors migrated to different continents or islands.

Look into the future. If the average person today had only 2 children, in a century they'd have 8 descendants, and in 1,330 years they (we) could have 1,000,000,000,000 descendants, which is a lot more population than this little old world could carry. In a

few thousand years it will be a rare person who can claim *not* to have been descended, more or less, from most of us—all 6+ billion of us—alive today. Kisses sweeter than wine.

Use your math. $2^2 = 4$, $2^3 = 8$,
$2^{10} = 2x2x2x2x2x2x2x2x2x2 = 1024$,
$2^{40} =$ one thousand billion
    (usually called "one trillion").

Subversive. Race mixing. See "We'll All Be A-Doubling," p. 207.

★ ★ ★

During WWII, a Mexican-American fellow soldier sang me a beautiful Mexican pop song "La Feria de las Flores." It was originally in 3/4 time, and supposed to be sung in two-part harmony.

One day in the '50s, I found myself humming the melody (top notes) to a Tennessee-type strummed banjo rhythm, 2/4 time. All of a sudden these words came out. I don't sing them often. Us New England types are kind of shy, you know. Good song, though.

Try singing my lyrics either to Mungo's original rhythm or to my new banjo melody which follows. (Indented verses use the "B" melody).

Note the asterisks. They indicate places you can add beats if you want to. Why? It's a Mexican tradition. The 3/4 rhythm stays steady. One guitar might play 3/8. One guitar may improvise on the top strings, another simultaneously on the bass strings. These asterisks show places where instrumental musicians can have fun, putting in instrumental runs or decorations, as is customary with Mariachi bands. After you get to know the melody, you too can improvise, adding or subtracting beats or measures as you wish. But keep the tempo constant.

MARIACHI COCULENSE, MEXICO

La Feria de las Flores A58

Me gus-ta can-tar-leal vien-to__ por-que
vue-lan mis can-ta-res__ y
di-go lo que yo sien-to__ en to-
di-tos los lu-ga-res.__ A-
qui vi-ne por-que vi-ne a la
fe-ria de las flo-res__ nohay
cer-ro que se meem-pi-ne__ ni cua-
co que se mea-to-re.

Words & music by Chucho Mungo
© 1942 (renewed) Promotora Hispano Americana de Musica.
Administered by Peer International Corp. Used by permission of CPP-Belwin Inc.
International copyright secured. Made in USA. All rights reserved.

Festival of Flowers A59

1. One sudden warm day in June,
   We drove far out in the country,
   We parked our car along the highway,
   And strolled across the meadows.

2. Just two of us hand in hand,
   Gathering armfuls of flowers,
   The sun rose high above us,
   We left our cares behind us.

3. There was a pool of clear water,
   Between the meadow and the forest,
   We stripped and bathed all over,
   And stretched out in the sunlight.

4. I'll remember this day forever—
   Our festival of flowers.
   Those short moments in our lifetime
   When we were one with nature.

5. Just two of us, hand in hand,
   Spending a few precious hours
   The sun rose high above us,
   In our festival of flowers.

Here's how I sing it with the banjo.

1. One sud-den warm day in June__ we drove far out in the coun-try,__ We parked our car a-long the high-way__ and strolled a-cross the mead-ow.__

2. Just two of us, hand in hand,__ gath-er-ing
5. Just two of us, hand in hand,__ spend-ing a
   arm-fuls of flow-ers.__ The sun rose high__ a-
   few pre-cious hours.__ The sun rose high__ a-
   bove us, we left our cares__ be-hind us.
   bove us, in our fes-ti-val__ of flow-ers.

3. There was a pool__ of clear wa-ter__ be-tween the mead-ow and the for-est.__ We stripped and bathed all o-ver,__ then stretched out in__ the sun-light. 4. I'll re-mem-ber that day__ for-ev-er,__ our fes-ti-val of flow-ers,__ those short mo-ments in our life-time__ when we were one__ with na-ture.

Words by Pete Seeger Music by Chucho Mungo
© 1942 (renewed) & 1993 Promotora Hispano Americana de Musica.
Administered by Peer International Corp. Used by permission of CPP-Belwin Inc.
International copyright secured. Made in USA. All rights reserved.

Years ago, visiting Marxist friends in Denver, I found these words to the next song, when fooling around on a guitar.

I thought I'd made up a good tune. Years later realized I'd swiped the tune from "Nearer My God To Thee."

Oh, Had I a Golden Thread

Words & music by Pete Seeger (1958)
© 1959 by Stormking Music Inc.

1. Oh, had I a golden thread
   And needle so fine
   I'd weave a magic strand
   Of rainbow design,
   Of rainbow design.

2. In it I'd weave the bravery
   Of women giving birth,
   In it I would weave the innocence
   Of children over all the earth,
   Children of all earth.

3. Far over the waters
   I'd reach my magic band
   Through foreign cities,
   To every single land,
   To every land.

4. Show my brothers and sisters
   My rainbow design,
   Bind up this sorry world
   With hand and heart and mind,
   Hand and heart and mind.

5. Far over the waters
   I'd reach my magic band
   To every human being
   So they would understand,
   So they'd understand.

REPEAT FIRST VERSE

Hardly any two people sing the exact same melody. Lots of folks have recorded their own versions, including Joan Baez, Judy Collins, Eva Cassidy, Peter, Paul and Mary, Dar Williams and Toshi Reagon, Leon and Eric Bibb, and the British group The Three City Four (Martin Carthy, Leon Rosselson, Ralph Trainer and Marion MacKenzie).

Well, my guess is that if a person likes a song well enough to want to keep it going longer, they'll make up new verses.

> I'd weave an end to guns and bombs,
> Bury them under concrete floors.
> The days of anger end,
> And there be no more wars,
> There be no more wars.
>
> (BILL GOODMAN, CHICAGO)

> I'd weave a land of parks
> Where people can be at peace.
> The land will be sparkling clean
> And there be a clear breeze,
> And there be a clear breeze.

> In it I'd weave the dignity
> Of folks in every land,
> In it I'd weave justice
> To strengthen every strand,
> Every strand.
>
> (PAULA BELSEY, OREGON)

As I told you in the first chapter, Bernice Reagon made up a good new version of the melody.

How Does a Melody Get Made Up? #1

One answer: When you're having fun with music. For years I've amused myself putting short melodies to highway signs, to advertisements, to newspaper headlines.

It helps to be able to write down a good tune so you don't forget it. Malvina Reynolds in her mid-forties went to school, brushed up on music notation just so she could do this.

Consider: Playing guitar or piano doesn't necessarily help. It can hinder. Some of the greatest melodies have come from parts of the world where melodies are sung unaccompanied. They have to be good enough to stand up by themselves, without a sea of harmony supporting them.

Someone asked me once, what does repeating the last line of a verse do for a song? I don't really know. Many song traditions do it. What does any repetition do? Perhaps it gives one time to savor different meanings in the words. Or time to think: "What the heck is the next verse?"

Maybe it reinforces an idea. Often it encourages a listener to join in. The blues form tends to repeat the first line, as do some old European songs.

In the musical *Hair*, they repeated the last line of one song so many times it became a song itself, "Let the sun, let the sun, let the sun-shine in." In a Washington, D.C. peace rally in '69, I heard 50,000 sing it for five or 10 minutes.

Why do ideas come to one at odd hours? The brain works in odd ways. Unexpected connections get made when you're relaxed. The Shakers said the angels guided their pen. Bob Dylan said he didn't know where the ideas came from. Arlo Guthrie believes there's a stream of song ideas flowing past us all the time, and we just have to know how to reach out and grab one. "I'm just glad I don't live down-stream of Bob Dylan," says Arlo.

I suspect there's more to it than this. Thomas Edison said, "Genius is 5 percent inspiration and 95 percent perspiration." And a famous painter said, "The test of an artist is to finish a work, long after the original moment of inspiration has passed." See pp. 89 and 258.

Here's ways to start writing melodies. Change old melodies slightly at first, altering their character with only a note or two. Don't just improvise aimlessly. Imagine you have to make a march into a blues, or vice versa. Try changing "Yankee Doodle" as it would be sung by three very different people.

Next, a love song for overly busy people. In this technological world it seems like half of us are trying to do three jobs, and the other half are unemployed.

I'm Gonna Sing Me a Love Song

Words & music by Pete Seeger (1954)
TRO - © 1967 Melody Trails, Inc., New York, NY.

Photo by Berenice Abbott

TOSHI-ALINE OHTA & PETE SEEGER, 1943

1. I'm gonna sing me a love song
      just in hopes you might be passing by.
   I'm gonna sing me a love song
      just in hopes you might be passing by.
   And if you're not too busy,
      perhaps I might catch you on the fly.

2. Oh, come along with me down by the spring,
   Won't you come along with me down by the spring,
   To see the waters gliding,
      and hear the nightingales sing.

3. What I got to say's so personal,
      can't say it to no one but you,
   What I got to say's so personal,
      can't say it to no one but you,
   It's just mm, mm, mm, ooh, ooh, ooh, ooh, ooh.

4. Now my song is over, but the melody lingers on,
   Now my song is over, but the melody lingers on,
   And should I ever leave you, remember when I'm gone.

People who know a "real blues" would dismiss this song. Yet I've sung it on and off for 40 years. Even had requests for it.

★ ★ ★

Next, a story I've told on stage. It's a ragtime tune, hence the piano part.

This Old Car

A friend of mine, we'll call him Joe, was driving home. He lives in New Jersey about an hour's drive from New York City. He was going up the West Side Highway. He was thinking of his old car, seven years old. Pretty soon he's going to have to turn it in, but he hoped he could hold out for another year.

He was thinking of his wife, Molly, who always sees that it's greased and oiled every 3,000 miles, and so on. If it wasn't for Molly, the car would have broken down long before. Before he got to the George Washington Bridge, he finished the verse:

> I been many a mile in this old car
> And I hope I got many more
> All — because little Molly
> Sees that it's well cared for
> The spark plugs spark, The carburetor carbs
> The pistons do what they're supposed to do.
> Oo-oo — and little Molly
> Keeps it lubricated all the time

TOSHI & PETE SEEGER, 1992

© Steve J. Sherman

Well you know as Joe went over the Washington Bridge he was feeling rather proud of himself for making up this song. He gaily gave the man in the booth his dollar and jammed his foot on the floor and brought up the clutch too quickly. He was stuck in high gear. He couldn't get the old fashioned stick shift out of high. By using the clutch very carefully, he got started and drove home that whole way. He figured, well if you have to go through life stuck in one gear, it's better to be stuck in high gear than low. Right? Well, he sung the song to himself all the way home.

He couldn't get up the hill to his home though. He drove downtown to the garage and said, "Bill, you have to help me here. I can't get out of third gear." His friend at the garage simply raised the hood — about ten seconds later he said, "Try her now." Son of a gun, it worked perfectly. Joe got the gear-shift into neutral — no trouble.

Bill, the mechanic, he says, "The parts are just getting a little worn down there. If it happens again, you just reach down and give it a little jiggle." So as Joe was driving home, he thought of a second verse:

> Now if things get a little out of kilter
> Here's how to fix it right away
> Reach down and give a little jiggle
> Everything will be okay
> The spark plugs spark, the carburetor carbs
> The pistons do what they're supposed to do.
> Oo-oo — and little Molly
> Keeps it lubricated all the time

Well, that's how a folk song gets made up. I asked Joe what did his wife think of it. He said with a smile, "Oh, she let me know she appreciated it."
(SING BOTH VERSES THROUGH)

This Old Car

1. I been man-y a mile_ in this old car,_ and I hope I got a man-y more._

All_ be - cause lit-tle Mol-ly sees that it's well cared for;_____ The

spark plugs spark, the car-bu-re-tor carbs, the pis-tons do what they're sup-posed to do,_ Oo -

oo_____ and lit-tle Mol-ly keeps it lu - bri-cat-ed all the time._

2. Now if things get a lit-tle out of kil-ter, Here's how to fix it right a-way,

Reach down and give a lit-tle jig-gle, Ev-'ry-thing will be o - kay;_____ The

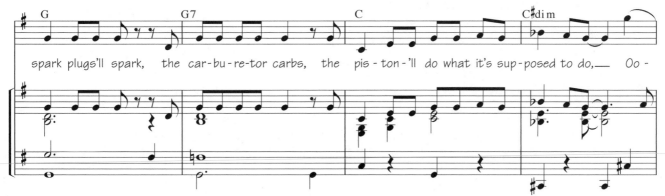

spark plugs'll spark, the car-bu-re-tor carbs, the pis-ton-'ll do what it's sup-posed to do,___ Oo-

oo_____ and lit-tle Mol-ly keeps it lu - bri-cat-ed all the time._____

Words & music by Pete Seeger (1962)   Piano arrangement by Joe Levin
© 1964, 1965 (renewed) Sanga Music Inc.

Lee Hays was a tall man, a good bass singer, and off and on an extremely good songwriter. He would play this tune on the piano occasionally. Said he got the idea for it back in Arkansas from two wayward young women who enjoyed playing something like it. He couldn't remember their song, and ended up making his own. But he couldn't complete it. By gosh, I came along and put together a "bridge" ("money, money," etc.).

Empty Pockets Blues   A64

Also known as "Barrel of Money Blues"
Words & music by Lee Hays & Pete Seeger (1930s-1950s)
© 1958 (renewed) by Sanga Music Inc.

1. I never had a pocket full of money,
   I never had a ruby red ring,
   All I ever had was you, babe,
   To sit and listen to me sing I've got those blues,
   Those empty pockets blues.

2. I never had a pocket full of money,
   I never had a big Cadillac,
   All I ever had was you, babe,
   And that's a fact I've got those blues,
   Those empty pockets blues.

BRIDGE:
   Oh, money, money, money, money
   When will I make the grade?
   I'm so broke that a dollar bill
   Looks big as a window shade.

3. Now some say the blues are sorrowful,
   Some say the blues are sad,
   But when I sing the blues to you,
   They come out feeling glad, I've got the blues,
   The empty pockets blues.

Incidentally, I sing the song in the key of A. Gets a nice diminished chord, with the A# bass note.

Money, Money, Money

The last line of the "bridge" is from a country blues I heard sung by a teenager in Alabama in 1940, and never forgot. "Traditional" blues? Joseph Shabalala, leader of Ladysmith Black Mambazo, told a friend of mine, "I have learned something in the last few years. When the word 'traditional' is used, it means the money stays in New York."

When a copy of this book is sold, where does the money go? About 40% to the bookstore, another 10 or 15% to the distributor, another 15% or so to the printer. Let's hope all workers involved got union pay. Of the remainder, if the book sells enough, *Sing Out!* will get back its investment and the book will help keep the magazine and the Resource Center going. *Sing Out!* is a not-for-profit corporation. Copyright owners of the songs in the book all get a token fee. The writer, yours truly, for whom these pages have been a labor of love or vanity depending on how you want to look at it, has decided to give the author's royalties to various places in Africa from which so much — and so many — has/have been stolen.

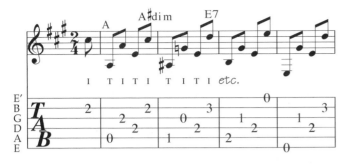

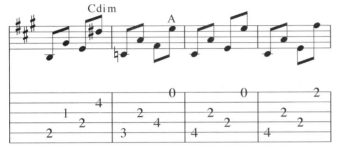

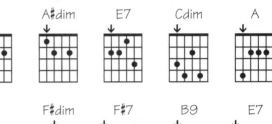

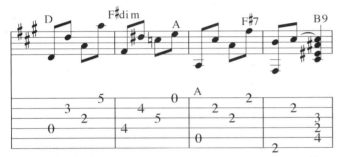

LEE HAYS PLAYING "EMPTY POCKETS BLUES," 1946

E. B. White, one of the great writers of the 20th Century, spent most of his life writing short anonymous essays for the weekly magazine, *The New Yorker*. He and his wife Katherine lived in Maine. This poem he once wrote her as a birthday gift; it was published years after he died.

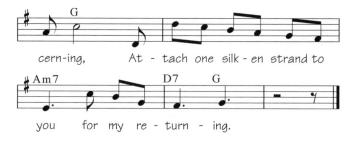

cern-ing, At-tach one silk-en strand to you for my re-turn-ing.

Words by E.B.White (1929) Music by Pete Seeger (1982)
Text © 1976 by E.B.White. Music © 1993 by Stormking Music Inc.

The Spider's Web
(original title: "Natural History")

A65

1. The spi-der, drop-ping down from twig, un-folds a plan of her de-vis-ing, a thin pre-med-i-tat-ed rig to use in ris-ing. 2. And all that jour-ney down through space, in cool de-scent and loy-al heart-ed, she spins a lad-der to the place from where she start-ed. 3. Thus I, gone forth as spi-ders do, in spi-der's web a truth dis-

1. The spider, dropping down from twig,
   Unfolds a plan of her devising,
   A thin premeditated rig
   To use in rising.

2. And all that journey down through space,
   In cool descent and loyal hearted,
   She spins a ladder to the place
   From where she started.

3. Thus I, gone forth as spiders do
   In spider's web a truth discerning,
   Attach one silken thread to you
   For my returning.

I'm not the first songwriter to use the same tune for different sets of words. (George M. Cohan did it, too.) Unwittingly, I put approximately the same tune to a famous 19th Century verse.

Flower in the Crannied Wall

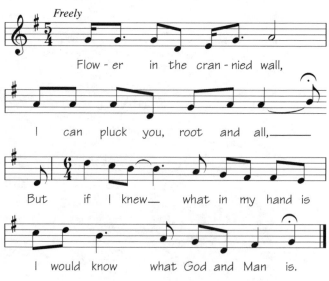

Flow-er in the cran-nied wall, I can pluck you, root and all,___ But if I knew___ what in my hand is I would know what God and Man is.

Words: Alfred Tennyson (1869) Music by Pete Seeger (1991)
© 1993 by Sanga Music Inc.

Starlight, Starbright

Star - light, star - bright, first star I
see to - night,___ I wish I may,___ I
wish I might___ have the wish I
wish to - night,___ That al - ways may your
love be shin - ing bright,___ Just like that
first star that I see to - night.

Words (original verse): traditional
Music & additional verses by Pete Seeger (1951); verse 2 by Paul Suchow
TRO - © 1962 (renewed) & 1965 (renewed) Ludlow Music, Inc., New York, NY.

1. Starlight, starbright, first star I see tonight,
   I wish I may, I wish I might, have the wish I wish
      tonight.
   That always may your love be shining bright
   Just like that first star that I see tonight.

2. Stars give, stars shine, makes our whole world
      seem fine.
   But stars can do just what they do, all the rest
      is up to you.
   So forever, never let peace out of sight
   Just like that first star that I see tonight.

3. Star song, love song, I hope it won't be long
   Before you're home and in my arms;
      then we'll both be safe from harm
   And then we'll know our love is shining bright
   Just like that first star that I see tonight.

REPEAT FIRST VERSE

This next song is part of a TV playscript I once wrote —never performed. But it's a usable song. What a great melody! The tune is "Shoals of Herring" by the late Ewan MacColl.

Once again I ask myself: How does one make up a melody? Ewan, a great singer of Scottish ballads, made up songs all his life, without thinking anything of it, borrowing old melodies and changing them a bit, to fit his new lyrics.

Read his autobiography, *Journeyman*, Sidgwick and Jackson, Publishers, England, 1990. Fascinating.

EWAN MacCOLL & PEGGY SEEGER WITH THEIR SON NEILL, CA. 1960

In the Stillness of My Heart

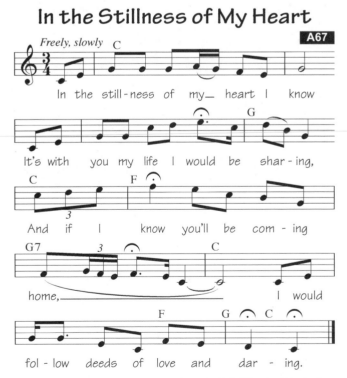

Freely, slowly

In the still - ness of my___ heart I know
It's with you my life I would be shar - ing,
And if I know you'll be com - ing
home,___ I would
fol - low deeds of love and dar - ing.

Words by Pete Seeger (1972) Music by Ewan MacColl ("Shoals of Herring")
© 1962 (renewed) & 1993 by Stormking Music Inc.

Copyrights & Robberies, Part 2

Canadian singer Alan Mills was in London and visited Cecil Sharp House, headquarters of the English Folk Song and Dance Society.

"Oh, so you are Alan Mills, the man who claims to have written 'The Old Woman Who Swallowed a Fly.'"

"But I did. I read the words in a magazine, put together by a woman who'd based her verses on an old children's rhyme. I added some verses and put a tune to it."

"Well, we've got a field recording in our library of an old man in Yorkshire singing it."

"Let me hear that recording," said Alan.

They checked. The man in Yorkshire was recorded one year after Burl Ives had a record out of the song — and Burl had learned the song a year earlier from Alan. The two versions were identical. It was obvious that the man in Yorkshire had somehow learned it from Burl's record.

When George Wein (founder of Newport Jazz Festival and Folk Festival) heard I'd listed "the Ballad of Barbara Allen" as P.D. (Public Domain— that is, not copyrighted), he emphatically said "You're wrong, Pete. You're giving money to Columbia Records. Columbia didn't write that song."

I can see his point. And in a social system where everything has to be owned and accounted for, to leave something "un-owned" means to simply abandon it and allow it to be mistreated.

Look what's happened to the air and water. (For more discussion on these issues, see pp. 61 and 90.)

Someone called bluesman Muddy Waters long distance from London to Chicago when he heard Eric Clapton play some of Muddy's riffs. Muddy's voice came back very relaxed, over the wire. "Oh, that's fine. When you steal, steal with taste."

Lee Hays pointed out a great melody in Carl Sandburg's *The American Songbag* (1927), which only had one partly-usable verse. He and I both worked on it through the years. Hey, check out the guitar part.

Times A-Getting Hard, Boys

1. Times are get-ting hard, boys.

Mon-ey's get-ting scarce. If times don't get no

bet-ter, boys, I'm goin' to leave this place,

Take my true love by the hand, lead her through the

After changing individual notes in this guitar arrangement several times, I realized that I never play it twice the same. Neither should you.

2. Look-ing for the prom-ised land, some-where be-yond the blue, When I did-n't find it, I came back to you.___ When I looked in-to your eyes, I knew that I was home. When I looked in-to your eyes, I knew that I was home.

Perhaps a melody without words is as good a love song as any.

THE SEEGER HOME, 1970

"Living in the Country," the guitar piece on the next page, is one of the half dozen "compositions" in this book which have been interesting enough to be picked up and sung or played by others. Leo Kottke plays it quite fast. George Winston made a best-selling piano recording of it. The accent marks in the first few measures indicate that hidden in all these notes is a syncopated melody.

The piece came to me 45 years ago after listening to my younger sister Peggy sing and play a song collected by folklorists from African-American dockworkers off the coast of Georgia 70 years ago.

Pay me, Oh pay me, Pay me my mon-ey down,— Pay me or go to jail,— Pay me etc.

If you analyze it, that's an Africanized version of one of the 19th Century's most famous English sea chanteys, "Blow the Man Down."

Blow the man down, bul-lies, blow the man down,

After I heard my sister, I found myself fooling around on the guitar, and developing variations. Before the week was out, I had a new piece of music. Like the "original," it starts on the fifth note of the scale, has mainly descending phrases, except for the third phrase in each section, which tends to go up.

Check the Appendix if you want to puzzle out the tablature. Or listen to some of the recordings. (See Discography).

Living in the Country

By Pete Seeger (1958)   © 1962, 1963 (renewed) by Sanga Music Inc.

Why do I put the song in this chapter? Because of a beautiful counter melody made up by Frank Hamilton when we recorded it on two guitars for Folkways Records. It's *made* for a love song.

A71

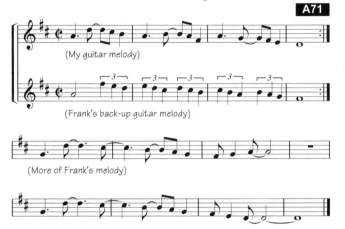

(My guitar melody)

(Frank's back-up guitar melody)

(More of Frank's melody)

Sooner or later someone will put words to it. Try these lyrics to Frank's "backup melody" **(slower):**

> If ... you would be patient and teach me
> I think that I could learn to dance (REPEAT THESE LINES)
> Who knows what then we might improvise?
> Who knows, who knows? We might improvise.

And who knows what other counter melodies may be improvised? Folk music is a very long chain.

Pete's 12-string guitar made by Bruce Taylor of Weston, CT. based on an earlier design by Stanley Francis of Liverpool, England.

Now comes an old Irish-American courting song. I made some sparkling banjo notes to introduce it.

The Leatherwing Bat **A72**

VERSE
1. Hi, said the lit-tle leath-er-wing bat,

I'll tell you the rea-son that, the

rea-son that I fly__ by night, is

'cause I've lost my heart's de-light.__

CHORUS
Ow-dy dow__ a - did-dle-o day,

Ow-dy dow__ a - did-dle-o day,

Ow-dy dow__ a - did-dle-o day, and a

hey lee lee_____ lee li lee-lo.__

Collected, adapted & arranged by John A. Lomax & Alan Lomax
TRO - © 1947 (renewed) Ludlow Music, Inc., New York, NY.

1. Hi, said the little leatherwing bat
   I'll tell you the reason that
   The reason that I fly by night
   Is 'cause I've lost my heart's delight.

CHORUS (AFTER EACH VERSE):
Owdy dow a-diddle-o day
Owdy dow a-diddle-o day
Owdy dow a-diddle-o day
And a hey lee lee__ lee li lee-lo.

2. Hi, said the woodpecker settin' on a fence
   Once I courted a handsome wench
   But she got saucy and from me fled
   Ever since then my head's been red.

3. Hi, said the little bird so blue
   If I'd 'a' been a young man I'd 'a' had two
   So if one got saucy and wanted to go
   I'd have me a new__ string to my bow.

4. Hi, said the owl with head so white
   A lonesome day and a lonesome night
   I thought I heard some pretty girl say
   Court all night and sleep all day.

5. Hi, said the lonesome turtle dove
   I'll show you how to gain her love
   Keep her up both night and day
   Never give her time to say "go away."

I put this little banjo run together four decades ago and never figured a way to use it, except before and after singing "Leatherwing Bat." It should go lightning fast. It's an example of something you can do on a 5-string banjo. Yes, for a love song!

The D Minor Flourish `A73`

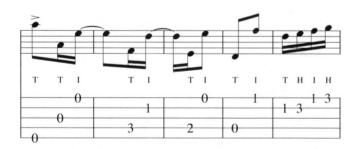

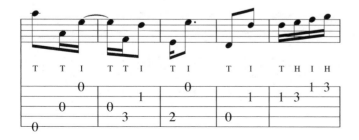

By Pete Seeger (1955)
TRO - © 1993 Melody Trails, Inc., New York, NY.

Sections #1, #2, and #3 can be juggled interchangeably. I played 'em for 40 years without analyzing what I was doing. Now it took me a whole day to try and write it down — still not correctly. For example, the three accented notes (> > >) in 2 should be more like triplets. Or maybe the four notes spread out over three short measures should be equal. I realize that as I play it, I'm still fooling around with the rhythm. It's fun to play.

The next tune I thought I made up. I worked it out 30 years ago on the top strings of a guitar, and kept asking Irish friends if they knew what the melody was. No one knew. I concluded that I must have made it up. The month this book first went to press, friend Ernie Marrs identified it: "The Memory of the Dead" or "Who Fears to Speak of 'Ninety-Eight," in Patrick Galvin's book *Irish Songs of Resistance*. But it could have been some other Irish melody.

I put it in this chapter because it has something of the yearning which Irish "slow airs" have. Here it is in the singable key of D.

Who'd Believe I'd Feel So Good?
(An Irish Air)

(Dropped D tuning is nice here)

...and who'd be-lieve I'd feel so good to dis-cov-er that I'd been wrong.

Music by Pete Seeger (1975) derived from "The Memory of the Dead" ("Who Fears to Speak of '98") by William Elliot Hudson (1843)
New words added by Pete Seeger (1993)
TRO - © 1993 Melody Trails, Inc., New York, NY.

As you see, I had a few ideas for words to it but so far have lacked the inspiration or perspiration to complete them. I liked the way the end of the second line (16th bar) led into the beginning of the third line, and I liked even better the way the last note of the third line (24th bar) literally became the first note of the last line. If one used an ABAB rhyme pattern, you'd need a first line to rhyme with "who'd" (rude? food? lewd?) and a second line to rhyme with "wrong" (song? long? See next page). Such technicalities. They destroy the spirit of love.

Well, here's the tune as I originally made it up, for guitar in the unsingable (for me) key of A. An electric guitar could get these sustained notes well.

The tune returns to me at odd times — when I'm looking at something beautiful, or in bed half asleep, or I find myself with guitar in hand and nobody around. I think now that what I'm looking for — what so many writers look for — is the right story. It's probably lying in wait somewhere, hiding, wondering if I'll find it. Meanwhile I get distracted by jokes, such as the following. I read in the '70s about a bill proposed in Congress by Senator Fong of Hawaii, to try and stop the importing of counterfeit pop records from Hong Kong — not paying money to publishers nor anyone else who created the original hit record. Senator Fong wanted the bill co-sponsored by Senator Long of Louisiana and Senator Spong of Virginia, so it could be called the Long-Fong-Spong Hong Kong Song Bill.

There. Try writing a love song after that. But perhaps someone somewhere will find the right story. If I'm still around, let me know. I've told my publishers not to object if people want to sing their own words, even on the air — unless they are racist, sexist, violent, or otherwise stupid. But not let the song be recorded, at least not right away. Eventually there might be several sets of words floating around. Good.

I do better writing tunes for other people's words.

Some other love songs in this book are not in this chapter. Such as "False From True" (p.151). "A Little a' This 'n' That" (p. 256) is my best love song to Toshi. I usually dedicate it to all the cooks in the world.

I confess I don't like to categorize songs closely. How do you separate love of home, country, kids, love of O.F. (Old Forever)? The last song in this chapter is another kind of love song. A love song for the earth.

This was written in 1967. I'd just returned from a tour in Japan. Early a.m., in a Hollywood motel, I pick up a copy of *Variety*, the entertainment business bible, famous for headlines like "STIX NIX HIX PIX."

I leaf through it, see an ad from Yamaha, "Win a free trip to Japan! World song contest! Fill out these music staves with your song and mail it in to us!"

TOSHI SEEGER, 1965

Photo by David Gahr

There was a page of blank music staves. I wrote this song and mailed it in. Never heard from them. But I won a prize — a song I've sung ever since. Here's a choral arrangement. (Choirs: enunciate clearly!)

This arrangement may not make sense to you. It starts with a 4-part SATB arrangement for a chorus, with altos taking the melody. Then comes a first verse normally sung by one or two persons. Then in a second chorus we see how a songleader could get a crowd singing it, by feeding them some words for each phrase. Next, a 2nd verse, and finally 1½ choruses, or 2½ or 3½! You take your choice of how to do it.

Rainbow Race   A75...

Words & music by Pete Seeger (1967)
© 1970 by Sanga Music Inc.

To you, the reader of this book, consider that once an audience gets to learn a good chorus, why not repeat it two or three times? In this case, end with one and a half a chorus so you end on the word "more" rather than the word "die."

CHORUS:
One blue sky above us
One ocean lapping all our shore,
One earth so green and round,
Who could ask for more?
And because I love you,
I'll give it one more try,
To show my rainbow race
It's too soon to die.

1.   Some folks...want to be like an ostrich,
     Bury their heads in the sand.
     Some hope that plastic dreams
     Can unclench all those greedy hands.
     Some hope to take the easy way:
     Poisons, bombs. They think we need 'em.
     Don't you know you can't kill all the unbelievers?
     There's no shortcut to freedom.
(REPEAT CHORUS)

2.   Go tell, go tell all the little children,
     Tell all the mothers and fathers too,
     Now's our last chance to learn to share
     What's been given to me and you.
(REPEAT CHORUS ONE AND A HALF TIMES)

*The asterisks show where I usually call out some words in advance so the audience can sing the chorus.

The Purposes of Music

In 1936 Charles Seeger was a bureaucrat in Washington, working for the Resettlement Administration music project. He assigned a young musician, Margaret Valiant, to a community organizing job in the South with these words. I've put my own comments in italics. He wrote before the Walkman Revolution.

1) Music, as any art, is not an end in itself, but is a means for achieving larger ends; *But many artists create for their own happiness.*

2) To *make* music is the essential thing — to listen to it is accessory; *But a mother sings, a baby listens.*

3) Music as a group activity is more important than music as an individual accomplishment.

4) Every person is musical; music can be associated with most human activity, to the advantage of both parties to the association.

5) The musical culture of the nation is, then, to be estimated upon the extent of participation of the whole population rather than upon the extent of the virtuosity of a fraction of it. *Many participate by dancing to the music. Perhaps others dance in their minds?*

6) The basis for musical culture is the vernacular of the broad mass of the people — its traditional (often called "folk") idiom; popular music and professional music are elaborate superstructures built upon the common base.

CHARLES LOUIS SEEGER IN HIS 70s

Photo by Robert Krones

7) There is no ground for the quarrel between the various idioms and styles, provided proper relationship between them is maintained — pop need not be scorned nor professional music artificially stimulated, nor folk music stamped out or sentimentalized.

8) The point of departure for any worker new to a community should be the tastes and capacities actually existent in the group; and the direction of the activities introduced should be more toward the development of local leadership than toward dependence upon outside help.

9) The main question, then, should be not "is it good music?" but "what is the music good for?"; and if it bids fair to aid in the welding of the people into more independent, capable and democratic action, it must be approved.

10) With these larger ends ever in view, musicians will frequently find themselves engaged in other kinds of activity, among them the other arts; this, however, promotes a well-rounded social function for them and ensures opportunity to make music serve a well-rounded function in the community.

You can see we're in little danger of getting overly sentimental in this chapter on love songs. Here's a story: Ammon Hennacy was a cheerful anarchist I met back in the 1950s. In the '60s, he ran a "halfway house" in Salt Lake City, called the Joe Hill House. I've quoted many times these next few sentences of his.

"Love. Courage. Wisdom. You need all three. Love alone is sentimentality, as in the average churchgoer. Courage alone is foolhardiness, as in the average soldier. Wisdom alone is cowardice, as in the average intellectual. You need all three."

Chapter 5: *Bells of Rhymney –*
New Tunes to Others' Words

Two hundred years ago in Scotland an old woman saw a man writing down the ballad she was singing, "Och, now ye've killed the song," she said. "Ye've wrote it down."

I'm glad to say she was wrong. Print and paper have sometimes crippled the folk process, but they haven't been able to kill it. What is this "folk process?" It is a process which has been going on for thousands of years. Ordinary people changing old things to fit new situations. Cooks translate old recipes to fit new stomachs. Lawyers translate old laws to fit new citizens. No, in spite of priest and politician, change goes on. In spite of tape, disc and computer, change goes on. And my hope is that if you like music (melodies, harmonies, rhythms) and if you enjoy using words, knowing that they also are slippery, changeable, unreliable things, you will enjoy using these songs to help build a world free of poverty, a world of peace, a world free of pollution. (Realizing too, that the last 18 words can mean 18 different things to different people.)

Tradition! The show *Fiddler on the Roof* had a whole song about it. Some traditions should live: our love for working together, playing, singing together. Some traditions deserve to live only in history books: the idea that you should put to death someone you think you hate.

When Woody Guthrie made up a song, more often than not he put new words to an old melody, often without thinking of what the old song was. He'd be thinking of his new words. In the back of his mind were a bunch of good old melodies floating around; he'd reach up, pull one down and try it out. In Oregon, in '41 he wrote:

Roll on, Co-lum-bia, roll on.

I said to him, Woody, isn't that almost the same tune as Lead Belly's "Irene"? He said "Sure 'nuff. Hadn't noticed it."

I - rene, good - night,_____

Brownie McGhee remembered singing with Woody an old gospel hymn:

Oh my lov-in' broth-er, when the world's on fi-re, do you want God's bos-om to be your pil-low?

Which is possibly where he got the tune for "This Land is Your Land." On the other hand, he might have been inspired by a similar song elsewhere. A half-dozen other songs have similar melodies.

Woody's "Union Maid" used the melody of "Red Wing" (whose 1907 author may have heard Robert Schumann's "The Happy Plowman.")

But I think it's more likely he (she?) remembered some old German folk tune which Schumann also remembered. But where did that great refrain come from? It was what people remembered: "Oh, the moon shines bright on pretty Red Wing." And with Woody's great new words ("Oh, you can't scare me, I'm stickin' to the union") it'll be remembered for centuries. ITAHRSH.*

*If there's a human race still here.

Woody heard Burl Ives sing "The Blue Tailed Fly" (which Alan Lomax taught to Burl).

Jim-my Crack Corn, and I don't care

And not one, but several of Woody's children's songs are based on this tune:

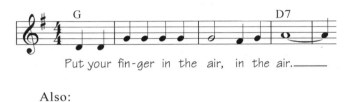

Put your fin-ger in the air, in the air._____

Also:

Jig, jig - a - jig - jig, Jig - a - long home,

"Put Your Finger in the Air" by Woody Guthrie TRO © 1954 (renewed) Folkways Music Publishers, Inc.
"Jig Along Home" by Woody Guthrie TRO © 1951 (renewed) Ludlow Music, Inc.

"Reuben James" might have been inspired by the tune of "Wildwood Flower," recorded by the Carter Family.

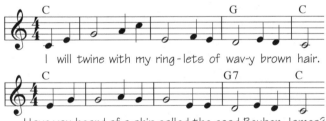

I will twine with my ring-lets of wav-y brown hair.

Have you heard of a ship called the good Reuben James?

But Woody's tune is more than a bit different.

"Reuben James" by Woody Guthrie © 1942 (renewed) MCA Music Publishing.

Woody once joked about another songwriter, "Oh, he just steals from me. But I steal from everybody. I'm the biggest song-stealer there ever was."

Nearly always he would change the old tune slightly to make it fit his words better. Sometimes he'd sing an old song and gradually change the earlier tune. He heard the record of Blind Lemon Jefferson's "One Dime Blues."

I'm broke and I ain't__ got a dime!__

I'm broke and I ain't got a dime_____

After a year of Woody's singing, it came out more like:

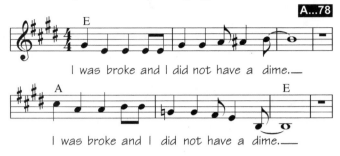

I was broke and I did not have a dime.__

I was broke and I did not have a dime.__

And then he made up some new verses. It ended up like a new song. He changed it to a four-line blues; the new first verse he'd sing like this:

Stand-ing down in New York Town one day,__

Stand-ing down in New York Town one day.__

Stand-ing down in New York Town__ one day,__ Well, it's hey, hey, hey, hey.

"New York Town" by Woody Guthrie TRO © 1961 (renewed) & 1964 (renewed) Ludlow Music, Inc.

Woody wrote the verses of "So Long, It's Been Good to Know You," using the melody of "The Ballad of Billy the Kid." Then he created a great chorus using some elements of that melody, but adding some wonderful new notes.

Same way with "Reuben James." He wrote about 10 or 15 verses telling the names of all 40 men who were drowned when the ship was sunk. The rest of the Almanac Singers, including me, complained that nobody but Woody would sing it that way. "Give us a chorus we can join in on." And he obliged, building his great singing chorus on some of the melodic elements of the verses (see p. 26).

Lead Belly did the same thing. Every song he ever sang he remolded to fit his voice and his 12-string guitar. Check p. 64, "Kisses Sweeter Than Wine."

After many decades and becoming slightly acquainted with the music traditions of several continents, I realized that some traditions assume that improvisation and change are the normal way to make music.

But keep in mind: some other traditions pride themselves on changing the music or words as little as possible. "I'm passing this song on to you exactly as I learned it. Don't you change it." And this is good too.

Forty years ago I learned the Seneca canoe song "Ka-yo-wa-ji-neh," from Tehanetorens (Ray Fadden). I have tried to teach it to others exactly as I learned it.

Kayowajineh `A79`

Use rattles or drum for accompaniment

Ka-yo-wa-ji - neh yo ho___ hey___ yo ho___

Ka-yo-wa-ji - neh_____ Ka-yo-wa-ji - neh - heh

Ka-yo-wa-ji - neh_____ yo ho___ hey___

Ka-yo-wa-ji - neh_____ Ka-yo-wa-ji - neh - heh

Traditional (Seneca)

Sometimes I'll play a melody on the recorder, knowing I'll never be able to sing the "original" words, but trying to play it (as near as I can remember) just as I heard it. Here's a "slow air" from Ireland or Scotland. A Catskill lumberman, George Edwards, remembered his mother singing it. He called it:

The Hills of Glenshee `A80`

Freely, slowly — unaccompanied

Traditional

And here's a slow air from Ireland as I heard Canadian Ed McCurdy sing it. (Old friend Ed in 1949 wrote the anti-war classic "Last Night I Had the Strangest Dream.")

My Lagan Love `A81`

Slowly, freely — unaccompanied

Traditional (Irish)

I've tried for decades to find words worthy of it. Failed. You try. I feel the melody is far greater than any words put to it so far, but here are some of the old words Ed sang.

> Where Lagan stream sings lullaby
> There blows a lily fair
> The twilight gleam is in her eye
> The night is on her hair...

One idea:
> We'll never know all the hows and whys
> But we know that we're here.

What does "freely" (at upper left) mean? An imperiodic rhythm (CLS). Some notes unexpectedly held longer or shorter than strict rhythm would have them. In other words, the notes never have twice exactly the same time value or meter. The time value of the notes can change — but beware changing more. *Don't* tap your foot.

Do you know any recorder players? Show them this. That's why I put it up in such a high key — for soprano or tenor recorders. Same fingering on an alto recorder gives you the key of A — much easier to sing in.

Here's another slow melody from halfway 'round the world. Unless you are familiar with Japanese traditions, again I'd suggest not changing it. (On the other hand as I was pasting this book together I heard a Led Zeppelin tape on which guitarist Jimmy Page improvised for six and a half minutes on the Irish air "She Moved Through the Fair." So maybe my theories are all wet.)

Nevertheless I've enjoyed playing "Kuroda Bushi" for a third of a century without wanting to change a note. It's a 400-year-old song, I'm told.

Kuroda Bushi

Traditional (Japanese)

When in Japan I asked them why they didn't ever try putting new words to some of their old melodies, they were shocked at the idea. I related this to my father. He replied, "You see, for them the old is so very old, and the new is so very new."

I think this is not the whole reason. It's also that the "old" songs for many people are regarded like religion. You tend to accept a religion or reject it; you don't try to change it. Except nowadays. Hooray for the folk process in religion. Politics, too.

In early times human beings lived in separate tribes with separate languages and folkways. It was unthinkable to adopt another tribe's way of dressing, eating, singing. But several thousand years ago around the Mediterranean Sea, different cultures started borrowing from each other on a large scale. Words, architecture, foods. From Africa, from Asia. After the Roman Empire fell, the tradition of borrowing continued in Europe. The windmill came to Holland from Persia in the 11th century. Soon after, gypsies brought the guitar to Spain. Genghis Khan's warriors brought the fiddle, and perhaps pasta, though Marco Polo, 90 (80?) years later, is usually credited with this.

So now you can see what led to the song on page 14 ("All Mixed Up"). One line in the song is disputed. "The stories behind the word 'Okay' are as varied as the imaginations of the lexicographers who penned them. A native American contender: In the Choctaw language 'okeh' meant 'it is' or 'it is so.' The Choctaw language served as the trade language in the Southeast and 'okeh' signified that the two parties were in agreement." (Jack Weatherford in *Native Roots*, © Crown Publishers).

At any rate, credit that old racist, President Andrew Jackson (he'd spent years in the Southeast Indian Wars), for signing state papers "O.K., Andrew Jackson" and starting its career as the world's most famous word.

Sometimes the folkways are so different that the people despise each other for centuries. (No. *Millennia.*) Irish poet Shaemas O'Sheel was infuriated by Beethoven's arrangements of Irish tunes. "That damn German stamping music! They never should have let him near those delicate Celtic melodies." In the years 300–600 A.D. the Celts fought the invading Angles and Saxons every inch of the way. The invaders must have despised the Celts too. There are only a few dozen Gaelic words in the English language ("Hooligan" is one).

I had an Irish great-great-grandmother, and a German great-great-grandfather, as I told you on p. 11.

I met Alex Comfort in London, 1959. Yes, the same guy who 15 years later wrote *The Joy of Sex*. He was a mathematician too. Another cheerful anarchist. Wrote some hilarious songs when part of the Campaign For Nuclear Disarmament led by Bertrand Russell in the 1950s. Described himself as a longtime writer of verses-sung-in-the-bathroom. Lo and behold, a year or so later I got these verses from him, asking if I could make up a tune. It's still sung, although not always with the same exact words, as you'll see.

Nina Simone started singing this next song in the '60s and kept singing it the way Alex Comfort wrote it. "One man's hands can't tear a prison down/Two men's hands can't tear a prison down/but if two and two…etc." Today I make so bold as to keep Alex's great three-syllable title but amend the rest of the words.

Of course you can switch things around as you want when you (I mean *you*) sing it. You might also consider

Alan Lomax's opinion that the American vowel "a" as in "cat" and "hat" is the most important vowel in American folk song — more than "oo" or "ee," which many lyricists aim at. ("June-Moon-croon-spoon" — also "thee, me, lea, sea.") Alan felt it's no accident that "This land is your land" proved so popular. And John Henry died with a hammer in his hand.

One Man's Hands

A83

1. Just my hands can't tear a pris-on down,___ Just your hands can't tear a pris-on down,___ But if two and two and fif-ty make a mil-lion, We'll see that day come round, We'll see that day come round.___

Original lyrics by Alex Comfort
Music (1961) by Pete Seeger Lyrics adapted by Staughton Lynd
© 1962 Sanga Music Inc.

Editor:
   In the October 1990 issue of this Magazine, pg. 262, the American folk singer Pete Seeger's "If two and two and fifty make a million" is followed by a suggestion for "readers...to try." Perhaps it is as simple as one-two-three: indeed 1, 2, 3 are exponents in the product $2^1 \times 2^2 \times 50^3$ which equals an exact million.

— Prem N. Bajaj
Wichita State University

1. Just my hands can't tear a prison down,
   Just your hands can't tear a prison down,

CHORUS (AFTER EACH VERSE):
   But if two and two and fifty make a million,
   We'll see that day come 'round,
   We'll see that day come 'round.

2. Just my voice can't shout to make them hear,
   Just your voice...etc.

3. Just my strength can't ban the atom bomb...

4. Just my strength can't break the color bar...

5. Just my strength can't roll the union on...

6. Just my feet can't walk across the land...

7. Just my eyes can't see the future clear...

REPEAT FIRST VERSE

Melodies #2

How *does* one think up a tune? Here's a few "melody games" you might try playing:

1) Try improvising variations on any tune you know, or are listening to. This is no more than any jazz musician does. Try imagining you are a musician from a different tradition or a different part of the world. How would *they* change that tune?

2) Try slowing a tune down, or speeding it up. Put it in a different "mode," major or minor. Start by changing one or two notes in the beginning, middle, or end. Then change whole phrases. You don't need to have accompaniment. Try it when driving a car, improvising changes in tunes you know. Of course, more often than not you'll decide the original tune was better. But you'll soon find what a different effect you get by just changing a few notes.

3) Here's a game I've often played when in a car: put tunes to words on highway billboards. Pretend it's a singing commercial you hear on the air. You can play the same game leafing through magazines or newspapers. Sing the headlines. What you'll decide is what the world's best composers have long known: it's easy to make up a half-good melody. But to make up an unforgettable one takes luck, and for all anyone knows, help from The Great Unknown. Nevertheless, I agree with Thomas Edison. ("Genius is 5 percent inspiration and 95 percent perspiration.") Practice may not make perfect, but it sure as hell makes for improvement.

Mbube
(Wimoweh)

I imagine that I am writing to the director of a high school chorus. Following are two intertwined stories, as true as I think I can get them, of how a South African song was changed and added to (and profited from) in the U.S.A. during the last 60 years. It's a musical story and a money story.

In 1929 a young Zulu sheepherder, Solomon Linda, made up a song consisting of a few wails and shouts, and a chanted background. It had a great bass part, repeated over and over:

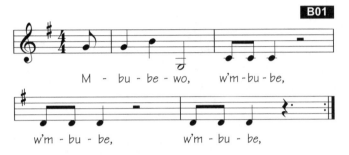

In 1939 Linda was in Johannesburg singing with five other young men. For a flat fee he recorded this song for the local record company, Gallo Records. It was the biggest hit of the decade, in South Africa: "Mbube," by Solomon Linda and the Evening Birds.

In 1948 Gallo sent a dozen of their recordings to Decca Records in New York City. Decca was not interested in promoting them, but folklorist Alan Lomax was working at Decca then grabbed the 78 rpm discs before they were thrown out, and gave them to me. I was in bed with a cold, got pencil and paper, transcribed the music, mispronounced the two words, and taught it to the Weavers, a quartet just organized.

In 1950 when the Weavers, to everyone's surprise, "hit the big time," we had a hit (Number 6 on the "Hit Parade") with "Wimoweh," accompanied by Gordon Jenkins' orchestra.

Flash forward to 1966. I was at a Newport Folk Festival committee meeting at the New York City apartment of Chairman George Wein. A telephone call came for me from a secretary at Columbia Records. "Mr. Seeger, I need to know copyright information for songs in your new records. She listed several titles, then listed

the British ballad "Barbara Allen." "That's public domain," said I.

"Oh, thank you," said she with surprise in her voice. Back at the meeting I told George of the call. He said, "Pete, I don't think you're being nice. I think you're wrong. Columbia Records didn't write 'Barbara Allen.' You gave them the money as if they did."

It was the first I knew that since about 1940 it had been standard practice in the music industry for performers, when recording an old song in the public domain, to copyright the song, because they had "adapted and arranged it." Now they received royalty payments as songwriters as well as performers.

Flash back to 1951. Howie Richmond, the Broadway publisher, had published "Goodnight Irene" and paid royalties to Lead Belly's family and to John and Alan Lomax, who first printed it. With the Weavers' (then) manager (not Harold Leventhal) he now published all the songs the Weavers "adapted and arranged." I distinctly remember being told, "Pete, money is coming in for "Wimoweh." Where should we send it? Gallo says send it to them."

"Oh, don't send it to them," says I. "Solomon Linda will never get a penny of it."

"Well, get his address. We'll send it directly to him." I didn't bother to ask exactly what "it" was. Foolish me. A year later I'd located Linda and a check for about $1000 was presented to him at a grand banquet in Johannesburg. I assumed this was the first of many such payments, and that a standard songwriter's contract had been signed with Linda. Again, foolish me. Linda received 12½%, not the usual songwriter's 50%. Gallo got the same 12½%. The Weavers' manager and the Weaver's each got 5%, and the Weavers' manager got another 37½% because he set up a new publishing company with Howie, to get most of the publisher's 50%.

Enough of money. Here's the song. Skip the nine-second intro in Zulu. The Weavers never sang it. Instead, have all the men in your chorus open with those four measures. If some cannot sing the low G, let them go down to B. After they've sung it twice, have all the women join them with these four measures. Tenors sang this in the original recording; alto Ronnie Gilbert and Fred Hellerman sang it for the Weavers.

It's important that those two or three notes be clipped short. Notice the rests. It's not "Wee-mo-wayyy!"

Now the soloist joins them. Perhaps you have a tenor who knows how to yodel. This opening wail should be done in falsetto, then the voice breaks to a "natural" tone. If you haven't such a tenor, then a soprano or several sopranos could take part. Perhaps you have a rough voice alto who can yodel down. (Some women can yodel.)

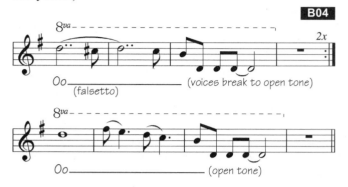

And now the shouter takes over. The Weavers called me a "split tenor" because I could yodel down from falsetto and also handle the shouting in key of G. But beware that your tenor doesn't get hoarse. Solomon Linda lost his voice; so did I after 30 years. The shouting and high wail, every eight measures, alternate throughout the song. The background continues without stopping.

After? Variations, of course, are possible, no matter who is the soloist. See the next four measures. Linda crooned this only once. I did it three or four times.

In 1958 the Tokens made it the central part of a new song. Jay Siegel added five notes; George Weiss made up ten words for the short melody. I haven't been able to get permission to reprint or put on this CD any of the Token's recording "The Lion Sleeps Tonight," but it's known worldwide. I didn't like it at first. There's no jungle near Johannesburg. Lions don't sleep at night. But now in my conservative old age I realize that for almost sixty years "Mbube" has been a testament to the power of joy over dark and bitter times, a lesson learned directly from black South Africa under apartheid.

After I left the Weavers in 1957 I found I could get audiences singing with me. I'd teach all the men the bass part, then ask all the women on my left to sing the lower of the two tenor parts, then ask all the women on my right to sing the higher tenor part.

On the very last measure I could slow them all down for an ending.

Words and music by Solomon Linda (1939)
Arranged and adapted by Ronnie Gilbert, Lee Hays, Fred Hellerman and Pete Seeger (1949)
TRO - © 1951 (renewed) & 1952 (renewed) Folkways Music Publishers, Inc., NY, NY.

SOLOMON LINDA (LEFT) & THE EVENING BIRDS IN 1941

At various times I've thought of making up new verses and then thought better of it. I'm mainly happy that Solomon Linda's children are now getting the full 50% songwriter's royalties. The contract has been re-written. How come? In 2004 out came the lead article in *Rolling Stone* magazine

IT IS ONE OF THE GREAT musical mysteries of all time: how American music legends made millions off the work of a Zulu tribesman who died a pauper. After six decades, the truth is finally told.

ONCE UPON A TIME, A LONG TIME ago, a small miracle took place in the brain of a man named Solomon Linda. It was 1939, and he was standing in front of a microphone in the only re-

Kaempfert. The New Zealand army band turned it into a march. England's 1986 World Cup soccer squad turned it into a joke. Hollywood put it in *Ace Ventura: Pet Detective*. It has logged

I wrote the editor, "Hooray for muckraking journalists and journals that will print their muck." The author, an anti-apartheid white South African, did not get every fact straight, but basically taught me how wrong I'd been to leave finances entirely in the hands of others. Soon after, lawyers representing Linda's children sued the Disney Corporation for royalties they should have received from *The Lion King*. They won a large out-of-court settlement. Here's the New York Times headline two years later.

Johannesburg Journal

In the Jungle, the Unjust Jungle, a Small Victory

By SHARON LaFRANIERE
JOHANNESBURG — As Solomon Linda first recorded it in 1939, it was a tender melody, almost childish in its simplicity — three chords, a couple of words and some baritones chanting in the background.

But the saga of the now known worldwide as "The Lion Sleeps Tonight" is anything but a lull-

Born in 1909 in the Zulu heartland of South Africa, Mr. Linda never learned to read or write, but in song he was supremely eloquent. After moving to Johannesburg in his mid-20's, he quickly conquered the weekend music scene at the township beer halls and squalid hostels that housed much of the city's black labor force.

He sang soprano over a four-part harmony, a vocal style that was soon

hit called "Mbube," Zulu for "The Lion." Elizabeth Nsele, Mr. Linda's youngest surviving daughter, said it had been inspired by her father's childhood as a herder protecting cattle in the untamed hinterlands.

"The lion was going round and round, and the lion was happy," she said. "But my father was not happy. He had been staying there since morning and he was hungry." The

And I hope that with the help of this book and the CDs, you the reader with a chorus of any group, may keep this song alive by singing it.

In '64, in Dar Es Salaam, East Africa, I sang for a group of exiled South Africans, and felt much honored when they asked me to sing this song. "I don't know the right words." "That's okay, you have the rhythm." And as they sang along, they put their arms around each other's shoulders and did a simple dance – a few steps forward, a few steps back.

They didn't want me to stop. I sang it for eight minutes. Was hoarse for a week.

How did I locate Solomon Linda? Through a friend in South Africa, I contacted Harry Bloom, a lawyer who defended Africans in Civil Rights cases. "I can't promise anything, but I'll try," wrote Bloom.

Four months later he found Linda. He'd lost his voice — probably sang "Mbube" too many times without a microphone — and was working as a stock clerk for Gallo for low wages.

In the course of trying to find Linda, Bloom met a number of musicians, including Hugh Masekela. Bloom said "I've got an idea for an opera. Can you do the music for it?"

The resulting show, about a prizefighter nicknamed *King Kong*, was a hit and ran for two years in Johannesburg. The female lead was a hitherto unknown singer named Miriam Makeba.

In the '60s Bloom had to flee the land of apartheid. I met him in London. He told me a story I'll never forget as long as I live. Once an African friend burst into his office, out of breath and in great agitation. Harry said, "What's the matter? Catch your breath. Can I do anything to help?" Finally his friend got his breath.

"No, there's nothing anyone can do ... But something terrible has happened ... I was on that long escalator in the department store across the street ... Just ahead of me was an elderly woman. She put her hand to her face and closed her eyes. I said to myself, 'That woman is going to faint.' I put my hand out to steady her, and saw my black hand next to her white skin, and thought 'What if she should scream?' There would be no help for me. I looked around. There was no on else on the escalator. I withdrew my hand. And she did faint."

"And she tumbled, tumbled, tumbled, all the way to the bottom."

And this is the problem for you, for me, for every soul. In a world of hate, doing a good deed may endanger your life.

★ ★ ★

The next song was written at the request of Moses Asch, head of Folkways Records. In 1950 he had paid Woody Guthrie a small stipend to go up to Massachusetts, do some investigating, and write songs about the famous Sacco-Vanzetti case. Two Italian anarchists, Nicola Sacco and Bartolomeo Vanzetti, were charged with murder, framed and executed in 1927. After Woody returned to New York, Moe asked me, "Do you think you could put a tune to this? It's a letter from Nicola Sacco to his 12-year-old son."

By omitting a word here and there, or adding one, I found I could make it scan, if not rhyme. I recorded it for Moe, and he added the song to the record of Woody's about the Sacco-Vanzetti case. Almost 30 years later a couple in Maryland, Terry Leonino and Greg Artzner, who sing as a duo called "Magpie," started singing it. I heard them rehearsing it at the People's Music Weekend one January. To my surprise and delight I realized what an Italian-type melody I'd put together; they sang it in two-part harmony, which I give here. The melody is on the bottom, that is, the lower of the two notes given. It's not so hard as it looks. Just keep the rhythm steady.

In the 1990s, Charlie King and Karen Brandow made a CD about Sacco and Vanzetti and included this song. For a different set of harmony, listen to them on **B8**.

Sacco's Letter To His Son

1. If no-thing hap-pens,___ they will e-lec-tro-cute us right af-ter
Don't cry,___ Dan-te,___ for man-y man-y tears have been
mid-night,___
wast-ed,___ As your moth-er's tears have been al-read-y wasted___
There-fore here I am,___ right with you,___ with
love and with o-pen heart,___ As I was yes-ter-day.___
for sev-en years,___ And nev-er did an-y good.___
So son, in-stead of cry-ing,___ be strong, be brave,___
So as to be a-ble___ to com-fort your moth-er.___

Words by Nicola Sacco (1927)   Music by Pete Seeger (1951)
Harmony by Greg Artzner and Terry Leonino
Transcription by Marcia Diehl and Greg Artzner
© 1960 (renewed) by Stormking Music Inc.

* The melody is the lower of the two notes. Add or subtract notes to fit the
syllables in the verses.
**Examples of where extra beats are needed to fit the lyrics. Sacco's spirit is worth it.

NICOLA SACCO & FAMILY, 1922

1. If nothing <u>happens</u> they will electrocute us right after <u>mid</u>night
   Therefore here I <u>am</u>, right with <u>you</u>, with love** and with open heart,
   As <u>I</u> was yesterday.
   Don't cry, <u>Dante</u>, for many, many tears have been <u>wasted</u>,
   As your mother's <u>tears</u> have been already <u>wasted</u> for seven years,
   And <u>never</u> did any good.
   So son, instead of <u>cry</u>ing, be strong, be brave
   So as to be <u>able</u> to comfort your mother.

2. And when you <u>want</u> to distract her from the discouraging <u>soleness</u>
   You take <u>her</u> for a long <u>walk</u> in the quiet countryside,
   Gathering <u>flowers</u> here and there.
   And resting <u>under</u> the shade of trees, beside the music of the <u>waters</u>,
   The <u>peace</u>fulness of <u>nature</u>, she will enjoy it very much,
   As <u>you</u> will surely too.
   But son, you must re<u>member</u>: Don't use all yourself.
   But <u>down</u> yourself, just one** step, to help the weak ones at your side.

3. The weaker <u>ones</u>, that cry for help, the persecuted and the <u>victim</u>.
   They are your <u>friends</u>, friends of yours and <u>mine</u>, they are the comrades that fight,
   <u>Yes</u>, and sometimes fall.
   Just as your <u>father</u>, your father and Bartolo have <u>fallen</u>,
   Have fought and <u>fell</u>, yester<u>day</u>, for the conquest of joy,
   Of <u>freedom</u> for all.
   In the struggle of life you'll <u>find</u>, you'll find more love.
   And in the <u>struggle</u>, you will be loved also.

For 40 years Lee Hays (1913-1981) and I knew each other, sang together off and on, tried making up songs together occasionally. This next poem of his I've often recited at concerts. I tried putting a tune to it; decided it was better simply recited as a poem.

To Know Good Will

If I should one day die by violence,
Please take this as my written will;
And in the name of simple common sense
Treat my killer only as one ill,
As one who needs far more than I could give,
As one who never really learned to live
In charity and peace and love for life,
But was diseased and plagued by hate and strife.
My vanished life might have some meaning still
When my destroyer learns to know good will.

By Lee Hays
© 1987 by Sanga Music Inc.

LEE HAYS, 1980

© David Gahr

I'm glad I was able to find a singable melody for this next gem of Lee's. He sent it as a letter to my wife, also a gardener.

In Dead Earnest
(Lee's Compost Song)

B09

Freely / Cm / Fm
If I should die be-fore I wake,
All that I am will feed the trees and

Bb / Cm
all my bone and sin-ew take.
lit-tle fish-ies in the seas. When

Fm / Eb
Put me in the com-post pile to
rad-ish-es and corn you munch, you

G7 / Cm / G7 / Cm
de-com-pose me for a while.
may be hav-ing me for lunch.

1. Cm / Fm
Worms, wa-ter, sun, will have their way, re-

Eb / G7
turn-ing me to com-mon clay.

2. Cm / Fm
And then ex-crete me with a grin,

Bb / G7 / Cm
chort-ling: There goes Lee a-gain.___

Cm / Fm
*Twill be my hap-piest des-tin-y to

Bb / G7 / Cm
die and live e-ter-nal-ly.

Words by Lee Hays (1979)   Music by Pete Seeger (1979)
© 1981, 1982 by Sanga Music Inc.
* I find I can omit the last two lines.

If I should die before I wake,
All my bone and sinew take
Put me in the compost pile
To decompose me for a while
    Worms, water, sun, will have their way,
    Returning me to common clay
    All that I am will feed the trees
    And little fishies in the seas.
When radishes and corn you munch,
You may be having me for lunch
And then excrete me with a grin,
Chortling, "There goes Lee again."
    'Twill be my happiest destiny
    To die and live eternally.

Lee was raised in Arkansas, son of a Methodist preacher. A great storyteller. In the mid-'30s, Lee taught at Commonwealth College, a small Arkansas labor

school. It was forced to close by the Ku Klux Klan. A good biography of Lee, *Lonesome Traveler*, by Doris Willens, is now available from the University of Nebraska Press, Lincoln, Nebraska. I used to think Lee was cantankerous. Now I think he was some kind of genius.

Lee Hays and I had a long friendship with Walter and Lillian Lowenfels of Philadelphia. Walter had been an expatriate avant-garde poet in Paris in the 1920s. Shared a poetry prize with e. e. cummings. Returned home a Communist, spent 15 years editing the Pennsylvania edition of *The Daily Worker*. In his last years went back to poetry, put out some wonderful books, such as *Walt Whitman's Civil War* and *Letters to My Twelve Grandchildren*.

Business

English translation by Walter Lowenfels (from the French of Guillevic)
Music by Pete Seeger (1961)
© 1963 (renewed) by Stormking Music Inc.

Two million bushels of North African grain
Resold to Germany for Swiss francs,
Paid for by a consortium of banks
With a deal in futures that the Stock Exchange
Unloads for coffee from Brazilian uplands
Destined for Paris. Before the whole deal sinks,
The checks written in indelible inks
Outrace Atlantic's winter hurricanes.

At last the coffee arrives, also the wheat,
Needless to say, the deal was a success.
Who can deny that all of us have gained?
Our benefactors? Three trusts. They compete
For honor, glory, power and of course,
Profits, where all happiness is contained.

WALTER LOWENFELS IN THE 1940S

Touring Japan in 1967 I met a young professor, Yuzuru Katagiri, publishing a literary magazine in English(!). I'm a magazinaholic; I subscribed. Shortly after, I read this poem. I got permission to record it back then for Columbia Records. Don't be scared off because it looks like a long song; it's got four short verses, each slightly different from the other.

When I Was Most Beautiful

Words by Noriko Ibaragi (1957) Music by Pete Seeger (1967)
TRO - © 1968 & 1970 Melody Trails, Inc., New York, NY.

1. When I___ was most beautiful,
   Cities were falling
   And from unexpected places

   Blue sky was seen
   When I___ was most beautiful
   People around me were killed
   And for paint and powder
   I lost the chance___

2. When I ___ was most beautiful
   Nobody gave me kind gifts.
   Men knew only to salute
   And went away.
   When I___ was most beautiful
   My country lost the war
   I paraded the main street
   With my blouse sleeves rolled high___

3. When I___ was most beautiful
   (IN TEMPO) Jazz overflowed the radio;
   I broke the prohibition against smoking;
   Sweet music of another land!
   (FREELY) When I___ was most beautiful
   I was most unhappy___
   I was quite absurd___
   I was quite lonely___

4. That's why I decided to live long
   Like Monsieur Rouault,
   Who was a
   Very old man,
   When he painted such terribly beautiful pictures,
   You see_____ (Dm, Dm/C, Gm/Bb, A7, Dm) ...?

*The guitar plays the accompaniment for the last five bars while the singer holds one high note, even after the accompaniment is over.

I accompany this in "Dropped D" tuning, and capo up so I'm really playing in F. Here's how the words to the 2nd and 3rd verses fit to the music:

*(C) – one string.

In case some reader knows Japanese, here's the original poem.

わたしが一番きれいだったとき
街々はがらがら崩れていって
とんでもないところから
青空なんかが見えたりした

わたしが一番きれいだったとき
まわりの人達が沢山死んだ
工場で　海で　名もない島で
わたしはおしゃれのきっかけを落してしまった

わたしが一番きれいだったとき
だれもやさしい贈物を捧げてはくれなかった
男たちは挙手の礼しか知らなくて
きれいな眼差だけを残し皆発っていった

わたしが一番きれいだったとき
わたしの頭はからっぽで
わたしの心はかたくなで
手足ばかりが栗色に光った

わたしが一番きれいだったとき
わたしの国は戦争で負けた
そんな馬鹿なことってあるものか
ブラウスの腕をまくり卑屈な町をのし歩いた

わたしが一番きれいだったとき
ラジオからはジャズが溢れた
禁煙を破ったときのようにくらくらしながら
わたしは異国の甘い音楽をむさぼった

わたしが一番きれいだったとき
わたしはとてもふしあわせ
わたしはとてもとんちんかん
わたしはめっぽうさびしかった

だから決めた　できれば長生きすることに
年とってから凄く美しい絵を描いた
フランスのルオー爺さんのように
ね

My guess is that no two people will accompany it in the same way — though I hope they won't tamper with the words. I make the accompaniment more rhythmical in the beginning of the third verse, where the words are about jazz. Sometimes I whistle an interlude between verses.

NORIKO IBARAGI

I'm told that the words are very good in Japanese — but I doubt they fit this melody. Noriko Ibaragi became a well-known poet. She wrote this when she was 31. Her publishers are Shicho-sha, 3-15, Sadohara-cho Ichigaya, Shinjuku-ku, Tokyo, Japan. In 1984 on another tour, she came to my concert, recited the original poem in Japanese, and then I sang this afterwards. She died in 2006.

Incidentally, most of my life I've been prejudiced against high endings. But this one works. Hold the word "see" under five chord changes and longer. Pianissimo.

The poem is a good answer to the English poet (male) who tossed off the line, "Women are. Men do."

★ ★ ★

Idris Davies, a coal miner in Wales, was a friend of Dylan Thomas. I came across his poem reprinted in one of Thomas' essays. After the failure of the British general strike of 1926, Idris Davies, then a teenager, determined to leave coal mining. He studied nights for four years, and finally passed his examination to Nottingham University. After graduation, he became a school teacher in London, and published three slim volumes of poetry. Died of cancer at the young age of 44.

In 1960 Toshi and I were able to visit Mrs. Davies, Idris's mother, still living in Rhymney — a typical coal mine town: 50 yards wide and one mile long. Caerphilly is nearby, famous for a type of cheese. Cardiff and Newport are on the Bay of Bristol. Wye is a more prosperous valley 50 miles east. Pronounce more like "Rummnee."

Bells of Rhymney

* See p. 101 for chords ** p. 100 Tablature *** See p. 101 for chords

3. Throw the van-dals in court, Say the bells of New - port. All would be well if if if if if if, Cry the green bells of Car - diff, Why so wor-ried, sis-ters, why?— Sang the sil - ver bells of Wye.— And what will you give me? Say the sad bells of Rhym - ney.

From Idris Davies: A Personal Memoir, by Islwyn Jenkins. Gomer Press

IDRIS DAVIES

I sang these three verses slowly, freely, then set the guitar into a fast rhythm and sang the same three verses again. See pp. 100-101.

Coda—Keep the rhythm going to the end

(whistle)

Words from *Gwalia Deserta* by Idris Davies (written ca. 1927, pub. 1938)
Music by Pete Seeger (1959)
TRO - © 1959 (renewed) & 1964 (renewed) Ludlow Music, Inc., New York, NY.

1. Oh what will you give me?
    Say the sad bells of Rhymney
    Is there hope for the future?
    Cry the brown bells of Merthyr.
    Who made the mine owner?
    Say the black bells of Rhondda.
    And who robbed the miner?
    Cry the grim bells of Blaina.

2. They will plunder willy-nilly,
    Cry the bells of Caerphilly.
    They have fangs, they have teeth,
    shout the loud bells of Neath.
    Even God is uneasy,
    Say the moist bells of Swansea.
    And what will you give me,
    Say the sad bells of Rhymney.

3. Throw the vandals in court
    Say the bells of Newport.
    All would be well if, if, if,
    Cry the green bells of Cardiff.
    Why so worried, sisters why?
    Sang the silver bells of Wye.
    And what will you give me?
    Say the sad bells of Rhymney.

Map by Peter Blood

The tune is another cousin of "Twinkle Little Star." It came to me once on tour, in Montreal. Thanks to my pocket notebook I had the rest of the words at hand. That night I stuck the words to the microphone and tried them out.

Pronounce Rhymney more like "Rhuhmney," Caerphilly like "Caffilly," and Swansea like "Swanzy." The "r's" tend to be rolled. Rhondda sounds more like "Rhundtha."

Here's tablature for the accompaniment:

The accents are to remind you that these syncopated notes are the ones which really sound out.

Then I strike some full chords up the neck:

After singing all three verses I usually break into a regular rhythm, thumb on bass strings, index and middle fingers on top strings.

At first you see a rhythmic version of the pattern given in the chord diagrams on the next page (***).

Continue this rhythmic pattern while repeating all or some of the three verses again. You can add or subtract beats as you want, while keeping the rhythm steady. I usually end by whistling a few measures against the pounding guitar.

My accompaniment for "Bells of Rhymney" was worked out on a 12-string guitar, which is customarily tuned lower than a 6-string. I get my heavier strings from La Bella in Newburgh, NY.

Thus D position turned out to sound B flat, a comfortable key for me to sing the song. On a 6-stringer, you either have to sing in a tenor range, or re-tune strings, or else capo way up (to sing it in G, for example). Or else figure out a new accompaniment. Here are my chords. Tuning: DADGBE.

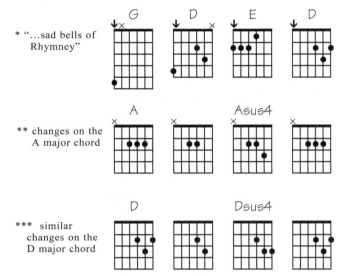

* "...sad bells of Rhymney"

** changes on the A major chord

*** similar changes on the D major chord

As a teenager I had a scholarship in an unusual prep school, Avon Old Farms, near Hartford, Connecticut. Ninety students. Best thing about it, for me, was 3,000 acres of woodland, with a small river. I could explore, camp out, snowshoe in winter. It also had some unusual teachers, including Harold Lewis Cook, poet and a friend of other poets like Edna St. Vincent Millay and Max Eastman. In Cook's English classes we'd spend three months reading and discussing in depth one Shakespeare play. One year it might be *Hamlet*, *Macbeth*, another year *Romeo and Juliet*, or *The Tempest*. Occasionally today I find myself rereading World Famous Will, impatient sometimes with his archaic language, his wordiness, but rewarded with some fantastic lines: "...to sleep,...perchance to dream...aye, there's the rub..." (Hamlet is contemplating suicide.)

In 1965 I stole his phrase for another idea:

To fight, perchance to win, aye, there's the rub
For victory brings power and prestige
And the children of the children of the fighters
Take all for granted, and in turn, oppress.

Around 1955, singing at another prep school, in Woodstock, Vermont, I found myself at another English class, with teacher Buffy Dunker. Together we all put a tune to the song of Ariel in *The Tempest*. I'm sure other musicians have tried also; I don't know how this tune compares. It has worked for me.

Full fath-om five thy fa-ther lies, Of his bones_ are cor-al made; Those_ are pearls that were his eyes: Nothing of him that doth fade, But doth suf-fer a sea change in - to something rich and strange. Sea nymphs hour - ly ring his knell, ding - dong.__ Hark, now,_ I hear them, ding - dong_ bell.__

Words by William Shakespeare (1611, from *The Tempest*)
Music by Pete Seeger & students of Woodstock School (1954)
© 1962, 1963 (renewed) by Sanga Music Inc.

Full fathom five thy father lies;
 Of his bones are coral made:
Those are pearls that were his eyes:
 Nothing of him that doth fade,
But doth suffer a sea-change
Into something rich and strange.
Sea-nymphs hourly ring his knell: ding-dong.
Hark! now I hear them — ding-dong, bell.

I and a friend recording it really thought long and hard about the above melody. Now we think we have it right. Keep the tempo. Singing, don't be afraid of shortening vowels and lengthening nice consonants like "m" and "l." Fathmmm. Knelllll. Dinggg. Belllll.

World Savers have to guard against being unremittingly serious, but in nearly every program I give for any age, I try to put in one deadly serious song. This is one – an English translation of the last poem by Victor Jara, brutally murdered by Chilean fascists in September 1973.[1]

VICTOR & JOAN JARA WITH THEIR DAUGHTERS

Victor was singing for students at the university when the whole area was surrounded. All within were taken prisoner and marched to a large indoor soccer stadium, Estadio Chile. For three days it was a scene of horror. Torture, executions.

An officer thought he recognized Victor, pointed at him with a questioning look and motioning as if strumming a guitar. Victor nodded. He was seized, taken to the center of the stadium and told to put his hands on a table. While his friends watched in horror, rifle butts beat his hands to bloody pulp.

"All right, sing for us now, you ..." shouted the officer. Victor staggered to his feet, faced the stands.

"Compañeros, let's sing for el commandante."

Waving his bloody stumps, he led them in the anthem of Salvador Allende's Popular Unity Party. Other prisoners hesitantly joined in.

RAT-TAT-TAT-TAT.

The guards sprayed him and the stands with machine guns.

This last poem of his was smuggled out of Chile, in several different versions. This translation was given to me by a woman at a Chicago concert in 1974. A few minutes later I stuck the words on a mic stand and improvised a guitar accompaniment as I recited them. Over a week of reciting, the chords took the form given here. (Dropped D tuning: DADGBE).

[1] On this date General Pinochet, with the assistance of the CIA and the ITT Corporation, took over the government of Chile, bombing the presidential palace of elected socialist Salvador Allende, and murdering him.

After reciting this, any applause is impossible.

I usually swing right into an upbeat song like "Guantanamera," which everyone can sing with me.

Years later I got Victor's original words. Mine are much shorter, as you see. It was a young mother, Joanne Fox-Przeworski ("shehVORski"), who made up the excellent translation. Gracias!

Estadio Chile   B16

Spoken poem with guitar accompaniment.
Exact timing of the words would have to be improvised,
or learned from the recording.

Sample accompaniment, verse:

We_____ are five thousand...

Accompaniment, bridge: B17

in march tempo

The military   carry out their

plans with precision   Blood   is...

Later: B18

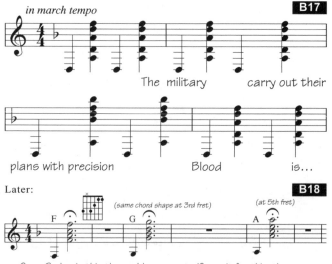

(same chord shape at 3rd fret)   *(at 5th fret)*

O my God... is this the world you created? was it for this, the...

Words by Victor Jara (1973), translated by Joanne Fox-Przeworski. Musical setting by Pete Seeger (1974)
© 1975 Mighty Oak Music Ltd., London, England
TRO - Cheshire Music, Inc., New York, controls all publication rights for the USA & Canada.

```
      Dm                  Dm/C
1.  We are 5,000 ..... here in this little part of the city .....
      G7/B                        Gm6/B♭
    We are 5,000 ..... how many more will there be? .....
          Dm/A                      A
    In the whole city, and the country ..... 10,000 hands .....
    B♭addE/A                       C/A
    Which could seed the fields ..... make run the factories .....
          BaddE/A                  B♭addE/A
    How much humanity ..... now with hunger, pain, panic
                    A
      and terror? .....


      Dm                      Dm/C
2.  There are six of us ..... lost in space among the stars .....
        G7/B              Gm6/B♭
    One dead ..... one beaten like I never believed a human

      could be so beaten .....
          Dm/A                      A
    The other four wanting to leave all the terror .....
              B♭addE/A                 C/B♭
    One leaping into space ..... others beating their heads

      against the wall .....
    BaddE/A            B♭addE/A        A
    All ..... with gazes ..... fixed on death .....
```
(In march rhythm)
```
Dm                          B♭/D  B♭/A
      The military ..... carry out their plans with precision .....
Dm                          B♭/D   B♭/A
      Blood is medals for them ..... Slaughter is the badge

      of heroism ..... (In march rhythm)
                    F         G
      Oh my God ..... Is this the world you created? .....
                A         (tacit)
      Was it for this ..... the seven days, of amazement

      and toil? .....
```
(Original chords)
```
Dm                  Dm/C              G7/B
3.  The blood ..... of compañero Presidente ..... is stronger
                  Gm6/B♭
      than bombs ..... is stronger than machine guns .....
Dm                                    A
    O you song ..... you come out so badly ..... when I must
    B♭addE/A  C/A
    sing ..... the terror! .....
          BaddE/A                  B♭addE/A
    What I see I never saw ..... What I have felt, and what I
          (tacit)
    feel ..... must come out! .....
          B♭addE/A
    "Hará brotar el momento! ..... Hará brotar

      el  momento!"*            *The moment will bloom
```

1. Somos cinco mil
    en esta pequeña parte de la ciudad.
    Somos cinco mil
    ¿Cuántos seremos en total
    en las ciudades y en todo el país?
    Solo aquí,
    diez mil manos que siembran
    y hacen andar las fábricas.
    ¡Cuánta humanidad
    con hambre, frío, pánico, dolor,
    presión mortal, terror y locura!

2. Seis de los nuestros se perdieron
    en el espacio de las estrellas.
    Un muerto, un golpeado como jamás creí
    se podía golpear a un ser humano.
    Los otros cuatro quisieron quitarse todos los
        temores, uno saltando al vacío,
    otro golpeándose la cabeza contra el muro,
    pero todos con la mirada fija en la muerte.

3. ¡Qué espanto causa el rostro del fascismo!
    Llevan a cabo sus planes con precisión artera
        sin importarles nada.
    La sangre para ellos son medallas.
    La matanza es acto de heroísmo.
    ¿Es este el mundo que creaste, dios mío?
    ¿Para esto tus siete días de asombro y de trabajo?
    En estas cuatro murallas sólo existe un
        número que no progresa,
    que lentamente querrá más muerte.

    Pero de pronto me golpea la conciencia
    y veo esta marea sin latido,
    pero con el pulso de las máquinas
    y los militares mostrando su rostro de matrona
        lleno de dulzura.

    ¿Y México, Cuba y el mundo?
    ¡Que griten esta ignominia!
    Somos diez mil manos menos
    que no producen.
    ¿Cuántos somos en toda la Patria?

4. La sangre del compañero Presidente
    golpea más fuerte que bombas y metrallas.
    Así golpeará nuestro puño nuevamente.

    ¡Canto qué mal me sales
    cuando tengo que cantar espanto!
    Espanto como el que vivo
    como el que muero, espanto.
    De verme entre tanto y tantos
    momentos del infinito
    en que el silencio y el grito
    son las metas de este canto.
    Lo que veo nunca vi,
    lo que he sentido y lo que siento
    hará brotar el momento...

As long as we're into deadly serious songs, here's another, which I sang when Marilyn Monroe killed herself with an overdose of pills. I read the poem in *Life* magazine, put a tune to it. Later on, met the author, got his permission. He knew Marilyn well; she was known as Norma Jean (her original name) to her friends.

I've written it all out, because though it has only two short melodies, there are important little variations in each verse. Nine soloists could sing this, each taking one verse.

MARILYN MONROE & NORMAN ROSTEN

Who Killed Norma Jean?

B19

1. Who killed— Nor-ma Jean? I, said the Cit-y,

As a civ-ic du-ty, I killed Nor-ma Jean.

2. Who saw her die? I, said the Night,—

And a bed-room light,— We— saw her die.

3. Who'll catch her blood? I, said the Fan,

With my lit-tle pan, I'll catch her blood.

4. Who'll make her shroud? I, said the Lov-er,

My guilt to cov-er, I'll— make her shroud.

5. Who'll dig her grave? The tour-ist will come and

join in the fun, He'll dig her grave.

6. Who'll be chief mourn-ers? We who repre-sent,— And

lose our ten per-cent.— We'll be the chief mourn-ers.

7. Who'll bear the pall? We, said the Press,— In

pain and dis-tress,— We'll— bear the pall.

8. Who'll toll the bell? I, screamed the moth-er,

Locked in her tow-er, I'll pull the bell.

9. Who'll soon for-get? I, said the Page,— Be-

gin-ning to fade,— I'll be first to for-get.

Words by Norman Rosten   Music by Pete Seeger
TRO © 1963 (renewed) & 1964 (renewed) Ludlow Music, NY, NY.

1. Who killed Norma Jean?
   I, said the City, as a civic duty,
   I killed Norma Jean.

2. Who saw her die?
   I, said the Night, and a bedroom light,
   We saw her die.

   3. Who'll catch her blood?
      I, said the Fan, with my little pan,
      I'll catch her blood.

4. Who'll make her shroud?
   I, said the Lover, my guilt to cover,
   I'll make her shroud.

5. Who'll dig her grave?
   The tourist will come and join in the fun,
   He'll dig her grave.

6. Who'll be chief mourners?
   We who represent, and lose our ten percent.
   We'll be the chief mourners.

7. Who'll bear the pall?
   We, said the Press, in pain and distress,
   We'll bear the pall.

   8. Who'll toll the bell?
      I, screamed the mother, locked in her tower,
      I'll pull the bell.

9. Who'll soon forget?
   I, said the Page, beginning to fade,
   I'll be first to forget.

NAZIM HIKMET

"It's difficult to write about Marilyn Monroe now that she is gone. The past tense just doesn't suit her somehow; she was too acutely alive. I knew her and was very fond of her. She was a strange, tormented, endearing girl, full of fun — a bravado fun, as though daring death to strike her down. Well, it did, finally. What can we say who saw her living in that shadowland of loveless Hollywood? She who had such love in her heart — love for people, animals, birds, trees — had to die for lack of it!

Who to blame? I thought of blame, even though it's always too late. My poem tried to say it for myself, anyway…for whatever it's worth for others."

—Norman Rosten

In the late '50s I got a letter: "Dear Pete Seeger: I've made what I think is a singable translation of a poem by the Turkish poet, Nazim Hikmet. Do you think you could make a tune for it? (Signed), Jeanette Turner."

I tried for a week. Failed. Meanwhile I couldn't get out of my head an extraordinary melody put together by a Massachusetts Institute of Technology student who had put a new tune to a mystical ballad "The Great Silkie" from the Shetland Islands north of Scotland.

Without his permission I used his melody for Hikmet's words. It was wrong of me. I should have gotten his permission.

But it worked. The Byrds made a good recording of it, electric guitars and all.

I'll never forget 6,000 young people in Lisbon, Portugal, in '84, singing it with me. The English words were on a screen. I played the melody first on a recorder, then with the help of some expert Portuguese back-up musicians, we sang the whole song through, all 6,000 of us.

I never met Jeanette Turner, who was a volunteer with a New York peace organization. She died soon after she wrote me. Bless your memory, Jeanette. And Hikmet, the Turkish Communist poet imprisoned for so many years.

And thank you, James Waters, later a professor in Vermont. Your melody is one of the world's greatest. I hope you will someday forgive me for using it without permission.

After Sept. 11, I often sing this song:

I Come and Stand at Every Door
(Girl of Hiroshima)

B20

I come and stand at ev-'ry door,

But none can hear my si-lent tread,

I knock and yet re-main un-seen,

For I am dead,— for I am dead.

Original Turkish poem by Nazim Hikmet   English translation by Jeanette Turner
Music by James Waters ("The Great Silkie")   Adaptation by Pete Seeger (1962)
Text © 1966 by Stormking Music Inc. Music © 1966 Folk Legacy Records.
All rights reserved.

1. I come and stand at every door
   But none can hear my silent tread
   I knock and yet remain unseen
   For I am dead, for I am dead.

2. I'm only seven, although I died
   In Hiroshima long ago.
   I'm seven now as I was then—
   When children die, they do not grow.

3. My hair was scorched by swirling flame;
   My eyes grew dim, my eyes grew blind.
   Death came and turned my bones to dust,
   And that was scattered by the wind.

4. I need no fruit, I need no rice.
   I need no sweets, or even bread;
   I ask for nothing for myself,
   For I am dead, for I am dead.

5. All that I ask is that for peace
   You fight today, you fight today.
   So that the children of the world
   May live and grow and laugh and play!

The opening three notes can be sung several different ways:

or

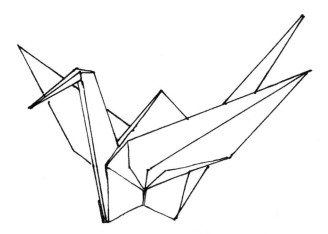

And, to try to make up to James Waters, here's the words to "Great Silkie," for which he originally wrote the melody. A "silkie" is a seal. A "nouris" is a nursing mother. An old Scottish song-story.

The Great Silkie

1. An earthly nouris sits and sings,
   And aye she sings, ba lily wean
   And little ken I my bairnie's father
   Far less the land that he dwells in.

2. For he came one night to my bed feet
   And a grumlie guest I'm sure was he,
   Saying, Here am I, thy bairnie's father,
   Although I be not com-e-lie.

3. I am a man upon the land
   As I am a silkie on the sea
   And when I'm far, and far frae land
   My home is in the Sule Skerrie.

4. It wasna' well, quo' the maiden fair,
   It wasna' well, indeed quo' she
   That the grey silkie of Sule Skerrie
   Should come and take my babe from me.

5. Now he has ta'en a purse of gold
   And he has placed it on her knee,
   Saying, give to me my little young son
   And take thee of thy nouris' fee.

6. And it shall come to pass on a summer's day
   When the sun shines bright on every stone
   I'll come and fetch my little wee son
   And teach him how to swim the foam.

7. And ye shall marry a gunner good
   And a right good gunner I'm sure he'll be
   And the very first shot that e'er he shoots
   Shall kill both my young son and me.

Traditional Scottish ballad

This has been a somber chapter. Now we cheer up.

I was lucky to have been acquainted with Malvina Reynolds, another of the great 20th Century songwriters. I am only sorry that because we lived on opposite sides of the continent, we didn't see each other often. Here's six of her songs.

Some song collaborators are close. Husband-and-wife teams. Some don't get along personally. Gilbert and Sullivan. A good many musicians work with people at long distance, as chance gets them together.

Mal and I agreed philosophically on most things. I usually deferred to her judgment, but not always.

I met her in the summer of 1947. I was 28 years old; she was 45, with beautiful white hair. She asked me if she could speak with me for a few minutes and perhaps give her some advice on the general subject of getting started as a singer and writer of songs. I usually make a practice of not discouraging people, but I have to confess that when I first met her, I didn't perceive her genius. I think I had in the back of my mind a feeling, "Gosh, she's pretty old to want to get started as a musician." I had a lot to learn.

I don't know if the advice I told her was any good or not. I probably described how I sang for a wide variety of community organizations and left-wing causes. For schools, churches, movements, and most anybody who called up. And how, if I ever was lucky to get a song written, I made copies of it; but I didn't expect any publisher to want to pay me for them nor print them and distribute them. I probably told her how Woody mimeographed the words of his songs and sold them for a few cents a copy. And I told her about our song magazine, *People's Songs*, in New York.

From time to time over the next 30 years I would receive copies of her new songs in the mail. She had bought one of those early office copying machines which could print up to 50 copies in purplish ink. And occasionally she would do me the honor of asking me to try writing a melody to her lyrics. Here are a few that I worked on. What a wonderful person. How I miss her. I'm only one of millions who have benefited from her wisdom and stick-to-it-iveness. Before she died, friends in Berkeley made a movie of her, *Love It Like a Fool*. The title comes from a line from one of her songs: "This old world is mean and cruel/Still I love it like a fool."

Her life should be an inspiration to many people in many places. She refused to be discouraged, and if she thought she had a song worthy of being sung somewhere, she'd get on the telephone and ask to sing. She would not be put down, even though some people called her "pushy."

I once joked that she made up a new song before breakfast every morning. She looked at me severely and said, "You *know* it's not that easy."

Because I recorded her song "Little Boxes," in 1963 and it was even on the Top 40 very briefly, some people thought I had written it. But all I did was sing it like she wrote it.

Little Boxes B21

Lit-tle box-es on the hill-side, Lit-tle box-es made of tick-y tack-y, Lit-tle *

By Malvina Reynolds © 1962 (renewed) by Schroder Music Co.

She made up "Little Boxes" when she was driving to Palo Alto to sing for a small meeting of the Friends Committee on Legislation. Driving past Daly City south of San Francisco, she looked up at the hillside, and said to her husband, "Bud, take the wheel. I feel a song coming on." When she got to Palo Alto, she had the song ready to sing.

Bud was a great guy, too. When I first knew him, he was working as a carpenter. In his early days, he'd been one of the heroic organizers of the automobile workers' union in Detroit. Later on he was an organizer for the Communist Party in Omaha. What a wonderful pair.

Photo by Joe Alper

BUD & MALVINA REYNOLDS AT NEWPORT, 1963

*Oh, a lot of readers will cuss me out for not printing all of this great song here. But I really hope people will write and get books with lots of Malvina's songs. She wisely set up a small publishing company named after the character in the comic strip *Peanuts*. You can order her recordings and songbooks from Sisters Choice, 704 Gilman Street, Berkeley, CA 94710, phone: 510-524-5804, fax: 510-528-9342. Or see their Web site: <www.sisterschoice.com>.

From Way Up Here

Words by Malvina Reynolds   Music by Pete Seeger and Pete Tchaikovsky
© 1962 (renewed) by Abigail Music Co. All rights reserved.

From way up here the earth looks very small,
It's just a little ball of rock and sea and sand,
No bigger than my hand.

From way up here the earth looks very small,
They shouldn't fight at all
    down there upon that little sphere.
Their time is short, a life is just a day,
You think they'd find a way.
You think they'd get along
    and fill their sunlit days with song.

(Whistle melody from *Swan Lake*)

From way up here the earth is very small,
It's just a little ball, so small, so beautiful and dear.
Their time is short, a life is just a day,
Must be a better way
To use the time that runs among the distant suns.

From way up here the earth is very small,
It's just a little ball, so small, so beautiful and dear.

Lovers of ballet will recognize that the notes whistled between the verses are the ones that I swiped from Tchaikovsky.

Seventy Miles

B24

MALVINA REYNOLDS

CHORUS (AND AFTER EACH VERSE):
Seventy miles of wind and spray,
Seventy miles of water,
Seventy miles of open bay—
It's a garbage dump.

1. What's that stinky creek out there,
   Down behind the slum's back stair—
   Sludgy puddle, sad and gray?
   Why man, that's San Francisco Bay! (CHORUS)

2. Big Solano and the Montecell',
   Ferry boats, I knew them well,
   Creak and groan in their muddy graves,
   Remembering old San Francisco Bay. (CHORUS)

3. Joe Ortega and the Spanish crew
   Sailed across the ocean blue,
   Came into this mighty Bay,
   Stood on the decks and cried, "Olé!" (CHORUS)

4. Fill it there, fill it here,
   Docks and tidelands disappear,
   Shaky houses on the quakey ground,
   The builder, he's Las Vegas bound. (CHORUS)

5. "Dump the garbage in the Bay?"
   City fathers say, "Okay.
   When cries of anguish fill the air
   He'll be off on the Rivière." (CHORUS)

Words by Malvina Reynolds   Music by Pete Seeger

Mrs. Clara Sullivan's Letter

B25

Dear Mis-ter Ed-i-tor, if you choose, Please
send me a cop-y of the la-bor news;
I've got a son in the In-fan-try, And
he'd be might-y glad— to see That
some-bod-y, some-where, now and then,
Thinks a-bout the lives of the min-ing men,
In Per-ry Coun-ty.

Words by Malvina Reynolds   Music by Pete Seeger

1. Dear Mister Editor, if you choose,
   Please send me a copy of the labor news;
   I've got a son in the Infantry,
   And he'd be mighty glad to see
   That somebody, somewhere, now and then
   Thinks about the lives of the mining men,
   In Perry County.

2. In Perry County and thereabout
   We miners simply had to go out.
   It was long hours, substandard pay,
   Then they took our contract away.
   Fourteen months is a mighty long time
   To face the goons on the picket line
   In Perry County.

3. I'm twenty-six years a miner's wife,
   There's nothing harder than a miner's life,
   But there's no better man than a mining man,
   Couldn't find better in all this land.
   The deal they get is a rotten deal,
   Mountain greens and gravy meal,
   In Perry County.

4. We live in barns that the rain comes in
   While operators live high as sin,
   Ride Cadillac cars and drink like a fool
   While our kids lack clothes to go to school
   Sheriff Combs he has it fine,
   He runs the law and owns a mine
   In Perry County.

5. What operator would go dig coal
   For even fifty a day on the mine pay-roll!
   Why, after work my man comes in
   With his wet clothes frozen to his skin,
   Been digging coal so the world can run
   And operators can have their fun
   In Perry County.

6. When folks sent money to the *Hazard Press*
   To help the strikers in distress,
   They gave that money, yours and mine,
   To the scabs who crossed the picket line,
   And the state militia and F.B.I.
   Just look on while miners die
   In Perry County.

7. I believe the truth will out some day
   That we're fighting for jobs at decent pay.
   We're just tired of doing without,
   And that's what the strike is all about,
   And it helps to know that folks like you
   Are telling the story straight and true,
   About Perry County.

To see what a poet can do changing prose to verse, contrast Mal's words, above, with the original letter.

Scuddy, Kentucky
January 21, 1963

Dear Editor:

I recently read a magazine of yours about the labor unrest in Perry county and surrounding counties. I would like very much to get one of these magazines to send to my son in the service. I don't have any money to send you for it, but would you please send me one anyway?

I am a coal miner's wife. I have been married 26 years to a coal miner and you can't find a harder worker than a coal miner. We have been treated so unfair by our leaders from the sheriff up to the president. I know what it is to be hungry.

My husband has been out of work for 14 months. He worked at a union mine at Leatherwood. Now the company has terminated the union contract (UMWA) and plans to go back to work with scab workers. It isn't just here that all this is happening. The company will say they have to close as they are going in the hole. Then they will

Photo by Alejandro Stuart

MALVINA REYNOLDS

re-open with scab laborers that will work for practically nothing as long as the boss smiles at them and gives them a pat on the back. These men just don't realize the amount of people they are hurting or just don't care.

The operators have the money and the miner doesn't have anything but a bad name. You couldn't find better people anywhere in the whole world. But we have our pride too. We are tired of doing without. The operators have beautiful homes, Cadillacs and aeroplanes to enjoy, and our homes (camp houses, by the way) look like barns.

We don't want what the operators have. All we want is a decent wage and good insurance that will help our families. Is this too much to ask?

The operators wouldn't go in a mine for $50 a day. I've seen my husband come home from work with his clothes frozen to his body from working in the water. I have sat down at a table where we didn't have anything to eat but wild greens picked from the mountain side. There are three families around me, that each family of seven only had plain white gravy and bread for a week is true. Is this progress or what? I just can't understand it.

I have two sons that go to school and they don't even have decent clothes to wear. No one knows our feelings and I'm quite sure the coal operators don't care as long as they get that almighty dollar. Of all the things that were sent here to the Helping Fund (Editor's Note: This is the "relief" fund administered by the Hazard newspaper. See story, January PL.) not one of these needy families received a thing nor did anyone here in camp. Where did it all go? Somebody got a real good vacation with it I suppose. All the newspapers are against us because of political pressure, but our day is coming.

The government talks of re-training. My husband went into the mines in Alabama at the age of 11 with only the second grade of schooling. How could he retrain now, and him 52? It is silly to even think this will help the older miner. All the state thinks about is building up the tourist trade. How will that help us? It would just put more money in the big shots' pockets — not ours. No one would want to spend money to come here for a vacation to see the desolate mine camps and ravaged hills.

Happy A.B. Chandler lost his election by siding against the laboring class of people; by sending the State Militia and State Police (by Don Steirgill, then head of the State Police) in here to use as strikebreakers in 1959. Wilson Wyatt lost because of Governor Combs doing the same thing, only in a more subtle way. How can he hope to get elected to the Senate? How does he think Ed Breathitt will fare by endorsing him?

The truth will [come] out someday. I'm sorry I have rambled on like this. It just seems so unjust, especially to the poor.

Please, sir, could you send me a magazine?

Thank you sincerely,

Mrs. Clara Sullivan
Scuddy, Kentucky
Perry County

You can make up a song out of many an item you read in the newspaper. The journalist has already done half your job for you. Woody made up "Reuben James," "Deportee" and "Isaac Woodward" from seeing short items in some paper. Malvina Reynolds was similarly helped to write "Andorra." It was a three-inch item in the *New York Times*. Years later I met the newspaper reporter in Andorra. He knew just what he was doing.

Andorra

B26

CHORUS (AFTER EACH VERSE):
I want to go to Andorra, Andorra, Andorra,
I want to go to Andorra, it's a place that I adore,
They spent four dollars and ninety cents
On armaments and their defense,
Did you ever hear of such confidence?
Andorra, hip hurrah!

1. In the mountains of the Pyrenees
   There's an independent state,
   Its population five thousand souls,
   And I think they're simply great.
      One hundred and seventy square miles big
      And it's awf'lly dear to me.
      Spends less than five dollars on armaments,
      And this I've got to see.

2. It's governed by a council,
   All gentle souls and wise,
   They've only five dollars for armaments
   And the rest for cakes and pies.
      They didn't invest in a tommy gun
      Or a plane to sweep the sky,
      But they bought some blanks for their cap pistols
      To shoot on their Fourtha July*

3. They live by the arts of farm and field
   And by making shoes and hats,
   And they haven't got room in their tiny land
   For a horde of diplomats;
      They haven't got room in their tiny land
      For armies to march about,
      And if anyone comes with a war budget
      They throw the rascals out.

Here's two verses I added:

4. I wandered down by the Pentagon
   This newspaper clipping in hand
   I said, "I want to see everyone
   In McNamara's band." **
      I said, "Look what they did in Andorra,
      They put us all to shame.
      The least is first, the biggest is last,
      Let's get there just the same."

5. The general said, "My dear boy,
   You just don't understand.
   We need these things to feel secure
   In our great and wealthy land."
      I said, "If security's what you need
      I'll buy a couch for you,
      A headshrinker is cheaper and quicker
      And a damn sight safer too."

Words by Malvina Reynolds
Music & final two verses by Pete Seeger

*On *their* independence day, not ours, of course.
**Robert McNamara, Secretary of Defense, 1962

The folk process continues. Am I proud. And I think Malvina would be proud, too, to know that Charlie King made up a new ballad, using some of her old song. Charlie also had a news item to start him. P.S.: The Republic of Andorra now has a population of 70,000. Progress. It's the Hong Kong of the Pyrenees – a beautiful valley.

Factories With Amenities Hinder Poland's Stark Turn to Capitalism

By STEPHEN ENGELBERG
Special to The New York Times

KEDZIERZYN KOZLE, Poland — Prime Minister Jan Krzysztof Bielecki recently visited the sprawling Azoty chemical works here, and what he saw chilled him to his free-market bones.

More than a year after the Government began its pioneering program to dismantle the centrally managed socialist economy, this state-run company seems frozen in an earlier time, when profits did not matter much and companies typically took on the role of municipal governments.

"It still conducts functions so typical for a socialist enterprise," Mr. Bielecki lamented in an interview. "They have an indoor skating rink, a very nice swimming pool, culture center, soft drink bottling plant and a very nice laundry. They maintain 1,000 free factory apartments, heat 80 percent of the town and still make a profit."

He continued: "This company has entered an international market and holds 5 percent of world production, yet it doesn't work at all on marketing, and the name of the enterprise" — Zakladv

Nawozowo-Azotowe w Kedzierzynie Kozlu — "is not pronounceable by anyone who doesn't speak Polish."

The factory, and its relationship to this squat, working-class town several hundred miles southwest of Warsaw, is a microcosm of the difficulties Poland faces in dismantling an encrusted system. In the last few weeks, Mr. Bielecki has repeatedly cited Azoty (ah-ZOH-teh), the 22d-largest enterprise in Poland, as a symbol of resistance to change.

I Want To go To Azoty

There's a factory in Silesia, in Poland's troubled land
5,000 working people and I think they're simply grand
They run the plant the old fashioned way—
    socialistically
And they're doing just fine on the bottom line, now this
    I got to see.

CHORUS:
    I want to go to Azoty (ah-ZOH-teh), Azoty, Azoty
    I want to go to Azoty, it's a fact'ry I admire
    Azoty people seem content—a job for all, free heat,
      free rent
    While turning a profit of 10%, Azoty, hip hoorah!

It's governed by a council, employees kind and wise
They've a tiny budget for marketing, the rest for cakes
    and pies
There's a beautiful pool to swim in, a wonderful rink
    to skate
A theater for concerts and dances and plays and I just
    think it's great!

The fact'ry churns out plastic for squirt guns, blocks
    and tops
There's a laundry to wash their working clothes
    and a shop for bottling pop
When they see something go to waste they try to plow
    it back
So they pipe steam down to heat the town that used to
    go up the stack.

It's all for one and one for all, they've lived that way
    for years
They haven't got room in their tiny town for the new
    free-marketeers
They haven't got room for prophets of doom or Wall
    Street eagle scouts
The Prime Minister came to play that game and they
    threw the rascal out.

Let's send a delegation and see if we take the hint
The Labor Czar, the Head o' the Fed, and maybe the
    Mayor of Flint
Tell 'em "Look what they do in Azoty, they put us all to
    shame,
It's wrong, it's Red, it's s'posed to be dead, let's try it
    all the same!"

New words by Charlie King
(adapted from the song "Andorra" by Malvina Reynolds & Pete Seeger)
© 1962 (renewed) & 1993 Amadeo-Brio Music Inc., PO Box 1770, Hendersonville TN 37077. Used by permission.

It's a well-known trick of wordsmiths to write parodies of well-known tunes. But I would not call this song of Charlie's a parody. A parody usually satirizes or at least subtly comments on the "original" song. See "Ole Time Religion," p. 136. But a song which stands on its own two feet I don't consider a parody.

Ring Like a Bell

Words by Malvina Reynolds   Music by Pete Seeger (1965)
© 1966 by Abigail Music Co. All rights reserved.

1.   Oh, if I could ring like a bell!
     If I could swing like a clapper on a bell!
     To tell the world that the wars are over,
     Wouldn't that be the day?

2.   Oh, if I could sound like the thunder!
     If I could sing out the glory and the wonder
     To tell the world that the wars are over,
     Wouldn't that be the day!

     BRIDGE # 1:

     Wouldn't that be the morning!
     Wouldn't that be the day!
     The faces of men would smile again
     And the bombs and the missiles would rust away.

REPEAT VERSES 1 AND 2

     BRIDGE # 2:

     Wouldn't that be the morning!
     Wouldn't that be the day!
     The news would sound the world a-round
     And the stars would dance in the Milky Way,
        Oh, oh, oh,

3.   Oh, if I could ring like a bell!
     If I could swing the clapper on a heavenly bell
     To tell the world that the wars are over
     Wouldn't that be the day.

I urge all songwriters to do what Malvina Reynolds did — send out lead sheets of words, at least, or words and melody, if possible, or a tape. Don't send a lot of songs; send one or two at a time, but send them to a number of people.

Above all, try singing the songs for family and friends and neighbors of all sorts. These will give you your best response. Woody Guthrie used to say that he'd try out his new songs on the folks in the local bar. If it wasn't good enough for them, then he'd go back and try again to improve it.

★ ★ ★

The words for the next song were found among Mal's papers after she died. I put a tune to them and we sang it at a memorial concert for her.

No Closing Chord

Words by Malvina Reynolds (ca.1976)   Music by Pete Seeger (1976)
© 1979 by Abigail Music Co. All rights reserved.

1. Don't play that closing chord for me, baby ba-by.
    I want a wake to wake the dead.
    Some rolling sounds with drums and rocking bass,
    And my good comrades dancing…all around
        the place.

2. Don't play that closing chord for me, baby, ba-by.
    I want rejoicing when I go.
    Celebrate my advent and that I had my day,
    With a roving melody to…send me on my way.

    BRIDGE:
        Don't play that closing chord for me, baby ba-by,
        Lugubrious is not my style.
        I favored grins and laughs, with loving on the side.
        So do a Moog type version of "Here comes
            the bride."

3. Don't play that closing chord for me, baby, ba-by,
    I'll bless the ground from whence I came,
    I'll make some daisy shine (daisy shine)
    Some grass grow green (grass grow green).
    And leave a sneaky dandelion to decorate the scene.

Some Proverbs

Before this chapter is over, some fragments. All songwriters must have fragments floating around in their brains. Most of these are proverbs.

B29

Eas-y come, eas-y go.

I know I'm in a melodic rut, but I found myself using the same phrase for other old sayings:

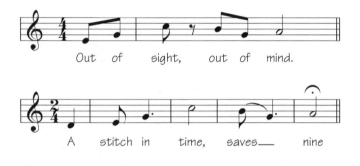

Out of sight, out of mind.

A stitch in time, saves— nine

Another melodic phrase I'm stuck on:

Bet-ter late than nev-er—

No fool— like an old fool

No news— is good news

If it ain't one thing it's an-oth-er

Here's one from Mother Jones:

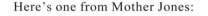

Pray for the dead and fight like hell for the living.

And one from John Donne:

Ask not for whom the bell tolls; it tolls for thee.

The next two proverbs I got from Carl Sandburg's novel *Remembrance Rock*.

B30

There's lots more to a mar-riage

than four bare legs in a bed.

To the storms to come, and to the

stars that fol-low the storm.

And I suspect this is an old blues:

Don't you know life is an on-ion,

when you peel it you have— to cry.—

This line I read 50 years ago in the *Reader's Digest*. Wish the author would get in touch. What a great metaphor!

The larg-er the is-land of know-ledge,—

the long-er the shore-line of won-der.

For the above songs, excepted as noted: Words by unknown authors Music by Pete Seeger
© 1993 by Sanga Music Inc.

Chapter 6: *Guantanamera –*
Translations Pro and Con,
New Words to Others' Tunes

© Len Munnik, Amsterdam

Robert Frost was once asked, "Mr. Frost, what is your definition of poetry?"

The great poet looks skyward, pauses, purses his lips.

"Poetry is — what gets lost in the translation."

And this is why some of the world's greatest songs may never be sung outside the language area where they were created.

Nevertheless, translation is not always impossible. Edward FitzGerald, who translated the Rubáiyát of Omar Khayyam, said, "Better a live sparrow than a dead eagle." In a sense, we all try to translate. Cooks translate old recipes for young stomachs. Lawyers translate old laws for new citizens. The Irish people have translated and found English words for some of their great melodies. Some European melodies have found new life in Japan and Korea. For example, the melody most of us know as "Auld Lang Syne" is known in Japan by a quite different name. It is the most popular song to sing when one is saying farewell at school graduations, at the end of a party, or when a ferryboat is pulling away and the relatives onshore wave to their friends on the boat until they can see them no more.

Max Colpet's German translation of "Where Have All The Flowers Gone" sings better than my original: "Sag' mir, wo die Blumen Sind" (See p. 169).

Hardest to translate into English are songs in some variety of the English language which cannot be easily understood, or people will misinterpret if you try and pronounce the original way. They might think you're making fun of "dialect." Some of my favorite songs, Scottish, or West Indian, I don't ever sing in public because the original pronunciation makes them unintelligible, and they are no longer such good songs translated into another kind of English.

I've urged people *not* to try to put English words to great songs like "Guantanamera," "De Colores," and "Amanece." It's only a matter of time before the USA, like most of the world, is some sort of a bilingual country. Learning songs in Spanish will hasten the day. And if a song is not too difficult, I urge people to try to learn the original, no matter what the country. "To learn a bit of another people's language is to get a glimpse of their soul." (Rockwell Kent).

I've been able to make only a few singable translations in my life. Here's one of them.

I learned the song in 1947, when I was singing for the Communist-led fraternal organization, the IWO (International Workers' Order), in and around Pittsburgh.

One evening after I sang, a man came up to me and said, "When I was young, we used to make up songs too."

I asked him if he would teach one of the songs to me.

"Oh, it wouldn't mean anything to you. It's all in Slovakian."

Fortunately, a friend of mine, Dr. Jacob Evanson, who was at that time the Superintendent of Music for the schools of Pittsburgh, was accompanying me, even though he mistrusted my politics. He immediately took the man aside and wrote down this song, music and words. The man's name was Andrew Kovaly; after he died I found out from his son that he had written many poems.

I didn't try to rhyme. You'll see that I simply took the literal meaning and tried to find syllables that were good to sing. And repeated them when necessary.

He Lies in the American Land

Freely—Drone bass—No chords B31...

1. Ah,_____ my God! What is this land of A-mer-i-ca? So_____ man-y peo-ple trav-el-ing there._____ I will go_____ too, for I am still young. God, the Lord will grant me_____ good luck there.

Original East Slovakian dialect words & music by Andrew Kovaly (early 20th c.)
Transcribed by Jacob Evanson
English lyrics by Pete Seeger (1951)
© 1983, 1993 by Sanga Music Inc.

1. Ah, my God! What is this land of America?
   So many people traveling there.
   I will go too, for I am still young.
   God, the Lord will grant me good luck there.

2. You, my wife, stay here till you hear from me.
   When you get my letter, put everything in order.
   Mount a raven-black steed, a horse like the wind.
   Fly across the ocean to join me here.

3. Ah, but when she arrived in this strange land,
   Here in McKeesport, this valley, this valley of fire,
   Only his grave, his blood, his blood did she find.
   Over it bitterly—she cried:

4. "Ah, ah, ah, my husband,
      what have you done to this family of yours?"
   "What can you say to these children,
      these children you've orphaned?"
   "Tell them, my wife, not to wait, not to wait,
      not to wait for me."
   "Tell them I lie here! In the American Land!"

The story? Andrew Kovaly was foreman in a steel mill when one of his crew was run over by an ingot buggy. His wife and children were arriving from the old country. Kovaly had to go down and meet them at the train and break the terrible news to them.

This is how the melody fits the rest of the verses.

2. You, my wife, stay here till you hear from me._____ When you get my let-ter_____ put ev-'ry-thing in or-der. Mount a ra-ven black steed, a horse like the wind. Fly a-cross the o - cean to join me here._____

3. Ah,_____ but when she ar - rived in_ this strange land,_____ Here in Mc-Kees-port, this val - ley, this val-ley of fire, On - ly his grave,_____ his blood, his blood did she find. O - ver it bit-ter - ly - - - - she cried.

4. "Ah, ah, ah, my hus-band, what have you done to this fam-'ly of yours?" "What can you say_____ to these chil-dren, these chil-dren you've or-phaned?" "Tell them, my wife,_____ not to wait, not to wait, not to wait for me." "Tell them I lie_____ here! In the A-mer-i-can Land!"

Here's one verse of the original, from *Pennsylvania Songs and Legends*, University of Pennsylvania Press. Don't attempt it unless you get a Slovakian to coach you.

B...31

Ej Božemoj cotej Ameriki!
Idze doňej narod preveliki,
Ija pojdzem, šak som mladi ešče.
Dami Panboh tam dajake scesce.

I usually accompany this song with just one low note, like a drone on a bagpipe. I go back and forth with the tip of my index finger. See p.122.

The original of the next can be found in *Norwegian Emigrant Songs and Ballads*, by Blegen and Ruud (Arno Press, New York). It was a famous drinking song both in Norway and among Norwegian-American men. The story behind it? In the 1840s, the famous Norwegian violinist Ole Bull toured the USA. Some real estate agents sold him 120,000 acres in northwest Pennsylvania, and when he returned home he announced there was free land for Norwegian emigrants. But the first settlers found it was mostly rocks. No good for farming. They headed west to places like Wisconsin. This satirical ballad was written in 1853 by Ditmar Meidel, a Norwegian newspaper editor. It had several dozen verses.

The tune is one more variant of what we know best as "Twinkle, Twinkle, Little Star," a melody with hundreds of different versions throughout Europe and the Americas. A slow, minor-key version is "Hatikvah," the national anthem of Israel. The gospel song "Come By Here" (Kumbaya) incorporates it. I suspect the tune was known by our cave-dwelling ancestors.

Oleanna

B32

Oh, to be in O-le-an-na,

That's where I'd like to be, Than be bound in

Nor-way to drag the chains of slav-er-y.

CHORUS

O-le, O-le-an-na, O-le, O-le-

an-na, O-le, O-le,

O-le, O-le, O-le, O-le-an-na,

Norwegian words & music by Ditmar Meidel (1853) Thanks Lillebjørn!
English lyrics by Pete Seeger (1953)
TRO - © 1958 (renewed) Ludlow Music, Inc., New York, NY.

1. Oh, to be in Oleanna,
   That's where I'd like to be,
   Than be bound in Norway
   To drag the chains of slavery,

CHORUS:
Ole, Ole-anna,
Ole, Ole-anna,
Ole, Ole, Ole, Ole,
Ole, Oleanna

2. In Oleanna land is free,
   The wheat and corn just plant themselves,
   Then grow four feet a day,
   While on your bed you rest yourself.

3. Beer as sweet as Münchener
   Springs from the ground and flows away,
   The cows all like to milk themselves
   And hens lay eggs ten times a day.

4. Little roasted piggies
   Rush about the city streets,
   Inquiring so politely if
   A slice of ham you'd like to eat.

(SPOKEN:) *"The moon is always full. I am observing it now, with a bottle for a telescope."*

(SPOKEN:) *"In Oleanna the women do all the work! If she doesn't work hard enough She takes a stick and gives herself a beating!"* *

5. Aye, if you'd begin to live,
   To Oleanna you must go,
   The poorest wretch in Norway
   Becomes a Duke in a year or so.

* This is a joke? In 1853.

For a recording of the original Norwegian, contact Skandisk Music online at <www.skandisk.com> or phone 1-800-468-2424.

Here's some of the original verses.
I Oleana der er det godt at være,
I Norge vil jeg inte Slavelænken bære!
 Ole - Ole - Ole oh! Oleana!
 Ole - Ole - Ole oh! Oleana!

I Oleana der faar jeg Jord for Intet,
Af Jorden voxer Kornet, og det gaar gesvint det.

Ja Bayerøl saa godt, som han Ytteborg kan brygge,
det risler i Bækkene til Fattigmandens Hygge.

Aa brunstegte Griser de løber om saa flinke
Aa forespør sig høfligt, om Nogen vil ha' Skinke.

Kronarbejde findes ej — nej det var saa ligt da!
Jeg sad nok ikke ellersen saa frisk her aa digta.

Aa Kjærringa maa brase aa styre aa stelle —
Aa blir hu sint, saa banker hu sig sjelv — skal jeg
 fortælle.

Ja rejs til Oleana, saa skal Du vel leve,
den fattigste Stymper herover er Greve!

Drawing by Eric von Schmidt

The old Russian folk song, "Stenka Razin," had a beautiful melody, but the words deserve to stay on the library shelf. It is the story of a legendary Cossack chief. He is rowing across the Volga with his band of warriors, and his bride, a Persian princess. He hears them grumble, "Ah, Stenka Razin has become a sissy; he's got married." Stenka Razin roars, "I'll show you who's a sissy. Mother Volga, see what a sacrifice I make for you!" He picks up his bride, throws her in the Volga and drowns her. So much for folklore. I put together some new words in 1950, while chopping trees along the banks of the Hudson.

River Of My People `B33`

Slow, sing unaccompanied

There's a riv-er of my peo-ple and its
flow is swift and strong, Flow-ing to some might-y
o-cean, though its course is deep and long,
(all voices join) Flow-ing to some might-y o-cean, though its
course is deep and long.

Words by Pete Seeger   Music: traditional Russian ("Stenka Razin")
© 1953 by Stormking Music Inc.

1. There's a river of my people
   And its flow is swift and strong,
   Flowing to some mighty ocean,
   Though its course is deep and long,
     Flowing to some mighty ocean,
     Though its course is deep and long.

2. Many rocks and reefs and mountains
   Seek to bar it from its way.
   But relentlessly this river
   Seeks its brothers in the sea.*
     But relentlessly this river
     Seeks its sisters in the sea.

3. You will find us in the mainstream,
   Steering surely through the foam,
   Far beyond the raging waters
   We can see our certain home.
     Far beyond the raging waters
     I can see our certain home.

4. For we have mapped this river**
   And we know its mighty force
   And the courage that this gives us
   Will hold us to our course.
     And the courage that this gives us
     Will hold us to our course.

5. Oh, river of my people,
   Together we must go,
   Hasten onward to that meeting
   Where my brothers wait I know,
     Hasten onward to that meeting
     Where my sisters wait I know.

*If a group of men and women sing this, have them sing different lines.
**We didn't map human history as well as we thought.

So there's another song repeating the last line. There's even more repetition in the next song. What's the purpose of repetition? I see at least five possible reasons:
   • It gives listeners a chance to join in.
   • It imprints an important phrase.
   • It gives the singer a chance to gather her/his thoughts ("what the heck *is* the next verse?").
   • It gives a first time listener time to savor and digest a thought.
   • Even those who've heard the song before can ponder other meanings of the words.

★★★

I found this next song in *The Treasury of Jewish Folk Song*, edited by Ruth Rubin back in the 1940s. She had Jewish songs from Israel, from Eastern Europe of the old days, from New York City of the old days ("Tumbalalaika"). And she also had songs from the Soviet Union. This song, as you'll see, was made up on a Jewish collective farm in the Crimea.

Djankoye

B34

English lyrics by Pete Seeger (1947)
Original Yiddish words & music: author unknown (Crimea, 1926)
© 1947 (renewed) by Stormking Music Inc.

1. Az men fort kain Sevastopol
   Iz nit vait fun Simferopol
   Dortn iz a stantziye faran.
   Ver darf zuchn naye glikn
   S'iz a stantziye an antikl
   In Djankoye, Djan, djan, djan.

CHORUS (AFTER EACH VERSE):
Hey Djan, Hey Djankoye,
Hey Djanvili, Hey Djankoye,
Hey Djankoye, Djan, djan, djan.

2. When you go from Sevastopol
   On the way to Simferopol,
   Just you go a little farther down.
   There's a little railroad depot
   Known quite well by all the people
   Called Djankoye Djan, djan, djan.

3. Enfert Yidn oif main kashe
   Vu'z main bruder, vu'z Abrashe
   'Sgayt bai im der traktor vi a ban.
   Di mume Laye bai der kosilke
   Bayle bai der molotilke
   In Djankoye, Djan, djan, djan.

4. Ver zogt az yidn kenen nor handlen,
   Esn fete yoich mit mandlen
   Nor nit zain kain arbetzman?
   Dos kenen zogn nur di sonim
   Yidn, shpait zay on im ponim!
   Tut a kuk oif Djan, djan, djan.

5. There's Abrasha drives the tractor
   Grandma runs the cream extractor
   While we work we all can sing our songs,
   Who says that Jews cannot be farmers?
   Spit in his eye, who would so harm us.
   Tell him of Djankoye, djan.

In 1964, years later, my family and I were in the Crimea. I was singing in nearby Simferopol when I found that "Dzhankoy" was nearby, a city of about 20,000 people. I went first to the newspaper office. The editor, a man in his 30s, said, "I'm not Jewish, but there are a lot of Jewish people who work here at the newspaper, and we're about to have lunch. Why don't you speak to them during lunch hour?" While I waited, I looked at the pictures around the room. Typical of socialist countries, they had awards to various workers for their good efforts, and I noticed names like Fagin and Cohen. At lunchtime there were over a dozen workers with their lunchboxes eating around a big table and chatting with each other when the editor introduced me.

I said, "I've sung this song now for 15 years and gotten audiences in the United States and other countries to sing it with me, but I'm curious to know if any of you know this song."

One woman raised her hand. She said that she didn't know the song herself, but she remembers hearing people sing it. As a matter of fact, she said, there was once a record out with this song on it. One of the other people at the table said, "It was probably made up on the Sholem Aleichem Collective Farm. That's now part of Rosseeya." (This is how the word "Russia" is pronounced in Russian.)

Said I, "I want to investigate the song. I've been told by friends now that Stalin's anti-semitism has been exposed, this song is a fake and should not be sung."

Laughter. Yes, laughter. They were not angry. They were a little incredulous. One said, "You go down to Rosseeya. See for yourself." And after lunch our car sped us five or 10 miles away. The manager of Rosseeya, a tall business-like fellow, shook hands. "We have 50,000 people, and thousands of hectares. We make wine, cognac, brandy."

"About 1/3 of Rosseeya is Ukrainian. A little over 1/3 are Jewish. A little less than 1/3 are Russian. I have to know all three languages. Why don't you wait a moment and I'll see if I can find one of the Jewish farmers." And a few minutes later a man in his 50s was introduced to us. It was his lunch hour now, but he took a few minutes to speak to us:

"Yes, I remember. It was about 1926. There was a crowd of young people who liked to make up songs then. During the terrible war, every Jew who was physically able was fighting. The women and children and old people were evacuated to the east to places like Tashkent, and some people never came back to live here again. There was not much to come back to. Everything destroyed. The only building left standing was the Stantsiya, the railroad station mentioned in the song. But we have a good life here."

The man sang the song to me with only very slight changes from the way I'd learned it out of Ruth's book.

(The above words were written decades ago, reprinted here. I wish I were able again to visit Djankoy. It's part of Ukraine now. I still sing the song. Mixing languages works.)

For a banjo to attempt a tune written for a symphony is a kind of translation. For a half-century I've played, mainly for my own amazement, a couple of Beethoven melodies. Here's four measures from one of them.

Ode to Joy
(last 4 measures)

B35

Music by Ludwig van Beethoven ("Ode to Joy", 1826) Banjo arrangement by Pete Seeger (1958) © 1993 by Sanga Music Inc.

*My middle fingernail is weak, so I usually pick up with my index finger and my ring finger.

Don West, longtime Appalachian radical, wrote three English verses for it and I, with a chorus to help, sang one on Paul Winter's 1996 CD *Pete*. I substituted the two words "Joy! Joy!" for his "Work beside me."

Build the road of peace before us
Build it wide and deep and long
Speed the slow, remind the eager
Help the weak and guide the strong

None shall push aside another
None shall let another fall
Joy! Joy!* Sisters and brothers
All for one and one for all!

B36

Build the road of peace be-fore us. Build it
wide and deep and long. Speed the slow, re-mind the
ea-ger, help the weak and guide the strong.
None shall push a-side an-oth-er. None shall
let an-oth-er fall. Joy! Joy!___ sisters and
broth-ers! All for one and one for all!

*Listen to the chorus on the recording. Is Beethoven rolling over in his grave?

That's from Beethoven's 9th Symphony. Next is a famous two-part melody in the 2nd movement of his 7th Symphony. For years I played it on the two middle strings of my banjo, with my finger going rapidly back and forth. My father was amused that I would attempt it on a banjo.

Music by Ludwig van Beethoven ("Symphony No. 7, in A major, Opus 92," 1812)

Visions of Children

HIGH VOICES

We'll work to-geth-er, though we work dif-frent.

When we con-sid-er all of the dan-gers

Vi-sions of chil-dren ask-ing— us to save them.

Build-ing their gar-dens, through all the world.—

In 1991 I tried putting words to that two-part melody in Beethoven's 7th Symphony, but never sang 'em till I improved 'em in May '99. The Green Guerrillas had a big rally on 42nd Street in New York City to try to save 115 beautiful community gardens that Mayor Giuliani wanted to sell to developers. The M.C. asked in advance, "Are there any women here who can read music at sight? Pete Seeger needs help on a song. Come backstage." I got six singers and divided 'em into altos and sopranos. It only took five or six minutes to rehearse. An hour later we're on stage together, sopranos around a mic on my right, altos around a mic at my left. In the center I softly said, "One, two, three, sing." I strummed the chords while they sang. Since the song was short, I then spoke the words clearly for the crowd and we sang it again a half-step higher. I've written it in Cm, but I usually capo up a bit and play it in Am. (The chords are Am E7, E7 Am, Am C, G7 C, C B7, BmE7 Am, Am E7Am, E7 Am.) In later concerts I asked for singers and rehearse 'em in the intermission.

P.S.: Thanks to Bette Midler and the Trust for Public Land, 112 of the gardens were saved!

LOW VOICES

We'll work to-geth-er, e-ven though we work dif-frent-ly.

When we con-sid-er all the ma-ny great dan-gers

Vi-sions of chil-dren ask-ing— us to— save— them.

Build-ing their gar-dens, all— through the— world.—

Words by Pete Seeger (1997) Music by Ludwig von Beethoven (1812)
TRO - © 1993 Melody Trails, Inc., New York, NY.

Here's another verse, again for 2 parts:

SOP.: Make your voice heard now, we all need gardens

ALTOS: Make your voice heard now, the city needs many more gardens

SOP.: Some can grow flowers, some can grow food

ALTOS: Some can grow bright flowers, some can grow fresh food to eat

SOP.: There's thirteen thousand other unused spaces

ALTOS: There's thirteen thousand other unused lots in New York Town

SOP. & ALTOS: Builders can build there; here keep it green!

I went back and listened to the 7th Symphony again, because several people said I left out a fantastic bass part. It might be nice to add a bass when repeating the last 16 measures. I also found that I liked one note ("great dan -") a half-step higher than Ludwig did it.

If a chorus wanted to try it, I suggest they try out several different keys. When it's sung by women, or by men, or by women and men. Or when a bass or other parts are added. I put it in B.

I bet it would sound best with just maracas or shakere rhythm for accompaniment. Let that extraordinary two-part melody stand in the clear. How eloquent it is, though it moves slowly through a narrow range. I'm sure Beethoven heard two-part Slavic melodies which also end one octave apart.

No matter. This 7th Symphony will inspire human beings as long as there are human beings to be inspired.

Is it necessary that song lyrics rhyme? Sometimes yes, often no. Look at the great old spirituals which sing so well. They stick in your memory. "Steal Away." "Didn't My Lord Deliver Daniel." Look at some traditional lullabies.

As you work on song lyrics you'll become more conscious of why one word fits the tune better than another. Sometimes the rhythm is helped by a lot of sharp consonants: "Oh you can't scare me, I'm stickin' to the union." Sometimes you want the phrase to flow more smoothly. Listen to the words. Over years of songwriting you'll see why some words work in one way and others work in another way.

★ ★ ★

Here are new words to a South African wedding song. In Cape Town Province, there was an old custom among the African people in which two choirs were formed: one by the friends of the bride, and the other by the friends of the groom. A traditional "competition" was held during the 24 hours or more of festivities in which certain traditional songs were always sung. This, including all the four-part harmony, was the original African music. I got the song out of the same book where I found the lullabye "Abiyoyo."

Here's To the Couple

Music: traditional (South African) transcribed by J.N.Maselwa & Rev. H.C.N.Williams   Original title: "Lo Mfan Unesongota"
English lyrics by Pete Seeger (1954)

1. Here's to the couple so valiantly wed,
   (BASSES: "…valiantly knotted untogether!")
   Here's to the years that for them lie ahead.
   We wish them good fortune and health of the best.
   We wish them good fortune and health of the best.
   (TENORS: "…and also have good neighbors")
   Strong children, good neighbors, and all the rest. (2x)
   (BASSES AND ALTOS: "Also good neighbors, and all
   the rest!")

2. Here's hoping that they never do part
   (BASSES: "…never have trouble with the baby")
   And all their quarrels be patched 'ere they start
   Let love be the teacher and make all the rules
   Let love be the teacher and make all the rules
   (TENORS: "Remember!")
   Let love be the doctor and cure the fools (2x)
   (BASSES & ALTOS: 'Love be the doctor and cure
   the fools')

3. They venture now out on life's stormy seas
   (BASSES: "…on the waves and the waters of
   the ocean")
   May they hold to their course, be it north, south
   or east.
   May they hold to their course though the tempests
   may blow
   And reach their goal, the goal of us all
   (TENORS: "Forever!")
   For them and their children, a world at peace (2x)
   (BASSES AND ALTOS: "And for their children, a world
   at peace")

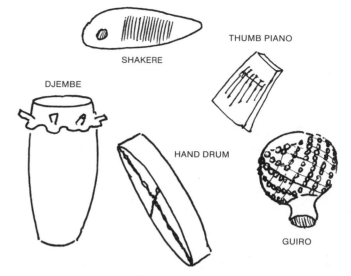

SHAKERE

THUMB PIANO

DJEMBE

HAND DRUM

GUIRO

Somewhere in West Africa there was a songwriter who should have gotten royalties for the next song. It was never a top-40 hit; but the Weavers sang it, and I've sung it for audiences in all sorts of places.

I learned it in 1949 from Bryant French, who learned it from some West African students in Los Angeles. In those days, they said, the British controlled Nigeria and Ghana, and slapped weekday curfews on nighttime fun. It was a song of social commentary. All he learned was one verse in English and one verse in a Nigerian language, I think Yoruba.

I sang it for some children; they asked, "Is that all there is to the song?"

"I don't know any more," said I, "but this is a good song. Let's sing it in different languages." Soon there

THE WEAVERS, 1950

Photo by Sonia Handelman Meyer, Sing Out! Resource Center

was a contest on between readers of *Sing Out!* magazine, in the early '50s, to see how many different languages we could sing it in. My only contribution to the situation was to realize that a really good tune doesn't need a lot of different verses, but maybe the same verse sung in different languages. You might consider this for other great melodies that you know.

Everybody Loves Saturday Night

West African song, adapted & arranged by Ronnie Gilbert, Lee Hays, Fred Hellerman & Pete Seeger (1948)
TRO - © 1953 (renewed) Folkways Music Publishers, Inc., New York, NY.

1. Ev'rybody loves Saturday night,
   Ev'rybody loves Saturday night,
   Ev'rybody, ev'rybody, ev'rybody, ev'rybody,
   Ev'rybody loves Saturday night.

2. Bobo waro faro Satodeh! (NIGERIAN—YORUBA)
   Bobo waro faro Satodeh!
   Bobo waro, bobo waro, bobo waro, bobo waro,
   Bobo waro faro Satodeh!

3. Tutti amano il Sabato sera, (ITALIAN)
   Tutti amano il Sabato sera,
   Tutti amano, tutti amano,
    tutti amano, tutti amano,
   Tutti amano il Sabato sera.

4. Yeder ener glacht Shabbas ba nacht, (YIDDISH)
   Yeder ener glacht Shabbas ba nacht,
   Yeder ener, yeder ener, yeder ener, yeder ener,
   Yeder ener glacht Shabbas ba nacht.

5. Tous le monde aime Samedi soir, (FRENCH)
   Tous le monde aime Samedi soir,
   Tous le monde , tous le monde ,
    tous le monde , tous le monde ,
   Tous le monde aime Samedi soir.

(COME BACK TO ENGLISH OCCASIONALLY)
Ev'rybody loves Saturday night,
Ev'rybody loves Saturday night,
Ev'rybody, ev'rybody, ev'rybody, ev'rybody,
Ev'rybody loves Saturday night.

6. El Sabado ama todo el mundo, (SPANISH)
   El Sabado ama todo el mundo...

7. Jedermann liebt den Samstagabend... (GERMAN)

8. Alle elsker Lordag asften... (DANISH)

9. Alle elsker Lordag kveld... (NORWEGIAN)

I'm sorry that we have no verses yet in Russian, Uzbek, Chinese, Japanese, Arabic, Hebrew, Finnish, Latvian, Swahili, Bengali, Urdu, Quechua, Portuguese, Mongolian, etc., etc. You get 'em! Hey I leave the space below for you to write 'em in.

I didn't add a word or a note to the next old German song. Why presume to include it? It's an example of a very successful translation. "Dear Willie" sings better than "Lieber Heinrich." I also invented a way for one man to sing it. It works. I ham it up, look ridiculous, singing the man's verse only. Then I pick the banjo ever more briskly, just the melody, and ask women in the audience to sing the answer-back part.

There's a Hole in the Bucket

B40

SONGLEADER (MALE)

There's a hole in the buck-et, dear

BANJO

Li-za, dear Li-za, There's a hole in the

buck-et, dear Li-za, there's a hole.

SONGLEADER

"All the wom-en sing, 'Then fix it, dear Wil-lie!'"

WOMEN IN AUDIENCE

Then fix it, dear Wil-lie, dear

8va

Wil-lie, dear Wil-lie, Then fix it, dear

(8va)

Wil-lie, dear Wil-lie, then fix it.

(8va)

Traditional (U.S., originally German)

(Who translated this? When? Where? Pennsylvania maybe? No matter. Great job.)

1. (MAN:) There's a hole in the bucket, dear Liza, dear Liza,
   There's a hole in the bucket, dear Liza, there's a hole.
   (I SPEAK:) (*"All the women sing, 'Then fix it, dear Willie.'"*)
   (WOMEN IN AUDIENCE:) Then fix it dear Willie, dear Willie,
   dear Willie,
   Then fix it dear Willie, dear Willie, then fix it

2. But how shall I fix it, dear Liza, dear Liza
   But how shall I fix it, dear Liza, but how?
   (SPOKEN BY THE SONGLEADER:) (*"With straw, dear Willie."*)
   (WOMEN IN AUDIENCE:) With straw, dear Willie, dear Willie,
   dear Willie
   With straw, dear Willie, dear Willie, with straw

3. But how shall I cut it, dear Liza, dear Liza
   But how shall I cut it, dear Liza, but how?
   (*"With a knife."*)
   (WOMEN:) With a Kni-ife, dear Willie, etc.

4. But the knife needs sharpening, dear Liza, etc.
   (*"Then sharpen it."*)
   (WOMEN:) Then sharpen it, dear Willie, etc.

5. But how shall I sharpen it, dear Liza, etc.
   (*"On a stone."*)
   (WOMEN:) On a stone, dear Willie, etc.

6 But the stone needs water, dear Liza, etc.
   (*"Then fetch it."*)
   (WOMEN) Then fetch it, dear Willie, etc.

7. But how shall I fetch it, dear Liza, etc.
   (*"In a bucket."*)
   (WOMEN:) In a bucket, dear Willie, etc.

8. (THE WHOLE AUDIENCE JOINS THE LEADER, FULL CHORDS,
   RITARD AT THE END:)
   There's a hole in the bucket, dear Liza, dear Liza,
   There's a hole in the bucket, dear Liza, there's a hole.

Often it's better not to try translating.

José Martí, born 1853, was one of the world's great writers. Seventy volumes of prose and poetry! Plays, novels, polemics. At age 17 he was banished from his home in Cuba because he was active in the movement for independence from Spain. For the next 25 years he made a living as a journalist, including 12 years in New York. In 1895 he went back to Cuba and was killed in an abortive uprising, age 42.

JOSÉ MARTÍ

Source: People's Weekly World

In Havana 1949 a classical pianist and composer, Julian Orbon, found that the stanzas in Martí's last book, *Versos Sencillos* ("Simple Verses"), could be sung to a well-known melody. "Guantanamera" was first made up to satirize the women in Guantanamo who went out with American sailors. In '49 it was sung on the Havana radio every afternoon by "Joseito," who would open up the daily newspaper and improvise verses on the latest scandal of the day. "Joseito" was the professional name of José Fernandez Diaz, who put together the original song back in the 1920s.

In 1961 a former student of Julian Orbon was in New York studying at the Manhattan School of Music. The student, Hector Angulo, had a summer job as a counselor in a children's camp in the Catskills, Camp Woodland. I visited to sing for the kids. The kids said, "Hey, we've got to teach you a great song we learned from our counselor." A shy, quiet young man was introduced to me.

I learned the song, taught it to the Weavers. A more commercial group, the Sandpipers, had a hit record of it. The song is known worldwide now —Martí's philosophic verses have ennobled the old melody. I urge people *not* to try translating it. Translations are not for singing.

Credit for the music should go to Joseito and to Orbon, who added an important note, the first note of the chorus (B, formerly A, for the syllable "Guan"). But Angulo deserves credit, too, for thinking long and hard to select the right stanzas out of a possible two hundred to teach to the children — and to me. All I did was to find a less complicated accompaniment and way to teach it to Anglo audiences. It's one of two or three songs I most often perform. I've sung it in 35 countries on four continents; it rings true in every one.

Guantanamera   B41

Original lyrics & music by José Fernandez Diaz (Joseito Fernandez)
Music arranged & adapted by Julian Orbon, Hector Angulo & Pete Seeger
Words (verses) by José Martí, lyrics adapted by Julian Orbon (1949)
© 1963, 1965 (renewed) by Fall River Music Inc.

1. Yo soy un hombre sincero
   De donde crece las palmas
   Yo soy un hombre sincero
   De donde crece las palmas
   Y antes de morirme quiero
   Echar mis versos del alma

   (I am a truthful man,
   From the land of the palms.
   Before dying, I want to
   Share these poems of my soul.)

CHORUS (AFTER EACH VERSE):
Guantanamera! Guajira!
Guantanamera!
Guantanamera, Guajira,
Guantanamera.

2. Mi verso es de un verde claro
   Y de un carmín encendido
   Mi verso es de un verde claro
   Y de un carmín encendido
   Mi verso es un ciervo herido
   Que busca en el monte amparo

   (My poems are light green,
   But they are also flaming red.
   My verses are like a wounded fawn.
   Seeking refuge in the mountain.)

3. Cultivo la Rosa blanca
   En junio, como en enero
   Cultivo la Rosa blanca
   En junio como en enero
   Para el amigo sincero
   Que me da su mano franca

   (I cultivate a white rose
   In June and in January
   For the sincere friend
   Who gives me his hand.)

4. Y para el cruel que me arranca
   El corazón con que vivo
   Y para el cruel que me arranca
   El corazón con que vivo
   Cardo ni ortiga cultivo
   Cultivo la rosa blanca

   (And for the cruel one who would tear out
   This heart with which I live.
   I cultivate neither thistles nor nettles.
   I cultivate a white rose.)

5. Con los pobres de la tierra
   Quiero yo mi suerte echar
   Con los pobres de la tierra
   Quiero yo mi suerte echar
   El arroyo de la sierra
   Me complace más que el mar.

   (With the poor people of this earth,
   I want to share my lot.
   The little streams of the mountains
   Please me more than the sea.)

In Cuba, 1983, I learned two more of Martí's verses from a black man, head of a research farm.

6. Rojo, como en el desierto
   Salió el sol al horizonte
   Rojo, como en el desierto
   Salió el sol al horizonte
   Y alumbra un esclavo muerto
   Colgado a un seibo del monte

   (Red, as in the desert,
   Rose the sun on the horizon.
   It shone on a dead slave
   Hanging from a tree of the mountain.)

7. Un niño lo vió, tembló
   De pasion por los que gimen
   Un niño lo vió, tembló
   De pasión por los que gimen
   Y al pie del muerto juro
   Lavar con su sangre el crimen.

   (A child saw it, trembled,
   With passion for those that wept,
   And swore that with his blood
   He would wash away that crime.)

In 2001 I read a translation of Martí's book *Versos Sencillos (Simple Verses)*. In the introduction he describes himself living in New York City in 1891. "I was in a state of great indecision. I want independence for Cuba, but I don't want to hurt Spain – Spain is the mother country. And if we do get independence for Cuba, how do we keep her out of the claws of the great eagle of the north?

"The doctor says, 'Jose, you need to get your health back. Go to the country; go walking in the woods.'"

Where did he go? Up the Hudson to the Catskills, rented a room in a little town called Haines Falls, and then wrote all the verses, over a hundred of them, of *Versos Sencillos*.

And 71 years later, I learned the song in the Catskills, only 13 miles south of Haines Falls!

In Cuba it is traditional to improvise new verses to Guantanamera. "Fidel's beard is a broom to sweep the Yankees out of Latin America." In Hanoi in 1972, I accompanied a roomful of Cuban sailors for half an hour, improvising many verses, as they danced in a Conga line. We woke up the whole hotel.

My guitar accompaniment:

throughout the song, except for the first measure of the chorus:

Between Orbon and me, this song was, in a sense, Europeanized a bit. In Cuba, the tradition is to tear the melody to shreds. We regularized it. And my guitar accompaniment is a bit gringo, too. Perhaps it helped spread the song. Whether it improves the song is open to question.

And Orbon's one-note change also took it a step away from the Afro-Cuban tradition. Joseito's original refrain was:

but Orbon changed it (and Hector taught it to me as)

The former keeps the traditional chord changes. Orbon changed one note and the chord that went with it. If one bad note can ruin a song, one good note can make it.

Orbon moved to New York in 1961 and got a share of writers' royalties. I've written the Cuban Authors' Rights Association that I will not accept any of the royalties. Most of the money, a large sum, sits in a N.Y. bank because a federal law will not allow money to be sent to Cuba. When it's repealed (soon, I hope) money can be sent to Hector Angulo, and to the family of Joseito, and to the Martí Library in Havana, I guess. The song is a world "standard" now.

★ ★ ★

One thing you learn if you're a guest on TV is that you have to be brief and to the point. Time is money.

Of course, maybe in the long run TV will learn that there is a limit to how fast everything can be, and somebody will have a popular program which is also leisurely. I know some churches where they wouldn't think of singing a song if it didn't last for four or five or even 15 minutes.

Nevertheless, there's a time for short songs, and it so happened that I made up a short one about 20 years ago and, by gosh, I had a chance to use it on TV. Once I was a guest on the *Dick Cavett Show*, but he was busy talking to James Brown, the "King of Soul," and then to Frank Borman, the astronaut. The show was almost over, and he still hadn't called on me. Suddenly he noticed the time and said to the audience, "Oh, I was going to have Pete Seeger sing a song. Pete, are you out there? Come on." I walked on the set. "Pete, do you have a very short song?" This is what I sang:

> Here we are knee-deep in garbage,
> Firing rockets at the moon...

The song took eight seconds. I sat down.

Cavett said, "Well, that *was* a short song. We have time for a question. What do *you* think of the space exploration program? Do you think it is worth the money that the taxpayers are putting into it?"

I replied, "It seems to me kind of silly to say that we can spend $60 billion going to the moon and then say we don't have enough money for schools or hospitals or job training and so on."

There was spontaneous applause from the audience. Poor Frank Borman didn't even have much time to say, "Well, that's very simplistic —." [1] The program was over. We were off the air. James Brown was sitting on the other side of Borman, but he reached right over to me in front of Borman and pumped my hand.

The tune for my song? One of the late Cole Porter's greatest hits, "You'd Be So Nice To Come Home To." I only used the first few bars.

Here We Are Knee-Deep in Garbage

Words & music adaptation by Pete Seeger (1974)
Adapted from the song "You'd Be So Nice to Come Home To" by Cole Porter
© 1942 (renewed) & 1993 by Chappell & Co. International Copyright Secured.
All rights reserved.

[1] Well, in a sense, most great songs are a triumph of oversimplification. Remember the saying of Alfred North Whitehead: "Strive for simplicity; learn to mistrust it."

We need more humor. Anger is good at times, but humor is too. Cruel as it may be. You know Charlie Chaplin's definition of humor? A newspaper reporter asked him, "Mr. Chaplin, what is your definition of humor?"

Pencil poised.

Charlie thought a second, reached into his pocket, pulled out a pocket knife. He reached across the table, cut the reporter's tie off.

"Hey, I didn't think that was funny!"

"I did," said Charlie.

There's probably not a joke one could tell anywhere that someone somewhere would not say seriously, "Hey, that's not funny."

But if another says, "You're too sensitive," tell this other: suppose your shoulder was rubbed raw and later I come along and just touch it. You wince with pain. It's not for me to say, "You're too sensitive."

Since this is a sort of musical autobiography, for historical honesty I've included many items of only passing interest. But is a song that lasts only a short time necessarily a bad song? Is a soufflé that lasts only five minutes any less a work of art? I'd like to see people through the world making up new songs for each other all the time, as well as remembering other songs that may be centuries old. A birthday, a wedding, a newspaper headline, is worth a song.

In 1951 I could see the Catskills, 45 miles away, when standing in Toshi's vegetable garden. Now only when the northwest wind blows can I see it. The next day smog has filled up the valley.

Thus, these new words to the national anthem of Canada. The music was written in 1880 by Calixa Lavallee, French-Canadian composer. A story of his life can be found in a back issue of *Sing Out!* magazine, v. 5 #2 (1955).

Here are my new words:

B43

O Canada
At last I breathe again
All thanks to you
Also your great north wind.
No customs tax, no border guards
Could keep your clean air out
So down here in the Polluted States
We all stand up and shout.
O Canada! O Canada!

O Canada—
The words stop in my mouth,
What happens to you when the wind blows
From the south?

O Canada
(Original Words)

French lyrics by Hon. A.B. Routhier (1880) English lyrics by R. Stanley Weir (1908)
Music by Calixa Lavallee (1880) New verse by Pete Seeger (1965)

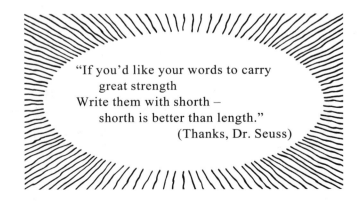

"If you'd like your words to carry
great strength
Write them with shorth —
shorth is better than length."
(Thanks, Dr. Seuss)

One of the best songwriters I know is Lorre Wyatt. He wrote "Somos El Barco," "Sailing Up/Sailing Down," and dozens more. Lorre started this song off. Had a good tune but too many verses. We made an appointment, set ourselves the task. It took us a day and a half. We boiled 'em down to this:

Huddie Ledbetter Was a Helluva Man

Words by Lorre Wyatt with additional lines by Pete Seeger
Music by Lorre Wyatt
© 1988 Roots & Branches Music (BMI), PO Box 21, Amherst MA 01004.
All rights reserved. Used by permission.

HUDDIE LEDBETTER ("LEAD BELLY")

*Lead Belly's wife Martha pronounced his name "Hew-dy" and most of us who knew him in the 1940s picked up this pronunciation.

**European music notation can't show how Lead Belly's voice would swoop and glide, rather than proceed in neat steps. I think of his voice rising through this measure in one steady motion.

1. Huddie* Ledbetter was a helluva man,
   Huddie got his music from the heart of the land,
   In his voice you could hear John Henry's hammer ring
   While his hands would "buck and wing" upon the big twelve string;
   Sometimes a lion, sometimes a lamb,
   Huddie Ledbetter was a helluva man.

CHORUS (AFTER EACH VERSE):
He's a long time gone (He's a long time gone)
But his songs live on (But his songs live on)
He's a long time gone (He's a long time gone)
But his songs live on (But his songs live on)

2. Down in Lou'siana, eighteen eighty-eight
    There was a black baby born into a
        white man's state;
    He saw the cane and the cotton stretch for
        miles around,
    He heard his mama's voice a-singing when the sun
        went down;
    Into a <u>world</u> where having dark <u>skin</u> was a crime,
    Huddie was born—and started serving his time.

3. Teenage Huddie went to Shreveport town
    There he got in trouble, he was jailhouse bound
    The odds were slim that he would get out alive
    But somehow Huddie and his music survived
    He escaped just once and was put back again
    He was called Lead Belly by the rest of the men.

4. A collector, name a' Lomax, brought a
        record machine,
    Huddie sang 'em sweet and high, he sang 'em low
        and mean;
    And for years to come, they would tell the tale
    Of how Huddie Ledbetter sang his way out-a jail,
    Sayin', "If I had you, Governor, like-a you got me
    I would wake up in the morning and-a set you free."

5. He got his farewell ticket back in '49
    He caught the Midnight Special on the
        Rock Island Line;
    And I'll bet you when he wakened from his
        earthly dream
    He was wakened with a kiss from a gal named Irene.
    Now millions of people the world around
    Are taking Huddie's hammer up and swinging it down!

REPEAT FIRST VERSE AND CHORUS

Lead Belly, "The king of the 12-string guitar," had a wonderful way with bass runs and melodies which his powerful right thumb picked out. In memory of him I made up this break for the guitar, tuned DADGBE, of course.

B45

LORRE WYATT

And as long as we're singing about Lead Belly, here's a verse to add to one of America's greatest songs, the Texas prison blues "Midnight Special," which he taught us all. (For tune, see p. 227)

Old Huddie Ledbetter
He was a mighty fine man
He taught us this song
And to the whole wide land
But now he's done with all his grieving
His whoopin', hollerin' and a-crying
Now he's done with all his studyin'
About his great long time.

Can't remember when I put the above verse together — in the '50s or '60s. Lead Belly had a verse ending with the last four lines. I tacked my four lines in front of them.

Now, some great songs — none written by me. All I did was add a verse. I got the idea from Woody Guthrie. His extra verse to the old spiritual, "You Got To Walk That Lonesome Valley" just makes that song for me.

An old tradition. It's been done for ages, I'm sure.

Lonesome Valley
(Woody Guthrie's extra verse)

B46

Now, though the road——

(though the road)— be rough and rock-y

(rough and rock-y), and the hills

(and the hills)— be steep and high— (steep and

high), We can sing (we can sing)— as we go

march-ing (we go march-ing) and we'll win that

One Big Un-ion by and by (by and by).

New words & music adaptation by Woody Guthrie
TRO - © 1963 (renewed) & 1977 Ludlow Music, Inc., New York, NY.

And here's my last verse to a great old Calypso song. Words and music are in v.4 #4 of *Sing Out!* magazine.

Money Is King

This song was written some time ago,
By a man called The Tiger in calypso,
But I've a few verses of my own
About who put King Money on his throne?
I did not crown him nor will I kneel today
Depose him now is what I say
Yes, money can still be a handy tool
But let's not allow King Money to rule
It's up to us to use our heads
And let sense and sisterhood rule instead.

(The last line is because in 2008 I'm convinced that the female tradition of nurturing may save the world.)

Here's one of the most widely known love laments in Britain. It has been in folk song collections for over a century or two. This version I learned from my sister Peggy. In 1955 I made a sing-along out of it, putting it in 4/4 time. Now it's well known throughout the U.S.A.

Incidentally, why is it that human beings can get a warm comfortable feeling as they all sing together about someone ready to kill themselves with despair?

Well, I get people harmonizing on it now. With a microphone I can call out the words to them, one phrase at a time, even though my voice is barely above a whisper. I added the sixth verse. The words and music can be found in my book, *American Favorite Ballads* (see Bibliography). My sister Peggy says this version was collected by Cecil Sharp in 1904.

The Water is Wide

B47

1. The water is wide, I cannot cross over,
And neither have I wings to fly,
Give me a boat that can carry two,
And both shall row—my love and I.
(CAN BE REPEATED AS A REFRAIN)

2. A ship there was, and she sails the sea,
She's loaded deep, as deep can be,
But not so deep as the love I'm in
And I know not—how, I sink or swim.

3. I leaned my back against some young oak
Thinking he was a trusty tree,
But first he bended and then he broke
And thus did my false love to me.

4. I put my hand into some soft bush
Thinking the sweetest flower to find
I pricked my finger to the bone
And left the sweetest flower alone.

5. Oh, love is handsome, love is fine,
Gay as a jewel, when first it is new,
But love grows old, and waxes cold,
And fades away, like summer dew.

6. The seagulls wheel, they turn and dive,
The mountain stands beside the sea.
This world we know turns round and round
And all for them—and you and me.

REPEAT FIRST VERSE

I often sing this song right after a gang has raised the roof on "If I Had a Hammer," saying, "All our militance, enthusiasm, bravery will count for nothing if we can't cross the oceans of misunderstanding between the peoples of this world…"

6. The sea-gulls wheel,_____ they turn and dive._____ The moun-tain stands_____ ___ be-side the_____ sea._____ This world we know_____ turns 'round_____ and 'round, and all for them, and_____ you and me._____

Traditional. New last verse by Pete Seeger (1982)
Guitar arrangement by Pete Seeger
© 1993 by Sanga Music Inc.

As I write down these notes, I realize I never sang it twice the same. The guitar keeps fast "arpeggios" going like this. But the measures may have three or five or six beats. The chords look tricky but aren't. Arrows point to the string the thumb plucks.

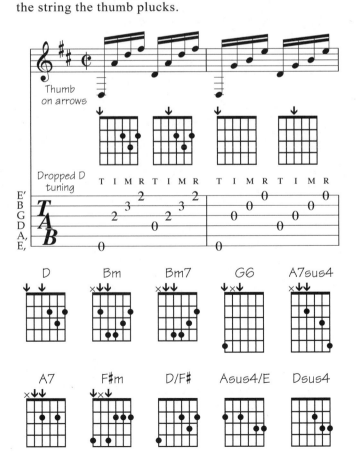

If you want to just strum, instead of playing jillions of fast little notes, it could turn out like this.

Free rhythm

Right Thumb throughout — A ship there was and she sails the sea, She's load-ed deep as deep can be But not so deep as the love I'm in, And I know not how I sink or swim.

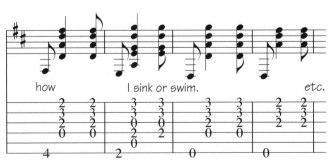

etc.

How do I get audiences to harmonize on it? Get the melody set firmly in people's minds, first.

I first play the great melody quite slowly, on a wooden recorder, or I whistle it along with the guitar. Then I tell folks how I can't sing it anymore, because my voice wobbles too much, but they can, because I'll give them the words.

"The water is wide, I cannot cross over…"

And then, very slowly, with the guitar leading, we start. Often, when it comes to the third or fourth line of a verse, I only give half a line at a time.

"But not so deep…" And while they are singing that wonderful word "deep" I'll give them the next five words, "…as the love I'm in…"

After they can sing the tune, for two or three verses, I encourage more harmony: "Some people are singing a nice high part." I hum a few notes.

"We can use more of this. There's no such thing as a wrong note if you are singing."

If I have a good microphone I don't need to speak loudly to be heard above thousands of people. By the time we get to my new last verse, my voice is hardly above a whisper.

"This world we know…"

"And all for them…"

"And — you — and me…"

"The — water — is — wide!"

By this time they are learning *from each other*. I don't need to give the words again. As an accompanist, and a 'conductor of the chorus' my main job is to keep the song from speeding up, to get them to hold out the last notes of phrases, to encourage them to improvise harmony.

★ ★ ★

For several decades a group of science fiction fans who like to write satirical verses to well known tunes have exchanged mimeographed (now photocopied) song-sheets which they call "filk songs." Who exactly started this one off, no one knows, but it has so far accumulated over 500 verses. (Send $ to John Boardman, 234 East 19th Street, Brooklyn, NY 11226. He may be able to send you some photocopies.) Judy Gorman taught it to me. I selected my own favorites and then added a last verse of my own. Keep it brisk.

The "Filk Song" Ole Time Religion

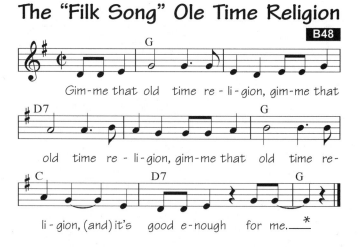

B48

Gim-me that old time re-li-gion, gim-me that old time re-li-gion, gim-me that old time re-li-gion, (and) it's good e-nough for me.____*

Words: Anonymous, 6th verse by Pete Seeger (1982)
Music: traditional (gospel hymn), adapted by Pete Seeger (& others)
© 1993 by Sanga Music Inc.

CHORUS:
Gimme that old time religion (3x)
It's good enough for me.

1. We will pray with Aphrodite
   We will pray with Aphrodite
   She wears that see-through nightie
   And that's good enough for me

2. We will pray with those Egyptians
   Build pyra<u>mids</u> to put our crypts in
   Cover subways with inscriptions
   And it's good enough for me

3. We will pray with Zarathustra
   Pray just like we used ta
   I'm a Zarathustra booster
   And it's good enough for me

4. We will pray with those old Druids
   They drink fermented fluids
   Waltzing naked through the woo-ids
   And it's good enough for me

5. Hari Krishna he must laugh on
   With my robes all trimmed in saffron
   And my hair that's only half on
   But it's good enough for me

(TIME FOR AN INSTRUMENTAL BREAK.
AND I ADD MY OWN VERSE)

6. I'll arise at early morning
   When my Lord gives me the warning
   That the solar age is dawning
   And that's good enough for me.*

(END WITH A ROUSING LAST CHORUS)

Both Sides Now

Words & music by Joni Mitchell, 4th verse by Pete Seeger (1975)

1. Rows and floes of angel hair,
   And ice-cream castles in the air,
   And feather canyons ev'rywhere,
   I've looked at clouds that way,
      But now they only block the sun,
      They rain and snow on ev'ryone,
      So many things I would have done,
      But clouds got in my way.
   I've looked at clouds from both sides now,
   From up and down, and still somehow
   It's clouds illusions I recall;
   I really don't know clouds at all.

2. Moons and Junes and ferris wheels,
   The dizzy dancing way you feel,
   As ev'ry fairy tale comes real,
   I've looked at love that way.
      But now it's just another show,
      You leave 'em laughin' when you go.
      And if you care, don't let them know,
      Don't give yourself away.
   I've looked at love from both sides now,
   From give and take, and still somehow
   It's love's illusions I recall;
   I really don't know love at all.

3. Tears and fears and feeling proud,
   To say "I love you" right out loud,
   Dreams and schemes and circus crowds,
   I've looked at life that way.
      But now old friends are acting strange,
      They shake their heads, they say I've changed.
      But something's lost but something's gained
      In living ev'ry day.
   I've looked at life from both sides now,
   From win and lose and still somehow
   It's life's illusions I recall;
   I really don't know life at all.

(NEW VERSE FOR AN OLDER PERSON TO SING:) **B51**
4. Daughter, Daughter, don't you know
   You're not the first to feel just so,
   But let me say before I go,
   It's worth it anyway.
      Some day we may all be surprised,
      We'll wake and open up our eyes,
      And then we all will realize
      The whole world feels this way.
   We've all been living upside down,
   And turned around with love unfound,
   Until we turn and face the sun;
   Yes, all of us, everyone.

I first heard Joni's song on a car radio, added a fourth verse suitable for my age, and got a nice letter from Joni permitting me to sing it.

Garbage

B52...

I'm only one of many people who have made up extra verses to this now famous song. Some people like to shout out the word at random. I like to get a gang to mutter it throughout (for our mutter country).

Dm
Mis-ter Thomp-son calls the wait-er, or-ders

steak and baked po-ta-ter, but he

leaves the bone and gris-tle and he

A7
nev-er eats the skins. The

bus-boy comes and takes it, with a

cough con-tam-i-nates it, and

puts it in a can with cof-fee

Dm
grounds and sar-dine tins. The

A♯dim
truck comes by on Fri-day, and

Dm
carts it all a-way, and a

Gm
thou-sand trucks just like it are con-

C   A7
verg-ing on the bay, Oh,

Dm
Gar-bage! (gar-bage, gar-bage, gar-bage)

Gar-bage (gar-bage, gar-bage) We're

A7
fill-ing up the seas with gar-bage!

A♯dim   A7
What will we do when there's

A♯dim   A7   Dm
no place left to put all the gar-bage? (garbage...)

Words & music by Bill Steele, 4th verse by Mike Agranoff and Pete Seeger (1977)
© 1969 William Steele. Copyright assigned 1992 to The Rainbow Collection, Ltd., PO Box 300, Solebury PA 18963. All rights reserved. Used by permission.

I find the A♯ diminished chord a very useful one in this song. Just one extra finger is needed to make the change. The third verse repeats this measure seven times, with slight variations, and the fourth verse nine times. See next column.

A♯dim   A7

1. Mister Thompson calls the waiter, orders steak and baked potater
   But he leaves the bone and gristle and he never eats the skins;
   The bus boy comes and takes it, with a cough contaminates it
   And puts it in a can with coffee grounds and sardine tins;
       The truck comes by on Friday
       and carts it all away;
       And a thousand trucks just like it are converging on the bay, oh,

   Garbage! (garbage, garbage, garbage) Garbage!
   We're filling up the sea with garbage (garbage...)
   What will we do
   When there's no place left to put all the
   Garbage? (garbage, garbage, garbage...)

2. Mister Thompson starts his Cadillac and winds it
      down the freeway track
   Leaving friends and neighbors in a hydro-carbon
      haze;
   He's joined by lots of smaller cars all sending
      gases to the stars.
   There they form a seething cloud that hangs for
      thirty days.
         And the sun licks down into it with an ultra-
            violet tongue.
         Turns it into smog and then it settles in our
            lungs, oh,

   Garbage! (garbage, garbage, garbage) Garbage!
   We're filling up the sky with garbage (garbage...)
   What will we do
   When there's nothing left to breathe but
   Garbage (garbage, garbage...)

3. Getting home and taking off his shoes he settles
      with the evening news,
   While the kids do homework with the TV in one ear
      (Garbage, garbage)
   While Superman for the thousandth time sells
      talking dolls and conquers crime,
   Dutifully they learn the date-of-birth of Paul Revere.
         In the papers there's a piece about the Mayor's
            middle name,
         He gets it read in time to watch the all-star
            bingo game, oh,

   Garbage, (garbage, garbage, garbage)
   * Garbage! (garbage, garbage, garbage)*
   We're fillin' up our minds with garbage
   * (garbage, garbage, garbage)*
   *What will we do when there's nothing left to read**
   And there's nothing left to need,
   Nothing left to watch,
   And nothing left to touch,
   There's nothing left to walk upon
   And nothing left to talk upon
   Nothing left to see
   And there's nothing left to be but
   Garbage? (garbage, garbage)

   B...52

4. In Mister Thompson's fac-to-ry
      they're making plastic Christmas trees
   Complete with silver tinsel and a geodesic stand
   The plastic's mixed in giant vats
      from some con-glom-er-ation that's
   Been piped from deep within the earth
      or strip mined from the land.
         And if you question anything they say,
            "Why, don't you see
            It's ab-so-lute-ly needed for the
            e-co-no-my," oh

Garbage (garbage, garbage)
* Garbage! (garbage, garbage)*
Their stocks and their bonds all garbage
What will they do
*When their system goes to smash***
There's no value to their cash
There's no money to be made
But there's a world to be repaid
Their kids will read in history books
About financiers and other crooks
And feudalism, and slavery
And Nukes and all their knavery
To history's dustbin they're consigned
Along with many other kinds of
Garbage (garbage, garbage, garbage...)

* Sing next seven lines to essentially the same line of music.
**Sing the next nine lines also to this same line of music.

Sample variations.

Mike Agranoff of New Jersey made up the first
seven lines of verse 4, disagreed with me about the rest,
but allowed me to sing his lines anyway. Thanks, Mike;
your complete verse is below. And, thanks Bill Steele.
Bill tells me that dozens of people have added verses to
his song, an underground classic.

   In Mister Thompson's factory
      they're making plastic Christmas trees
   Complete with silver tinsel and a geodesic stand.
   The plastic's mixed in giant vats
      from some conglomeration that's
   Been piped from deep within the ground
      or strip mined from the land.
         The residue gets flushed away
            through pipes beneath the ground,
         Gets dumped into the river
            and fills up Long Island Sound.

Garbage, (garbage, garbage, garbage)
* Garbage, (garbage, garbage, garbage)*
We're killing off the fish with garbage,
* (garbage, garbage, garbage)*
What will we do when there's no fish left to catch
And nothing left to swim in
And nothing left to drink but garbage!

God Blessed America
This Land Was made for you + me

This land is your land, this land is my land
From the California to the New York Island,
From the Redwood Forest, to the Gulf stream waters,
   God blessed America for me.

As I went walking that ribbon of highway
And saw above me that endless skyway,
And saw below me the golden valley, I said:
   God blessed America for me.

I roamed and rambled, and followed my footsteps
To the sparkling sands of her diamond deserts,
And all around me, a voice was sounding:
   God blessed America for me.

Was a big high wall there that tried to stop me
A sign was painted said: Private Property.
But on the back side it didn't say nothing —
   God blessed America for me.

When the sun come shining, then I was strolling
In wheat fields waving, and dust clouds rolling;
The voice was chanting as the fog was lifting:
   God blessed America for me.

One bright sunny morning in the shadow of the steeple
By the Relief Office I saw my people —
As they stood hungry, I stood there wondering if
   God blessed America for me.

*all you can write is
what you see.

Woody G.
N.Y., N.Y., N.Y.
Feb. 23, 1940
43rd st + 6th Ave,
Hanover House

original copy
of this song

Above is the song "This Land Is Your Land" as Woody first wrote it down. Sometime between 1940 and 1949 he changed the last line and then recorded verses 1, 2, 3, and 5 for Folkways Records. A later handwritten version amended the words to one verse slightly to read:

Was a great high wall there that tried to stop me;
Was a great big sign there says "Private Prop'ty…"

Arlo sings this line as "A great big sign says 'No Trespassing.'" And Woody later added a good new last verse:

Nobody living can ever stop me,
As I go walking my freedom highway.
Nobody living can make me turn back.
This land was made for you and me.

It was this last verse along with the 4th and 6th verses which Woody taught young Arlo in the early 1950s saying, "Arlo, they're singing my song in the schools, but they're not singing all the verses. You write 'em down now."

What comes next is an article I wrote about this song a few years back for *The Village Voice.*

This Land Is Your Land
(Portrait of a song as a bird in flight)

"A notation of folksong in a book is like a picture of a bird in a bird book. It was changing before the picture was taken, and changed afterward." (CLS)

"This Land Is Your Land," with its deceptively simple melody, was put together by Woody Guthrie in the 1940s. When he first got the idea for it, "God Bless America" was getting a big play on the radio. In his own handwriting in the 1940s, you see how he first wrote it. In the next nine years he changed the last line, added a few verses. In the late 1940s he recorded it for Disc Records (now Folkways) in the three-verse version printed below, now widely known. Around 1949, the Jewish Young People's Folksingers Chorus directed by Robert DeCormier in New York started singing it. They spread it. When Woody Guthrie went into the hospital in 1952, he signed over the rights to the then-little-known song to a publisher who now collects royalties for it and turns them over to Woody's family. Indirectly much of the royalties go to the Committee to Combat Huntington's Disease, which was set up by Marjorie Mazia Guthrie.

By the mid-1950s a few school song books dared include it. By 1971 they all did. But only a chorus and three verses.

WOODY GUTHRIE & FAMILY, CONEY ISLAND, 1951

B53

This land is your land, this land is my land, From Cal-i-for-nia to the New York Is-land, From the red-wood for-est to the Gulf Stream wa-ter, This land was made for you and me.

Words & music by Woody Guthrie (1940)
TRO - © 1956 (renewed), 1958 (renewed) & 1970 Ludlow Music, Inc., New York, NY.

(The three best-known verses were printed here. See page at left for all five of Woody's original verses, plus another one he taught Arlo).

The other three verses are not so generally known. When Arlo Guthrie was a child his father visited home from the hospital and had Arlo write down the verses which didn't get in the school songbooks.

I and others have started singing them. We feel that there is a danger of this song being misinterpreted without these new/old verses being added. The song could even be co-opted by the very selfish interests Woody was fighting all his life. Washington big wheel Clark Clifford in March 1950 addressed the wealthy businessmen at Chicago's Executive Club: "...The people have to feel that their small share of this country is as much theirs as it is yours and mine..." With only half of Woody's verses, "This Land Is Your Land" falls right into Mr. Clifford's trap. In other words, "Let people go ahead and sing the song. Meanwhile you and I know who really controls the country."

The song has now been used in movies and TV, and has been used to accompany television commercials. Today every American has heard the song at some time or another, even though it has never been at the "top of the charts." A few far rightists look upon the song as part of "the International Communist Plot," but the daughter of Ronald Reagan liked to include the song in her repertoire as a "folk singer" in the 1970s. It was sung at Ronald Reagan's inauguration party.

OK. Was Woody a Communist? Were Woody alive today I believe he would scorn to use the Bill of Rights to protect himself. "Sure I'm a communist" he once wrote in the mid-'40s in a personal letter. And at the time he wrote "This Land Is Your Land," he was writing a regular column "Woody Sez" for the *Daily Worker* and *People's World*, the two U.S. Communist newspapers. He once applied to be a member of the party but was turned down. He was always traveling, hated meetings and political discussions which used long words. Keep in mind that he considered Jesus was basically a Communist. In his own way Woody was very religious. When he went into a hospital in 1952, he said intently to us, "Only God can help me." When a nurse asked him what religion he was so she could fill out a form, he replied, "All." She asked him again and said he must give one or another; his reply was, "All or none."

Fred Hellerman went with Harold Leventhal (who set up the Woody Guthrie Trust Fund) to visit Woody at the first mental hospital he was sent to. "Is the food OK? Being treated all right?"

Woody said everything was fine. "Besides, I can get up here and shout 'I'm a Communist' and everybody'll shrug and say 'Aw, he's crazy' You try doing that on the outside and they'll arrest you. Why this is the last place in America that's really free."

Would Woody call himself a Communist today? Read his writings, prose and poetry. Decide for yourself.

Back to the song.

One young fellow wrote me that he was starting a campaign to make the song the national anthem. I wrote him, "Please stop! Can't you see U.S. Marines marching into another little country playing this song?" In any case, I for one would be sorry to see it made an official anthem. A song is not a speech. Like any work of art, it has many meanings for many people. It reflects new meanings as life shines new lights upon it. To make "This Land Is Your Land" an official song would be to rob it of its poetic career and doom it to a political straitjacket, no matter how well-fitting the jacket might seem to be at the time.

When I sing the song now, I still usually end up with the gloriously optimistic verse, "The sun came shining and I was strolling." But before this I do a lot of singing and talking and often throw in a couple new verses of my own.

Maybe you been working just as hard as you're able
And you just got crumbs from the rich man's table
Maybe you been wondering, is it truth or fable
This land was made for you and me.

My friend from Louisiana, Brother Frederick Douglass Kirkpatrick, sang "You just get crumbs from the white man's table."

Dozens of other verses have been written to the song within the last 10 years. Some of them simply change a few words to make the chorus apply to Canada or to England or Australia. There have been verses sung from New Mexico in Spanish. There have been anti-pollution verses. I always encourage anyone who loves any song not to be ashamed to try making up verses for it. Try some language other than English, if only to remind ourselves that this America of ours is a multi-national place. I'd like to hear verses in the Cherokee language, or Navaho, or Mohawk.

Consider the following verse made up a few years ago.

This land is your land, but it once was my land
Before we sold you Manhattan Island
You pushed my nation to the reservation,
This land was stole by you from me.

(BY CAPPY ISRAEL)

When I am on stage and sing the previous verse, it often gets applause, but still I find it hard to go right into the well-known chorus after that, so I tell them the story of how in May 1968 in Resurrection City, Washington, D.C., Jimmy Collier, a great young black singer from the midwest, was asked to lead this song. Henry Crowdog of the Sioux Indian delegation came up and punched his finger in Jimmy's chest. "Hey, you're both wrong. It belongs to me." Jimmy stopped and added seriously, "Should we not sing this song?" Then a big grin came over Henry Crowdog's face. "No, it's okay. Go ahead and sing it. *As long as we are all down here together to get something done.*" And then Jimmy sailed into the chorus and the crowd roared it along with him.

How can a disinherited people possess their future? Who are the disinherited? Certainly Native Americans are. Certainly African-Americans. I say the whole of industrialized, polluted humankind has, to a certain extent, sold our birthright for a mess of pottage. If we are to survive, we must build a world in which the children of every human being on earth can share. Struggling, sure. But cooperating too, not threatening to kill each other. This song can help us in our search and our joyous struggle to possess our future:

Where poisons no longer fill our waters
Where peace and justice fill our borders
When hunger and hatred are past disgraces
This land was made for you and me.

As I was sailing that Hudson River
I saw around me the tow'ring timber
I saw beneath me all New York's litter
Still this land was made for you and me.

(BY JEAN WILCOX, ILLINOIS)

JIMMY COLLIER & PETE SEEGER

Photo by Julie Snow

Many have written sarcastic verses.

As I was walking that ribbon of highway
I heard the buzzing of a hundred chain saws
And the redwoods falling, and the loggers calling
This land was made for you and me.
(BY COUNTRY JOE McDONALD)

We've logged the forests, we've mined the mountains
We've dammed the rivers, but we've built fountains!
We got tin and plastic, and crowded freeways,
This land was made for you and me.
(BY JERRY J. SMITH)

I've roamed and rambled, and followed the beer cans
From the toxic cities to the flooded canyons
And all around me were the billboards reading
"This land was made for you and me."
(BY ???)

On the other hand, they'd say to me, "Pete, you're sentimental. Be realistic."

As I went walking the oil-filled coastline
Along the beaches fishes were choking
The smog kept rolling, the populations growing
This land was made for you and me.
(BY COUNTRY JOE McDONALD)

Several people have made verses in Spanish.

Es vuestra tierra, es nuestra tierra
De la llanura a la sierra
De la mar Pacífico a la mar Atlántico
Fue hecha para tí, para mí.
(BY TIM MAY, 1990)

Esta Es Mi Tierra

Aquí llegaron mis antecesores.
Cruzaron aguas grandiosamente.
Montaron caballos hasta Santa Fe.
Mi bella tierra es para mí.

Esta es mi tierra, esta es tu tierra
Tierra de hombres exploradores
Poblaron pueblos entre los Indios
Mi bella tierra es para mí.

Conquistador Hernando Cortes
Cabeza de Vaca y Coronado
Honorables hombres de nuestra Raza
Mi bella tierra es para mí.

Colonizador fue Juan de Onate
Diego de Vargas también lo fue
Hombre valiente fue Santa Ana
Fue gran ejemplo para mí.

Esta es mi tierra, esta es tu tierra
Desde California hasta el Río Grande
Esas fronteras del Sudoeste
Mi bella tierra es para mí.

Esta es mi tierra que hermosos valles
Sierras muy altas, montes muy verdes
Cielos muy claros, aires muy limpios
Mi bella tierra es para mí.

Esta es mi tierra, esta es tu tierra
Sangre mezclada Indo-Hispana
Mi lindo idioma es español
Mi bella tierra es para mí.
(ALBERTO O. MARTINEZ, ESPANOLA, NM

PUBLISHED IN *EL GRITO DEL NORTE*, JUNE 1969.)

Some verses I made up when singing along the Hudson River, in the Clearwater campaign.

This river is your river, this river is my river
She'll return to us just as much as we all give her
She needs our love, more than gold or silver
This land was made for you and me.

I come a long way here, I got a long way to go yet
I got things to learn here, I got seeds to sow yet
So many sisters and brothers, we still don't know yet
This land was made for you and me.

Woodland and grassland and river shorelines
To everything living, bugs, snakes and microbes
Fin, fur, and feather, we're all here together
This land was made for you and me.

One final note: remember what I wrote on p.16. "Add, subtract. But beware of multiplying."

The publishers of this song, who have the difficult job of collecting royalties for its use and seeing that it is not misused, are probably wincing by now. I am certainly not making their job any easier. Let me say simply that all the verses printed in this article are copyrighted by the same company that copyrighted the original song. And I suggest that if you make more changes yourself, you send them in to the company so at least they'll have a complete list of all the good new verses. Here's their address: TRO, 266 W. 37th St., 17th Floor, New York, NY 10018; <info@songways.com>.

Hey, I've counted at least 22 other songs in this book which have new words to old tunes. Check out, for example, the Clearwater version of "Blue Skies" on p. 222. Also see pp. 14, 21, 23, 25, 28, 31, 35, 45, 56, 63, 64, 66, 148, 180, 192, 194, 207, 208, 216, 218 and 223.

Note: The last three pages have been adapted from an article in a New York City weekly © Copyright 1971 by *The Village Voice*. Reprinted by permission.

After this long discussion of one famous song, someone will say, "Why don't we just sing Woody's song like he wrote it? His verses are better than any that have been added."

Good point. It's true that sometimes a group of people get singing a good song and want to make it longer and longer. They add all the verses they know, and make up new ones. But maybe one of the more creative things a singer can do to a song is to forget.

Forget the verses which are forgettable.

Forget words, phrases. Substitute better ones.

Forget whole songs except for one unforgettable phrase which then gets incorporated into another song.

And finally the songs which a nation remembers are truly called folk songs, because so many folks have had a hand (or a throat) in shaping them.

The word "Revolution" means different things to different people. When people learned how to be farmers, instead of hunters and gatherers of food, that was the Agricultural Revolution. It started in the Near East about 10,000 years ago, more recently in other parts of the world. Then there was the Industrial Revolution. By contrast, the more common meaning of the word is when the government of a country is taken over by some kind of force. It is taken away from one group of rulers and then a different group of rulers is in charge. Which, compared to the Agricultural or Industrial Revolutions is more like a "Coup d'etat" (French term), a state takeover.

Now we're in the middle of an Information Revolution. If the human race is still here in a hundred years we'll grow in generosity, grow in common sense, grow in the ability to talk with people we disagree with. But won't grow in size or numbers.

And of course, there's always pros and cons to everything. In my conservative old age, I confess that if I'd been there when someone invented the wheel, I woulda said "Don't."

Chapter 7: *Waist Deep in the Big Muddy —*
The Vietnam War

"Any mule can kick a barn down. It takes skilled hands to build it up again."

>Lyndon Johnson, 1967
>(Give credit where credit is due)

There's nothing like a crisis to bring out the urge to write poetry. The 1960s were a productive period for me. I had been inspired by the Civil Rights movement. Every week I was singing at different colleges and was able to test out a new song on a live-wire audience. I knew I was doing O.K. when some person would loudly boo a line and then was promptly drowned out by thousands of cheers. The poor guy who booed probably looked around in astonishment, saying "What's happening to our country when traitorous words like that are applauded?" I hope I started him thinking.

I could remember that way back in 1954 when the French were being defeated in Vietnam, I read in the *Daily Worker*, "The U.S. establishment will move in now to try to control things there." President Eisenhower said, "The USA must have that tungsten."

But the first song I wrote about Vietnam, "King Henry," was 11 years later. It was inspired by a letter in a local newspaper. I took the words of the third, fourth, and fifth stanzas directly from it. The woman writing the letter was quoting her husband, who had been a U.S. "adviser." I couldn't get her letter out of my head. I had taken my family skiing for two days. My conscience was getting to me. The words of the verses came to me on a ski slope. The tune is an ancient great one.

Ten months after I wrote it, this song got me in hot water. Toshi and I were on tour in Europe, east and west. In the Soviet Union I had sung songs of the Civil Rights Movement and the Labor Movement but purposely stayed away from the subject of Vietnam. In Moscow I was asked by one of the students at Moscow University if I'd give an extra concert for them. "None of us have been able to get tickets to your regular concert. It is sold out."

Peter Grose, the *New York Times* correspondent in Moscow, asked if he could accompany me to the concert. "They won't let me on the campus."

"Sure," said I, all innocence, "come along. You can carry my guitar for me."

The short article he wrote was first printed in the Paris edition of the *New York Herald-Tribune*. He ignored all the positive songs I'd sung and mentioned only this one, which had actually been sung during the question-and-answer period, when one of the Moscow students asked, "What kinds of songs are being sung in American universities these days?" I told them about the songs of Phil Ochs and Bob Dylan and sang "King Henry."

Grose's article was picked up a couple days later by the *New York Times* and given the headline "Seeger Sings Anti-American Song in Moscow." The headline and the article were then picked up by my hometown paper in Beacon, New York, population 13,000, 60 miles north of the Big Apple. I called up the editor of the *Times*, and quoted the words of the song. He agreed they were not "anti-American," and said the headline had been changed in later editions. But the damage had been done.

King Henry

B54

King Hen-ry marched forth, a sword in his hand, Two thou-sand horse-men all at his com-mand;— In a fort-night the riv-ers ran red through the land,— The year fif-teen hun-dred and twen-ty.——

Words by Pete Seeger (1965) Music traditional (Scottish) "I Once Loved a Lass"
© 1965 (renewed), 1966 by Sanga Music Inc.

1. King Henry marched forth, a sword in his hand,
   Two thousand horsemen all at his command;
   In a fortnight the rivers ran red through the land,
   The year fifteen hundred and twenty.

2. The year it is now nineteen sixty-five
   It's easier far to stay half alive.
   Just keep your mouth shut when the planes zoom
       and dive
   Ten thousand miles over the ocean.

3. Simon was drafted in '63,
   In '64, sent over the sea;
   Last month this letter he sent to me,
   He said, "You won't like what I'm saying."

4. He said, "We've no friends here, no hardly a one,
   We've got a few generals who just want our guns;
   But it'll take more than that if we're ever to win,
   Why, we'll have to flatten the country."

5. "It's my own troops I have to watch out for,"
       he said,
   "I sleep with a pistol right under my head";
   He wrote this last month; last week he was dead,
   And Simon came home in a casket.

6. I mind my own business, I watch my TV,
   Complain about taxes, but pay anyway;
   In a civilized manner my forefathers betray,
   Who long ago struggled for freedom.

7. But each day a new headline screams at my bluff,
   On TV some general says we must be tough;
   In my dreams I stare at this family I love,
   All gutted and spattered with napalm.

8. King Henry marched forth, a sword in his hand,
   Two thousand horsemen all at his command;
   In a fortnight the rivers ran red through the land,
   Ten thousand miles over the ocean.

I was due to sing at the local high school in two weeks. Some local "patriots"[1] started a petition campaign to stop the concert. They went up and down Main Street and got 700 signatures. Somebody started a forest fire at one end of our mountainside land one Sunday, and a week later another forest fire at the other end of our property. A liberal doctor in Beacon urged me, "You should cancel the concert. You know this is fascism. You're going to be run out of town."

Toshi and I decided it was worth making a stand, and sure enough, we were right. The Beacon High School students stuck up for me, and so did a few of the shopkeepers that we had traded with. I remember one elderly hardware store owner who was personally extremely conservative and had voted for Barry Goldwater in '64. He said, "Well, I don't know your politics, young man, but it's America. You got a right to your opinion."

The head of the school board, also an elderly man, said he could not legally refuse to allow the use of the high school. The New York State Supreme Court had only recently handed down a decision that if the schools rented to anybody, they had to rent to anybody regardless of their opinions. (The court's decision actually was related to the attempt of the John Birch Society to stop my concert in East Meadow, Long Island, a few years earlier.)

So it all turned out pretty well after all. With all this publicity, the high school auditorium was jam-packed, and the folks sang along well. Me, I learned an important lesson.

I realized belatedly that for 18 years I'd treated my home town like a hotel. I'd gone down to pick up my mail and groceries and gone back to our mountainside cabin. Most people in town didn't really know who the heck I was.

Well, the *Clearwater* campaign forced me to change my way of doing things. More of that later.

[1]Why do I use quotes? Because too often these types think they are the only patriots.

Bring 'Em Home

B55

Words & music by Pete Seeger (1966)
© 1966 by Stormking Music Inc.

1. If you love your Uncle Sam,
    Bring 'em home, Bring 'em home.
    Support our boys in Vietnam,
    Bring 'em home, Bring 'em home.

2. It'll make our generals sad, I know,
    (REFRAIN: Bring 'em home…, etc.)
    They want to tangle with the foe.
    (REPEAT REFRAIN THROUGHOUT)

3. They want to test their weaponry,
    But here is their big fallacy:

4. Our foe is hunger and ignorance,
    You can't beat that with bombs and guns.

5. I may be right, I may be wrong,
    But I got a right to sing this song.

6. There's one thing I must confess,
    I'm not really a pacifist.

7. If an army invaded this land of mine,
    You'd find me out on the firing line.

In 2003, the year our country invaded Iraq, I recorded a new version of this song with Billy Bragg, Ani DiFranco, Steve Earle, Anne Hills and Tom Pacheco. We added a couple of verses supplied by Jim Musselman. And in 2006 Bruce Springsteen sang it:

So if you don't want to fight for oil
Bring 'em home …
Underneath some foreign soil
Bring 'em home …

So if you love this land of the free (Bring …)
Bring all troops back from overseas (Bring …)

YES, if you love this FREEDOM LAND (Bring …)
From Iraq and Afghanistan
BRING 'EM HOME, BRING 'EM HOME

I admit I'm not a military expert. But have you heard the French definition of an expert? "Someone who avoids all the little mistakes on the way to the big fallacy."

Not one of my best, this. An editorial in rhyme. I always caution beginning songwriters, "Beware of editorials in rhyme. Better: Tell a story." Nevertheless it did its job, got thousands singing that short refrain. And some life-long passions got into the verses.

And I may be wrong. In 2006 this became widely listened to because Bruce Springsteen recorded it, with words about Iraq. See p. 157.

★ ★ ★

A year later the next song took a couple weeks to write. I saw a photo of troops in the Mekong Delta and the last line came to me all at once — words, tune, rhythm. I wrote it down in my pocket notebook: then, as usual, I was unable to finish it. But it kept coming back to haunt me. Had to do something about it. In two weeks of tussling, I got it finished. I sang it everywhere I could. At colleges it got an explosive reaction. This was early in '67.

In the fall I got a phone call from two friends, Tommy and Dick Smothers, who had started in night clubs as comedians making fun of "folk singers," and now had a successful weekly national TV show. In early '67 their bosses at CBS, overjoyed at their high ratings, had asked what they could do to make their stars happier. "Let us have Seeger as a guest on our show," shot back Tommy.

"Well—hm—let's think about that."

In October CBS said O.K. I flew to L.A., sang a medley of soldier songs on the show, starting with "The Riflemen of Bennington" (1778), "John Brown's Body" (1863), "The D-Day-Dodgers" (1944) and ended with "Big Muddy." The videotape was flown to New York City for the CBS brass to check it before it went out over the network. When it was aired a couple days later, "Big Muddy" had been cut out of the tape. One moment I had a guitar in my hand; a second later I had a banjo in my hand — it was an obvious cut.

The Smothers Brothers took to the print media, "CBS is censoring our best jokes; they censored Seeger's best song." Finally in January CBS said, "O.K., O.K., you can have Seeger sing it." On 24 hours' notice, I again flew to L.A., taped the song. Seven million viewers saw it. Only a Detroit station deleted the song.

This was one time in my entire life I really wished I had been able to properly promote a song and get it heard by the whole country. It could have saved lives. John Hammond, then overseeing my recording at Columbia, agreed to release the song as a single. But neither he nor I had much influence with the sales department. In Denver a young man told me, "Pete, I was working in the office of the local distributor for Columbia Records when your single of 'Big Muddy' came in. My boss took one listen and exploded, 'Those guys in New York must be nuts to think I can sell a record like this.'"

"Pete, your record never even left the shelves," said my friend.

However, a month after the TV program, LBJ threw in the sponge, said he would not run for re-election. Did this song help? Who knows?

Waist Deep In The Big Muddy

(Also known as "The Big Muddy")
Words & music by Pete Seeger (1967)
TRO - © 1967 Melody Trails, Inc., New York, NY.

1. It was back in nineteen forty-two,
   I was a member of a good platoon.
   We were on maneuvers in-a Loozianna,
   One night by the light of the moon.
   The captain told us to ford a river,
   That's how it all begun.
   We were—knee deep in the Big Muddy,
   But the big fool said to push on.

2. The Sergeant said, "Sir, are you sure,
   This is the best way back to the base?"
   "Sergeant, go on! I forded this river
   'Bout a mile above this place.
   It'll be a little soggy but just keep slogging.
   We'll soon be on dry ground."
   We were—waist deep in the Big Muddy
   And the big fool said to push on.

3. The Sergeant said, "Sir, with all this equipment
   No man will be able to swim."
   "Sergeant, don't be a Nervous Nellie,"
   The Captain said to him.
   "All we need is a little determination;
   Men, follow me, I'll lead on."
   We were—neck deep in the Big Muddy
   And the big fool said to push on.

4. All at once, the moon clouded over,
   We heard a gurgling cry.
   A few seconds later, the captain's helmet
   Was all that floated by.
   The sergeant said, "Turn around men!*
   I'm in charge from now on."
   And we just made it out of the Big Muddy
   With the captain dead and gone.

5. We stripped and dived and found his body
   Stuck in the old quicksand.
   I guess he didn't know that the water was deeper
   Than the place he'd once before been.
   Another stream had joined the Big Muddy
   'Bout a half mile from where we'd gone.
   We were lucky to escape from the Big Muddy
   When the big fool said to push on.

6. Well, I'm not going to point any moral;
   I'll leave that for yourself.
   Maybe you're still walking, you're still talking,
   You'd like to keep your health.
   But every time I read the papers**
   That old feeling comes on;
   We're—waist deep in the Big Muddy and the
   Big fool says to push on.

7. Waist deep in the Big Muddy
   And the big fool says to push on,
   Waist deep in the Big Muddy
   And the big fool says to push on.
   Waist deep! Neck deep! Soon even a
   Tall man'll be over his head, we're ***
   Waist deep in the Big Muddy!
   And the big fool says to push on!

Variant melodies:

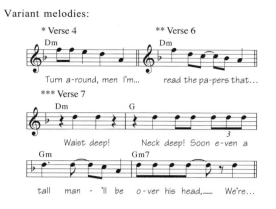

P.S.: After singing in a Midwest college, I stayed over-night at the home of a professor. At lunch he came in laughing, "At my first class I started briskly announcing that we had to get cracking the books; from the rear of the room I heard some student mutter, 'The big fool says to push on.'"

★ ★ ★

In April the civil rights coalition was falling apart. Dr. King was assassinated; Robert Kennedy soon after. The Democratic Party convention in Chicago ignored the anti-war protests. In the fall Nixon was elected. Soviet tanks rolled into Prague. I was 49 years old.

As in any blues, the melody changes from verse to verse, and every time you sing it. Incidentally, I usually do it down in G or A. The banjo gets better blue notes. You've heard it asked, "Can a white man sing the blues?" Randolphe Harris counters, "Can a blue man sing the whites?"

False From True

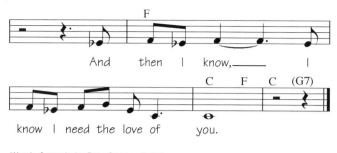

1. When my songs turn to ashes on my tongue,
   When I look in the mirror and see I'm no longer young,
   Then I got to start the job of separating
       false from true,
   And then I know, I know I need the love of you.

2. **When I found tarnish on some of my brightest
       dreams,
   When some folks I'd trusted turned out not quite
       what they seemed;
   Then I got to start the job of separating
       false from true,
   Then once more I know, I know I need the love of you.

3. No song I can sing will make Governor Wallace
       change his mind,*
   No song I can sing will take the gun from a
       hate-filled man;
   But I promise you, and you, brothers and sisters
       of every skin,
   I'll sing your story while I've breath within.

4. *** We got to keep on keeping on, even when the
       sun goes down,
   We got to live, live, live until another day
       comes 'round;
   Meanwhile, better start over, separating
       false from true,
   And more and more, I know I need the love of you.

*Hey, I wrote this nearly 40 years ago. Maybe he *did* change his mind.

The next song was sparked by one line in a poem in a popular magazine: "In April they sent us the bill for the burning of the children." Now I've lost the poet's name. I sent her a copy of my song, thanked her, and got a nice letter in reply. In the 1990s the Short Sisters (Kim Wallach, Fay Baird and my niece, Kate Seeger) recorded it.

The Calendar **B58**

1. May, May, the flow-ers bloom;— a
June wed-ding, an emp-ty room.—
Ju-ly— was ver-y warm-O,
Li-lo, lull-o, li-lo.—

2. Au-gust, we beat the heat,—
Fled the sub-urbs for the beach.—
Sep-tem-ber, bought a car-O,
Li-lo, lull-o, li-lo.—

3. Oc-to-ber, red and gold;—
No-vem-ber, turn-ing cold.—
De-cem-ber, 'round the tree-O,

Li-lo, lull-o, li-lo.—

4. Jan-u-a-ry brought the snow,—
Next month, ski-ing all did go.—
March, my God, how did the wind blow!
Li-lo, lull-o, li-lo.—

5. A-pril, cru-el, sweet A-pril!—
Now they pre-sent to us the bill.—
For the burn-ing of the chil-dren,
For the burn-ing of the chil-dren.
Lie* low, Lie low, Lie low.

Words & music by Pete Seeger (1969)
© 1969 by Sanga Music Inc.

*Pronounce "Lie-low" at the end — La-ee-lo.

Postscript: Singers in many parts of the world like to give out sounds that have no strict meaning. Why? Why do we like music anyway? Some Native American songs are mostly "vocables." Irish songs and some English and Scottish songs are full of "nonsense words." "Hey diddle diddle, Too-ri-oo-ri-ay." I think it's a little like repeating the last line of a song (see p. 120). In a narrative song with compact words, they slow down the action so you can savor it.

African-American songs have a lot of it, too, but of a different type — more "Ohhs" and "Heys." Gospel songs will have a lot of repetition instead.

Sometimes, as in scat singing, the "nonsense" words end up meaning more than the listener thought, at first hearing. In this song, "The Calendar," it comes out in the last line of the last verse.

In 1969 I took a nap in a student dormitory before singing in a small southern college. At the foot of the bed was a huge American flag. At the head of the bed was a huge photo-enlargement of Leon Trotsky. Couldn't sleep. Got up. Wrote verses. The first line is swiped from a poem by my uncle, Alan Seeger, who was one of the first Americans killed in World War I — he was a volunteer with the French Foreign Legion. My father, his older brother, had written him: "Alan, you're a damn fool. Don't you know the class of people that run France is the same class that runs Germany? You should have stayed out of it. I don't expect to see you again." And he didn't. But my uncle's poem was widely reprinted. I sometimes recite both together. Here's Alan's original.

ALAN SEEGER (1888–1916)

I Have a Rendezvous with Death

I have a rendezvous with Death
At some disputed barricade,
When Spring comes back with rustling shade
And apple blossoms fill the air —
I have a rendezvous with Death
When Spring brings back blue days and fair.

It may be he shall take my hand
And lead me into his dark land
And close my eyes and quench my breath —
It may be I shall pass him still.
I have a rendezvous with Death
On some scarred slope of battered hill,
When Spring comes 'round again this year
And the first meadow-flowers appear.

God knows 'twere better to be deep
Pillowed in silk and scented down,
Where Love throbs out in blissful sleep,
Pulse nigh to pulse and breath to breath,
Where hushed awakenings are dear ...
But I've a rendezvous with Death
At midnight in some flaming town,
When Spring trips north again this year,
And I to my pledged word am true,
I shall not fail that rendezvous.

By Alan Seeger (1916)
From his *Collected Poems* published by Charles Scribner's Sons in 1916.

So now after that great poem, I make so bold as to put my lesser poem of 1969. Tried and failed to get a worthwhile melody for it. It has been of use, though. I've been reciting it more the last few years, at the request of African-American friends.

The Torn Flag

At midnight in a flaming angry town
I saw my country's flag lying torn upon the ground.
I ran in and dodged among the crowd,
And scooped it up, and scampered out to safety.
    And then I took that striped old piece of cloth
    And tried my best to wash the garbage off.
    But I found it had been used for wrapping lies.
    It smelled and stank and attracted all the flies.
While I was feverishly at my task,
I heard a husky voice that seemed to ask;
"Do you think you could change me just a bit?
Betsy Ross* did her best, but she made a few mistakes.
    My blue is good, the color of the sky.
    The stars are good for ideals, oh, so high.
    Seven stripes of red are strong to meet all danger;
    But those white stripes: they, they need some
      changing.
I need also some stripes of deep, rich brown,
And some of tan and black, then all around
A border of God's gracious green would look good there.
Maybe you should slant the stripes, then I'd not be so
  square."
    I woke and said: "What a ridiculous story.
    Don't let anybody say I suggested tampering with
      Old Glory."
    But tonight it's near midnight, and in another
      flaming town
    Once again I hear my country's flag lies torn upon
      the ground.

By Pete Seeger (1969)
TRO - © 1970 Melody Trails, Inc., New York, NY.

*Research of Earl Williams, Jr., of Washington, D.C., has discovered that Francis Hopkinson actually proposed the design.

Some parts of the world (Japan is one) like songs in a minor mode. Some individuals also. Most of us now go back and forth easily — too easily? — from one mode to another. The next song, like the last two, is in a minor key.

The weakness of any allegory, here, or in the Bible or anywhere, is that it can be too pat. The "meaning" of a work of art should shift, change, expand. However, this allegory worked. I had requests for it 20 years later. Today the "eggheads" are warning us about the ozone layer, global warming, overpopulation, etc.

All My Children of the Sun

Words & music by Pete Seeger (1969)
© 1969 by Sanga Music Inc.

1. The navigator said to the engineer,
   I think our radio's dead.
   I can hear but I can't send,
   And there's bad weather ahead.
      The pilot said to the co-pilot,
      Our right engine's gone.
      But if we can make it over these mountains,
      Perhaps I can set her down.
   All my children of the sun!

2. Five hundred miles from nowhere
   We bellylanded on a river.
   We bid a quick goodbye
   To that ship of silver.
      Twenty-five piled out the window,
      Twenty reached the shore.
      We turned to see our metal bird
      Sink to rise no more.
   All my children of the sun!

3. We found some floating logs,
   We found some sharp stones.
   We cut some vines and made a raft.
   It was our only hope.
      The navigator said he thought there was
      A town somewhere downstream.
      So now each tried to do his best
      To paddle as a team.
      (OMIT LAST LINE)

4. All except one young guy
   Who kept arguing with the navigator.
   He said he'd read about a waterfall
   We would come to sooner or later.
      At a river's bend he persuaded us
      To bring our craft to beach.
      But a search party found the river smooth
      As far as eye could reach.
   All my children of the sun.

5. Once again he persuaded us to stop.
   We cursed at the delay.
   Once again we found the river
   Flowing on the same old way.
      We said, shut up your arguing.
      You give us all a pain.
      Why don't you pitch in and do your part—
      Be constructive for a change?
   All my children of the sun.

6. Still egghead kept on talking
   In the same longwinded way.
   We said, if you won't paddle,
   Get the hell out of our way.
     We told him to go sit
     Far back at the stern.
     Then we strained to paddle harder,
     And then the river made a turn.
   All my children of the sun.

7. One paddler heard sound of tapping
   And what he saw, when he did turn,
   Was egghead with a sharp stone,
   Cutting the vines that bound the stern.
   (THE FOLLOWING FOUR LINES USE SAME TUNE AS THE PREVIOUS FOUR)
     With a cry of rage the paddler
     Leaped up to his feet.
     He swung his long pole
     Knocked egghead into the deep.
       But now the logs were splaying out.
       The raft had come unbound.
       Like mad we paddled for the shore,
       Before all would drown.
     All my children of the sun.

8. A search party went out to find more vines
   To tie the raft up tight.
   In twenty minutes they returned,
   Their faces pale with fright.
     They said a quarter mile down river
     We <u>did</u> find a waterfall.
     It's over a hundred feet in height.
     It would have killed us all.
   All my children of the sun.

9. And that is why on the banks
   Of a far off wilderness stream,
   Which none of us, none of us,
   Will <i>ever</i> see again,
     There stands a cross for someone,
     Hardly older than a boy.
     Who, we thought, was only
     Trying to destroy.
   All my children of the sun.

My accompaniment to this was some fast banjo picking, as on a Kentucky mountain ballad. Tuning was "Mountain minor" — EBEAB (I have a long-neck banjo) and so the Am6 and B7 chords are fretted as below. Without this exciting accompaniment, this is a boring melody.

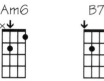

The fast banjo rhythm sets the tense feeling for this story. Below are the notes I play between the verses. You may want to work out something different.

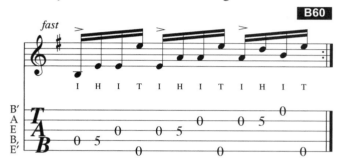

About the same time I made up a verse to sing to Bob Dylan's song, "The Times, They Are A-Changin'."

    Yes, this is me,
    Old stick-in-the-mud
    Still shovelling away
    At a mountain of crud,
    Still hoping that songs
    Can stanch rivers of blood
    Though the evidence I may be evading
    But till this throat is choked
    And I'm drowned in the flood
    It will sing for the times ever changing.

Two Against Three: A Rhythm Skill
(A Musical Interlude)

When people sing two-part harmony, they sing two notes at the same time. Can you also beat two different rhythms at the same time?

From Mexico down to Chile and Argentina it is common to see one guitar playing 3/4 time, like a waltz, and another guitarist nearby playing 6/8 time, that is, two beats per measure.

Technically, "two-against-three" is called "hemiola." It's not unknown in European music, but it's rare.

Here's a way to learn how to get the feel of it. Count off six rapid beats over and over, and pat with your left hand on your knee on the first and fourth beat only.

↓   ↓

"ONE two three FOUR five six   **B61**
ONE two three FOUR five six
ONE two three FOUR five six."

After about 20 seconds stop patting with your left hand but keep counting to six over and over. Now with your right hand tap your right knee on the first, third, and fifth beats:

↓   ↓   ↓

"ONE two THREE four FIVE six
ONE two THREE four FIVE six
ONE two THREE four FIVE six."

Now here's the tricky part. Bring down *both* hands on the beat "ONE." When it comes to "three four five," do a "right-left-right." Keep counting to six over and over without changing speed. Eventually you can stop counting "two" and "six." Once you get it into your muscles (so your brain can forget counting), you've got it made.

Chopin also once composed an A♭ piano "Etude" ("study") where the left hand played in 2/4 time and the right played two sets of triplets in each measure.

Franz Schubert wrote "Marche Militaire." It's become a well known melody. But I remember it this way. This is the two-against-three pattern.

(One way to remember the above notes is to sing "Big bagashit, Big bagashit, Big bagashit now ..." After a while you'll get the rhythm in your head and hands, which is where music should be.)

★ ★ ★

Back to the subject of this chapter.

In November 1969 in Washington, D.C., the "two-against-three" skill came in handy when I faced one of the largest crowds I've ever sung for. A half million people, all protesting the Vietnam War. Music, speeches alternated all afternoon. Suddenly it was my turn with Brother Fred Kirkpatrick, the great civil rights singer. We tried getting the crowd to join in on "Bring 'Em Home" (p. 149). No luck. By the time the beat got way out to that huge crowd, it came back a beat and a half late. Sound only travels 1,200 feet a second.

We tried Kirk's song, "Everybody's Got a Right To Live." Same problem. I looked over at Cora Weiss, holding a stopwatch on the proceedings. With a questioning look, I held up one index finger, meaning "OK, to sing one more song?"

She nodded.

I decided it was worth a gamble to try the short refrain by Yoko Ono and John Lennon, which I'd heard only three days before, and only sung once. Slow.

Give Peace a Chance   **B62**

All we are say - ing, _____ is

Give Peace a Chance.

Words & music by John Lennon & Paul McCartney

That's all there is to it. A song only ten seconds long. We sang it over and over. After 30 seconds a few thousand were singing it with us. After a minute tens of thousands. Peter, Paul and Mary suddenly joined us on our left. Half a minute later Mitch Miller (yes, "Sing along with Mitch") jumped up on our right and helped, waving his arms to keep everyone in rhythm. Two, three, four minutes went by as 500,000 sang it over and over.

Looking out at that sea of faces, it was like a huge ballet, flags, banners, signs, would move to the right for three beats (one measure) and then left for the next measure. Parents had children on their shoulders, swaying in rhythm.

I used the pauses to shout out short phrases. At first:

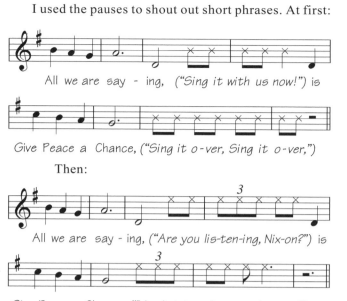

All we are say - ing, ("Sing it with us now!") is

Give Peace a Chance, ("Sing it o-ver, Sing it o-ver,")

Then:

All we are say - ing, ("Are you lis-ten-ing, Nix-on?") is

Give Peace a Chance, ("You bet-ter lis-ten, Ag-new.")

It went on for five or six minutes. A litany! Everyone got caught up in it. Finally we let it end softly as in a gospel church when a hymn has been sung till no one can add more.

How does all this relate to a "two-against-three rhythm"? Simply this: I accompanied it in 6/8 time, that is two strong beats against the 3/4-rhythm of the melody. I had a big 12-string guitar. Sonorous bass notes. My usual "Dropped D" tuning, even though we were in the key of G. I got one rich low "D."

The hemiola gave it a rhythmic bite it would not have had otherwise. You try it, see if I'm not right.

B63

G
Melody
All we are

Guitar

D

say - ing,_____ is Give Peace a Chance.

etc.

Words & music by John Lennon & Paul McCartney
Adaptation and guitar arrangement by Pete Seeger

Postscript: Dozens of television cameras recorded the afternoon's songs and speeches. A few days later I asked a friend at CBS if there was a chance to get a copy of the tape of that song. He said that one day after the demonstration orders came down from the top to destroy all the tapes.

TOSHI & PETE,
WASHINGTON MONUMENT, NOVEMBER 1969

Lisa Kalvelage

B64

Steady tempo

1. My name is Li-sa Kal-ve-lage, I was born in Nu-rem-berg, And when the trials were held there, nine-teen years a-go___ It seemed to me ri-dic-u-lous to hold a na-tion all to blame___ For the hor-rors that the world did un-der-go.___ A short while lat-er when I ap-plied to be a G.I. bride, An A-mer-i-can con-sul-ar of-fi-cial ques-tioned me. He re-fused my ex-it per-mit, said, my ans-wer did not show I'd learned my les-son a-bout res-pon-si-bil-i-ty.___

Originally titled "My Name Is Lisa Kalvelage"
Words adapted & music by Pete Seeger (1972)
© 1966 by Sanga Music Inc.

1. My name is Lisa Kalvelage, I was born in Nuremberg,
And when the trials were held there 19 years ago
It seemed to me ridiculous to hold a nation all
    to blame
For the horrors that the world did undergo
A short while later when I applied to be a G.I. bride
An American consular official questioned me
He refused my exit permit, said my answer did not
    show
I'd learned my lesson about responsibility

2. Thus suddenly I was forced to start thinking on
    this theme
And when later I was permitted to emigrate
I must have been asked a hundred times where I was
    and what I did
In those years when Hitler ruled our state
I said I was a child or at most a teenager
But that only extended the questioning
They'd ask, where were my parents my father,
    my mother
And to this I could answer not a thing.

3. The seed planted there at Nuremberg in 1947
Started to sprout and to grow
Gradually I understood what that verdict meant
    to me
When there are crimes that I can see and I can know
And now I also know what it is to be charged with
    mass guilt
Once in a lifetime is enough for me
No, I could not take it for a second time
And that is why I am here today.

4. The events of May 25th, the day of our protest,
Put a small balance weight on the other side
Hopefully, someday my contribution to peace
Will help just a bit to turn the tide
And perhaps I can tell my children six
And later on their own children
That at least in the future they need not be silent
When they are asked, "Where was your mother,
<u>when?</u>"

This story was in a newspaper clipping sent me from San Jose, California. Lisa Kalvelage and two other women, dressed in their Sunday best, stopped a shipment of napalm by standing on a loading platform and refusing to budge. Arrested, and in court she told this story to a newspaper reporter. She remained active in the peace movement there. I've done a few benefit concerts for them. Lisa died in March 2009.

LISA KALVELAGE WITH FAMILY

I sing the song with a steady tempo, as Woody might have. I heard Rutthy Taubb in a street demonstration (she had a mic) do it unaccompanied, with a more free rhythm. It was beautiful to hear her voice floating above the street noise.

No two people would sing it exactly the same, and as you see here, the details of rhythm and pitch changed from verse to verse. This is standard practice, I suspect, when singing narrative ballads in various countries, in various traditions.

Seymour Hersh broke the story on the My Lai massacre. Later there was a trial and the two officers most immediately responsible got light sentences. I sang the song during the '70s. The American media ignored it, but the song got on Swedish TV. Nuremberg refers to the 1945-46 war-crimes trials of some of Hitler's accomplices.

Last Train to Nuremberg

All on board.

1. Do I see Lieu-ten-ant Cal-ley? / Do I see Pres-i-dent Nix-on?
Do I see Cap-tain Me-di-na? / Do I see both hous-es of Con-gress?
Do I see Gen-'ral / Do I see the
Kos-ter and all his crew? / vot-ers, me and you?

Words & music by Pete Seeger (1970)
© 1970 by Sanga Music Inc.

CHORUS (AND AFTER EACH VERSE):
Last train to Nuremberg!
Last train to Nuremberg!
Last train to Nuremberg! All on board!

1. Do I see Lieutenant Calley?
   Do I see Captain Medina?
   Do I see Gen'ral Koster and all his crew?
   Do I see President Nixon?
   Do I see both houses of Congress?
   Do I see the voters, me and you?

2. Who held the rifle? Who gave the orders?
   Who planned the campaign to lay waste the land?
   Who manufactured the bullet? Who paid the taxes?
   Tell me, is that blood upon my hands?

3. Go tell all the young people, tell all the little children
   Don't, don't you get aboard this train!
   See where it's come from, see where it's going.
   Don't, don't you ride it ever again.

4. If five hundred thousand mothers went to Washington
   And said, "Bring all of our sons home without delay!"
   Would the man they came to see,
   say <u>he</u> was <u>too</u> bizz<u>ee</u>?
   Would he say he had to watch a football game?

Ho Chi Minh, who died in 1969, is one of my all-time heroes. Could he have humanized bureaucracy? I think so. A poet, a storyteller with a great sense of humor. The son of a small town school teacher, he got a job on a ship, made his way to France to study this thing called socialism, while working in a restaurant. Attending socialist conferences after WWI he chided the French proletariat for not pushing to give French colonies their freedom. Toshi and I learned about him when we visited Hanoi in '72. Here's one of the many stories circulating about "Uncle Ho."

He's visiting an army camp, sees all the officers seated in the front row, the non-coms behind them, and the privates in back of them. He immediately goes to the rear of the hall, shouts "about face" and gives a short speech to the effect that the rank-and-file are the most important part of the army, the country, the world. And by his example he showed his generals that the best leaders are those that can inspire the rank-and-file to do their best.

HO CHI MINH

Teacher Uncle Ho   **B66**

He ed-u-cat-ed all the peo-ple.

He dem-on-strat-ed to the world: If a

man will stand for his own land— he's

got the strength of ten.   (Bass acc.)

And if we'd on-ly learn the les-son,

It could e-ven be a bless-in'.

He and me might dis-ag-ree— but we

need-n't go to shoot-ing a-gain.— And if

sol-dier boys— in ev-'ry land— said:

Hell no, we won't go ("what did you say?")

Hell no, we won't go ("say it a-gain")

HELL NO, WE WON'T GO. I'll have to say— in

my own way,— the on-ly way— that I

know, that we learned pow-er to the peo-ple and the

po-wer to know— from Teach-er, Un-cle Ho!

Words & music by Pete Seeger (1970)
© 1970, 1993 by Stormking Music Inc.

He educated all the people.
He demonstrated to the world:
If a man will stand for his own land,
He's got the strength of ten.

And if we'd only learn the lesson,
It could even be a blessin',
He and me might disagree,
But we needn't go to shooting again.

And if soldier boys in every land say,
"Hell no, we won't go," ("what did you say")
"Hell no, we won't go," ("say it again!")
"HELL NO, WE WON'T GO!"

I'll have to say in my own way,
The only way that I know,
That we learned power to the people and the power
     to know
From Teacher Uncle Ho!

Incidentally, this tune is one of my best. It's basically a steel drum melody, although it could be played by a mandolin, or nowadays a keyboard. I composed it years before I found words for it.

I used to get a college audience shouting, "Hell no, we won't go." See where I capitalize the words fourth staff up.

After singing the song once, I'd whistle the interlude below and then sing the song again. But it was a difficult song to perform. No one but me ever tried it, to my knowledge. The main difficulty, besides spitting the words out clearly, is to find the proper key. If it's comfortable to sing it, it's difficult to whistle. Perhaps the solution is to play the "Whistling Interlude" on some instrument, and just pitch it where you can sing it.

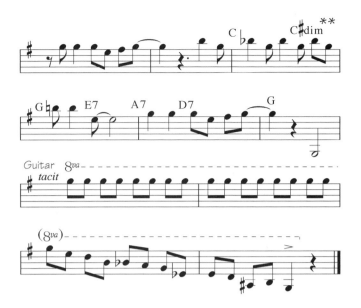

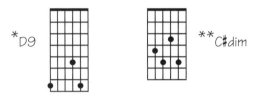

Here's a couple of unusual chord positions which are fun to try if you used Dropped D tuning (see asterisks).

The song is fun to play on an instrument, but has a bigger range than the "Star Spangled Banner."

Well, at the moment the song is mainly of historical interest. Maybe someone will find another use for the tune someday. It sounds good on steel drums.

© Ezio Peterson

And this next song was inspired by a line in a student newspaper.

Our Generation

1. Our gen-er-a-tion___ has san-dals
like Vi-et-nam-ese.___ Our gen-er-
a-tion___ wears long hair.___
with our clob-bered minds.___
We still wink an eye to say,___
Meet me, meet me___ at the
bot-tom of the stairs.___

Words & music by Pete Seeger (1970)

1. Our generation has sandals like Vietnamese.
Our generation wears long hair.
With our clobbered minds, we still wink an eye to say
Meet me, meet me at the bottom of the stairs.

2. Our generation whistles in the dark, has faith
In faithlessness and in blue sky.
Our heroes now are either none, or ev'ryone.
Our saints also are only you and I.

3. Our generation won't remake this ravished world.
Our generation can only try
To wink an eye at ev'ryone, yes, ev'ryone.
Saying meet me at the beginning of the sky!

In 1970 I knew students, black and white, who were convinced that a bloody uprising was soon coming. But students are often over-enthusiastic about revolution. In '71 in Spain I was forbidden by the Franco government to sing for the students at Barcelona University. Later a student asked me what I thought of Spain. I replied, "I think it is like a steam engine when someone has tied down the emergency release valve and the pressure is building up so there is danger of the boiler exploding."

"Oh, I hope it comes soon," said the student enthusiastically. An older man and woman standing near him didn't look so enthusiastic. They'd lived through three years of bloody civil war.

Hence the song below.

If a Revolution Comes To My Country
(Hear the Thunder! Hear the Thunder!)

If a rev-o-lu-tion comes to my coun-try,
let me re-mem-ber now.___
I mean, if blood-y con-flict rag-es,
I bet-ter learn right now.___ How to
catch and skin and cook a rat,___

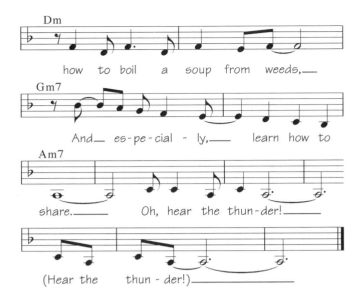

how to boil a soup from weeds,—

And— es-pe-cial - ly,— learn how to

share.— Oh, hear the thun-der!—

(Hear the thun - der!)—

Words & music by Pete Seeger (1971)
TRO - © 1976 Melody Trails, Inc., New York, NY.

1. If a revolution comes to my country,
   Let me remember now.
   I mean if bloody conflict rages,
   I better learn right now.
   How to catch and skin and cook a rat,
   How to boil a soup from weeds,
   And especially learn how to share.
   Oh, hear the thunder… (Hear the thunder!)

2. If a revolution comes to my country,
   Let me remember now.
   I mean if civil war breaks down everything,
   I better learn right now.
   How to sleep ten in one room,
   How to keep dry outside when it rains,
   And especially learn how to share.
   Oh, hear the thunder… (Hear the thunder!)

3. If a revolution comes to my country,
   Let me remember now.
   There'll be sickness, epidemic,
   I better learn right now.
   How long to boil water safe to drink,
   How to recognize gangrene,
   And especially learn how to share.
   Oh, hear the thunder… (Hear the thunder!)

4. If a revolution comes to my country,
   Let me remember now.
   Old dollar bill, you won't mean much,
   I better learn right now.
   What in life has true value,
   And, oh, if we'd only learn to share,
   Then, oh, then would be the revolution.
   Oh, hear the thunder… (Hear the thunder!)

5. If a revolution comes to my country,
   Let me remember now. (END)

JOAN BAEZ & PETE SEEGER, U.S. CAPITOL

Photo © 1975 by Shia, Washington, D.C.

At the same time the previous songs were being sung, the *Clearwater* project was starting up, and I was starting to do more work with young folks in my own hometown. I realized that the tragedy of small towns is that often the best people of each generation leave town for better opportunities elsewhere. I wrote this for high school students, black and white, that I saw leave Beacon, New York.

Snow, Snow   B70

Capo up 3 Frets—use Am chords, they sound Cm

Words & music by Pete Seeger (1964)
TRO - © 1965 (renewed) Melody Trails, Inc., NY, NY.

CHORUS (AND AFTER EACH VERSE):
Snow, snow, falling down;
Covering up my dirty old town.

1. Covers the garbage dump, covers the holes,
   Covers the rich homes, and the poor souls,
   Covers the station, covers the tracks,
   Covers the footsteps of those who'll not be back.

2. Under the street lamp, there stands a girl,
   Looks like she's not got a friend in this world.
   Look at the big flakes come drifting down,
   Twisting and turning, round and round.

3. Covers the mailbox, the farm and the plow.
   Even barbed wire seems—beautiful now.
   Covers the station, covers the tracks.
   Covers the footsteps of those who'll not be back.

When the Soviet magazine *Krugozor* (Horizon) printed one of my songs, this is the one they chose. The guitar part is also one of the better pieces I ever put together. You play the melody with the index finger on the top strings, while the thumb keeps a steady rhythm with the bass and middle strings. On the next page I give chord diagrams for left hand of the guitar, arrows point to the melody string for the index finger. Thumb keeps bass-chord pattern going. Single strings sound best.

If, like me, you find it easier to read chord diagrams than tablature, try deciphering this. Here the arrows point to the melody notes.

Postscript: I've rarely refused copyright permission for someone to change one of my songs. After all, I've changed so many other people's songs, what right have I to be picky about my own?

But when someone wanted to record this as "my little old town," I said, "No." The whole point of the song is the contrast between the clean snow and the dirty town.

Is that unfair to towns that really try to keep clean? No. The folks trying to clean 'em know that try as we might, we've only half succeeded.

Keep in mind that I'd only sing one or two or at most three of these songs during a concert, even at the height (depth!) of the Vietnam War. I'd try to touch base with a variety of people in the audience, as always singing "something old, something new, something borrowed and something blue."

And not forgetting something funny. What a stupid race we are. The gods must be laughing. We have the know-how to provide education and other necessities for every soul on earth. Instead we waste most of it fighting.

Few people but me recorded any of the songs in this chapter. Country Joe McDonald's song "Fixing To Die Rag" (One-two-three-what are we fighting for?) was the best known song against the war; it got in the movie *Woodstock*. If my country was as free as it claims to be, his song would have been "at the top of the charts" in 1971.

But one song of mine, written back in '55, spread from soldier to soldier. When Gen. John Paul Vann was buried with military honors in Arlington Cemetery, his widow had the band play it.

October 1955, I was sitting in a plane bound for Ohio to sing for the students at Oberlin College. Half dozing. Found in my pocket three lines copied a year before when reading (in translation) *And Quiet Flows the Don*, the Soviet novel by Mikhail Sholokhov. He describes the Cossack soldiers singing as they galloped off to join the Tsar's army.

Where are the flowers? The girls have plucked them.
Where are the girls? They've taken husbands.
Where are the men? They're all in the army.

Something clicked in my subconscious. I remembered the phrase I'd thought of a couple years earlier, "Long time passing." A singable three words. Then I added the handwringer's perennial complaint, "When will they ever learn?" Twenty minutes later it was completed; that evening I taped it to a mic and tried it out. Three verses.

I originally wrote it a little shorter and differently than most people know it now.

Where Have All the Flowers Gone
(Original Version) `B71`

Words & music by Pete Seeger (1955)
© 1961 (renewed) by Sanga Music Inc.

1. Where have all the flowers gone?
   Long time passing,
   Where have all the flowers gone?
   Long time ago —
   Where have all the flowers gone?
   Girls have picked them ev'ry one.
   Oh, when will you ever learn?
   Oh, when will you ever learn?

2. Where have all the young girls gone?
   Long time passing,
   Where have all the young girls gone?
   Long time ago —
   Where have all the young girls gone?
   They've taken husbands every one.
   When will they ever learn?
   When will they ever learn?

3. Where have all the young men gone?
   Long time passing,
   Where have all the young men gone?
   Long time ago —
   Where have all the young men gone?
   They're all in uniform.
   Oh, when will <u>we</u> ever learn?
   Oh, when will <u>we</u> ever learn?

Slightly different melody, last 3 lines of verse 3:

Recorded it this way for Folkways in '56 with several other short songs. A year later stopped singing it, thinking it one more not-too-successful attempt. But Joe Hickerson, leader of the Oberlin College Folksong Club, picked it up. Next summer Joe was the music counselor at Camp Woodland in the Catskills. The kids liked it.

He gave the song some rhythm. He tried out all sorts of verses even, "Where have all the counselors gone? Broken curfew every one…"

In Greenwich Village, New York City, Joe's rhythmic version got to Peter, Paul and Mary, who started singing it at the beginning of their career. The Kingston Trio picked it up from them, recorded it a year later. My manager, Harold Leventhal, asked me, "Pete, didn't you write a song called 'Where Have All the Flowers Gone?'"

"Yeah, three or four years ago."

"Did you ever copyright it?"

"No, I guess I didn't."

"Well, the Kingston Trio have just recorded it."

I got on the phone to Dave Guard.

"Oh, Pete, we didn't know you wrote it. We thought it was an old song. We'll take our name off of it."

It was really nice of them. Technically, legally, I had "abandoned the copyright." But I knew Dave well. About four years before, I had got $1.59 from him and sent him a copy of my self-mimeographed book, *How to Play the 5-String Banjo*. A year later I got another letter from Dave: "Dear Pete, I've been putting that book to hard use. I and two other students here at Stanford have a group we call the Kingston Trio."

The song is usually sung now with Joe's extra two verses and rhythm, and with Peter, Paul and Mary's tune changes. (See verses 4 and 5 at right.)

Where Have All the Flowers Gone
(Adapted Version) **B72**

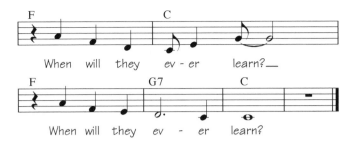

Words & music by Pete Seeger (1955) with new 4th & 5th verses by Joe Hickerson
© 1961 (renewed) by Sanga Music Inc.

1. Where have all the flowers gone,
   Long time passing.
   Where have all the flowers gone,
   Long time ago.
   Where have all the flowers gone?
   The girls have picked them every one,
       When will they ever learn?
       When will they ever learn?

2. Where have all the young girls gone,
   Long time passing.
   Where have all the young girls gone,
   Long time ago.
   Where have all the young girls gone?
   They've taken husbands every one.
       When will they ever learn?
       When will they ever learn?

3. Where have all the young men gone,
   Long time passing.
   Where have all the young men gone,
   Long time ago.
   Where have all the young men gone?
   Gone for soldiers, every one.
       When will they ever learn?
       When will they ever learn?

4. Where have all the soldiers gone,
   Long time passing.
   Where have all the soldiers gone,
   Long time ago.
   Where have all the soldiers gone?
   Gone to graveyards, every one.
       When will they ever learn?
       When will they ever learn?

5. Where have all the graveyards gone,
   Long time passing.
   Where have all the graveyards gone,
   Long time ago.
   Where have all the graveyards gone?
   Covered with flowers every one.
       When will <u>we</u> ever learn?
       When will <u>we</u> ever learn?

JOE HICKERSON AND SON MIKE, 1970

Photo by John Dildine

My phrase, "Where has all the (something) gone?" seems to have entered the English language. Toshi and I spot it at least once a month, in a headline or an ad. The way I usually sing the song now is to start the first line quite slowly with no accompaniment and no rhythm, more as I originally sang it.

But soon the rhythm starts, and from here on the audience sings the song for me, the accompanist.

On the last verse, whether I sing five verses or the original three-verse way (pithier), I get them to slow down at the end as I originally sang it.

Yes, when will we ever learn — to once again combine work with fun, to make a dance out of sweeping floors, making beds. We have songs for putting a baby to sleep. Why not songs for other jobs? We have songs for singing at church, at a rally, a meeting, a party. Why not songs to sing while waiting for a bus, while waiting for a game to start, when pushing a car out of a mudhole, for picking up litter, for calling a meeting together? (See pp. 219–220.)

Incidentally, *Sing Out!* magazine[2] offered a prize for anyone who could locate the original Russian song. A. L. Lloyd in England won the prize, sending in this.

Traditional Russian folk song

1. Koloda Duda, (Koloda Duda*
Ee-dye-zh tih bihla? Where have you been?
Konei steregla. Minding the horses.)

2. Chevo vysteregla? (Which were you minding?
Konya s sedlom, The horse with the saddle
s zolotym makhrom. With the golden fringe.)

3. A ee-dye-zh tvoi kon? (But where is your horse?
Za vorotami stoit. Standing by the gate.)

4. A ee-dye-zh vorota? (And where is the gate?
Voda unesla. Carried away by the water.)

5. A ee-dye-zh gusi? (And where are the geese?
V kamyh ushli. They've gone to the reeds.)

6. A ee-dye-zh kamysh? (And where are the reeds?
Devki vyzhali. The girls have gathered them.)

7. A ee-dye-zh devki? (And where are the girls?
Devki zamuzh ushli. The girls have gotten married and gone away.)

8. A ee-dye-zh kazaki? (And where are the Cossacks?
Na voinu poshli. They've gone to war.)

*a woman's name

[2]P.O. Box 5460, Bethlehem, PA 18015-0460; 1-888-SING-OUT; <www.singout.org>. Quarterly, $30 a year or $60 with a CD in each issue. (It's worth it!)

I originally thought that I wrote the tune all by myself. Around 1960 Ernie Marrs of Atlanta pointed out that I got the first two lines from an Irish-American lumberjack song collected by Marjorie Porter.

John-son says he'll load more hay,

Says he'll load ten times a day—

More than any song I ever put together, the song has crossed borders, been translated. I'm a lucky songmaker.

Photo by Gunther, courtesy of FPG International

MARLENE DIETRICH

Here's the German translation of "Where Have All the Flowers Gone." It sings better in some ways than the English original. Marlene Dietrich got Max Colpet to do it. When she returned to Germany on a tour in 1959 the old Nazis were out to put her down. ("She sang for the American troops fighting us!")

But her recording of this song became a #1 hit on German radio. She didn't need to say a thing. The song said it for her: "It's not me who is out of step with the German people." She had a triumphal tour. The 1993 Berlin musical show about her life used this as its title.

Sag' mir, wo die Blumen Sind

1. Sag' mir, wo die Blumen sind? *
   Wo sind sie geblieben?
   Sag' mir, wo die Blumen sind?
   Was ist geschehn?
   Sag' mir, wo die Blumen sind,
   Mädchen pflückten sie geschwind.
   Wann wird man je verstehn?
   Wann wird man je verstehn!

2. Sag' mir, wo die Mädchen sind?
   ... Männer nahmen sie geschwind ...

3. Sag' mir, wo die Männer sind?
   ... Zogen fort, der Krieg beginnt ...

4. Sag', wo die Soldaten sind?
   ... Über Gräber weht der Wind ...

5. Sag' mir, wo die Gräber sind?
   ... Blumen blühn im Sommerwind.
   Wann wird man je verstehn?
   Ach, wird man je verstehn?

German translation by Max Colpet (1958)
© 1961, 1962 (renewed) by Sanga Music Inc.

* This line is unbeatable. Pronounce it "zahg meer vo dee bloomen zint"

And here's a French version.

Que Sont Devenues les Fleurs

1. Que sont devenues les fleurs
   Du temps qui passé
   Que sont devenues les fleurs
   Du temps passé
   Les filles les ont coupées
   Ell's en ont fait des bouquets
   Apprendrons-nous un jour
   Apprendrons-nous jamais

2. Que sont devenues les filles
   ... Ell's ont donné leurs bouquets
   Aux gars qu'elles rencontraient ...

3. Que sont devenues les gars
   ... A la guerre ils sont allés
   A la guerre ils sont tombés ...

4. Que sont devenues les fleurs
   ... Sur les tomb's ell's ont poussé
   D'autres fill's vont les couper ...

French translation by Guy Béart
© 1961 by Sanga Music Inc.

In most nations, in most ages, the local or national establishment tries to warp almost any good idea to its own ends. Music, art, science, humor. Religion, too.

What are its own ends? Roughly, "We are the best qualified ones to be in charge here. It only complicates matters to have others arguing and confusing the issues, and trying to go 50 different directions at once."

And the funny thing is, quite often they are right — in the short run. Are all people created equal? Nonsense. We are different heights, widths, shapes. We are more or less talented and untalented in sports, arts, patience, energy, honesty, mathematics, perseverance, health, languages and a hundred other things.

But in the long run, ever since civilization started, technology has enabled a few talented individuals to bequeath their power to their less talented offspring. In a little while the establishment is being run by the untalented. Considering that the original talent was often a talent for piracy, the end result is pretty bad. There never was much talent for honesty, farsightedness, generosity. Now there is next to none.

Not that the establishment doesn't try from time to time to co-opt talent. It tries very hard. The talented poor youth is often encouraged to rise — not "to the top" — but rise pretty damn high — *if* he or she is willing to accept the establishment. But to outspokenly speak truth to power is usually judged a crime, or at least cannot be permitted.

Our job now is to learn *how* to speak truth to power — without being thrown in jail too often. Don't say it can't be done. We can do it in a thousand ways. I've tried it with banjos and boats. Others are doing it with cooking and clothing, quiltmaking, paint and paper, games and gardens, swimming and science. We just have to be aware that it is a struggle, all the way, to keep from being co-opted. And that brings us back to where we started, 340 words ago.

— written in 1974

The Long March

Words & music by Pete Seeger (1974)
TRO - © 1993 Melody Trails, Inc., New York, NY.

By Pete Seeger (1988) TRO - © 1993 Melody Trails, Inc.

"Behind the ostensible government sits enthroned an invisible government owing no allegiance and acknowledging no responsibility to the people. To destroy this invisible government, to befoul the unholy alliance between corrupt business and corrupt politics, is the first task of the statesmanship of the day."

— Theodore Roosevelt,
April 19, 1906

I find it easier to think of a refrain than to put together the verses to precede it. These few lines keep returning to me, though. Maybe someone will be able to use them.

In the '70s the women's movement started up again in a new kind of way. I, like a lot of other men, started learning things I should have learned long before. So here's another chorus needing a song.

Which leads us into another song and another chapter.

Chapter 8: *Turn, Turn, Turn –*
Songs from the Great Old Book

This song, inspired by Genesis, in the Bible, was originally meant to be a dialogue between a pacifist and a freedom fighter. Then it got changed to be more a song for women everywhere.

Letter to Eve

B76

Words & music by Pete Seeger (1967)
© 1967 by Sanga Music Inc.

1. Oh, Eve, where is Adam, now you're kicked out
    of the garden? (2x)
   Been wandering from shore to shore,
   Now you find there's no more
      Ohh, Pacem in Terris, Mir, Shanti, Salaam, Hey Wa.

2. Don't you wish love, love alone, could save this
    world from disaster? (2x)*
   If only love could end the confusion—
   Or is it just one more illusion? Ohhh, ...etc.

3. Well if...you want to have great love, you got to
    have great anger (2x)
   When I see innocent folk shot down,
   Should I just shake my head and frown? Ohhh, ...etc.

4. Well if...you want to hit the target square, you
    better not have blind anger (2x)
   Or else it'll be just one more time
   The correction creates another crime. Ohhh, ...etc.

5. Oh Eve, you tell Adam, next time he asks you (2x)
   He'll say, "Baby, it's cold outside;
   What's the password to come inside?"
   You say, Ohhh, Pacem...etc.

6. Oh, Eve, go tell Adam, we got to build a new
    garden (2x)
   We got to get workin' on the building
   Of a decent home for all o' God's children. Ohh, ...

7. If music...could only bring peace, I'd only be a
    musician (2x)
   If songs could do more than dull the pain,
   If melodies could only break these chains
   Ohh, Pacem...etc. (SPOKEN:) ("Keep on singing")

8. Ohh, Pacem in Terris, Mir, Shanti, Salaam,
    Hey Wa! (2x)
   Four thousand languages in this world,
   Means the same thing to every boy and girl
   Ohh, Pacem...etc. (CHANTED:) ("Sing it over")**

If you want to get erudite, here's the way to write

PACEM IN TERRIS

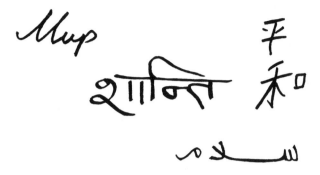

If you are leading this song with folks who don't know it, well, take time to teach 'em the last line:

"Those strange words are really the same word spoken in five of the world's many languages. The first is the Italian way of pronouncing Latin. Patchem In Terris… repeat…PATCHEM IN TERRIS. Next, Meer…MEER. That's Russian for 'Peace.' Shahnti…SHAHNTI. One billion people in India would understand that. Salaam…SALAAM. That's known not only in the mid-East; most of Africa knows it too, Indonesia, Pakistan, etc. as well. 'Hey Wa' is the Japanese way of pronouncing two Chinese characters that mean the same thing: peace in the world."

If you find yourself wanting to make the song even longer, here's a possible verse.

9. Oh, when it's stormy weather good people got to
       gather together***
   Oh, when it's stormy weather, good people got to
       gather together
   We know there's no place to hide,
   Still in friends one can confide
   Ohh, Pacem in Terris, Mir, Shanti, Salaam, Hey Wa.

Sample variations in the melody:

If human civilization (and the biosphere) survives, I think it will be partly because the feminine tradition of nurturing takes precedence over the male tradition of adventure, achievement, of power and glory. The '70s and '80s were a big education for me. And as a songwriter I was — and am — fascinated by the wealth of great songs being made up by women — by wives and mothers — by independent types and lesbians. I've told you about Malvina Reynolds. In my own family I've seen examples of strong, independent-thinking women in several generations. Through *Sing Out!* magazine, through the People's Music Network, and Clearwater folks, I learned the songs of Holly Near, Bernice Reagon, Cris Williamson, Pat Humphries, Joni Mitchell, Ysaye Barnwell, Ruth Pelham, Sis Cunningham, Gretchen Reed, Luci Murphy, and many others. Not just writing new songs, but rewriting old ones. I've sung their songs, and occasionally tried adding my words, as you know.

THE BYRDS

Funny story how the next song came to be put together. About 1959 I got a letter from my publisher complaining, "Pete, can't you write another song like 'Goodnight Irene'? I can't sell or promote these protest songs."

I angrily tore off a note to him, "You better find another songwriter. This is the only kind of song I know how to write." I leafed through my pocket notebook to some verses I'd copied down a year before, verses by a bearded fellow with sandals, a tough minded fellow called Koheleth, but in the King James translation called Ecclesiastes. He lived in Judea, like about 252 B.C.E. I added one line ("a time of peace, I swear it's not too late"), omitted a few lines, and repeated the first two lines as a chorus, plus one new word repeated three times. Taped it. Mailed it next morning.

Got a letter from the publisher two days later, "Wonderful; just what I hoped for." Myself, I was delighted by the version of the Byrds: all those electric guitars. Like clanging bells. And maybe this is a good place to say clearly that when Bob Dylan switched to an electric guitar at Newport in 1965 I was not upset with him. I *was* furious at the sound system. I wanted to cut the cable. Bob was singing "Maggie's Farm," one of his best songs, but you couldn't understand a word, because of the distortion.

I wonder what Ecclesiastes looked like. I bet he was short, wiry, irascible. I thought no one knew his/her real name — but then I read it was "Koheleth," 252 B.C.E.

Turn! Turn! Turn! B77...
(To Everything There Is a Season)

Words from the Book of Ecclesiastes
Music & additional words by Pete Seeger (1954)
TRO - © 1962 (renewed) Melody Trails, Inc., New York, NY.

*See p. 174

CHORUS:
>   To everything (Turn, Turn, Turn)
>   There is a season (Turn, Turn, Turn)
>   And a time for every purpose under heaven.

1.   A time to be born, a time to die
>   A time to plant, a time to reap
>   A time to kill, a time to heal
>   A time to laugh, a time to weep.

2.   A time to build up, a time to break down
>   A time to dance, a time to mourn
>   A time to cast away stones
>   A time to gather stones together

3.   A time of war, a time of peace
>   A time of love, a time of hate
>   A time you may embrace
>   A time to refrain...from embracing

4.   A time to gain, a time to lose
>   A time to rend, a time to sew
>   A time of love, a time of hate
>   A time of peace...I swear, it's not too late.

Here's some verses to sing for children, Toshi made them up.

>   A time for work, a time for play
>   A time for night, a time for day
>   A time to sleep, a time to wake
>   A time for candles on the cake.

>   A time to dress, a time to eat
>   A time to sit and rest your feet
>   A time to teach, a time to learn
>   A time for all to take their turn.

>   A time to cry and make a fuss
>   A time to leave and catch the bus
>   A time for quiet, a time for talk
>   A time to run, a time to walk.

>   A time to get, a time to give
>   A time to remember, a time to forgive
>   A time to hug, a time to kiss
>   A time to close your eyes and wish.

>   A time for dirt, a time for soap
>   A time for tears, a time for hope
>   A time for fall, a time for spring
>   A time to hear the robins sing.

A day or so after writing the melody, I worried that I was getting into a rut with my melodies — it was so similar to the melody I'd found for "Bells of Rhymney" (p. 98), which I'd worked out less than a year before. And a couple others.

And on closer examination I realized that both tunes owed more than a little to that ancient mother-of-tunes, "Twinkle, Twinkle, Little Star," starting on the first note of the scale, going up to the fifth note and working their way back down to the first note again.

Both the melodies "Rhymney" and "Turn, Turn, Turn" are fairly conventional, one might even say "cautious," except that they are more rhythmically adventurous. Some singers have tried to even out the irregularities.

I've urged them not to. However, in the 21st Century I decided that since most people know the Byrds' version of the melody (slightly different from mine), I'd go along with them. These days when my own voice is 90 percent gone, I give three or four words in advance to the crowd and they sing the whole song* while I play the accompaniment. On CD **B77...** you can hear it as I wrote it. On **B...77** you can compare my original and the Byrd's changes. The notes given here are a combination.

B...77

Me: time for ev'-ry pur-pose un-der heav-en.

Byrds: time for ev'-ry pur-pose un-der heav-en._

Me: A time to laugh, a time to weep.

Byrds: A time to laugh, a time_ to weep._

★ ★ ★

Words, Words, Words **B78**

1. Words, words, words, in my old Bi-ble. How much of truth re-mains?_

_ If I on-ly un-der-stood_ them,

While my lips pro-nounced them,

Would not my life be changed?_

Words & music by Pete Seeger (1967)
© 1967 by Sanga Music Inc.

1. Words, words, words,
   In my old Bible
   How much of truth* remains?
   If I only understood them,
   While my lips pronounced them,
   Would not my life be changed?

2. Words, words, words
   In Tom's old Declaration**
   How much of truth remains?
   If I only understood them,
   While my lips pronounced them,
   Would not my life be changed?

3. Words, words, words
   In old songs and stories
   How much of truth remains?
   If I only understood them,
   While my lips pronounced them,
   Would not my life be changed?

4. Words, words, words
   On cracked old pages
   How much of truth remains?
   If my mind could understand them,
   And if my life pronounced them,
   Would not this world be changed?

*Truth? See p. 12.

**Variant melody

B79

In Tom's old Dec-la-ra-tion,

How much of truth re-mains?_

I've read somewhere that Gandhi said "I like your Christ. But I do not always like your Christians. They are very unlike your Christ."

When Thoreau at age 44 was about to die from tuberculosis, his aunt said, "Henry, have you made your peace with God?" He replied, "(cough) I didn't know we had ever quarreled."

Well, I've finally decided I have made my peace with at least the word "God." Most of my youth, thinking religion was the opiate of the people, I disliked using the word. But I found, like many other European-Americans, that I truly loved the religious songs of African-Americans. It was as though I rediscovered my own humanity through them. I knew Mahalia Jackson. She sang, "I've seen God; I've seen the sun rise." I'm with you, Mahalia. I feel my heart lift every time I see the sun rise. Or the moon. Really, every time I see anything I feel I see God. Now this will no doubt offend some. They'd say, "You see the *handiwork* of God." But I think if I looked on the screen of an electron microscope and saw some molecule only one millionth of an inch in size, I see God. And I believe God is infinite, so compared to something infinitely small, that molecule is infinitely large. (see pp. 197–198). And if I looked at the screens of one of the big radar telescopes that my older brother, Charles, helped design, and saw a galaxy of stars five billion light years distant, I believe I'd be seeing God. And compared to something infinitely large, those five billion light years are an infinitely short distance. How lucky we are to be so spaced out.

In the book *Number: The Language of Science* by Tobias Danzig, I read that a "googol" is the number one followed by 100 zeroes. A googol is more than all the molecules in the known universe.

But imagine a "ga-gahll" — the numeral one followed by a line of zeroes stretched five billion light years away. And realize that, compared to Old Infinity Herself, this number is infinitely small. See p. 198 The Beethoven Phenomenon.

No. In a sense all of us have some kind of faith. Some are very dangerous faiths. Many scientists have faith that an infinite and uncontrolled increase in empirical knowledge is a good thing. But if the world were destroyed by misuse of this knowledge, would one say it was a good thing to be a scientist? Is it a good thing to be a musician? Sometimes. Sometimes not. (When you're trying not to wake the baby. When there are important other jobs that can't wait.) There are limits to everything.

My mother's father was a doctor, a gentle, conservative man. His favorite motto was "Everything in Moderation." Today I'd argue with him. Even moderation in moderation. There are limits to everything.

Limits to earning money, or stealing it. Tell that to would-be billionaires.

Limits to freedom of speech — we don't shout "Fire" in a crowded theater. We learn not to use words that insult some race or ethnic group — and we learn why.

Limits to freedom of press: If some clever chemist discovered a new, super powerful plastic explosive which could be made by mixing three new but commonly available products, would we want the recipe published in the *National Enquirer*?

Few of us like to be disciplined. But if we are lucky enough to live long lives, we realize that sometimes discipline has been good for us. When we get angry, don't reach for a weapon. We hold our tongues at times.

But one can have too much discipline. Here, too, moderation. Art is long, life is short.

Malvina Reynolds once printed this poem in a little booklet, with calligraphy by her daughter Nancy Schimmel, and mailed it to friends across the country. Oh, how we need her wisdom now!

You have been directed to look inside yourself for the meaning of life, for your soul.
You may find nothing there.
Because the soul is not inherent. The soul is something we accumulate in the course of living.

Living means love.
Living includes work and conflict.
How can you love if you do not face and resist the forces of destruction?
Such a course requires courage, and courage is a true value.

How can you live if you do not create, in return for the sustenance you need?
This requires effort, and effort is a true thing.
It is the source of food and beauty, and, in its use, of a resilient mind and body.

The valid community is mutually supporting.
You are not alone. You are nothing alone.
Living together, working, communicating, has made us what we are — a meaning.
In the monster cities of our time, communities disappear. People are alien to one another. The system of values of now prevents them from helping one another.

I believe that a new community is happening. It is smothered many times by the establishment, but it is bound to grow again.

Conversation is thinking in its natural state.
Thinking is the conversation within us.

Words distinguish us from the blessed beasts.
Words began in human beings in the process of transforming gregariousness into cooperation.
But words corrupted to manipulate others for selfish purposes are as poisonous as polluted water.

Being is the process of becoming.
Now is all that went before and the direction in which it is going.

The soul is not an inner pearl.
It is a patina created as an individual functions in a community.
Not knowing, people called it God, for it was not in the unique self nor in the world, so they could not explain it.
The soul is a function of communal being.

There's an honorable and long Christian tradition of songs that don't mention the name of God or Jesus, of heaven or hell. "Dona Nobis Pacem." "Amazing Grace." Likewise, many 19th Century hymns, still sung by people who use the "shape note" hymnbooks — so-called because they used square and triangular shapes for the music notes, as well as the oval shape.

The day…is past and gone;
The evening shades draw nigh.
O may we all (O may we all)
O may we all remember now
The night of death is near.

Here's another, collected in 1927 by Vance Randolph from Mrs. Francis Hall in the Ozark mountains. The song as Randolph collected it was printed in *Sing Out!* magazine, Spring 1992. I've changed it only slightly.

Only Remembered

Ozark variation of 19th Century hymn

1. Up and away like the dew of the morning.
   Up and away, born aloft by the sun
   So we take leave of earth's treasures and toiling,
   Only remembered for what we have done.

CHORUS: *
Only remembered, only remembered,
Only remembered, for what we have done.
Only remembered, only remembered,
Only remembered for what we have done.

2. Shall we be missed when others succeed us?
   Reaping the field that in springtime we've sown
   No, for the sowers can rest from their labors
   Only remembered for what they have done.

3. Only the truth that in life we have spoken
   Only the seeds that on earth we have sown
   These shall live on and live on forever
   And we'll be remembered by what we have done.

*The chorus could be written in 4/4 time. The original song had "I" for the first verse, "they" for the second, "we" for the third. I decided I liked "we" throughout and changed a dozen words.

JOHN SWENEY, 1878

In 1993 I heard from my friend Joe Hickerson, who wrote the extra verses to "Where Have All the Flowers Gone." For 30 years Joe was in charge of the Archive of Folk Culture in the Library of Congress.

He sent me this copy of the "original" song, printed in Philadelphia in 1886. Reverend Bonar wrote the original words, except for Mrs. Halls' third verse. Several people put the words to music, but this setting by John R. Sweney appears to be the ancestor. Sweney was a famous Methodist songleader and songwriter. He led choruses of hundreds, with sing-along audiences of thousands – with no mic! And his granddaughter was Joe Hickerson's mother. Interesting that Rev. Horatius Bonar's original version is mostly first person singular; Mrs. Hall's version is mostly first person plural. I've made it all "we."

★ ★ ★

We are born in simplicity and die of complications. The next song was an attempt to wrestle with the contradictions of the last verse of "All Mixed Up" (p. 14). I've sung it only a few times in my life, but it keeps coming back to me.

Once upon a time when we lived in small villages and tribes, there were only a few levels on which people lived: infancy, childhood, the men's hunting party, the women's work party.

Now there are hundreds (thousands?) of "vertical and horizontal" divisions in modern society.

Different rooms.

My wife's Virginia grandmother, a genteel daughter of the Old South, once when asked where she'd been (she'd been sitting on the toilet), replied, "I've been talking to God."

And lovers usually close the door of the room — or the car.

Now we recognize dozens of kinds of rooms, in order to try and make sense of our complicated 20th Century life.

The first line is from John 14:2.

Such sonorities. Such rhythms. Such certainties.

The committee put together at the request of King James in the early 17th Century was humble: "We aim only to make an earlier translation better." They decided to be anonymous. Only scholars know their names.

They took several years for the job. Individuals took responsibilities for different sections, then brought their efforts to a subcommittee for improvements, and the larger committee for final approval. I wonder: they were all men. Did they check anything with wives, daughters, mothers? With local congregations, students? I still shake my head in wonderment. Such sonorities. Such rhythms. Such certainties.

In any case, I stayed away from churches much of my earlier life, but at various times dip into the Great Old Book.

My Father's Mansion **B82**

Freely (suggest singing in unison with no accompaniment)

1. My fa-ther's man-sion has man-y rooms, With room for all of his chil-dren, As long as we do share His love,____ And see that all are free.____

2. And see that all are free to grow, And see that all are free to__ know, And

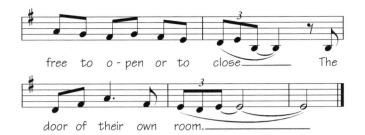

free to o-pen or to close____ The

door of their own room.____

Words & music by Pete Seeger (1966)
© 1966 by Stormking Music Inc.

1. My father's mansion has many rooms,
   With room for all of his children
   As long as we do share His love
   And see that all are free.

2. And see that all are free to grow,
   And see that all are free to know,
   And free to open or to close
   The door of their own room.

(ALL THE REST OF THE VERSES ARE SUNG TO THE MELODY FOR VERSE 2.)

3. What is a room without a door
   Which sometimes locks or stands ajar?
   What is a room without a wall
   To keep out sight and sound from all?

4. And dwellers in each room should have
   The right to choose their own design
   And color schemes to suit their own
   Though differing from mine.

5. Yes, and each room has its own design
   To suit the owner's state of mind
   And those who'd want them all the same
   Don't understand—the human game.

6. My family's mansion's many rooms
   Have room for all of His children
   If we do but share in His love
   And see that all are free.

7. The choice is ours to share this earth
   With all its many joys abound
   Or to continue as we have
   And burn God's mansion down.

NOTE: Some have urged me to change the title. They can if they wish.

Rev. Maurice McCrackin, pacifist preacher of Cincinnati, told me of a young minister being hired after a long session with a board of elderly deacons. One of them warns him: "Young man, you can glorify. You can edify. You can testify. But don't you specify."

Did you know when books stopped being on scrolls, and got rectangular pages? It was in the 2nd Century A.D. In the city of Pergament in the eastern Mediterranean, someone found how to split layers of sheepskin, and dry them flat. The word "parchment" came from there. What a great invention! Do you suppose the first page numbers were in Roman numerals?

Playwright George Bernard Shaw once said that English-speaking countries tend to read the *Bible* more than other countries. Why? Because the King James version is such a superb translation. People have often wondered if Shakespeare had ever helped with it, but in three centuries of looking they did not find the slightest shred of evidence. No "paper trail." Scholars long ago concluded, "No, Shakespeare did not help in any way with the *King James Bible*."

But a few decades ago, some woman said, "Hmmm, Shakespeare was 46 years old in 1610. "That's when the king told the committee to hurry up and finish the job. They'd been working at it for over five years."

She looked up the 46th Psalm of David, counted 46 words from the beginning. There's the word "shake." She counted 46 words from the end of that same psalm. There's the word "spear."

A coincidence? One word I could believe. But not two words. I have amused myself imagining how it could have happened. Someone from the committee managed to secretly contact the poet. "Master Shakespeare, we need your help. But you are a member of a scandalous profession. Not even my colleagues know that I am speaking to you now. It would not be approved that you have helped us in any way." Shakespeare is amused, and promises not to tell a soul of their meeting, nor of his help.

But then comes his 46th birthday.

★ ★ ★

The Sower of Seeds
(Minuit)

Most of my life I thought of a song as lasting two or three minutes, at most four or five. This song goes best if it lasts five or six minutes, perhaps seven or eight. It has two refrains, one best sung by women, the other best sung by men. Each short verse is sung twice.

In the 1970s I heard it, fell in love with an African song played by the Paul Winter Consort. "Minuit" means Midnight" in French. Words below are pronounced "mee-noo-wee sah-moo-zay mee-noo-wee."

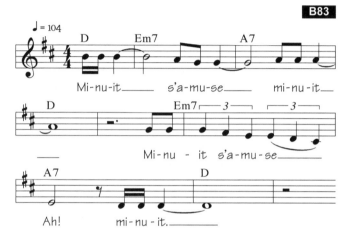

Translation: "Midnight pleases itself, midnight."

Paul learned it from the Ballets Africains from Guinea, West Africa, when they performed in New York City in 1966. The song tells a tragic love story pantomined by the dancers, and includes a court trial scene where the clerk calls for order, "Oyez, oyez" (Listen, listen) which becomes a refrain. Paul added a second refrain, suggested by South African folklorist Andrew Tracy. It's very simple; audiences can easily join in on it. But Paul doesn't translate anything, nor sing other verses; it's mainly an instrumental, vocal piece for him. He's done it around the world.

One of my life's most memorial music experiences was in the 1980s when I witnessed tall Jim Scott teach it to 1000 people at a fundraising concert for the Great Peace March. It was late at night. We had started at 8:00 P.M., but too many performers had been invited; Jim didn't go on till 12:30 A.M. With only his nylon-string guitar for rhythm, he started teaching three different parts of the song to different parts of the audience. After five minutes it was going better and Jim added a fourth part. After eight minutes, people were dancing in the aisles; some soprano stood in her seat and started improvising high counter-melodies. After ten minutes, he got us to gradually quiet down and he closed it.

After hearing that, I got the idea of putting some English words to the music, using the parable of the sower; it's in all the gospels except the Book of John. My words were printed in the first edition of this songbook in 1993. But nobody picked up on them. Nobody. Now I think I know why; I didn't teach the rhythm first.

If you have a guitar, don't just play chords, wham, wham. Nor just bass-chord, bass chord. Work out something with eighth notes.

Here's a more complicated pattern you might try:

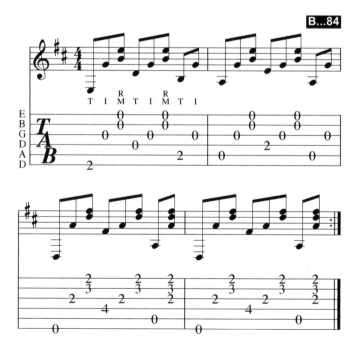

The same four measures are repeated from beginning to end without dropping a single beat:

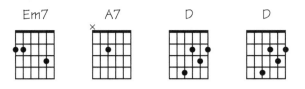

If you have someone who is experienced in playing marracas they can help:

Claves, guiro, shakere, etc., etc., all can contribute. Keep it soft.

Piano: The left hand part of this piano part has the notes played by the kora, the 21-string banjo-harp.

Paul Winter adds these notes played by a guitar:

The spoken introduction can be declaimed by one or more persons, done quite freely, as long as the words are heard clearly. Ideally you will have a mixed chorus leading this song, and hopefully some children. Note that each verse is sung first followed by the women's refrain (I print it as "Oh-yey, oh-yey" then the verse is repeated by all, hopefully with the audience joining in).

After that comes a simpler second refrain which men in the audience will sing with you.

Notice that the lines of the verses, and the first refrain usually come in two full beats before the downbeat. A few exceptions: "Ah" in the 2nd line of the verse, and the 3rd and the last "oyez" in the first refrain, are on-the-beat.

Here we go! Rhythm starts, gradually builds, builds, builds. Then introductory lines are declaimed by one or several soloists:

Consider the sower in the field...
With her arm she scatters the seeds ...
True, some seeds fall in the pathway and get
   stepped on.
They don't grow ...
And some seeds fall on stones.
They don't even sprout ...
But some seeds fall on fallow ground ...
(MEN SING THE FIRST VERSE)

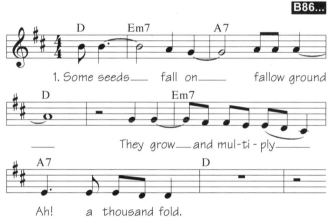

Without dropping a beat, sopranos and altos now sing the first refrain, which we hope will be picked up and sung by women in the audience before the song is over. Perhaps by arm movements they can be invited to try it. Notice that the 3rd "oh-yey" and the last "oh-yey" are both *on* the downbeat.

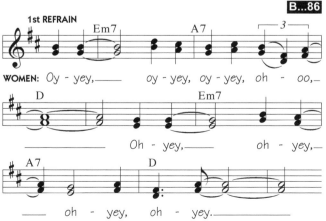

All men and women (and children) sing the 1st verse a second time. Right after the word "Thousand-fold" a man calls to the audience: "You men out there! Sing this with us!"

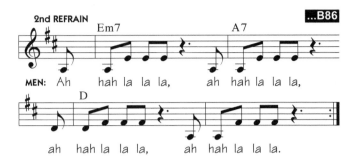

2nd REFRAIN

MEN: Ah hah la la la, ah hah la la la,

ah hah la la la, ah hah la la la.

Without dropping a beat, now some women sing the 2nd verse, followed by altos and sopranos singing the first refrain, then the whole chorus sings the repeat of the 2nd verse, followed by men leading the men in the audience in the second refrain.

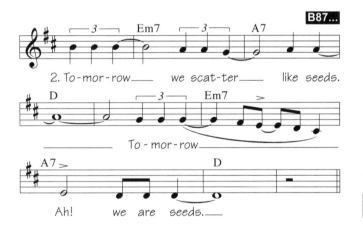

2. To-mor-row___ we scat-ter___ like seeds.

To-mor-row___

Ah! we are seeds.___

Oh-yey... ...oh-yey, <u>oh</u>-yey. oh-oo... ... ...
Oh-yey... ...oh-yey... ...oh-yey <u>oh</u>-yey... ...
Tomorrow... ...we scatter... ...like seeds... ...
TomorrooooooooooooooooAh! ...we are seeds... ... ...
    Ah HAH la la la, ah HAH la la la
    Ah HAH la la la, ah HAH la la la
    (A MAN AND A WOMAN SING VERSE 3)

The third verse and fourth verse follow the same pattern with only slightly different music. Don't drop a beat!

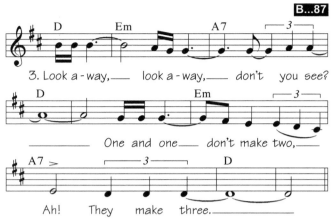

3. Look a-way,___ look a-way,___ don't you see?

One and one___ don't make two,

Ah! They make three.___

Oh-yey... ...oh-yey, <u>oh</u>-yey. oh-oo... ... ...
Oh-yey... ...oh-yey... ...oh-yey <u>oh</u>-yey... ...
Lookaway... ...lookaway... ...don't you see... ... ...
One and one don't make twoooooooAh! ...they make
  three... ... ...
    Ah HAH la la la, ah HAH la la la
    Ah HAH la la la, ah HAH la la la
    (GET KIDS FOR THE NEXT VERSE!)

Do you have children you can get to sing the fourth verse? Maybe by this time the whole audience can join on the repeat.

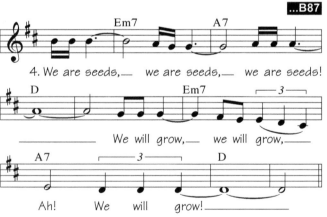

4. We are seeds,___ we are seeds,___ we are seeds!

We will grow,___ we will grow,

Ah! We will grow!___

Oh-yey... ...oh-yey, <u>oh</u>-yey. oh-oo... ... ...
Oh-yey... ...oh-yey... ...oh-yey <u>oh</u>-yey... ... ("Sing with us!")
We are see-eeds, we are see-eeds, ...we are
  seeds! ... ...
WE will grow, we will growwwAh!... We will grow... ... ...
    Ah HAH la la la, ah HAH la la la
    Ah HAH la la la, ah HAH la la la

At this point, the song is just getting started. The crowd is learning the refrains, and can sing along. But the original African song had a beautiful counter-melody for altos to sing. Susan Osborn, who also used to sing with the Paul Winter Consort, with recording engineer John Guth, made up some words in English to fit this melody, and it comes in now as a fine contrast to what has gone before:

B88

Words & Guinean lyrics by Keita Fodeba
English lyrics by John Guth & Susan Osborn
2nd Refrain by Andrew Tracy
Verses by Pete Seeger (1982)
© 1989 & 1993 Umpawaug Music (ASCAP).
All rights reserved.
Courtesy of Living Music

On the third repeat men start singing at the same time "Ah HAH la la la." On the fifth repeat sopranos and altos sing "Oh-yey, oh-yey." Now 3 parts are being sung at the same time. On the seventh repeat the audience can help the children sing their verse again, "We are seeds..." and the miracle is that all these 4 parts harmonize with each other. Repeat them!

But the songleader holds hands out palms down, moving them slowly up and down, indicating that all should sing more softly. And more and more softly.

And more softly. Till all singing and accompaniment is barely audible. And marracas bring it all to a close with a long:

B89

SHHHHHHHH

I've gone into such detail with this song, because I believe that 50 years from now the music will be known around the world, with words in many different languages.

Future historians will record that in these troubled times the riches of African music helped the people of the world to get together with each other.

In 1949, when Guinea was still a French colony, Keita Fodeba was a young African student in Paris. He put together a program of African dances with some fellow African students, "Ballets Africain." It was so well received that they did a program in Brussels, too. Several years later Guinea was an independent republic, and the government funded him to enlarge the troupe to

include women as well as men. Ballets Africain successfully toured Europe and America in the '60s.

But governments change. In 1969, Fodeba was arrested, charged with conspiracy, and executed. His wife fled with their children to neighboring Mali. Now his grown son, an engineer, is back in Conakry, the capital city of Guinea. Mme Fodeba is in touch with Paul Winter, and receiving copyright royalties on this song.

Bless your memory, Keita Fodeba, executed unjustly in 1969.

KEITA FODEBA

My father called it "the lingocentric predicament" — similar to the phrase used by ethnologists — "the ethnocentric predicament," meaning that a person raised in one culture can probably never completely understand another culture. Try as they might, they are always looking through their own colored glasses so to speak.

Similarly, said my father, people using words tend to forget that others hearing those same words have different meanings for them.

Religious leaders, philosophers, politicos, write whole books trying to define one word.

Or, they pick on one disputed word and tell us "don't ever say it."

My solution here is the comedian's — smile at our different definitions. Learn to take all words with a grain of salt. See "English Is Cuh-ray-zee," p. 266.

I was about 10 or 11 years old when I read that H.G. Wells said, it's a race between education and disaster. A great many members of my family have been teachers, and so am I, after a fashion. This chapter might be a good place for another quote from that English mathematician and philosopher, Alfred North Whitehead.

When one considers in its length and in its breadth the importance of this question of the education of a nation's young, the broken lives, the defeated hopes, the national failures, which result from the frivolous inertia with which it is treated, it is difficult to restrain within oneself a savage rage. In the conditions of modern life the rule is absolute, the race which does not value trained intelligence is doomed. Not all your heroism, not all your social charm, not all your wit, not all your victories on land and sea, can move back the finger of fate. Today we maintain ourselves. Tomorrow science will have moved forward yet one more step, and there will be no appeal from the judgment which will then be pronounced on the uneducated.

We can be content with no less than the old summary of an educational ideal which has been current at any time from the dawn of our civilization. The essence of education is that it be religious.

…A religious education is an education which inculcates duty and reverence. Duty arises from our potential control over the course of events. Where attainable knowledge could have changed the issue, ignorance has the guilt of vice. And the foundation of reverence is this perception, that the present holds within itself the complete sum of existence, backwards and forward, that whole amplitude of time, which is eternity.

— Alfred N. Whitehead, *The Aims of Education.*

So I give you now the chorus of an old spiritual Alan Lomax taught me in 1959. I found that I could use it as a refrain to a series of four or five short stories. You could use it for a different set of parables.

Seek and You Shall Find

Traditional (African American hymn) Adapted & arranged by Pete Seeger
TRO - © 1993 Melody Trails, Inc., New York, NY.

I usually first get the crowd to learn this chorus well, with a little harmony, repeating the last line. On the word "knock," I often point right at them. It's not hard to teach a little high harmony.

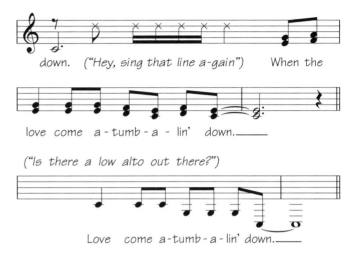

Once there was a king who had three sons, and he wanted to give them a good education. He called in his wise men. He said, "I want you to boil down all the world's wisdom into one book; I'll give it to my sons and have them memorize it." It took them a year; they came back with a volume bound in leather, trimmed in gold. The king leafed through it. "Hm, very good." He turns to his sons. "Learn it!" Now he turned to the wise men. He said, "You did such a good job with that, see if you can boil down all the world's wisdom into one sentence."

It took them five years. They came back and bowed low. "Your majesty, the sentence is 'This too shall pass.'" The king didn't like that so well. He said, "See if you can boil down all the world's wisdom into one word." It took them ten years. When they came back, their beards were draping on the ground.

They bowed low. "Your majesty!
The word is, (PAUSE) *'Maybe.'"*

> Seek and you shall find
> Knock, and the door shall be opened
> Ask and it shall be given
> When the love come a-tumblin' down

(Here are some more stories — you'll have to pick the ones you want to tell. There are others scattered through this book.)

There was another king in another country sitting in his palace. A messenger comes, out of breath. He said, "Your majesty, your majesty, a sea captain has landed his vessel on your coastline, and in the hold of the ship is a strange animal called an elephant." The king was busy enjoying himself; so he called in his wise men. He said, "Go down. Bring back a report on this beast." The wise men got into the carriages. Clip clop, clip clop, they went down to the seacoast, and they were taken out to the ship.

You know, they had been reading books so long, they were all blind as bats. And one felt the side of the elephant. "Hm," says he. The next felt the ear of the elephant. "Hm." And the next felt the tusk; the next felt the trunk; and the last one pulled on the tail. Then they all got back in the carriage, clip clop, clip clop, and went back to the palace. "Your majesty," says the first, "this elephant is very like unto the side of a building." "Oh, you're quite wrong," says the next. "I felt it myself. It's like the trunk of a small tree." The third one was shouting, "No, you're both wrong. I felt it myself. It's like a large leaf of a large plant." Now they are all shouting. The next says, "Your majesty, it's like a smooth spear." "No, no, your majesty, it's like a big snake." And the last one says, "Your majesty, it's like a rope hanging down from heaven. You pull on it, and the heavens open up with waste."

> Seek and you shall find ... etc.
> (Get the crowd singing with you)
> Knock, and the door shall be opened
> Ask and it shall be given
> When the love come a-tumblin' down

There were once two little maggots, two little worms. They were sitting on the handle of a shovel, and the shovel was in a workshop. Early in the morning a workman came, put the shovel on his shoulder, and started down the street to work. The two little maggots held on as long as they could, but finally they jiggled off. One fell into a crack on the sidewalk, and the next one fell onto the curb. And from the curb he fell into a cat, a very dead cat. Well, the second maggot just started in eating. And he ate and ate and ate for three days until he could eat no more. Finally he straightened up, said, "Huhh, I guess I'll go hunt up my sister." And the second maggot humped himself up over the curb and along the sidewalk until he came to the crack.

"Hello, you down there, sister?"

"Yes, I've been here three days without a bite to eat or a drop to drink. I'm nearly starved to death. But you, you are so sleek and fat. To what do you attribute your success?"

"Brains and personality, sister. Brains and personality."

> Seek and you shall find ... etc.
> Knock, and the door shall be opened
> Ask and it shall be given
> When the love come a-tumblin' down

Early one morning a man got up and went out for a walk. He saw a lion. The lion saw him. The man started running. The lion started running. Faster. The man came to a cliff. There was no place to go but down. He saw a branch sticking out from the cliff a few feet down, and he climbed down and hung onto that branch. Looking up, he saw the lion snarling at the brink of the cliff. Looking down, he saw another lion at the bottom of the cliff. Out at the end of the branch he saw a beautiful red strawberry. He reached out and plucked it. You know, it was the sweetest thing he'd ever tasted in all his life.

> Seek and you shall find ...
> Knock, and the door shall be opened
> Ask and it shall be given
> When the love come a-tumblin' down

With scientific surety the math professor detailed the processes of working with negative and positive numbers, and ended "...thus you see, it is impossible in any way for two positives to make a negative."

From the back of the room could be heard a derisive mutter.

Yeah, yeah.

> Seek and you shall find ...
> Knock, and the door shall be opened
> Ask and it shall be given
> When the love come a-tumblin' down

This story was originally in Yiddish. A hundred years ago, in a small city in Russia, a traveling salesman got measured by a tailor, to make a pair of trousers. "I'll pick them up next month when I'm back here again," said the salesman.

But next month the trousers were not ready. "No matter," said the salesman. "I'll pick them up next month."

But next month they were still not ready — nor the next, nor the next. Nor the next! "See here," said the salesman, "either finish these trousers or give me my money back." The tailor knew the heat was on. Next month the trousers were finished when the salesman knocked.

He tried them on. They fit _perfectly_. "Tell me, though," asked the salesman, "Don't you think seven months is a little long to make a pair of trousers? After all, the Lord made the world in seven _days_."

Said the tailor, "That's true ... but look at the world ... and look at my trousers!"

> Seek and you shall find
> Knock, and the door shall be opened
> Ask and it shall be given
> When the love come a-tumblin' down

A woman driving down a narrow country dirt road saw a car come around a curve ahead. To be polite she pulled off, two wheels in the ditch. As the other car passed her, a man stuck out his head and hollered "Pig!"

Outraged, she put her foot on the gas, zoomed out of the ditch, down the road, around the curve. And ran into a pig.

Seek and you shall find ...
(By now I trust the crowd is singing well with you, maybe adding harmony)
Knock, and the door shall be opened
Ask and it shall be given
When the love come a-tumblin' down

Who should I give credit to for the stories in this book? I've forgot where I heard most of them. Except the next: my father told it to my sister decades ago.

Jesus and the Devil were walking down Fifth Avenue. Jesus looked down, and saw Truth written on a stone. He reached down and picked it up. Looked at it. Held it to his bosom.

"With this stone I shall found my church," said Jesus.

"I'll help you," said the Devil.

Seek and you shall find ...
Knock, and the door shall be opened
Ask and it shall be given
When the love come a-tumblin' down

A musical note:

The tempo (speed) of this song should be about ♩ = 88. That means take about 22 seconds to sing this 16-bar chorus (without any repeat of the last line).

Standard military marches are ♩ = 120, meaning two steps per second. Square dancers usually like ♩ = 125, ♩ = 130 or faster. Most people's hearts beat about 72 times a minute (♩ = 72).

Now, as to the complicated notation on p. 184.

Once upon a time I would have written these notes much more simply.

Seek   and   you shall find

Or, slightly more accurately,

Seek__   and__   you shall find

But for the sake of those who just have these pages in hand — no tape recording to help, I really wanted to get it right. As in so much African-American music, you should feel the pulse under a long-held note, like "seek." Without this pulse the note could droop at the end, if you can imagine an arrow falling.

Not good, it should be more like:

If I was a choral director, I'd be waving my hands:

On the very last chorus, the last line can have a ritard, which could be written

When the love come - a - tumb - a - lin' down.

but would sound more like

When the love   come-a-tumb-a-lin' down.___

I guess I should just urge you to tap your foot, sway your body, snap your fingers as you sing — and realize that your body could move in several different ways, and there could be many ways of singing the word "seek."

The vowel "ee" can be made in several different ways, depending on how you shape your lips, or how far back in your mouth you shape your tongue. Try pushing out your lips, as when saying "Sh-h" and put the "ee" in the forward part of your mouth.

Enough of all this technical talk. Too confusing.

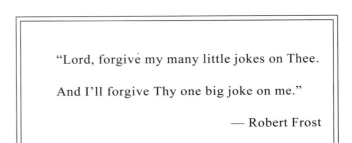

"Lord, forgive my many little jokes on Thee.

And I'll forgive Thy one big joke on me."

— Robert Frost

New England Puritans disapproved of carol singing. It probably originated as a European pagan custom. A carol was a dance.

In mid-19th Century England, people were moving to cities and forgetting their country ways. Some young preachers in London decided to revive carol singing. They translated "The First Noël" from French. They found a Swedish Easter carol melody and made up words to it about a Bohemian king named Wenceslas. And they translated this Welsh New Year's carol into English. One of my favorites for 70 years. Thinking that other guitar pickers might like to try deciphering the tablature, here 'tis.

Deck the Halls **B91**

Dropped D tuning

Music: Welsh New Years carol
Guitar arrangement by Pete Seeger (1956)
© 1993 by Sanga Music Inc.

My mother's grandmother was a good pianist at age 17. A local church committee asked her parents if they might rent a hall and sell tickets for a concert.

"Absolutely *not*!" said her parents. "A lady does not appear on stage." (Her father was a Philadelphia banker.)

"But we want to raise money for the church, and no one's home is big enough for all the people that want to hear her play."

A compromise was finally reached. She would be allowed to give the concert on the stage, but a screen had to be put between her and the audience. This was about the year 1850.

She lived to a ripe old age, raised six children. My father and mother remembered her in her eighties, with hands rippling up and down the piano keys.

© Len Munnik, Amsterdam

This North American version of an old English Christmas carol has long been a favorite of mine. I think I heard John Jacob Niles sing it first. The Weavers liked it too, and they asked me to play the recorder along behind it.

Surely many artists must feel as perplexed as I am when I am asked, "How do you write a good melody?" Melodies seem to spring out of the subconscious. God had something to do with it, perhaps. All I know is that one of the best melodies I ever invented was a little piece for the recorder as an introduction to this song.

If you want the ancient words, look them up under the title, "The Coventry Carol." If you want the verses Lee Hays made up for the Weavers to sing, write our music publisher (TRO, 266 West 37th Street, New York, NY 10018; <info@songways.com>). I purposely leave them both out here, hoping that in the next few decades some woman or man will find words for a new soul arriving in a world trembling on the brink of extinction. This could be a refrain.

Lulloo, Lullay

B92

Part for soprano or tenor recorder, in C.
Or a harmonica. Or whistle it.

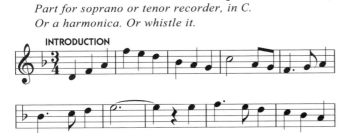

1. Lul - loo, lul - lay, my ti - ny child,
Bye, bye, lul - loo, lul - lay.
Lul - lay, my ti - ny lit - tle child,
Bye, bye, lul - loo, lul - lay.

Traditional English Christmas carol

When do you breathe in this song? Whenever you feel like it. If several people sing it together, they can breathe at different times, so the melody seems to flow without stop.

My older brother John taught me this old English carol back in the 1940s. You can sing the high part or the low part of the last line – they harmonize.

We Wish You a Merry Christmas

When singing it with the Weavers, I got the idea for an introduction and an ending to give it a "performance framework." I'm proud that it has caught on and others now sing these extra parts. The old English carol was just three short choruses, far too short for a song so much fun to sing.

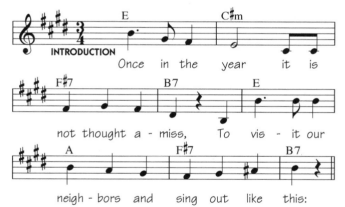

1. We wish you a merry Christmas,
   We wish you a merry Christmas,
   We wish you a merry Christmas
   And a happy New Year.

2. We want some figgy pudding (3x)
   And a cup of good cheer.

3. We won't go until we get some (3x)
   So bring it out here.

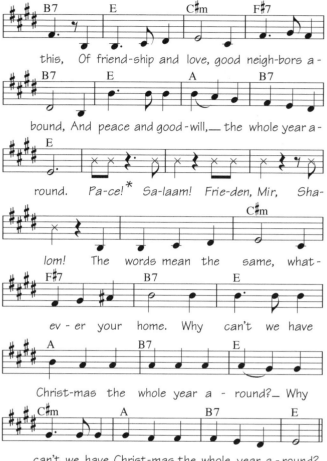

REPEAT VERSE 1

Original verses: traditional (English carol) Words & music to introduction and closing by Ronnie Gilbert, Lee Hays, Fred Hellerman & Pete Seeger (1950)
TRO - © 1951 (renewed) Folkways Music Publishers, Inc., New York, NY.

*Latin, then Arabic, German, Russian, Hebrew.

With a ritard at the end, the whole crowd should sing it with you.

We wish you a merry Christmas,
We wish you a merry Christmas,
We wish you a merry Christmas
And a happy New Year.

★ ★ ★

It's almost sacrilegious to draw into this profane volume one of the greatest musicians of all time, Johann Sebastian Bach. He, the heavenstormer, born over 300 years ago in Germany. But he loved rhythm. I believe he would have delighted in the needle-like tones of the banjo. This particular arrangement (of the organ obligato to one of his chorales) sounds best when played rather softly, and not too fast.

Bach wrote it in the key of G. With my rusty voice I usually capo up and sing it way down in B flat. But read on.

Jesu, Joy of Man's Desiring

Music by Johann Sebastian Bach (1716)
Arranged with English words by Pete Seeger (1989)
© 1993 by Stormking Music Inc.

1. Jesus bleibet meine Freude,
   Er ist meines Herzens Trost und Saft.
   (Jesus remains my joy,
       He is my heart's consolation and life blood.)

PRONOUNCE:
   "Yayzoos bly-bet my-neh Froydeh
   "Air ist my-ness Hair-tzenz Trohst oond Sahft."

   In 1989 I thought of some verses in English to try with Clearwater's Walkabout Chorus.

2. We will love or we will perish.
   We will learn the rainbow to cherish.

3. Dare to struggle, dare to danger,
   Dare to touch the hand of a stranger.

4. Dare to struggle, dare to danger.
   Dare to touch the soul of a stranger.

REPEAT VERSE 2

(Tenors and altos have the melody)

Play it through again. Of course, if you have a good organist or pianist, Bach modulated it beautifully.

Did you know that in the year 1717, at the age of 32, Bach was thrown into prison by Wilhelm Augustus, the new Duke of Saxe-Weimar. Bach threatened to quit the Duke's service to accept an offer as the chief organist and composer at the court of Bach's more appreciative friend, Prince Leopold of Anhalt-Cothen. Despite his growing fame and talent, Bach was dissatisfied with his lot at Saxe-Weimar and wanted to leave. The Duke had him locked up for nearly eight months — from April 6 to December 2, 1717 — but when Bach persisted in quitting, the Duke was finally forced to let him go.

The above information is from an article by Dave Platt in the magazine *Jewish Currents* — New York City. Which leads us to the next song. Platt quotes a poem by the late Yuri Suhl, with Suhl's introduction. Treblinka was one of the Nazi death camps. An orchestra of prisoner musicians was compelled to play each morning when prisoners marched off to their slave labor details. See also p. 237.

Ode to a Composer

You're one of us now
Johann Sebastian Bach
your statues stand
but you
chained in your own score
were dragged to Treblinka
where murder and music
go hand-in-hand.

Bach at Treblinka

Poem ("Ode to a Composer") by Yuri Suhl (1973)   Music by Pete Seeger (1983)
TRO - © 1973 & 1993 Yuri Suhl & Melody Trails, Inc., New York, NY.

The Weavers used to sing another Bach chorale, "O Sacred Head Now Wounded," with English lyrics by Tom Glazer (degenderized by Tom in 1987).

The Whole Wide World Around

C02

Because all men are brothers, wherever men may be,
And women all are sisters, forever proud & free,
No tyrant shall defeat us, no nation strike us down,
And all who toil shall greet us the whole wide world
around.

My brothers & my sisters, forever hand in hand,
Where chimes the bell of freedom, there is my native land.
My brothers' fears are my fears, yellow, white or brown,
My sisters' tears are my tears the whole wide world
around.

Let every voice be thunder, let every heart be strong,
Till tyrants be unseated, our work will not be done.
Let every pain be token, the lost years shall be found.
Let slavery's chains be broken the whole wide world
around!

Words by Tom Glazer   Music by J.S. Bach ("St. Matthew Passion")
© 1948 Tom Glazer. Copyright assigned Songs Music, Inc., Scarborough, NY
10510. Renewed 1975. Lyrics reprinted herein by permission.

Next are additional words by me.

O Sacred World Now Wounded

C03

O sac-red world now wound-ed, we
pledge to make you free Of hate, of war, of
hun-ger, and self-ish cru-el-ty. And
here— in our small cor-ner we
plant a ti-ny seed, And it— will grow to
beau-ty to shame the face of greed.

Words by Pete Seeger (1988)
Music by Hans Leo Hassler (1601)   Harmonized by J.S. Bach (1719)
TRO - © 1993 Melody Trails, Inc., New York, NY.

In the early '70s, on the cobblestone streets of an old English town, I thought of this next tune, wrote it down. Worked out a spare way of playing it on the guitar. It is intended to be soft, with open notes on high strings as well as low strings, ringing out as long as possible. I wiggle my left hand as violinists do, to get a bit of vibrato.

The Emporer Is Naked Today-O!

C04...

A few years later I was able to fashion the lyrics. I was glad to hear Barbara Dane sing it in a jazz tempo.

The test of a usable song is its ability to be sung several different ways. I usually alternate playing the tune, then singing it, then end by playing it again.

Originally titled "As the Sun"   Words & music by Pete Seeger (1970)
© 1977, 1979 by Sanga Music Inc.

1. As the sun
    Rose on the rim of eastern sky,
    And the one
    World that we knew was trying to die.
        We said: Stand!
        And sing out for a brand new day-O!
        Your child may be the one to exclaim:
        The emperor is naked today-O!

2. Four winds that blow
    Four thousand tongues, with the word: survive
    Four billion souls*
    Striving today to stay alive —
        We say: Stand!
        And sing out for a brand new day-O!
        Why don't we be the ones to exclaim:
        The emperor is naked today-O?

3. Men — have failed
    Power has failed, with papered gold.
    Shalom-salaam
    Will yet be a word where slaves were sold**
        We say: Stand!
        And sing out for a brand new day-O!
        Why don't we be the ones to exclaim:
        The system is naked today-O!

*In 2008, 6+ billion.
**Jerusalem, which is why I put the song in this chapter.

Only in my eighties did I read what I consider *the* most important section of the *Bible* for everyone to read. I know there are many important and beautiful parts, but I believe everyone must read Leviticus. It's near the beginning, right after Exodus.

In it we are told we must sacrifice a bull to the Lord. There is a certain special way it must be killed, and if you do not kill it the right way *you* will be killed. No ifs or buts. Once you have read Leviticus, you are better prepared to read the whole *Bible*, cover to cover.

I was about age nine when my father mentioned to me that one of the world's great melodies was nicknamed "Old Hundred." Years later I learned more about it.

In the 16th Century, the hymn got its start in Switzerland. Louis Bourgeois was songleader for the Protestant leader, John Calvin. And I'll bet he got the idea for the tune from some old French dance tune, and just slowed it down. He probably thought as John Wesley did: "Why should the Devil have all the good tunes?"

In the 17th Century it got English words, several sets of them. One was nicknamed "Old Hundredth" because the words were based on the 100th Psalm. Here the melody is given on the middle staff. Altos can sing the bass part or go even lower to sing the tenor part, one octave below the soprano. Sopranos and tenors should try to reach the high notes printed on the top staff. Or make up new parts.

My first line is part of the old hymn. The rest of the words I made up in 1984.

Words & music arrangement by Pete Seeger (1984)
From the original hymn by Louis Bourgeois (ca. 1510–1561)
© 1985 by Sanga Music Inc.

Incidentally, if you have no super high or super low voices, try raising the key a fourth, to C. Yes, now *all* men sing the bass part, sopranos sing the high part a fifth lower, and *altos* sing the melody. Try it!

1. All people that on earth do dwell,
    Sing out for peace 'tween heav'n and hell.
    'Tween East and West and low and high,
    Sing! peace on earth and sea and sky.

2. Old Hundred, you've served many years
    To sing one people's hopes and fear,
    But we've new verses for you now.
    Sing peace between the earth and plow.

3. Sing peace between the grass and trees,
    Between the continents and seas,
    Between the lion and the lamb.
    Between young Ivan and young Sam.

4. Between the white, black, red and brown,
    Between the wilderness and town,
    Sing peace between the near and far,
    'Tween Allah and six-pointed star.

5. The fish that swim, the birds that fly,
    The deepest seas, the stars on high,
    Bear witness now that you and I
    Sing peace on earth and sea and sky.

REPEAT FIRST VERSE

If the song is going well I'll add another verse and get a crowd to sing the first verse still one more time.

6. Old Hundred, please don't think us wrong
    For adding verses to your song.
    Sing peace between the old and young,
    'Tween every faith and every tongue.

REPEAT FIRST VERSE
(Ah…women and men…and children!)*

If you're singing this song for church folks I'm sure they would appreciate your adding at least one of Thomas Ken's verses (1674):

Praise God from whom all blessings flow
Praise Him all creatures here below
Praise Him above, ye heavenly host
Praise Father, Son and Holy Ghost.

The idea for this "unorthodoxology" actually came to me when listening to Grupo Moncotal. The Nicaraguan band played at a huge "Festival de la Nueva Canción" (Festival of New Song) in Ecuador, 1984. With that tremendous pulsing rhythm going on stage I wondered what it would be like to superimpose, right on top of it, some north-European long slow melody like this one.

When all is cooking — drum, guiro, maracas, claves, etc. then start the hymn in full harmony. But *not* in regular meter. It should float, as a Kentucky ballad does above the driving rhythm of a banjo. I'll try to write it below — first word slow, next three or four syllables fast, then slower, so the last syllable of each line is held out, thus:

After having described it to you, I confess —I've never heard it done. When I perform the song I usually first play the melody on the guitar, in a lower key — D

or E flat. I don't want to discourage anyone from singing because it seems too high.

That last line is fun to play. Here's the chord diagrams for: "Sing peace on earth and sea and sky."

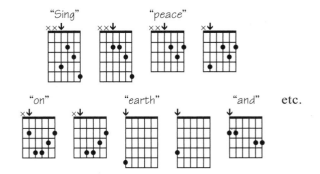

*See below, p. 196.

After I've played the tune on the guitar, I call out, "A lot of you know this melody. I'll give you some new words for it. All people that on earth do dwell!" Then I sing it, hoping a few will join in.

A small percentage do sing the first line with me. "Sing out for peace 'tween Heaven and Hell." A few more join in, sing the second line with me, "'Tween east and west and low and high" Now more are singing. I'm shouting now. "Sing peace on earth! And sea! And sky!"

After they sing this line I say, "There must be some people here who like to sing tenor or soprano. It's not hard; just three notes above the melody."

And although only a few may attempt it, I go through the whole four lines again, singing them, each line twice in the tenor-soprano part, so they can sing them back to me.

"Very good! Now, altos and basses! You have the best part of all."

I sing the first line of the bass part, but, of course, in the key of D it's much too low. Only a few basso profundos can make the last low note.

"Uh oh. I guess we better come up out of the cellar." I change the capo on the guitar if necessary, so we can sing it in F or G. "Let's try that again."

Now basses and altos learn the four lines, as I sing them out, one line at a time.

"Now let's put it all together."

"If you know your part well, sing out strong, so those who are not so certain will take courage from your efforts. That's how it is in this world. Them as knows must lead. If you can only decide who knows."

"If you hear too many people singing high, you sing low, and vice-virtue and here we go. Some start up here. All —" (I sing a B note). "The rest start here. All —" (I sing a G note).

Now we sing Verse 1 in three parts, with me feeding them the words one line at a time. Sometimes I have to encourage the high voices after the word "dwell."

...do   dwell   ("Where's   the   ten - ors?")

Or I encourage the basses.

...and____ hell   ("Where's   the   Bass-es?")

We get a fine ending on "sky." Then I sing the second verse briskly by myself.

2. Old Hun-dred, you've served man-y years___
To sing one peo-ple's hopes and fears,___
But we've new vers-es for you now.___
Sing___ peace bet-ween the earth and plow.

— and the third, fourth and fifth verses also briskly, before calling out the line that brings them all back for a repeat of the first verse.

5. The fish that swim, the birds that fly,
The deep-est seas, the stars on high,___
Bear wit-ness now that you and I___
Sing peace on earth and sea and sky.

SONGLEADER |—————— 5 ——————|

"All peo-ple that on earth do dwell!" 6. All...

After some grand harmony, if all is going well, I'll sing verse 6 by myself, and bring them back for another repeat of verse 1 and finally end, with a pun on the word "Amen." If children are in your chorus, they can give it a final tag.

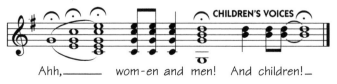

Ahh,___ wom-en and men! And children!___

In a hall with a lot of echo, people are often surprised how good it sounds. "You didn't know you were such a good chorus, did you? Well, it's like the whole world doesn't know what a great world we can make it if we start trying to work together."

In this book I go into some detail to show you how I teach the songs to audiences, not because I think others should slavishly try to copy my songleader techniques. I think there could be dozens of different ways to sing the songs. Slow. Fast. High. Low. Long. Short. With a bagpipe drone. Modulating to different keys. Using different accompaniments. Or none.

In 1984, when writing new verses for this I let imagination run amok. Then I found myself unable to make a proper selection. It was Arlo Guthrie who glanced over the lot, and unerringly checked off the six verses I sing now. "Sing these; forget the rest." He was right, as you can see. Here's the discards.

> Between the cats and rats and mice
> Between the fire and the ice
> Between what we've seen and what we've heard
> Between the rhythm and the word
> > 'Tween rank and file and the elite
> > Between the tofu and the meat
> > 'Tween short and tall and fat and thin
> > Between the solar and the sin
> 'Tween fast and slow and in and out
> Between the whisper and the shout
> 'Tween Yankee North and Latin South
> Between the stomach and the mouth
> > 'Tween what we squelch and what we say
> > Between the wide and narrow way
> > Sing peace before we're laid away
> > Between tomorrow and today
> Old hundred please don't think us wrong
> For adding verses to your song
> We all need shadows and the light
> Before we bid you all good-night
> > All people that on earth do dwell
> > Sing out for peace 'tween heaven and hell
> > Not bombs nor guns nor ancient pride
> > Let honest discourse now decide
> We see the world we see the shame
> Of cruel deeds in freedom's name
> Sing peace 'tween Luther and the Pope
> Sing peace between despair and hope
> > For snakes and snails and stars on high
> > Sing peace on earth and sea and sky
> > Let laser beams and poison gas
> > Join spears and arrows of the past
> All people now, both old and young
> Sing peace 'tween every skin and tongue
> An end to bombs and poison schemes
> We'll build the world which poets dreamed
> > Between our hands and our machines
> > 'Tween what we've felt and what we've seen
> > 'Tween what is read and what is heard
> > Between the rhythm and the word
> When every soul can sing as one
> I'll know my work on earth is done
> Though mortal shell is dead and gone
> My spirit shall go singing on
> > The struggle now in every breast
> > Will give each living soul no rest
> > Till bombs and guns are put aside
> > And reasoned discourse now decide.
> All people that on earth do dwell
> Sing peace between old heaven and hell
> For snakes and snails and stars on high
> Sing peace on earth and sea and sky.

> (A verse for Clearwater)
> > By peace we mean one simple thing
> > An end to bombs and all such things
> > Like sharpened knives between the ribs
> > And now let's raise mainsail and jib.

> So here's to motion slow or swift
> Here's to continents that drift
> Let Marx and Pope now sing the worth
> Of peace 'tween continence and birth
> > Between the water and the rock
> > Between the shepherd and the flock
> > Sing peace between the hand and wheel
> > Between the willow and the steel
> The struggle now in every breast
> Will give each living soul no rest
> Till poison hate is put aside
> And reasoned discourse now decide.
> > I find I still have one more rhyme
> > Praise be to women of all time
> > May women lead as now we build
> > A world where hopes can be fulfilled

At the end of this chapter I have a question for Christians. Why did you leave Rabbi Hillel out of your Bible? He lived in Jerusalem a little before the time of Jesus. He put together three of the world's greatest questions,

> If I am not for myself, who will be?
> If I am only for myself, what am I?
> If not now, when?

Above is how it was taught to me by Jo Schwartz. Vlad Pozner points out that the Oxford Dictionary of Quotations has it differently:

"If I am not for myself, who is for me, and being for my own self, who am I? If not now, when?"

> "What is peace? Respect for the rights of others."
> > Benito Juarez (1806-1872),
> > the greatest president of Mexico.

In any case, I'm no longer so shy of the word "God."

> I will not be dismayed
> Through all the sun and shade
> We're finding our human soul
> As we struggle on.

God, in my opinion, is infinitely small as well as infinitely large. Hence the science fiction fantasy following. (Turn the page!)

The Beethoven Phenomenon

It's the 100th birthday party of a famous nuclear scientist. The large room is filled with other scientists, men and women from four continents. After the speeches, toasts, the old guy rises shakily to his feet, peers over his glasses, clears his throat, raises a glass, speaks slowly.

"Friends...all! I toast <u>you</u> with this glass of the world's most precious liquid; you know what it is. And I have a present for <u>you</u>. Yes, I see the red light of the United Nations TV camera on me. Hello out there! This present is for all of you, too. I've avoided TV most of my life, because of a well-known rule that fame reduces one's ability to think logically. But these days I don't think logically anyway. Only romantically. My close partner of seventy years died ten years ago, but she is here in spirit. Like Joe Hill, she is at my side. She was the one who, using the World Women's Network, made the breakthrough in the invention of the Super High Speed recording machine. And it is this Super High Speed recording machine that has enabled me — us! — to give this present to you tonight.

"For the benefit of those out there looking at me on an electronic screen, I remind you that in this mid-Twenty-First Century, the Big Bang has been verified by thousands of observations. All of our hundreds of billions of galaxies, some as distant as 10 billion light years away, started our journey at one instant about 13.5692 billion years ago. Also verified has been what is called the Beethoven Phenomenon — the fact that before the Big Bang there were three large crunches, as in the 5th Symphony of the German composer Beethoven: Ba...ba...ba...BOOM!

Ba - ba - ba BOOM!

'But I always liked to call it the Great Sneeze, as in 'ah...ah...ah...CHOO!' I agreed with Bertolt Brecht, that Beethoven's Fifth Symphony reminded him of paintings of battles, and he didn't like battles. Nor do I. But I'm wandering. Centenarians are garrulous.

"As most of you know, I've spent my life's work not with radar telescopes, but rather at the small end of the space-time scale, with the electron microscope and now with the quarkscope.

"Until now, we were certain that there are no particles smaller than a subquark, of which there are over a hundred to each hydrogen atom. They seem to appear and disappear about ten thousand times a second. What I am able to give you tonight is the <u>sound</u> of a <u>subquark</u> just as it starts its brief period of expansion and contraction. I have in my hand the button which will activate the Super High Speed recording machine. What you are about to hear has been slowed down by a factor of 21 billion, so our ears can hear it."

The old scientist presses a button. A faint hum. He points at the TV camera, cupping his ear with the other hand, as though urging TV viewers to listen. The room is silent.

Suddenly is heard clearly, as if in a child's voice: "Ah...Ah...Ah...CHOO!"

(God is infinitely small, infinitely large.)

★ ★ ★

My best songwriting in the year of '73 was to find three words which could be used for a new last line to this 19th Century African-American "spiritual." It took me 20 years to find 'em.

The old last line, "Soldiers of the cross," is good, but I wanted to sing the song for many different kinds of people, reminding them that heaven (and revolutions) are achieved neither in one big bang, nor by the throwing open of gates.

My voice prefers the song in the key of C, as here, though a group of women might prefer it a shade lower. And for a crowd that is really warmed up I'd do it in D, urging the crowd to harmonize.

Harmonize! This is what musicians can teach the politicians: not everyone has to sing the melody.

I know most songbooks give the song in 3/4 time, but 4/4 gives a songleader a few extra seconds to call out the new words and verses, and exhort basses, altos, etc. to do their best. Arlo Guthrie and I used to close a concert with it. Note the harmony on the last two measures. Of course no two verses will have exactly the same melody, and verses may be added or subtracted. This is traditional. It's also traditional for tempo to stay rock steady. Sometimes I sing four verses, sometimes eight, and repeat the first verse at the end.

Since I have a long-necked 12-string guitar tuned low, I can use a D tuning (see Appendix) but it sounds in C, and I start a rhythm on just the lowest pair of strings. In parentheses I give words such as I use to get a crowd singing, but you use what words you think best. My favorite verses are 1, 2, 4 and 5, and then repeat the 1st verse.

Jacob's Ladder

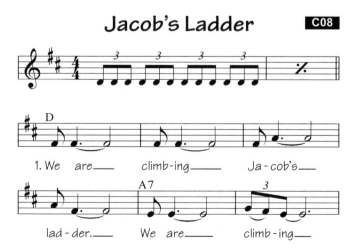

Ja-cob's__ lad-der.__ We are__

climb-ing__ Ja - cob's lad-der,__

Broth-ers,__ sis-ters,__ all.__

("Ev-ery rung goes high-er 'n' high-er")

2. Ev - ery__ rung goes__

high-er,__ high-er. ("Sing it o-ver")

Music: traditional (African-American spiritual). Additional words by Pete Seeger (1973)
© 1993 by Sanga Music Inc.
Verses 4 and 5 from women in Milwaukee,
verses 9 and 10 by Bill Goodman in Chicago.

1. We are climbing Jacob's Ladder (3x)
   Brothers, sisters, all.

2. Every rung goes higher, higher (3x)
   Brothers, sisters, all.

3. Every new one makes us stronger (3x)
   Brothers, sisters, all.

4. We are dancing Sarah's circle...*
   Sisters, brothers, all.

5. Every round a generation...*
   Sisters, brothers, all.

6. Struggle's long but hope is longer...
   Sisters, brothers, all.

7. People all need jobs and justice...
   Sisters, brothers, all.

8. We are climbing Jacob's ladder...
   Brothers, sisters, all.

9. Peace and love can conquer anger...
   Brothers, sisters, all.

10. Peace and justice will bring freedom...
    Brothers, sisters, all.

* A priest liked these marked verses so much he wrote a whole
long sermon on the value of going in circles.

As you see, I'm hoping that a crowd will feel the spirit so strongly that they can sing harmony, even if they never did it before. Of course, you don't have to sing all the verses. No two songleaders will do it the same.

If I'm with any group that knows how to harmonize I'll hold up four fingers, on the word "all," indicating to switch to the G chord ("subdominant") at the end. Then one finger pointed high indicates back to D ("tonic").

Singing in Chile and Argentina in 1988 I got help and we found Spanish words for this song.

1. Ya su-bimos… todos… juntos (3x)
   Todos… juntos… ya.

2. Es muy… larga… la esca-lera (3x)
   Todos… juntos… ya.

3. Los pel-daños… suben… suben (3x)
   Todos… juntos… ya.

4. Pan, jus-ticia… nuestra… meta (3x)
   Todos… juntos… ya.

5. Larga… lucha… hemos… vivido (3x)
   Todos… juntos… ya.

6. No más… larga… la esper-anza (3x)
   Todos… juntos… ya.

> "We are all bastards, but God loves us anyway."
> —Rev. Will Campbell, Mount Juliet, Tennessee

Overleaf: This highly simplified slant view of a spiral galaxy reminds us of our position in the universe. Earth and our sister planets, asteroids, and comets all revolve around the sun, a common type of star. Our Solar System revolves around the center of our spiral galaxy, "the Milky Way," once every 200,000,000 years or so. At approximately 27,000 light years from the center, the Sun is about halfway from the galactic center to the outermost observed members of the galaxy. Keep in mind that there is a lot more space between stars than is implied by this picture. If the sun were a large grain of sand, the nearest other star would be another grain of sand 50 miles away.

The spiral arms in our galaxy are clumpier than shown. Our galaxy is a fairly large one, as galaxies run, but noticeably smaller than the largest. Spiral galaxies seem to outnumber the non-spiral ones.

Because of interstellar dust clouds we cannot see much of our galaxy, including the center, but it is estimated that between 100 billion and 400 billion stars rotate. As the sensitivity of our telescopes increases, the number of galaxies observed in the universe increases. Current estimates are that there are at least as many galaxies in the universe as there are stars in our galaxy.

YOU ARE HERE

Chapter 9: *Sailing Down My Golden River –*
Think Globally, Sing Locally

POLLUTION

Drawing by Paul Loring

In the "Frightened '50s" I sang a variety of songs out of American history, going from college to college, summer camp to summer camp. I relayed songs of Woody and Lead Belly to a batch of younger folks. It was probably the most important job of music I'll ever do. I could have kicked the bucket in the early '60s — my job was mostly done. A lot of talented new songwriters came along to pick up where Woody and Lead Belly left off.

In 1962, Rachel Carson's book *Silent Spring* made a turning point in my life. As a kid I'd been a nature nut. Age 15 and 16, I put all that behind me, figuring the main job to do was to help the meek inherit the earth, assuming that when they did the foolishness of the private profit system would be put to an end.

But in the early '60s I realized that the world was being turned into a poisonous garbage dump. By the time the meek inherited it, it might not be worth inheriting. I became an eco-nik; started reading books by Barry Commoner and Paul Ehrlich.

About this time I also fell in love with sailing. I'd started earning money and got a little plastic bathtub of a boat. Such poetry! The wind can be from the north, but depending how you slant your sails, you can go east or west. (Don't let anyone tell you, "I had to do it." The same pressures will make one person do the right thing, another a stupid thing.)

Also, 500 years ago African sailors showed European sailors that if you used triangular sails instead of square sails, you could actually use the power of a north wind to sail towards the north, first northeast, then northwest. You can zigzag into the very teeth of the gale that's trying to force you back. That's good politics, too. Martin Luther King used the forces against him to zigzag ahead.

But sailing on the Hudson, I saw lumps of toilet waste floating past me. The ironies of "private affluence and public squalor" (thanks, J.K. Galbraith) got to me. I wrote the next two songs, then a string of others.

Sailing Up My Dirty Stream

C09

1. Sail-ing up my dir-ty stream,___ Still I love it and I'll keep the dream That some day, though maybe not this year, My Hud-son Riv-er___ will once again___ run clear. She starts high in the moun-tains of the north,___ Crys-tal clear and i-cy, trick-les forth, With just a few float-ing wrap-pers of chew-ing gum,___ Dropped by some hik-ers, to warn of things to come.___

Also known as "My Dirty Stream" or "The Hudson River Song"
Words & music by Pete Seeger (1961) © 1964 (renewed) by Sanga Music Inc.

1. Sailing up my dirty stream,
   Still I love it and I'll keep the dream
   That some day, though maybe not this year,
   My Hudson River will once again run clear.
   She starts high in the mountains of the north,
   Crystal clear and icy trickles forth,
   With just a few floating wrappers of chewing gum
   Dropped by some hikers to warn of things to come.

2. At Glens Falls five thousand honest hands
   Work at the Consolidated Paper Plant.
   Five million gallons of waste a day,
   Why should we do it any other way?
   Down the valley one million toilet chains
   Find my Hudson so convenient a place to drain.
   And each little city says, "Who, me?
   Do you think that sewage plants come free?"

3. Out in the ocean they say the water's clear
   But I ... live right at Beacon here*
   Halfway between the mountains and the sea,
   Tacking to and fro, this thought returns to me:
   Sailing up my dirty stream,
   Still ... I love it and I'll dream
   That some day, though maybe not this year,
   My Hudson River and my country will run clear.

* OR: "But we... live on the river here."

I was learning to sail, and spent my first night alone on the river, seeing the evening light go from golden to rose, to purple, to night. Made up a tune as I went along, and only realized a month later that I'd swiped the first part of the melody from one of my favorite Christmas carols, "Deck the Halls." (See p. 187.)

Sailing Down My Golden River

C10

1. Sail-ing down my gold-en riv-er, Sun and wa-ter all my own,___ Yet I was nev-er___ a-lone.___ Sun and wa-ter, old life-giv-ers, I'll have them where-e'er I roam,___ And I was not far from home.___

Originally titled: "Sailing Down This Golden River"
Words & music by Pete Seeger (1962)
TRO - © 1971 Melody Trails, Inc., New York, NY.

1. Sailing down my golden river
    Sun and water all my own
        Yet I was never alone.
    Sun and water, old life-givers
    I'll have them where'er I roam
        And I was not far from home.

2. Sunlight glancing on the water
    Life and death are all my own
        And I was never alone.
    Life to raise my sons and daughters
    Golden sparkles in the foam
        And I was not far from home.

3. Sailing down this winding highway
    Travelers from near and far
        Yet I was never alone.
    Exploring all the little by-ways,
    Sighting all the distant stars,
        Yet I was not far from home.

REPEAT FIRST VERSE

This song has been sung many different ways. As I put it down above, it might be taught to a group of people who never heard it, but are willing to try learning it out of a book.

When I first made it up, I sang it very freely; I opened with the guitar.

Arlo Guthrie used to sing it rhythmically with his pounding electric band, Shenandoah. Now his daughter Sarah Lee sings it with her husband Johnny Irion.

I guess if I had a voice and was able to sing it now, I'd like to put in more triplets.

You who read this, decide for yourself what's the best way.

Ernie Marrs, one of the best wordsmiths I know, sent me these lyrics and I put a tune to 'em.

The People Are Scratching

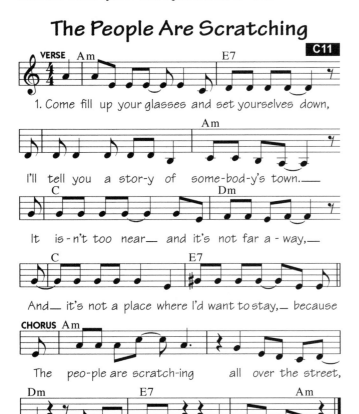

Words by Ernie Marrs & Harold Martin   Music by Pete Seeger (1962)
© 1963 (renewed) Sanga Music Inc.

ERNIE MARRS

© David Gahr

1. Come fill up your glasses and set yourselves down,
    I'll tell you a story of somebody's town.
    It isn't too near and it's not far away
    And it's not a place where I'd want to stay, because

CHORUS (AFTER EACH VERSE):
The people are scratching all over the street
Because the rabbits had nothing to eat.

2. The winter came in with a cold icy blast.
    It killed off the flowers, and killed off the grass.
    The rabbits were starving because of the freeze
    And they started eating the bark off the trees, now

3. The farmers said, "This sort of thing won't do,
    Our trees will be dead when the rabbits get through;
    We'll have to poison the rabbits, it's clear,
    Or we'll have no crops to harvest next year," now

4. So they bought the poison and spread it around
    And soon dead rabbits began to be found.
    Dogs ate the rabbits, and the farmers just said,
    "We'll poison those rabbits till the last dog is dead,"
    now

5. Up in the sky there were meat-eating fowls
    The dead rabbits poisoned the hawks and the owls,
    Thousands of field mice the hawks used to chase
    Were multiplying all over the place, and

6. The fields and the meadows were barren and brown,
    The mice got hungry and moved into town.
    The city folks took the farmers' advice,
    And all of them started to poison the mice, and

7. There were dead mice in all the apartments and flats,
    The cats ate the mice, and the mice killed the cats.
    The smell was awful, and I'm glad to say
    I wasn't the man hired to haul them away, and

8. All through the country and all through the town
    There wasn't a dog or a cat to be found,
    The fleas asked each other, "Now where can we stay?"
    They've been on the people from then till this day,
    yes

9. All you small creatures that live in this land,
    Stay clear of the man with the poisonous hand!
    A few bales of hay might keep you alive,
    But he'll pay more to kill you than to let you survive,
    oh

In 1964 I took my youngest daughter, then age nine, canoeing on a beautiful lake in Maine. We camped on a little island, and were dismayed to see the beach littered with bottles and cans. We picked 'em all up. I had a magic marker with me and wrote this graffiti on a flat stone.

Cursed Be The Nation

Cursed be the Nation of any size or shape
Whose citizens behave like naked apes
And drop their litter where they please
Just like we did when we swung through trees.

But blessed be the nation, and blessed be the prize
When citizens of any shape or size
Can speak their mind for whatever reason
Without being jailed or accused of treason.

By Pete Seeger (1967)
© 1993 by Fall River Music Inc.

(No, I never made up a tune for it. Someone else can try. Remember, you can change words, add words.)

Drowned In Paper `C12`

Words & music by Pete Seeger (1962)
© 1963 (renewed) by Sanga Music Inc.

CHORUS:
Drowned in paper, strangled in wire,
Our civilization is bound to go down.
And the birds and the bees and the bugs will take over
And the old green world go spinning around.

1. Some say the world will be ended in fire.
   Some say it'll be frozen in ice to the heart.
   But I think I know how our race will expire
   It'll be our own doing from being so smart.

(I made up some forgettable verses for this, but the chorus comes back to haunt me. You try.)

In '63 an artist friend, Vic Schwarz, told me they used to have sloops on the river with a boom 70 feet long.

"Oh, don't give me that," says I, unbelieving. "There never was a sloop that big, except an America's Cup racer."

"No, I've got a book all about them; I'll lend it to you," says Vic. Soon after he sends a dog-eared volume, *Sloops of the Hudson*, written in 1908 by two middle-aged gents, William Verplanck and Moses Collyer. "Before we die we want to put down what we can remember of these sloops, because they were the most beautiful boats we ever knew, and they will never be seen again."

I read it through twice. Wrote a long "poem" about sloops (next page). Finally after a couple years couldn't stand the temptation. Stayed up till 2 a.m. typing a seven-page letter to Vic. "Why don't we get a gang of people together and build a life-size replica of a Hudson River sloop? It would probably cost $100,000, but if we got enough people together we could raise it."

Then I forgot about the letter. Four months later I happen to meet Vic on a railroad station platform. "When are we going to get started on that boat?" says he.

"What boat?" says I.

"You wrote me a letter!"

"Oh, that's as foolish as saying let's build a canoe and paddle to Tahiti."

"Well, I've passed your letter up and down the commuter train; we've got a dozen people who don't think it's foolish."

"Hm. Maybe if there are enough nuts, we just might do it."

This isn't the place to go into more detail, except to say that three years later the sloop *Clearwater* was launched. It's owned by a democratic non-profit organization of several thousand members. Since 1969, it has taken 400,000 schoolkids out on educational sails, 50 at a time. The Hudson is noticeably cleaner, and *Clearwater* is one of the reasons why.

My violinist mother once said, "The three Bs are Bach, Beethoven and Brahms." I retorted, "For me they are ballads, blues and breakdowns." But now I guess it's boats, banjos and biscuits. Because one of *Clearwater*'s main education devices has been riverside festivals, with lots of good food and music. Along the line, people get some ideas about getting together to clean up a beautiful river.

Hudson River Sloops

"I can see them now," said old Verplanck in 1908,
65 to 75 feet long, 20 to 25 feet wide.
Draught 7 or 8 (13 with centerboards down),
Mast 90 to 100 feet, topmast another 30 to 50,
Boom 70 to 90 feet, bowsprit 25
Capacity 50 to 200 tons of cargo
Crew of six, including captain, cabin boy, and cook."

Four hundred plied the river in 1860
Often built in small yards, in towns like
Cornwall, Marlborough, New Hamburg.

"When the wind was fair we could compete with
steam — and even beat her!"
But with no wind,
It could be five days drifting up to Newburgh
And longer, back to New York.
Or, five hours, with the right wind and tide.

Cargo? Grain, pickles, salt meat in barrels, livestock,
hay for New York's horses, bricks, plaster, slate for
sidewalks. In early times panelled staterooms for the
rich. (Poor folk walked to Albany.)

The Highlands were beautiful but tricky. If the wind
was from the west, as many as 50 sloops might be
waiting near Peekskill, unable to breast the narrows
with wind and tide against them. When the tide
changed, off they'd race. By Newburgh, they'd be
stretched out a mile or more.

Most treacherous was the "Worragut"
Four miles from West Point to Pollopel Island
(Bannerman's)
Here the Neptune overturned in 1824 on a gusty day
And 35 of its 50 passengers drowned.

The railroad took passenger and mail service after 1847.

"The river teemed with sturgeon in those days—big
fellows weighing 250 pounds would be seen leaping
several feet in the air. Now and then one would fall
on the deck of a small boat. Catching and packing
these fish was an important industry. Sturgeon was
known as 'Albany Beef.'"

By the early 20th century, sloops finally abandoned
the river.

"They were the most beautiful boats we ever knew.
And they will never be seen again."

By Pete Seeger (1964)
© 1993 by Fall River Music, Inc.

Don McLean, who was on the first crew of the
Clearwater, sang an old hymn which gave me the idea for
a tune to use for a short piece of poetry quoted by Robert
Boyle in his book, *The Hudson, A Natural and Unnatural
History*. The original was in Dutch, about the year 1640
— Bob got the translation from the book *Portrait of New
Netherland* by Ellis L. Raesly, © 1945 in New York City.

This Is a Land `C13`

Slowly, free rhythm

Original Dutch words by Jacob Steendam (1635)
English translator unknown   New music adaptation by Pete Seeger (1971)
TRO - © 1975 Melody Trails, Inc., New York, NY.

This is a land
Of milk and honey flowing
With healing herbs
Like thistles, freely growing
Where buds of Aaron's Rods are blowing
Oh! This is Eden!

When I'm singing on stage, I'll follow this song
immediately with "Little Boxes."

★ ★ ★

As a child I learned an old spiritual called "The Old
Ark's A-Movering." It was collected and printed over a
hundred years ago. I haven't the faintest idea when it
was put together — probably sometime in the mid-19th
century by slaves or recently freed slaves. My new
words for it below were put together about 1970 after I
read in the book *The Population Bomb*, by biologist
Paul Ehrlich, that the human race was doubling every 32
years. I think Karl Marx would have liked the song. He
is the one who pointed out that the capitalist economic
system was in trouble any time it could not expand; so
sooner or later it would be in big trouble. Now I read
that if an investor can't double his money in 10 years, he

thinks he's doing something wrong. Growthmania needs a better song than this, but it's all I have right now.

We'll All Be A-Doubling

Words by Pete Seeger (1965)
Music: traditional ("The Old Ark's A-Movering")
TRO - © 1970 Melody Trails, Inc., New York, NY.

CHORUS (AND AFTER EACH VERSE):
We'll all be a-doubling, a-doubling, a-doubling,
We'll all be a-doubling in thirty-two years.

1. Two times two is four.
    Two times four is eight.
    Two times eight is sixteen,
    And the hour is getting late.

2. Twice sixteen is thirty-two.
    Next comes sixty four.
    Next a hundred and twenty-eight.
    Do we need to hear more?

3. Next is two hundred fifty-six.
    Next five hundred and twelve.
    Next one thousand and twenty-four.
    So figure it out yourself.

4. Keep doubling ten generations.
    You can have children over a million.
    Keep going another twenty.
    Your children would be over a trillion.

5. Give it another three hundred years,
    Your children number a billion;
    Keep doubling another millennium,
    You can have another quadrillion.

6. Either people gonna have to get smaller
    Or the world's going to have to get bigger;
    Or there's a couple other possibilities,
    I'll leave it to you to figger.

Along the Hudson River new verses should be written. The *Clearwater* (see below), having helped to partially clean up the waters, is now having to fight to save the shores. If we don't watch out, it will be an unbroken chain of high rises from Albany to the sea, walling off the river from the less affluent behind them. One of my local Democratic politicians (a really nice guy) says to me, "Pete, what can you do? If you don't grow, you die." Only late at night I realized the answer. "Yes, I suppose that's true. Doesn't it then follow that the quicker you grow, the sooner you die?"

Now: can we learn to grow in generosity, in common sense, in ability to talk with people we disagree with?

One of the more stupid things that Mao Tse-tung did 50 years ago was not alerting his countrymen to the need to keep the population down. Now it has reached panic proportions and has led to terrible things like infanticide.

In the "good old days," face it, perhaps each tribe kept the other tribe's population down.

An Arab story. Arabs are proud that the whole world uses their system of numbers.

If you have your health, put down the number one. If you have a family, put a zero next to it. Ten! How lucky you are. If you have land, put another zero down. One hundred! Who could want more? Well, if you have a good reputation, put down another zero. You have health, family, land, a good reputation! But take away the "one," and what have you left? Three zeros.

Bud Foote (1930-2005), professor of English at Georgia Tech, was a first-rate songmaker. He was at the Newport festival in 1969 when the Clearwater, on its maiden voyage, tied up at the Newport dock.

Bud later became famous in his home community near Atlanta, Georgia, for helping to stop a freeway with a song:

> Plant a little tree for Jesus
> And another for the Brotherhood of Man

It was on everybody's lips. Bud was deeply proud when he was told that in the Georgia State Department of Transportation he was known as "... the sonofabitch who writes the songs."

Ballad of the Sloop Clearwater

Words by Bud Foote, 7th verse by Pete Seeger (1969)
Music: traditional ("The Great American Folk Melody")
© 1971 by Sanga Music Inc.

1. I was sitting on my front porch as I watched this
   river rot,
   Thinking about the sturgeon that are gone but not
   forgot,
   And the buffalo all restless underneath the
   prairie sod,
   And the smoke stacked up to heaven so's it hid the
   face of God.

   There were soldiers marching past my door and
   a tap upon my phone,
   A freeway inching tow'rd me that would someday
   take my home.
   And the smokestacks hid a sunset that would
   never come again,
   When they brought the sloop Clearwater
   sailing 'round the bend.
   ("Sing it over.")
   When they brought the sloop Clearwater
   sailing 'round the bend.

2. The Captain had a moustache that was nineteen
   inches long.
   The shanty master paced the deck, roaring out
   a song.
   The man who held the tiller wore his hair down to
   his knees,
   And a hundred tons of canvas billowed out into
   the breeze.

But the redwood trees are crashing down out on
  the western coast,
An angry shadowy army follows Crazy Horse's ghost.
The eagle's nest is barren as the mountain lion's den.
As they brought the sloop Clearwater
  sailing 'round the bend. (2x)

3. The Sloop cut through the sewage lying on the
      river's face.
    They docked her mid the garbage that was all
      around the place.
    The crew struck up a hornpipe, and the boots
      rang on the wood,
    It echoed on the river, and the river found it good.

But there's lightning in the Asian skies and thunder
  in the slums.
You can hear the Indians tuning up their
  long-forgotten drums.
Children clap their hands and laugh while men
  are killing men,
As they brought the sloop Clearwater
  sailing 'round the bend. (2x)

4. I said, "You people must be fools to dance and sing
      and shout
    When your ship's so deep in liquid shit, it never
      can get out.
    Right now children cry from hunger, grown men
      get mean with shame.
    A war rages in every heart; the very ground's in
      flame.

"You sail your dirty river; you sing your little songs.
You dance your pretty dances and recite your
  petty wrongs.
Don't you know that Abiyoyo's making footprints
  in the fen?
While you bring your Sloop Clearwater
  sailing 'round the bend." (2x)

5. The crew just laughed and danced some more, and
      beads began to ping.
    Beards were lifted to the skies as the crew began
      to sing,
    A black man rose upon the deck and preached a
      sermon there,
    And a crewman capered on the mast like a
      dancing grizzly bear.

I said, "You people all are fools, but I guess I am one too."
Suddenly the guns went quiet. The river all was new.
The smoke clouds cleared. I almost wept to see
  the sky again.
When they brought the sloop Clearwater
  a-sailing 'round the bend. (2x)

6. Well, the mountains rang, the children laughed,
      the women sang a song.
    The bison thundered down the plain a hundred
      thousand strong.
    The ghost dance tent was raised again,
      The lion wandered free.
    The river ran like silver from the mountains to
      the sea.

There was love and joy and brotherhood, and peace
  the whole world 'round,
Life and paint and energy, and trees and taste
  and sound,
And Abiyoyo danced a solemn waltz out in the fen
When they brought the sloop Clearwater
  a-sailing 'round the bend. (2x)

7. Now, the Sloop is gone, once again I'm ready
      to watch that river rot
    While others feel the skyfire, and others hug
      the shot.
    But some folks in town are up and around
      asking, "What–how–why–and–when!"
    Ever since that Sloop Clearwater
      came sailing 'round the bend.
    Ever since that Sloop Clearwater
      came sailing 'round the bend.

Recycle

T-Shirt design by Tinya Seeger

The 1899 Rivers and Harbors Act said that nothing can be dumped in the waters without permission of the Corps of Engineers. The law was rediscovered in 1967 by Fred Danback of Yonkers when cleaning out the files of the Yonkers Lifesaving Corps with a friend. "Hey, Gus, listen to this. Wouldn't it be great if we had a law like this nowadays? It says the person who turns in the polluter gets half the fine!"

Gus said, "How do you know it's not still a law?" Fred wrote to the government printing office, and two weeks later got a letter to the effect: "Dear Mr. Danback, so far as we can discover that law is still on the books and has not been repealed."

Fred went now to see his Congressman, Richard Ottinger. "Hey, when I come to a red light, I got to stop. How come these guys are not stopping?"

Within a few years there were 500 cases in the U.S. courts. Bounty hunters were canoeing up waterways, taking test tube samples from every pipe. Manufacturers descended on Congress. "Do something! Repeal that law! We didn't know anything about it. We're all sitting ducks!"

Congress says, "Well, we can't repeal it now while everybody's talking about pollution. But we'll do something." So in 1972 they passed the Water Pollution Amendments to the Clean Water Act. It just incidentally superseded "old 1899."

The new law wasn't all bad though, and slowly citizen pressure started cleaning up the waters. By the 1990s, the Hudson was safe to swim in again from Yonkers to Catskill. I call it a 50 percent cleanup with a five percent effort. The next century will see a long, slow struggle to rid the river of toxic chemicals from industry, agriculture, and surface run-off as well. I think it's a sure thing that the river will be clean as a whistle 100 years from now. But it can happen in one of two ways. The human race will get rid of wars, injustice, and pollution. Or it won't, and there will be no more people around to pollute it. We don't have another 2,000 years to learn the Sermon on the Mount.

This song has far more verses than it needs. I've a habit of "over-writing," then paring things down to a usable size. For purposes of this book, though, I decided to print all verses, and put parentheses in front of the verses I ended up not singing. In a distant city, 15 years after writing the song, I found a total stranger singing it.

In '74 I'd borrowed a shad net, thinking to learn something about fishing. In '75 I thought of the opening line of this song when I saw it hanging unused in my garage.

> "Today's problems were created by yesterday's ingenious solutions."
>
> — Anonymous

Throw Away That Shad Net
(How Are We Gonna Save Tomorrow?)

Throw a-way that shad net, get rid of hook and line. There's no more Hud-son fish-ing, not for a long, long time. The poi-son's in the riv-er-bed, no mat-ter whose the crime.____ But how are we gon-na save to-mor-row?____

Also known as: "The PCB Song"
Words & music by Pete Seeger (1975)
TRO - © 1976 Melody Trails, Inc., New York, NY.

1. Throw away that shad net, get rid of hook and line.
   There's no more Hudson fishing, not for a long
      long time.
   The poison's in the riverbed, no matter whose
      the crime.
   But how are we gonna save tomorrow?

2. One thousand honest workers need that paycheck
      every week,
   Way up in Fort Edward where the PCBs did leak.
   And the GE Corporation knows the profits it must
      seek,
   But how are we gonna save tomorrow?

3. The river was looking cleaner, it was starting to
      get clear,
   We looked forward to the fishing getting better
      every year.
   Now the scientists tell us, things are not what they
      appear,
   But how are we gonna save tomorrow?

(4.) PCB was a clever thing, 'way back in twenty-nine.
   Transformers and capacitors got turned out
      on the line.
   Nobody suspected what they'd do to us in time,
   And now we got to worry 'bout tomorrow.

(5.) Well, the purpose of technology is gonna take a
   different turn,
   We'll test each new thing carefully, that's one thing
   we have learned,
   We need a clean world for all to share, and all
   to work and earn,
   Then, maybe, we can save tomorrow.

6. Well, the experts knew about it, so why not you
   and me,
   Who controls the information in this land of
   the free?
   The laws didn't seem to help in stopping PCB,
   So how are we gonna save tomorrow?

(7.) The longest journey taken needs a first step to begin.
   This cleanup's gonna take a while, but now we
   must begin.
   Clearwater says to lend a hand, a claw, a paw, a fin,*
   'Cause now we got to work to save tomorrow.

SPOKEN: *"This song's too sad."*

8. Here's to the lowly blue crab, because he has no fat
   And so he's got no PCB (hardly) we say, hooray
   for that,
   So I'll not quit my crabbing, you can stick that
   in your hat.
   Somehow, we're gonna save tomorrow.

SPOKEN: *"In the old days, coal miners took a canary
down to test the air."*

9. Here's to the canary we took down in the mine.
   Here's to the Hudson stripers, may their warning
   be in time.
   Here's to all the young folks singing, "This land
   is yours and mine."
   That's how we're gonna save tomorrow.

(10.) Oh, the glory's on the river, and the struggle's
   on the shore
   Next year is 1976; let's start a little war
   Anyone who thinks we're quitting better take just
   one think more
   And that's how we're gonna save tomorrow.

11. So don't throw away that shad net, don't junk that
   hook and line
   We're gonna make some changes, we're gonna start
   in time
   Clearwater sings to all of us, "This land is yours
   and mine"
   And that's how we're gonna save tomorrow.

*This line is by the late Bud Foote of Decatur, Georgia.

1975 news item: "Environmental Commissioner
Ogden Reid declared in August that polychlorinated
biphenyls (PCBs) in Hudson striped bass made them
now unfit to eat. John Cronin, working then for the
Clearwater, discovered that EPA investigators knew
about the industrial discharge of PCB's and did not stop
them. The Clearwater initiates a campaign to phase out
use of PCBs nationally and internationally."

In 1985 Clearwater clubs started up shoreside shad
festivals again, because PCB levels in shad had sunk to
2 parts per million (ppm). Arguments have since started
up again, because it's been found that PCB is more
liable to cause birth defects than they once thought. The
Beacon shadfest was cancelled.

Striped bass from the Hudson have 30 ppm of PCB.
And eels, 200 ppm. And Hudson snapping turtles, 2,000
ppm! They're higher on the food chain. We are, too.

Engraving: Frank Leslie's Illustrated Newspaper, 1878

A STURGEON GOT CAUGHT IN THE SHAD NET!

We have some good jazz musicians among the Hudson River sloop singers. A young woman who is a good dancer would tap dance between the second and third verses.

It's a true story. I drove my daughter past the little station and saw it being renovated. "Hooray, we turned the clock back," I exclaimed first. And second, "Hey, I got a song."

The New Hamburg Clockback

Words & music by Pete Seeger (1981)
© 1993 by Sanga Music Inc.

1. There's a railroad station here at New Hamburg,
   That closed ten years ago.
   The railroad bosses said, "Uneconomic!
   It's adding to the railroad's woes."
   But some folks in town, they didn't give up.
   They passed a petition around.
   And what do you know! It's open again.
   And we can take a train to town.

CHORUS (AFTER EACH VERSE):
   Hooray, (Hooray!) We turned the clock back,
   In one more little way.
   Hooray, (Hooray!) We turned the clock back,
   That's progress for today.
   Hooray, (Hooray!) We turned the clock back,
   There's a little more hope now, that's a fact.
   And when the nuclear maniacs get the sack,
   That'll be the clockback day, Hooray!
   That'll be the progress day.

2. New Hamburg's just about two hundred souls,
   On the river near Wappinger Falls.
   Thank God, they didn't believe that lie,*
   "You can't fight City Hall"
   Here's to the folks that didn't give up,
   And passed that petition around.
   Who knows, who knows, with spirit like that,**
   We could have progress the world around.

3. Look out the window, there's old Mama Hudson,***
   Rolling on down to the sea.
   And no matter what shape—size—color you are,
   She's got a message for you and me.
   We oughta quit being petroleum junkies
   And get on the track again.
   The locomotive of history is the people
   When we sing out loud and plain.

Again, no two singers will sing the exact same notes. Here are some of the variant melodies I use.

Verse 2   **C18**
Thank God they did-n't be-lieve that lie

Verse 2
Who knows, who knows, with spirit like that,
We can have progress the world a-round!

Verse 3
Look out the win-dow, There's old Ma-ma
Hud-son roll-ing on down to the sea.

Verse 3
And no matter what shape, size, color you are—

2nd & 3rd choruses 6th & 7th lines
There's a lit-tle more hope and that's a fact, And when the
nu-cle-ar ma-ni-acs get the sack etc.

© Len Munnik, Amsterdam

The best of the *Clearwater* songs are not in this book. Such as the new words Lorre Wyatt put to one of Jimmy Reed's rocking blues:

   Sailing Up (Sailing Up)
   Sailing Down (Sailing Down)
   Up! (down!) Down! (up!)
   Up and down the river
   Sailing on (sailing up, up, sailing up)
   Stopping all along the way
   The river may be dirty now
   But it's getting cleaner every day.

—also Rick Nestler's "River That Flows Both Ways"
   "I could be happy, spending my days   **C19**
   On the river that flows both way-y-ys."

Bob Killian's "Wind On the Water"   **C20**

Wind on the water, blowin' across the bay!

— and Bob's "There'll Come a Day"

There'll come a day the riv-ers will run a-gain

Favorites with every crew are songs by Bill Staines, like "River, Take Me Along." And his

All God's critters got a place in the choir

— and Lorre Wyatt's

So-mos el bar-co, so-mos el mar

— also Pat Humphries' "Swimming to the Other Side," Bob Reid's "Animals Need Water," Dan Einbender's "It Really Isn't Garbage." And many, many others. Some old ones are still favorites: "Drunken Sailor," "Shenandoah," "Bound for South Australia," "Roll the Old Chariot Along."

For these and hundreds of other Clearwater songs, try to find a copy of *For the Beauty of the Earth: An Environmental Songbook to Benefit the Hudson River Sloop Clearwater*, edited by Liza DiSavino. It's currently out-of-print, but look around for a copy. Or visit the Clearwater office.

The following song excerpts are used by permission:
"Sailing Up, Sailing Down" by Lorre Wyatt © 1984 Roots & Branches Music (BMI)
"River That Flows Both Ways" by Rick Nestler © 1983 Sanga Music, Inc.
"Wind on the Water" by Bob Killian © 1979 Bob Killian (ASCAP)
"There'll Come a Day" by Bob Killian © 1981 Bob Killian (ASCAP)
"A Place in the Choir" by Bill Staines © Mineral River Music (BMI)
"Somos El Barco" by Lorre Wyatt © 1984 Roots & Branches Music (BMI)

I saw a movie made by an anthropologist in the western Pacific, showing islanders strumming and a small crowd singing a friendly-sounding song. Said to myself, why couldn't we have a friendly-sounding song like that along the Hudson? Doesn't need a fancy melody. Just leave some ways a gang can join in without having to memorize a lot of words.

Broad Old River

C21

Friendly rhythm. Lots of harmony needed.

Come a-long with me___ (come a-long with me).
___ Up-on this broad old riv-er. Come a-long with me.
___ (come a-long with me)___ Up-on this
broad old riv-er. We will see (we will
see) What we can do (what we can do) For when we
work to-geth-er, in all kinds of
weath-er, There's no tell-ing what the pow-er of the
peo-ple And the riv-er can do (and the riv-er can do).

Music by Pete Seeger   Words by Pete Seeger and others
TRO - © 1993 Melody Trails, Inc., New York, NY.

1. Come along with me (come along with me)
Upon this broad old river.
Come along with me (come along with me)
Upon this broad old river.
And we will see (we will see)
What we can do (what we can do)
For when we work together, in all kinds of weather,
There's no telling what the power of the people
And the river can do (and the river can do).

2. Don't you be scared (don't you be scared)
Upon this broad old river.
Don't you be scared (don't you be scared)
Upon this broad old river.
Rockin' and rollin' (rockin' and rollin')
On all those waves (on all those waves)
For when we work together, in all kinds of weather,
No matter how the wind's gonna blow
We can be saved (we can be saved).

"We have an acronym, W.I.F.T.I., W.A.F.T.I.—Wind Is Fickle, Tide Implacable, Winds Are Fickle, Tides Implacable."

3. It's wifty wafty (it's wifty wafty)
Out on this broad old river.
It's wifty wafty (it's wifty wafty)
Out on this broad old river.
You can't half tell (you can't half tell)
What the future brings (what the future brings)
But if we work together, in all kinds of weather,
When the fickle winds fail we still
Got songs to sing (got songs to sing).

4. Lotsa songs to sing (lotsa songs to sing)
Upon this broad old river.
Lotsa songs to sing (lotsa songs to sing)
Upon this broad old river.
And we can sing (and we can sing)
When the old wind fails (when the old wind fails)
For when we sing together, in all kinds of weather,
With the power of the people and the voices
We can fill the sails (we can fill the sails).
(VERSE BY DAN EINBENDER)

5. Don'tcha give up hope (don'tcha give up hope)
Upon this broad old river.
Don'tcha give up hope (don'tcha give up hope)
Upon this broad old river.
Sooner or later (sooner or later)
The tide will turn (the tide will turn)
And when we work together, in all kinds of weather,
The teachers and the students
They both will learn (they both will learn).
(VERSE BY ???)

6. Come for a swim (come for a swim)
Into this broad old river.
Come for a swim (come for a swim)
Into this broad old river.
Bring the family down (bring the family down)
To the river shore (to the river shore)
You can see we're winning, just by going swimming,
You can see what we mean 'cause it's
Cleaner than it was before (than it was before)
(VERSE BY CAPT. TRAVIS JEFFREY)

7. We're gonna learn the ropes (gonna learn the ropes)
   Out on this broad old river.
   We're gonna learn the ropes (gonna learn the ropes)
   Out on this broad old river.
   Bowline and longsplice (long...splice)
   Clove hitch and square (clove hitch and square)
   And when we work together, in all kinds of weather,
   Like a lotta little fibers of rope we're
   Gonna hang in there (gonna hang in there).

8. Come fish with me (come fish with me)
   Out on this broad old river.
   Come fish with me (come fish with me)
   Out on this broad old river.
   And we will see (and we will see)
   What we can hook (what we can hook)
   But if we work together, in all kinds of weather,
   We know someday they'll be
   Clean enough to cook (clean enough to cook).

   (VERSE BY AL NEJMEH)

9. And you can help (and you can help)
   Clean up this broad old river.
   And you can help (and you can help)
   Clean up this broad old river.
   You'll never know (you'll never know)
   Until you try (until you try)
   But if we work together, in all kinds of weather,
   With the power of the people and the river
   We can turn the tide (we can turn the tide).

   (VERSE BY DAN EINBENDER)

Photo by Gretchen McHugh

10. Gotta lift your heart (gotta lift your heart)
    Out on this broad old river.
    Gotta lift your heart (gotta lift your heart)
    Out on this broad old river.
    Y'gotta understand (gotta understand)
    We got a job to do (got a job to do)
    But if we work together, in all kinds of weather,
    Before you know it this mighty river
    Will run clear through (will run clear through).

    (VERSE BY ROY DIGGIT)

(REPEAT FIRST VERSE FROM TIME TO TIME AS A CHORUS)

The Beacon Sloop Club is a sociable gang that likes to sing at its monthly meetings. It was a pleasant surprise to find others making up extra verses, such as:

> Lotsa songs to sing...
> Lotsa people to meet...
> Be prepared for storms...
> Read the book of nature...
> Gotta lift your eyes...
> Gotta lift your heart...
> Lift your feet...etc.

The second and fourth lines stay the same; the seventh and eighth lines usually also, but change sometimes as in Verse 4.

Clean Up the Hudson   C22

Calypso beat

1. Well, you know it was twen-ty years a-go, In-to New York har-bor there sailed a boat. Peo-ple laughed at such a fool - ish thought, to try to clean up the Hud-son. (spoken) ("Sing it with me now")

CHORUS

Clear-wa-ter, da da da da, Clear-wa-ter, da da da da, Clear - wa-ter, you kept your prom-ise to try to clean up the Hud - son!

Words by Pete Seeger (1989)   Music by Norman Span ("Matilda")
© 1953 (renewed), 1993 by MCA Music Publishing, a division of MCA, Inc.,
New York, NY 10019 and Colgems-EMI Music, Inc. International copyright secured.
All rights reserved. Used by permission.

1. Well, you know it was twenty years ago.
   Into New York Harbor there sailed a boat.
   People laughed at such a foolish thought,
   To try to clean up the Hudson.

   SPOKEN: *"Sing it with me now."*
   CHORUS (AFTER EACH VERSE):
      Clearwater, Da da da da,
         Clearwater, Da da da da,
      Clearwater, You kept your promise
         To try to clean up the Hudson!

2. Some people said we were a bunch of reds.
   Some said we smoked dope and were pot heads.
   But we ignored them and we pushed ahead
   To try to clean up the Hudson.

3. We held festivals in all the river towns.
   The young and old would gather 'round,
   With food and music to break the barriers down,
   And try to clean up the Hudson.

4. The beauty was there for all to see.
   It broke all resistance and eventually
   Even politicians began to agree
   To try to clean up the Hudson.

5. We taught classes in a brand new way
   While floating on the water on a breezy day.
   Kids caught fish, 'n' learned that it would pay
   To try to clean up the Hudson.

6. To raise the money we invented a way —
   The kids sail for free during the day.
   But for the evening sail the parents pay
   To try to clean up the Hudson.

7. Now so many schools want us to take them out.
   From Albany to New Jersey you hear them shout.
   Clearwater, you have to build more boats
   To try to clean up the Hudson.

8. Think globally, act locally.
   Sing and shout for a world that's free
   Of war and toxics and bigotry
   Once more for the Hudson.

9. These words were written in Albany jail.
   Goddess of Inspiration! You did not fail.
   Judge Keegan, send Pete there again without bail
   To try to clean up the Hudson.

Written while I was on a week's vacation, guest of Albany County jail, along with Rev. Al Sharpton and six others, as a result of protesting the Tawana Brawley decision and demanding a special prosecutor in racial bias cases. In jail I had time to write a song. No telephone calls. No mail. No dishes to wash.

One of my favorite American folk songs, learned from Alan Lomax over 50 years ago, was "Long John" — an African-American axe-chopping song (tune is right out of West Africa). With Captain Travis Jeffrey's help, the *Clearwater* got a rope-hauling song.

It's a Long Haul   C23

1. Uh-one day, one day (one day, one day), I was walk-ing a-long (I was walk-ing a-long), I

heard a lit-tle child (I heard a lit-tle child), Just a-

sing-ing a song___ (just a-sing-ing a song),*

CHORUS

It's a long haul,___ It's a high haul,___

It's a job for the man-y, Not just for the few,

It's a job for ev-'ry-bo-dy, That's

me and you,___ It's a long haul,___ It's a

high haul,___ It's a hard haul.___

Words & music adaptation by Pete Seeger & Travis Jeffrey (1987)
Adapted from the song "Long John (Long Gone)", collected & arranged by
John A. & Alan Lomax
TRO - © 1934 (renewed), 1993 Folkways Music Publishers, Inc. & Melody Trails,
Inc., New York, NY.

* The crowd repeats each line.

1. One day one day
   I was walking along
   I heard a little child
   Just a-singing a song.

2. About haulin' together,
   Keepin' in time.
   Hauling on a halyard,
   Making up a rhyme.

CHORUS (AFTER EVEN-NUMBERED VERSES):
It's a long haul
It's a high haul
It's a job for the many
Not just for the few
It's a job for everybody
That's me and you
It's a long haul
It's a high haul
It's a hard haul.

3. Now don'tcha get weary
   And don'tcha get tired
   If you don't keep hauling
   You all get fired

4. We're cleaning up a river
   So we all can swim
   Yes the rich and the poor
   Yes the her and the him.
   (CHO.)

5. We got Captain _____
   He's/she's got a sharp eye
   And we all call him/her
   Captain Bligh.

6. Yes Captain _____
   Will make you toe the mark
   If you don't do your job
   You get thrown to the
   sharks. (CHO.)

7. It's haulin' all together
   Each doin' what they can
   In all kindsa weather
   Each woman and man.

8. It's haulin' in the sunshine
   Haulin' in the rain
   When we haul together
   Then there's no pain. (CHO.)

9. So—sail the river
   Spring to fall
   Don't give up the struggle
   For us all.

10. It's a beautiful life
    Flowing down to the sea
    Got to get this world
    In harmony. (CHO.)

11. Yes it's a beautiful boat
    And a beautiful place
    And a beautiful thing
    We call the human race.

12. And a beautiful river
    So many beautiful things
    It can make you shiver
    It can make you sing. (CHO.)

*This song needs a group, a gang, to repeat each line after the
song leader, no matter what he/she sings. The chorus, sung after
every two or three verses, can use some high harmony.

Variant melodies in subsequent verses:

(repeat) (repeat)

(repeat) (repeat)

Harmony ideas:

It's a long haul

Photo by John Putnam

This is a *Clearwater* version of a song put together by Lead Belly. He took a field holler with verses about "Old Riley" who escaped (from prison, from slavery) and combined them with a rhythmic axe-chopping song with verses about a man who escaped, even though the hound dogs were hot on his trail. It made a great performance piece for him. After he died, the Weavers used to sing it with full harmony. The slow opening and closing make a framework for the rhythmic center section. The notes here are basically the Weavers' arrangement. I just rewrote the words for *Clearwater*.

Haul, Make Her Go High

Words & music adaptation by Pete Seeger (1978)
Tune: "Old Riley (In Them Long Hot Summer Days)" by Huddie Ledbetter, collected & arranged by John A. Lomax & Alan Lomax
TRO - © 1936 (renewed), 1992 Folkways Music Publishers, Inc. & Melody Trails, Inc., New York, NY.

INTRODUCTION (AND ENDING):

Clearwater's on the river,
Clearwater's on the river,
And it's a long haul you better believe.

2. Well it's a little piece o' pumpkin, little piece of pie
     Haul, Make her go high!
   I want to see clear water before I die
     Haul, Make her go high!

REFRAIN (AFTER EACH VERSE):
   Well it's hey! Clearwater!
     Haul, Make her go high!
   Hey, Clearwater!
     Haul, Make her go high!

3.   Albany's up but the Battery's down (Haul, etc.)
   Now we're headed to Kingston town (Haul, etc.)

4. We'll heist her high without delay (Haul, etc.)
   A few more pulls and then belay (Haul, etc.)

Add more verses as needed. End by repeating the slow introductory verse.

Any experienced arranger of music for choruses will recognize from the above that I am not an experienced arranger of music for choruses. Nevertheless I've helped many to sing in harmony, and have tried to indicate here how adding a few notes above or below the melody can make the music more fun for everybody. The choral music I most admired was that of African Americans — sacred or sinful. It was rarely written down, and it changed from verse to verse.

Nowadays I try and persuade choruses that sometimes they should try and find notes which audiences can sing with them. Bach did it, why can't we?

★ ★ ★

Now We Sit Us Down `C25`

A two-part song to pull folks together and get them ready for some sort of meeting.

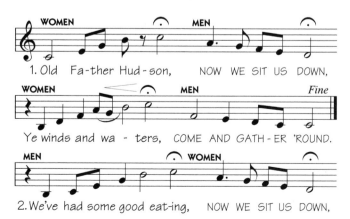

Words & music by Pete Seeger (1985)
TRO - © 1993 Melody Trails, Inc., New York, NY.

1. Old Father Hudson
   NOW WE SIT US DOWN
   Ye winds and waters
   COME AND GATHER
      'ROUND.

2. We've had some good eating
   NOW WE SIT US DOWN
   So let's start the meeting
   COME AND GATHER
      'ROUND.

3. Mighty full agenda
   NOW WE SIT US DOWN
   It's quite a mind bender!
   COME AND GATHER
      'ROUND.

4. But if we all choose our
      words well
   NOW WE SIT US DOWN
   We'll avoid the too-long-
      talker's hell
   COME AND GATHER
      'ROUND.

REPEAT FIRST VERSE

Of course, if this song works, it should eventually get rich harmony on the last four words:

THE SLOOP *CLEARWATER* WITH SCHOOLCHILDREN

The last song proved hard to teach, so I put similar words to a friendlier melody (see p. 180, where it's given in detail):

Take a Seat, Everybody

Words & music arrangement by Pete Seeger (1986)
Music adapted from "Minuit" by Keita Fodeba & Paul Winter

1. Take a seat... ev'rybody... sit down!...
   The meeting... won't be long... just gather 'round...
   Oyey... oyey, oyey, oh—oo...
   Oyey... oyey... oyey, <u>oyey</u>...

2. You see... what the agenda... will cover...
   If we are brief,... it will soo...<u>oon</u> be over...
   Oyey... oyey, oyey, oh—oo...
   Oyey... oyey... oyey, <u>oyey</u>...

3. And <u>if</u> we all... choose... our words well...
   We'll avoid... the too...oo long talker's Hell...
   *Ah ha la la la (4x)
   (INTERRUPT:) "OK, Let's get started."

*See p. 180

★ ★ ★

A musical digression.

For a century or more there's been a practice with many commercial songs: the well-known performer's name gets added to the unknown songwriter's name, for a share in the royalties. The justification? "This song wouldn't have gone anywhere without my help; I should share in the future profits."

The legal situation is almost the opposite. Singer B changes songwriter A's song, which now "takes off." But the law says that all of B's changes belong to A.

Here's a f'rinstance:

In the 1930s two African-American jazzmen, Slim Gaillard and Slam Stewart, liked to make up scat versions of popular tunes. They'd keep the original chords, and the main outlines of the melody, and add a lot of nonsense words. A popular swing band, Johnny Long's Orchestra, had hit records playing them. In '88 I spoke with Slam Stewart on the phone. "No, we didn't get a dime of royalties. Not even label credit. But that's life." He laughed.

"Slim and Slam" did have one big hit, "Flat Foot Floogie with a Floy, Floy." They've both gone to jazzmen's heaven now. But here's two samples of what they did with pop songs. The first is the 1932 slow, sentimental "Shantytown."

"In a Shanty in Old Shanty Town" Words by Joe Young Music by Jack Little & John Siras
© 1932 (renewed) Warner Bros. Music. Used by permission.

They'd first play the song "straight." Then they'd speed up the tempo almost twice as fast for their version.

Shantytown

Slim and Slam also improvised on Irving Berlin's 1926 hit song "Blue Skies." Here's the original. What a gem!

Blue Skies

Blue skies___ smiling at me.___ Nothing but

blue skies___ do I see.___

Blue-birds___ singing a song;___ nothing but

blue - birds___ all day long.___

Never saw the sun shining so bright. Never saw things

going so right. Noticing the days hurrying by;

when you're in love, my how they fly. Blue days,

___ all of them gone.___ Noth-ing but

blue skies___ from now on.

A Clearwater volunteer with a little help from me made up these new words to Slim and Slam's considerably changed melody. Now you can see why this musical digression got put in this chapter.

Blue Skies
(Clearwater Version)

Well it rained all night and I'm

feel-in' up-tight when I face this cit-y and I'm

feel-in' kind-a grit-ty, Oh, blue days!

Do I, do I, do I,___ do I need a new be-

gin-ning. Got-ta push, got-ta shove, got-ta

scratch a-round for love, got-ta squeeze my frame in a

slow com-mut-er train, Oh, blue days!

What else is there to do?___ I'm bushed.

Then I see that sloop

sail-ing up-stream. Take heart,__ take heart,__ it

ain't just a dream. Breath-in' in the breeze,

smell-in' the air.___ Gon-na do some-thing, work___

___ for what I care so sing out the good news!

Bye Bye Blues!— Take it slow, take it slow, you nev-er have to go, An' it's Blue Skies! — for me, from now on. ("Blue skies smiling at me!") Blue skies...etc.

Words & music by Irving Berlin   Adaptation by Slim Gaillard & Slam Stewart
New lyrics by Pete Seeger & Michael Scherker (1989)
© 1927 (renewed) by Irving Berlin. International copyright secured. Used by
permission. All right reserved.

When Clearwater's Walkabout Chorus does it, we start off singing Berlin's original song, uptempo. Then quite fast, we sing the Clearwater words:

Well it rained all night, and I'm feelin' uptight, when I
I face this city feeling kinda gritty, Oh, blue days!
　Do I, do I, do I, do I need a new beginning.
Gotta push, gotta shove, scratch around for love,
Gotta squeeze my frame in a slow commuter train,
　Oh, blue days! What else is there to do? I'm bushed.
Then I see that sloop sailin' up stream
Take heart, take heart, It ain't just a dream,
Breathin' in the breeze, smellin' the air,
Gonna do something, work for what I care
So – sing out the good news! – Bye bye blues
Take it slow, take it slow, You never have to go
'Cause it's blue skies for me from now on
　　(CALLED OUT: "Blue skies smiling at me")

The songleader, calling out the words in parentheses cues the whole audience to join in, without skipping a beat, singing Berlin's original song again real slow. The chorus adds a lot of high harmony.

Blue skies...smiling at me! ("nothing but blue skies")
Nothing but blue skies ("do I see") do I see ("bluebirds")
Blue...birds... ("singin' a song") singin' a song... (etc.)

When it comes to the bridge, the songleader's words almost overlap with the audience singing but if the tempo is slow, the words of each short phrase can be called out while the audience is holding out the long note:

Noticing the days ("hurrying by")
Hurrying by ("when you're in love")
When you're in love... ("my how they fly") (etc.)

And it all ends with a great ritard. G ... Cm ... G!
Well, if there's a human race here 500 years from now, this will be called an old folk song, just as is "Greensleeves," a 16th Century English pop song.

In 1972 shad fisherman Ron Ingolds gave us free shad for *Clearwater*'s first shad festival. Every spring he and a few helpers lived on the waterfront for a month, setting nets or taking them in every six hours when the tide changed, while only snatching a few hours sleep at a time. I wrote these words for him and his helpers, using a great old German melody. At age 88 I still got audiences singing this song.

Of Time and Rivers Flowing

C31

1. Of time and rivers flowing
   The seasons make a song.
   And we who live beside her
   Still try to sing along
   　Of rivers, fish, and men
   　And the season still a-coming
   　When she'll run clear again.

2. So many homeless sailors,
   So many winds that blow.
   I asked the half blind scholars
   Which way the currents flow
   　So cast your nets below
   　And the gods of moving waters
   　Will tell us all they know.

3. The circles of the planets,
   The circles of the moon,
   The circles of the atoms,
   All play a marching tune,
   　And we who would join in
   　Can stand aside no longer
   　Now let us all begin.

Words by Pete Seeger (1973)
Music: "Es ist ein Ros entsprungen" (Lo How a Rose Ere Blooming)
© 1974, 1993 by Sanga Music Inc.

Here's the German melody, "Es ist ein Ros entsprungen." College choirs know the English translation, "Lo, How a Rose Ere Blooming."

The melody is from an old German Christmas carol harmonized by Praetorius — too pretentiously, in my opinion. After 25 years of experimentation, I feel that a driving syncopated rhythm with an audience sing-a-long is the best way to do it — at least for me. I wrote it out for our Clearwater Walkabout Chorus. But as a soloist I call out the words and can get a large crowd to join in.

In 1972 when I first wrote the song, I tried singing it slowly. The song was a failure, at least with my voice. Fifteen years later I started singing it less pretentiously, with a fast rhythm. All of a sudden it "worked" — and I could get a crowd to sing it with me. Again, you'll see how I give words to the crowd, line by line (*italics*).

Of Time and Rivers Flowing
(For a Songleader and Group)

*I've written it out for a chorus, but any soloist and guitar can get a crowd joining the refrain (**boldface**). Ritard at end.

**In primary schools I have to sing "the spirits of moving waters."

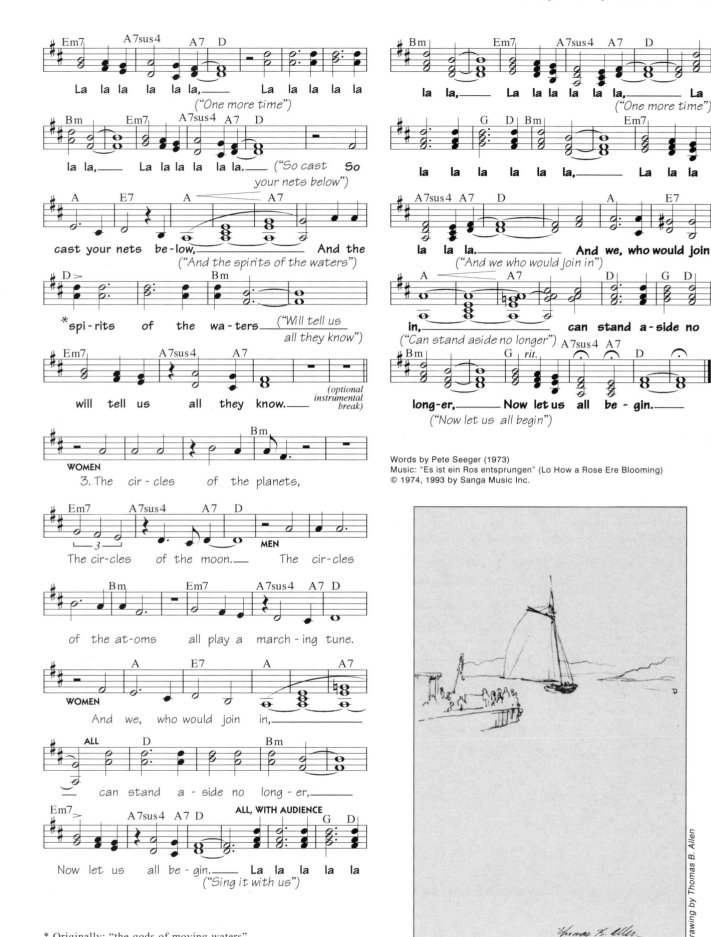

La la la la la la,_____ La la la la la

la la,_____ La la la la la la._____ ("So cast So

("One more time")

cast your nets be-low,_____ And the

("And the spirits of the waters")

*spi - rits of the wa - ters_____

("Will tell us all they know")

will tell us all they know._____

(optional instrumental break)

WOMEN

3. The cir - cles of the planets,

The cir - cles of the moon._____ **MEN** The cir - cles

of the at-oms all play a march - ing tune.

WOMEN

And we, who would join in,_____

ALL

can stand a - side no long - er,_____

ALL, WITH AUDIENCE

Now let us all be - gin._____ La la la la la

("Sing it with us")

la la,_____ La la la la la la,_____ La

("One more time")

la la la la la la,_____ La la la

la la la._____ And we, who would join

("And we who would join in")

in,_____ can stand a - side no

("Can stand aside no longer")

long-er,_____ Now let us all be - gin._____

("Now let us all begin")

Words by Pete Seeger (1973)
Music: "Es ist ein Ros entsprungen" (Lo How a Rose Ere Blooming)
© 1974, 1993 by Sanga Music Inc.

* Originally: "the gods of moving waters"

Drawing by Thomas B. Allen

Martha + Huddie ②   Somewhere at Sea
                 Dec 13, 1943

We have been awful lucky in some ways. We have been able to meet thousands of the very best kind of friends and they have always made their home our home, all because they liked the songs we sang and because you people are so nice. We've had some hard knocks and some rough going, but no matter how hard and rocky the road, our friends never quit us, never let us down, and they're the kind of people that will stick with us always. I know you already know this, but I just want you to know how you made me feel tonight when I heard you on the radio. (Of course Martha knows that what I say goes for her, too, because she is really what makes Leadbelly keep going.) It is now that we're apart that I really see how close we are together. Your guitar and mine both talk the same language - the language of the working people. When our guitars come in there together they talk their own language. I just wish I could have played my guitar along with you tonight, but I couldn't get to it. You can just imagine how I sweated and shook all over, hearing you play, and not able to play with you. The last time we played together was up at Pete & Toshi's wedding party - we had 3 banjos - boy - we really raised the roof that night, didn't we? I want to say I am speaking for our whole crew here on the ship - we all enjoyed your program. How much, I don't guess I could ever write it down.

  Well, just remember, we're out here listening to you and thinking about you. Here's to a couple of the nicest folks I ever hope to know -

         Your friend as ever
         Woody Guthrie

LETTER TO LEAD BELLY FROM WOODY GUTHRIE, SOMEWHERE AT SEA, DECEMBER 13, 1943

Chapter 10: *Well May the World Go*

You like this cartoon? Check out Bülbül's book, *Drawing My Times*, Arachne Pub., P.O. Box 4100, Mountain View, CA 94040. $14.95 + shipping.

I think we judge time by how long we've been on earth. When I was 13, six of us school friends pledged a reunion 10 years later. Those 10 years seemed about as long to me then as the 50 years that have flicked by since I was questioned by the House Un-American Activities Committee in '55. Which is logical; 10 years then was about half my conscious lifetime.

As you know, as a kid, I was a nature nut. Between age seven and twelve I read every single book by Ernest Thompson Seton, the Canadian author of *Wild Animals I Have Known, Rolf In the Woods* and others. Then I started reading more widely. Age 16, came a turning point in my life. My mother was teaching violin to the teenagers in a Jewish family (Kantrovich – some of them later became well-known scientists).

At a weekend at their house in Connecticut we got in a long discussion on what to do with one's life. I announced that I was going to be a hermit, because in this world full of hypocrisy that was the only way to stay an honest man. They jumped on me like a load of bricks. That's your idea of morality? You're going to stay nice and pure and let the rest of the world go to hell? They posed their traditional Jewish social conscience against my more New England Thoreau way of thinking.

I decided they were right. Started getting more involved, and have been ever since. But still my favorite way to relax is a walk or a work session in the woods.

I've com-mit-ted crimes against Na-ture, stay-ing in-doors on sun-ny days.

And about every April I feel like singing this verse, to the tune of "Midnight Special."

Bright Yellow Forsythia

1. Bright yellow for-sythia, just pretty as you please. Daf-fy-dils and li-lacs, and all the dogwood trees.— So— many colors, makes your heart want to sing. You can thank your luck-y stars— for giv-ing one more spring.—

Here's a good example of how changing a few notes can make quite a different melody, for words following a different purpose. Do you know someone building a community garden in some city? Tell 'em to get a gang together to complete this song.

Sing it in their local schools, or churches, unions or other organizations. Change my words as needed. Add specifics, such as the name and address, and when their garden was started and by whom. Tell their hopes for the future, and their plans to thwart the developers who will want to bulldoze it all and build a highrise when you have improved the neighborhood.

New lyrics & adaptation by Pete Seeger (1980)
Adapted from "The Midnight Special" by Huddie Ledbetter
Collected & arranged by John A. Lomax & Alan Lomax
TRO - © 1936 (renewed) & 1993 Folkways Music Publishers, Inc. & Melody Trails, Inc., New York, NY.

The words of the next song are by that close friend, a Communist poet, now dead, Walter Lowenfels. See p. 95.

Tomorrow's Children C33

English translation by Walter Lowenfels (from the French of Guillevic)
Music by Pete Seeger (1964)
© 1964 (renewed) by Stormking Music Inc.

1. But you who know days of a diff'rent kind,
   Tomorrow's children for whom work is more like play,
   And living is what poems are for me today,
   A passionate utterance carefully designed.

2. Remember us, the lame, the deaf, the blind,
   Not for the stupid things we've done and can't forget;
   Nor the endless dull jobs over which we all sweat,
   Nor all the sad chronicles that we leave behind.

   BRIDGE:
   But that we loved as much as anyone ever did,
   That we knew joys, the little deeds, the grand design.
   The dream of changing the world to something new.
   Believe us, in our way we loved to live.

3. Know that many, many things we loved,
   and of all of these,
   Our greatest joy was in opening the way for you.

Lest you think all of Walter's poems were serious or political here's another of his, a short one.

These bones you see
    so cold, so white and dead
Were once a young
    and agile girl in bed.

It was back in the late 1960s the telephone rang: "This is Otto Preminger speaking. (Thick Viennese accent.) Are you the Pete Seeger who makes up songs and sings them?"

"Yes," I reply.

"Well, I want to know if you can write me a song about the will to live."

"Why, that's my business."

"I have a movie which is about the will to live, and I want a song. Can you come to New York? You can see a screening of the rough cut of the movie."

A few days later Toshi and I were sitting in a comfortable apartment eating a very good meal with Hollywood producer Otto Preminger and his wife. He was a heavy-set man, 10 or more years older than I. A direct and honest way of speaking.

We saw the movie screened in his living room. It had been made from a novel, written by a nurse, about three people who leave a hospital at the same time. They decide to pool their meager resources and get a house. One is a young man, gay, who will be in a wheelchair the rest of his life as a result of a beating. A young woman has her face permanently scarred because of car battery acid splashed in her face by a man she had spurned and then laughed at. The third is a young man who is an epileptic and will never know when one of his seizures may kill him. The story showed the capacity of ordinary people to survive.

"I need a song to go under the titles of the movie at the beginning of the picture. Will one month be enough for you? Can we set the date now for you to fly out to California for the song to be filmed?"

I said, "Yes," and during the month spent numerous hours trying this idea and that, but not really being satisfied completely with any one idea. Toshi was a little worried. "Do you think you have Preminger's song ready?"

"Yes, I think so." (I lied.)

We landed at Los Angeles to meet Preminger and a camera crew of four or five people. "Can I hear the song now while we are waiting for the plane to Fresno?"

"Well, I have actually several songs. We'll see which one you think is best." I believe I sang three or four to him — some old folk songs with some new verses. I can't remember which ones. They might have been Gospel songs or spirituals. "There are still a couple more I have in mind." I could see Preminger was not enthusiastic about any one of them.

We had a one-hour plane flight to Fresno. It was now or never. I borrowed pencil and paper from Toshi. With the airplane drone in my ears, I managed to compose a "new" song. Nothing like a deadline to force something out of you. From the dregs of my subconscious, I scraped five verses. Used some repetition, and a melody derived from old ballads.

In the Fresno airport, I sang it for Preminger and the rest.

Old Devil Time

1. Old Devil Time, I'm— gonna fool you now!— Old Devil Time,— you'd like— to bring me down!— When— I'm feeling low,— my lovers gather 'round— And help me rise— to fight you one more time!—

Words & music by Pete Seeger (1969)
© 1969, 1970 by Sanga Music Inc. & Sigma Productions Inc.

1. Old Devil Time, I'm goin' to fool you now!
   Old Devil Time, you'd like to bring me down!
   When I'm feeling low, my lovers gather 'round
   And help me rise to fight you one more time!

2. Old Devil Fear, you with your icy hands,
   Old Devil Fear, you'd like to freeze me cold!
   But when I'm sore afraid, my lovers gather 'round
   And help me rise to fight you one more time!

3. Old Devil Pain, you often pinned me down,
   You thought I'd cry, and beg you for the end.
   But at that very time, my lovers gather 'round
   And help me rise to fight you one more time!

4. Old Devil Hate, I knew you long ago,
   Then I found out the poison in your breath.
   Now when we hear your lies, my lovers gather 'round
   And help me rise to fight you one more time!

5. No storm or fire can ever beat us down,
   No wind that blows but carries us further on.
   And you who fear, oh lovers, gather 'round
   And we can rise and sing it one more time!

REPEAT THE 5TH VERSE WITH EVERYBODY JOINING IN

"Yes, that will do very well, I think," said he. "Why didn't you sing that one to me first?"

"I only just made it up in the plane."

"Oh, don't tell me that. You had it all along."

Next day we drove out to the Sequoia groves in the Sierras, where they filmed me singing the song while tromping through the underbrush around the huge trees, even as a light snow was starting to fall. The next afternoon in Los Angeles with the film fresh from the developers, I recorded it again, "lip-sync," with studio quality. A few months later the film was out: *Tell Me That You Love Me, Junie Moon*, with Liza Minnelli. It was not a "hit," but it was a good movie. I am glad it is being seen now on DVD.

Preminger paid what was for me a huge sum — something like $1,500 or $2,000 for the first-rights use of the song, but I have been repaid many times over in getting a good song to sing from time to time in a program. I find I can do without the third verse, but I like to repeat the last verse a couple times so the audience can sing it with me.

I speak, "No storm or fire can ever beat us down." Then I sing it and hope some will sing it with me. "No wind that blows but carries us further on." Then more start to sing it with me.

I keep the soft rhythm going while I speak the next lines, "And you who fear, oh lovers, gather round. And we can rise and sing it one more time." And then the crowd will sing those two lines, and I call out, "And we can rise and sing it." And with a slight ritard at the end, I can usually get nearly everybody to join in.

"And we can rise and sing it — one more time."

I'm a lucky songwriter. Thank you, Otto, wherever you are.

I said the tune was derivative. See its similarity to the famous old English ballad "Barbara Allen," and its first-cousin-melody, "Come All Ye Fair and Tender Ladies."

Barbara Allen C35

Freely! (notes can be shortened as well as lengthened)

In Scar-let Town, where I was born,

There was a fair maid dwel-lin',

Made man-y a youth cry: Well-a-day,

And her name was Bar - b'ry Al-len.

Traditional English ballad

Come All Ye Fair and Tender Ladies

Come all ye fair____ and ten-der la-dies,____ Take warn-ing how____ you court young men. They're like the____ stars of a sum-mer's morning. They'll first ap-pear____ and then they're gone.

Traditional Southern Appalachian

I'm glad to see others singing "Old Devil Time" now, but I'm sorry so many seem to miss one of my favorite notes.

I wrote it: Somebody musta recorded it:

When I'm feeling low____   When I'm feeling low____

It's an old trick of melody writers to outline a chord by the notes of a melody. Hoagy Carmichael's great 1930 song "Stardust" did it.

Fiddle tunes do it all the time. Remember "The Irish Washerwoman"?

Marion Wade added a good new verse.

Old Devil Time, we're gonna fool you now
With words and tunes, the love we leave behind
And before our time is done, we think of those to come
Our voices rise to sing it one more time.

If I'm sitting around, improvising on the guitar, one of my favorite keys is A. That's how "Mexican Blues" was made up, also the next two.

Maple Syrup Time

1. First you get the buck-ets read-y,

clean the pans and gather fire-wood, Late in the winter,

it's ma-ple syrup time._____ You need warm and

sun-ny days_ but still a cold and freezing night-time

For just a few weeks, maple_ syrup time. We

boil and boil and boil and boil it all day long._

Till nine-ty sev'n per-cent of wa-ter e -

vap - o - rates just like this song, And when

what is left is syr-up-y_ don't leave it too long._

Watch out for burning! Maple_ syrup time.

Words (1975) & music (1967) by Pete Seeger
© 1977, 1979 by Sanga Music Inc.

1. First you get the buckets ready, clean the pans and
      gather firewood,
   Late in the winter, it's maple syrup time.
   You need warm and sunny days but still a cold and
      freezing nighttime
   For just a few weeks, maple syrup time.
   We boil and boil and boil and boil it all day long,
   Till ninety sev'n percent of water evaporates just
      like this song
   And when what is left is syrupy don't leave it
      too long—
   Watch out for burning! Maple syrup time.

(IF THERE'S ANYONE LISTENING TO ME, I ASK THEM TO MAKE THE
SOUND OF MARACAS WITH THEIR LIPS):
   sh-sh-sh-sh—"keep it up through the whole song."

2. I know it's not the quickest system but each year I
      can't resist it.
   Get out the buckets, and tap the trees in time—
   Making it is half the fun, and satisfaction when
      it's done.
   Keep up the fire! Maple syrup time.
   My grandpa says perhaps it's just a waste of time.
   Ah! but no more than this attempt to make a happy
      little rhyme,
   So pat your feet or swing your tail, but keep in
      good time.
   Keep up the fire! Maple syrup time.

3. I'll send this song around the world with love to
      ev'ry boy and girl,
   Hoping they don't mind a little advice in rhyme.
   As in life or revolution, rarely is there a quick
      solution,
   Anything worthwhile takes a little time.
   We boil and boil and boil and boil it all day long.
   When what is left is syrupy, don't leave it on the
      flame too long.
   But seize the minute, build a new world, sing an
      old song.
   Keep up the fire! Maple syrup time.

I got the idea for this tune 40 years ago when trying
to help steel bands become better known. No steel band
ever picked up my tune, but 15 years later I found words
for it, to send as a Christmas present to old friends in
Maine.

The original words were, "I'll send this song to
Scott and Helen/Up in Maine where they are dwellin',"
for Scott and Helen Nearing who wrote *The Maple
Sugar Book*, and got me started syruping.

Here's a fun way to play it on the guitar.

Maple Syrup Time
(Guitar Part)

C39

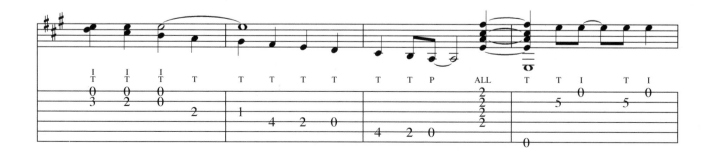

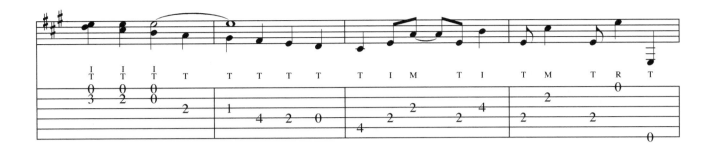

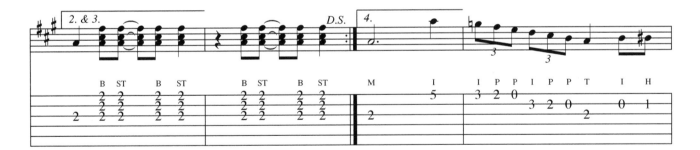

Guitar arrangement by Pete Seeger
© 1977, 1979 by Sanga Music Inc.

This tune I've never played on a stage, but I play it often when riding in a train or waiting in an airport. I can't remember when it began to take shape.

Spring Fever

By Pete Seeger (1973)
© 1993 by Sanga Music Inc.

(The last four measures I usually save for a final ending. Meanwhile I can experiment with variations in the piece. Below are just two possibilities)

*Variant first measure:

**Variant:

*** It's less difficult than it looks. The left middle finger frets both the 5th and 4th strings, sliding up and holding it for the next note.

Sour Cream

C41

My name is Pat-rick Spud-nut, pho-
tog-ra-pher by trade. I
trav-el this world o-ver, some think I got it made.
But while I film the world of fash-ion, I
Yes...
real-ly have a se-cret pas-sion,
I spend all my cash on so-ur cream.

Words & music by Pete Seeger (1976)
TRO - © 1979 Melody Trails, Inc., New York, NY.

1. My name is Patrick Spudnut* photographer by trade.
   I travel this world over, some think I got it made.
   But while I film the world of fashion,
   I really have a secret passion.
   I spend all my cash on sour cream.
   Yes, while I film the world of fashion,
   I really have a secret passion,
   I spend all my cash on sour cream.

2. Sour cream forever, emblazoned on my heart
   You know I can't forget you, I told you from the start.
   But if I ramble now and then,
   You know I will return again,
   Because I can't forget you, sour cream.
   Yes, if I ramble now and then,
   You know I will return again,
   Because I can't forget you, sour cream.

3. Sour cream, in salad or in soup,
   With you inside me I can really loop the loop the loop.
   Civilization will flower.
   Black, brown and buff can have cow power,
   When we all have plenty of sour cream.
   Civilization will flower.
   Black, brown and buff can have cow power,
   When we all have plenty of sour cream.

*Fake name. No need to libel a good friend. But he did arrive with a whole
quart of sour cream, saying, "I knew you wouldn't have enough."

Variants:

2. So-ur cream for-ev-er, em-bla-zoned in my heart...

3. So-ur cream, in sal-ad or in soup

About 10 years ago, chopping a dead tree down for
firewood, I had to face the fact that I was getting more
and more out of condition. Getting out of breath. Found
myself carrying on a tradition, making up a chopping
song — based on an older tune.

Lord Ha' Mercy On Me

C42

Lord ha' mer-cy on me! Chop me down
like I do this old tree. Take me 'way when I've
o-ver-reached my time. Yes, take me
'way when I've o-ver-reached my time.

Words by Pete Seeger (1988)   Music: traditional ("Old Reuben")
© 1993 by Fall River Music Inc.

Where'd I get the tune? Alan Lomax heard it from
the Golden Gate Quartet, like 70 years ago. Taught it to
me. It's also similar to "Keep Your Eyes on the Prize."

Old Reuben

Well they got old Reu-ben down and they stole his watch and
chain. It was all that poor boy ev-er had. It was
all that poor boy ev-er had. Cry-in' Reu-ben, cry-in'
Reu-ben. Say-in' Where have you been so long?

Traditional (U.S.A.)

(European harmonies aren't really needed for this African-
American melody. I bet it *is* an African tune.)

In the early 1930s, those deep Depression days, Lawrence Gellert came back from a trip down south with some extraordinary songs which were later printed by Communists in a book, *Negro Songs of Protest*. Years later, when he was an old man, I found these lyrics which he'd collected then, now reprinted in Dr. Philip Foner's mammoth volume, *Labor Songs of the 19th Century*. I wrote Larry for the tune, but his notes were indecipherable. I ended up making a new tune for them, and was proud when Brother Fred Kirkpatrick started singing this song about the 1831 Nat Turner rebellion of African slaves in Virginia.

BROTHER FRED KIRKPATRICK

The Gainin' Ground C43

("Nat Turner") Words: author unknown (1831) Music by Pete Seeger (1977)
TRO - © 1993 Melody Trails, Inc., New York, NY.

1. You might* be rich as cream,
   Drive you a coach and a four-horse team.
REFRAIN:
But you can't keep this world from turnin' round,
   turnin' round.
Nor Nat Turner from the gainin' ground, gainin' ground.
No you can't keep this world from turnin' round,
   turnin' round.
Nor Nat Turner from the gainin' ground, gainin' ground.

2. You might* be reader and writer too.
   Wiser than old Solomon the Jew. (REFRAIN)

3. And your name might* be Caesar, sure.
   You got cannon can shoot shoot a mile or more.
   (REFRAIN)

*Gellert's spelling was "mought." A more common southern pronunciation would be "maht."

THE CAPTURE OF NAT TURNER, 1831

Contemporary newspaper engraving

At Christmas time I sing carols, but I also sing "Chanukah, Oh Chanukah" and "In My Window," the song my niece, Kate, named "The Chanukah Chase." I love the few Yiddish folk songs I've heard. "Oyfn Pripichik." "Tumbalalaika." If I have a recorder with me, I may play the Yiddish lullaby written in New York in the late 19th Century, "Rozhinkes Mit Mandeln (Raisins With Almonds)" or the partisan song "Shtille di nacht." This last is a song I'll never forget. In 1943 Poland, Hirsh Glick, age 19, wrote a song for a girl:

Originally in Yiddish: "Shtille di nacht"

The night was still
And the stars shone
On the frosty ground.
Oh do you remember
I taught you to hold
A pistol in your hand.

In memory of them, the next song.

Embers of the Martyrs
(The Smoke of Treblinka)

`C44`

1. And still I choke on the smoke of Treblinka.
Wild winds weep over the bones of the dead.
In those gray spaces sacred souls are soaring
The hot ashes of the martyrs rain upon my head.
Forever these sacred ashes will wail in my heart.
In their searing my soul forever will groan,
Endless will be the Kaddish of my song.
In my blood, forever, a Kaddish will moan.

Those words were written by a man older than I. I put a tune to it after I read his poem in the magazine *Jewish Currents*.

Could a non-Jew presume to add anything to this? Ber Green died before I could show him my verse. It's for a children's chorus to sing. Modulate to a key good for kids.

Verse 2: But We Are Here

2. But we are here and we'll not forget you.   `C45`
We are here to build and to say:
The martyrs' ashes circle all the world now,
And we, yes we will find a way.
We'll remember; we will build, and you will live on
And your soul, your soul will mingle with theirs
Endless will be the brokhe that we bring...
In our blood, forever, your song will still... sing.

Thanks to Morris U. Shappes, editor of *Jewish Currents* for supplying the word "brokhe." It means "blessing" in Yiddish, derived from the Hebrew.

Poem in Yiddish by Ber Green   English translation by Martin Birnbaum
Music by Pete Seeger (1978)
TRO - © 1975 & 1993 Melody Trails, Inc., New York, NY.

"The truth will set you free, but first it will piss you off."

— Gloria Steinem

People think that what makes America strong is military might, powerful industry, mechanized agriculture. But I think it's the ancient tradition of forming organizations of all sorts, to get a job done. De Tocqueville pointed this out in the 1830s. Put a couple hundred Americans out on a prairie to start a town. Six months later they have religious and social organizations, political and business organizations, sports organizations, educational organizations. Keep in mind: the test of any organization is its ability to renew itself.

© Saul Steinberg

I drifted out of the Communist Party in the early '50s when I moved to the country. In the deepest sense of the word, I guess, I'm still a communist. I'd like to see a world without millionaires.

I often joke that I became a communist at age seven when I read about American Indians. No rich, no poor. Life and death decisions made around a council fire. And I've been fascinated to visit communes of one sort or another around the world to see how they attempt to solve problems. Including a kibbutz in Israel, a Christian commune in New York State. I admit, like most book writers, perhaps I'm a capitalist of the imagination, investing time and money to put out a book, then sitting back hoping it sells. Actually, a lot of songwriters look on themselves as gamblers, losing money most of the time, but hoping once in a while to hit the jackpot.

The problem: how to balance the positive values of competition with the positive values of cooperation. Locally, worldwide. Such thoughts led to the next song. As the Civil Rights coalition started to break up, I was also involved in helping some good people I knew who were in prison.

I still sing this when I sing in prisons.

Walking Down Death Row

1. Walk-ing down death row, I sang for three men, des-tined for the chair; Walk-ing down death row, I sang of lives and loves in oth-er years. Walk-ing down death row, I sang of hopes that used to be. Through the bars, in- to each sep-'rate cell, Yes, I sang to one and two and three: If you'd on-ly stuck to-gether you'd not be here! If you could have loved each oth-er's lives, you'd not be sit-ting here! And if on-ly this you could be-lieve, You still might, you might still be re-prieved!

Words & music by Pete Seeger (1966)
© 1966 by Stormking Music Inc.

1. Walking down death row,
   I sang for three men, destined for the chair;
   Walking down death row,
   I sang of lives and loves in other years.
      Walking down death row, I sang of hopes that
         used to be.
      Through the bars, into each sep'rate cell,
      Yes, I sang to one and two and three.
   "If you'd only stuck together you'd not
      be here!
   "If you could have loved each other's lives,
      you'd not be sitting here!
   "And if only this you could believe,
   "You still might, you might still be reprieved!"

2. Walking down death row,
   I turned a corner and found to my surprise;
   There were women there as well,
   With babies in their arms, before my eyes.
      Walking down death row,
      I tried once more to sing of hopes that
         used to be.
      But the thought of that contraption,
         down the hall,
      Waiting for whole fam'lies, one dozen,
         two or three,*
   "If you'd only stuck together, you'd not be here!
   "If you could've loved another's child as well as your
      own, you'd not be sitting here!**
   "And if only this you could believe,
   "You still might, you might still be reprieved."

3. Walking down death row,
   I concentrated, singing to the young.
   I sang of hopes that flickered still;
   I tried to mouth each sep'rate human tongue.
      Walking down death row,
      I sang of life and love that still might be.
      Singing, singing, singing down death row,***
      To each sep'rate human cell,
      One billion, two or three, or six or seven or
         eight soon!
   "If we'd only stick together, we'd not be here!
   "If we could learn to love each other's lives,
      we'd not be sitting here!
   "And if only this we could believe,
   "We still might, _we_ might still be reprieved."

Variants:

C47

*Verse 2

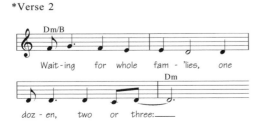

Wait-ing for whole fam - 'lies, one
doz - en, two or three:____

**Verse 2

If you could have loved an-oth-er's child as
well as your own you'd not be sit-ting here!__

***Verse 3

Dm/C

Singing, singing, singing down death row,— to each

Dm/B   Dm

sep'rate human cell, one bil-lion, two, or three (or

four or five__ or six or seven):

I usually end with a discord (Dropped D tuning):

A couple hundred years ago a shipwrecked sailor drifted for weeks till he saw land. He crawled up the beach not knowing what country or continent he'd landed on. He staggered up the bluff, and at the top found himself in a large field where there was a gallows and a man hanging. He exclaimed, "Thank God! I'm in a Christian country."

© Len Munnik, Amsterdam

Quite Early Morning `C48`

1. Don't you know it's dark - est___
before_ the dawn,___ And this thought keeps me_
mov - in' on.___ If we could heed
these ear-ly warn - ings, The time is now,
quite ear - ly morn-ing! If we could
heed these ear-ly warn - ings,___ The time is now,
___ quite ear - ly morn-ing.

Words & music by Pete Seeger (1969)
© 1969 by Sanga Music Inc.

1. Don't you know it's darkest before the dawn
   And it's this thought keeps me moving on
   If we could heed these early warnings
   The time is now quite early morning
   If we could heed these early warnings
   The time is now quite early morning.

2. Some say that humankind won't long endure
   But what makes them so doggone sure?
   I know that you who hear my singing
   Could make those freedom bells go ringing
   I know that you who hear my singing
   Could make those freedom bells go ringing.

3. And so we keep on while we live
   Until we have no, no more to give
   And when these fingers can strum no longer
   Hand the old banjo to young ones stronger
   And when these fingers can strum no longer
   Hand the old banjo to young ones stronger.

4. So though it's darkest before the dawn
   These thoughts keep us moving on
   Through all this world of joy and sorrow
   We still can have singing tomorrows
   Through all this world of joy and sorrow
   We still can have singing tomorrows.

(PLAY THE TUNE ON BANJO OR GUITAR, THEN REPEAT FIRST VERSE)

I usually strum along fairly fast while singing these verses.

I never thought anyone but me would ever sing this, but Magpie and the Mammals and others have picked it up. One never knows. Over the years I've had so much fun picking it three-finger style that for any banjo picker trying to puzzle through this, here 'tis. Don't be scared of the irregular barring of 16th notes. John Roberts, whose computer printed all this music, figured it would be easier to pick the melody out from all those other notes, and I think he's right. John knows a lot more about music notation than I do, and he's been like a consultant on this book.

JOHN ROBERTS, 1993

Photo by Mark Schmidt

In 1957, I'm strolling down Chicago's Michigan Avenue, and I hear this song coming out of a loud-speaker — a top hit record by the Ames Brothers. Till 1993 I didn't know the words, but for 36 years I played it on the banjo, mostly to myself. When a banjo plays softly, you can hear the strings ring out longer, and found I really liked the unison sound of two strings sounding the same note at the same time. Note the unusual tuning. The piece is impossible to play without lowering the fifth string by three frets, to E.

Melodie D'Amour

C50

*If I'm playing soft as I like, I can sound this note by hammering on — H

Music by Henri Salvador
Banjo arrangement by Pete Seeger (ca. 1952)
© 1957 (renewed) by Rightsong Music, Inc. and S.D.R.M.
International copyright secured. All rights reserved.

In case you or anyone with you would like to sing the words to this song, here they are:

Melodie d'Amour,
Take this song to my lover,
Shoo shoo little bird
Go and find my love.
Melodie d'Amour,
Serenade at her/his window,
Shoo shoo little bird
Sing my song of love.
 Oh, tell her/him I will wait
 If she/he names the date,
 Tell her/him that I care
 More than I can bear,
 For when we are apart   Maladie d'Amour
 How it hurts my heart,   Maladie de jeunesse
 So fly, oh fly away   Si tu n'aimes que moi
 And say I hope and pray   Reste tout près de moi
 This lover's melodie   Maladie d'Amour
 Will bring her/him back   Me fie toi des caresses
   to me.   Si tu n'aimes que moi
Oh, Melodie d'Amour,   Viens, mais prends garde à toi
Take this song to my lover,   Quand l'amour est petit
Shoo shoo little bird   C'est joli, si joli
Go and find my love.   Mais quand il devient fort
Melodie d'Amour,   Me fiez vous mes amis
Serenade at her/his   Cache sous le feuillage
 window,   C'est comme un serpent gris
Shoo shoo little bird   N'allez pas quand il dort
Tell her/him of my love.   Surtout le reveiller
            N'allez pas car il mord
            Si vous le reveillez
         Oh, Maladie d'Amour
         Maladie de jeunesse
         Si je n'aimes que toi
         Je reste près de toi
         Maladie d'Amour
         Qui nous grise et nous blesse
         Si je n'aimes que toi
         Rien ne m'en pechera
          Quand l'amour est petit
          C'est joli, si joli
          Mais quand il devient fort
          C'est plus beau que la vie
          J'irai sous le feuillage
          Chercher le serpent gris
          Car l'amour c'est la mort
          Mais c'est le paradis
          Car l'amour c'est la mort
          Mais c'est le paradis
         Maladie d'Amour...

English lyrics by Leo Johns, French lyrics by Marc Lanjean,
© 1949 by Editions Transatlantiques, Paris, France.
Originally "Maladie D'Amour"

★ ★ ★

It was a family Christmas party. Some of the crowd were playing Monopoly. Others were off in corners talking. I was sitting on the floor, experimenting with a tune that had just come to me with a nice bass line:

This is actually played in "Dropped D" tuning, again, even though it's in the key of A. You hook your thumb over on the sixth string and play the A chord or the E chord. Arrows point to bass notes plucked by the right hand thumb.

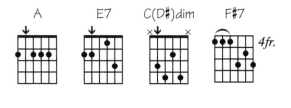

The left thumb solves a lot of problems, but it can't help with the C#7, except to mute the sixth string.

I knew I had a good tune and wrestled with words for it for several weeks, even trying to get friends like Lee Hays to help. No luck. Finally had to be content with one verse. And suddenly realized I was like many another pop song writer—lucky to get one verse which rippled off the tongue nicely. And when I perform it, I usually sing it once myself, then a second time with the crowd (lining out the words, one phrase at a time), then whistling it through once or twice, and finally doing it with the crowd one more time.

Anyway, playing it in A is a little high for some people. This is one reason I use a 12-stringer, tuned two or more frets below normal. The D tuning, as you'll see (note measures marked with an asterisk) is fine for getting barred chords of a certain sort up the neck. Not so good for C#7.

I've put the left hand bass runs in a second staff with a bass clef for the convenience of piano players.

shine through all__ our tears.

And when we sing an-oth-er lit-tle

vic-to-ry song,__ Precious friend,

__ you will be there,__ Sing-ing in har-mo-ny,

Pre-cious friend,__ you will be there..

there.__

Words & music by Pete Seeger (1974)
© 1974, 1982 by Stormking Music Inc.

Just when I thought
All was lost, you changed my mind.
You gave me hope, (not just the old soft soap)
You showed that we could learn to share in time.
  (You and me and Rockefeller)
I'll keep pluggin' on,
Your face will shine through all our tears.

And when we sing another little victory song,
Precious friend, you will be there, singing in harmony,
Precious friend, you will be there.

I'm a lucky songwriter. Till recently I didn't know where I stole the melody from, but Arlo Guthrie discovered one day when we were rehearsing "Precious Friend" that it uses the same chords as "I've Been Working on the Railroad." You can sing both melodies at the same time. So maybe I didn't steal the melody. Just stole the chords.

This is a little like the trick I learned when I was a child. One person can sing, "Way Down Upon the Swanee River" at the same time another sings the melody of "Humoresque" ("Passengers will please refrain from flushing toilets while the train…etc.").

ARLO AT CLEARWATER FESTIVAL, 1983

★ ★ ★

It was around 1961. Singing in Wisconsin with my younger brother and sister, Mike and Peggy, I found the next verses on the back of the menu of a roadside diner. I had never seen them before except for the first two lines, which I had once seen scrawled on the door of a public toilet.

When I put a tune to it and added a couple lines, I wrote to the hash house. I had stolen their menu. They told me they got the words from a newspaper column in a Milwaukee paper. I wrote to the columnist; he couldn't remember who had sent it to him.

I have since found that the poem has been widely reprinted in different versions. Nobody knows for sure who originally wrote it. It could be from anywhere in the English-speaking world. Probably sometime in the late 19th or early 20th century. I heard from people who remembered it from before WWI. It's sometimes titled "I'm Doing Quite Well For The Shape I'm In."

All I contributed besides the melody were a couple of lines and the idea of repeating the first four lines as a chorus. You'll find that you can do this with many poems that were written originally to be read but need more repetition if they are going to be successfully sung.

Get Up and Go

CHORUS
How do I know my youth is all spent,
My get up and go has got up and went,
But in spite of it all I'm a - ble to grin
And think of the pla-ces my get up has been.

VERSE
1. Old age is gold-en so I've heard said,
But some-times I won-der as I crawl in-to bed,
With my ears in a draw-er, my teeth in a cup,
My eyes on the ta-ble, un - til I wake up.

* START 3RD VERSE HERE
As sleep dims my vi-sion I say to my - self:
Is there an-y-thing else___ I should lay on the shelf?
But tho' na-tions are war-ring and busi-ness is vexed,
I'll still stick a-round to see what hap-pens next.

Words collected, adapted & set to original music by Pete Seeger (1960)
Original poem ("I'm Doing Quite Well for the Shape I'm In") by Ms. A.N. Onymous
TRO - © 1964 (renewed) Melody Trails, Inc., New York, NY.

CHORUS (AND AFTER EACH VERSE):
How do I know my youth is all spent?
My get up and go has got up and went.
But in spite of it all I'm able to grin
And think of the places my get up has been.

1. Old age is golden so I've heard said.
   But sometimes I wonder as I crawl into bed,
   With my ears in a drawer, my teeth in a cup,
   My eyes on the table until I wake up.
   As sleep dims my vision I say to myself:
   Is there anything else I should lay on the shelf?
   But though nations are warring and business
     is vexed,
   I'll still stick around to see what happens next.

2. When I was young my slippers were red,
   I could kick up my heels right over my head.
   When I was older my slippers were blue,
   But still I could dance the whole night through.
   Now I am older my slippers are black.
   I huff to the store and I puff my way back.
   But never you laugh; I don't mind at all.
   I'd rather be huffing than not puff at all.

(SING TO THE MELODY OF THE LAST 4 LINES OF THE VERSE:)
3. I get up each morning and dust off my wits,
   Open the paper and read the obits.
   If I'm not there I know I'm not dead.
   So I eat a good breakfast and go back to bed.

Eleanor Walden of Berkeley sent a new ending for
"Get Up and Go" to me in 1990.

I get up each morning and dust off my wits,
Open the paper and read the obits.
If I'm not there I know I'm not gone.
So I eat a good breakfast and plan to go on.
For life is a blessing and love is a hope.
There's too much to do now to sit here and mope.
So I tie my Adidas and answer the call.
I'll die in the struggle or I won't die at all.

How do I know I'm ready to fight.
My get up and go is still within sight.
In spite of my body my spirit is strong.
And I'm passing the torch from the old to the young.

★ ★ ★

In 1958 I sang at the funeral of John McManus, co-editor of the radical newsweekly, *The Guardian*, and regretted that I had no song worthy of the occasion. So this next got written. I print the song here as I do if I send it to the family of someone who has died — with a hand-colored flower alongside it.

To My Old Brown Earth

C53

Freely—slowly

To my old brown earth

And to my old blue sky

I'll now give these last few mol-e-cules

of "I"

And you, who sing,

And you who stand near - by,

I do charge you not to cry:

Guard well our hu-man chain,

Watch well you keep it strong,

As long as sun will shine,

And this our home,

Keep pure and sweet and green,

For now I'm yours

And you are al - so

Mine.

You could enlarge it on a photocopy machine so it would fit on an 11" by 17" piece of paper. Then color it or make your own picture. Trim off this paragraph of type before enlarging. Note that I wrote the words "Freely-slowly" at upper left. So while I've tried to give the time value to the notes as I sing them — purposely irregular in length — you sing it like you feel it. End on a long held "n-n-n-n" (the word "mine").

Words & music by Pete Seeger (1958)
© 1964 (renewed) by Stormking Music Inc.

A little old lady in New York took her dog out for a walk every night. As a good citizen she always obeyed the law that says, "Scoop up your dog's poop; don't leave it sitting on the curb."

One evening as she and the dog were returning after their evening stroll, she had a small suitcase with her. She was walking close to the curb when a car slowed down beside her. An arm reached out and grabbed her suitcase. The car zoomed off into the city traffic.

And the little old lady laughed and laughed and laughed, just to think what the people in that car thought when they opened that suitcase and saw what was in it.

"If you're in a coalition and you feel comfortable it's not a broad enough coalition."
— Bernice Reagon

"Steal from one person, it's plagiarism; steal from ten, it's scholarship," a girl at Oberlin College told me in the '50s. Added her friend, "Steal from a hundred, it's original research."

"I came to America from Italy," said the old man. "Through Ellis Island. I came because I was told the streets were paved with gold. I found out three things. One, they're not. Two, they're not even paved. Three, I'm expected to pave them."
— learned from Randolphe Harris

An old woman had lost almost all her teeth. But she said triumphantly, "I got two left. Thank God, they're hitters."
— from Lee Hays

"At times I cannot decide on a tune to use with my words for a song. Woe is me! I am then forced to use some old family style tune that hath already gained the reputation as being liked by the people."
— Woody Guthrie

"Anything too stupid to be said, can be sung."
— Voltaire

"Plagiarism is basic to all culture." (CLS)

Well May the World Go

Words & music by Pete Seeger (1973)
© 1973 by Stormking Music Inc.

CHORUS (AND AFTER EACH VERSE):
Well may the world go,
The world go, the world go.
Well may the world go,
When I'm far away.

1. Well may the skiers turn,
   The swimmers churn, the lovers burn
   Peace, may the gen'rals learn
   When I'm far away.

2. Sweet may the fiddle sound
   The banjo play the old hoe down
   Dancers swing round and round
   When I'm far away.

Paul Suchow made a good verse:

3. Long may we sing this song
   As younger voices carry on
   Let all nations get along
   When I'm far away.

4. Fresh may the breezes blow
   Clear may the streams flow
   Blue above, green below
   When I'm far away.

Here's 5 different ways you could sing that first line:

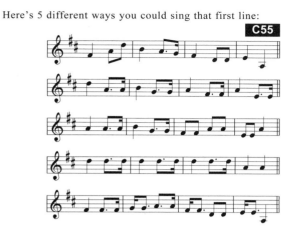

These new words to a traditional English song occurred to me one day, and in a few hours I'd got the verses set. It was such an easy song to write, I was surprised to find how usable it is.

The "original" song was "Weel May the Keel Row" (well may the boat row) from Newcastle-on-Tyne, northeast England. Different rhythm.

The Keel Row

C56

As I went thro' Sand-gate, thro' Sand-gate, thro' Sand-gate, As I went thro' Sand-gate, I heard a las-sie sing. Weel may the keel row, the keel row, the keel row, Weel may the keel row, that ma— lad-die's in.

Traditional Geordie song, Newcastle-on-Tyne, England

I now give tablature for the tune as played on a five-string banjo "double thumb." Later I speed up, strum it or frail it. I play it in the G tuning, although G is an impossible key to sing it in, except for a low alto or high tenor. What to do? Capo up or tune down. My friend Lois Pinetree, an alto, sings it in the key of A. I pitch it in E which is where my long neck banjo is in G tuning. Southern fiddlers know the tune as "Bile Them Cabbage Down." It's also a cousin of "Hard, Ain't It Hard," "Bury Me Beneath the Willow" and "Woody's Rag." Same chords suit 'em all. But different speeds.

Well May the World Go
(Banjo Arrangement)

C57

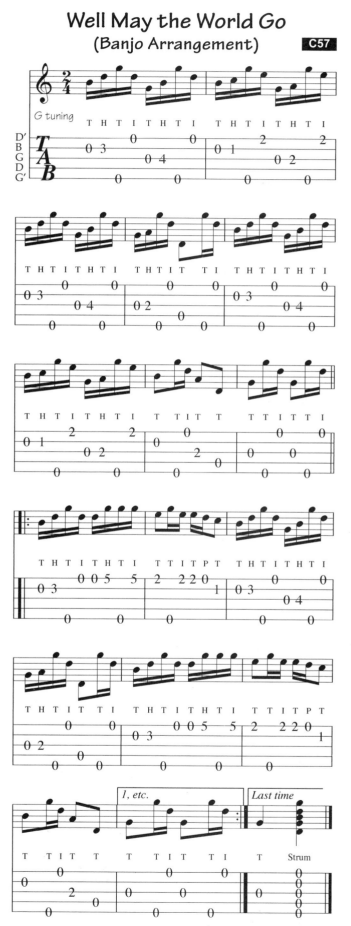

Rockin' Solidarity
(A Chorus Version)

`C58`

Dave Welsh of San Francisco is a barrelhouse piano player with a high tenor voice. He worked out new ideas for melody and rhythm to this famous old song. All I contributed was the choral arrangement and the idea that new verses could be added (and got some women to work on 'em). The key of G is fine for altos. A few tenors can reach it. The key can be made higher, A or even B, but beware of making it as low as E or F. The larger crowd will growl the famous chorus too low.

If the men shout out the third verse and the women a new fourth verse, then as large a gang as possible should do the fifth verse together.

Any hand clapping should be on the "offbeats."

(clap)   (clap)

The reason I put some words for the chorus to shout is that the whole audience should be singing the famous old melody, while the high voices are singing the new melody.

Words by Ralph Chaplin (1916) Tune: "Battle Hymn of the Republic"
New music & additional words by David Welsh (1987)
Choral arrangement by Pete Seeger
© 1988 & 1989 David Welsh. Used by permission.

1. When the union's inspiration
   Through the workers' blood shall run,
   There can be no power greater
   Anywhere beneath the sun,
   Yet what force on earth is weaker
   Than the feeble strength of one?
       But it's the union, yes, the union
       Makes us strong.
       ("Everybody sing it out, Sing it with us")

CROWD (CHORUS AFTER EACH VERSE):
Sol-i-da-ri-ty For-e-ver ("Gotta have it now")
Sol-i-da-ri-ty For-e-ver ("Ev'rybody's talkin' 'bout")
Sol-i-da-ri-ty For-e-ver
For it's the union, yes, the union
Makes us strong.

2. They have taken untold millions
   That they never toiled to earn.
   Yet without our brain and muscle
   Not a single wheel would turn.
   We can break their haughty power,
   Gain our freedom when we learn
       That it's the union, yes, the union
       Makes us strong,
       ("Got to have it, Everybody's got to have it.")

(SUNG BY MEN:)
3. It is we that plowed the prairies.
   Built the cities where they trade.
   Dug the mines and built the workshops,
   Endless miles of railroad laid.
   Now we stand outcast and starving
   'Midst the wonders we have made,
       But it's the union, yes, the union
       Makes us strong,
       ("Sing it over, Everybody sing it over.")

(SUNG BY WOMEN:)
4. It is we that raised the families
   Scrubbed the floors and chased the dirt,
   Fed the kids and sent them off to school,
   And then we go to work
   Where we work for lower wages
   With a boss that likes to flirt.
       But we will make it,
       Yes, we'll make the union strong.
       ("Everybody join in, join in now.")

This fourth verse is by Marcia Taylor, Faith Petric, and others. Whatever other verses you add, have the entire chorus sing this famous last verse together:

5. In our hands is placed a power
   Greater than their hoarded gold,
   Greater than the might of armies,
   Magnified a thousand fold.
   We can bring to birth a new world
   From the ashes of the old.
       'Cause it's the union, yes, the union
       Makes us strong,
       ("Sing it once more, Sing it once more now.")

   Sol-i-da-ri-ty For-e-ver   (A GOOD PLACE
   Sol-i-da-ri-ty For-e-ver   FOR SOME
   Sol-i-da-ri-ty For-e-ver   JAZZ BREAKS)
   For it's the union, yes, the union
   For it's the union, yes, the union
   For it's the union, yes—
   The union makes us strong.

Here's a sample of a piano part. I'm no piano player but I know that anyone who can play jazz piano would feel right at home here. The left hand does some sort of "walking bass," the right hand gets the offbeat chords. And if there's trumpet players around, this song can use 'em.

Frank's Yodel

By Pete Seeger (1975)
© 1993 by Sanga Music Inc.

★ ★ ★

My brother Mike has recorded southern farmers who do extraordinary yodels when in the fields. Here are two of my own favorite yodels — a quiet one I used to hum to myself, and a loud one for ship to shore or vice versa. The small ○ over a note indicates falsetto.

Can't remember when I made that yodel up. For 35 years I've yodelled it at the beginning of concerts. And from ship to shore and shore to ship. The harmony works.

Frank Morrison was my neighbor, a teenager. We'd yodel to each other, across 500 feet of wooded mountainside.

Now that my voice is mostly gone, I more often whistle. Artists, professional and amateur, will doodle on paper napkins and scratch paper while telephoning. Musicians play similarly at odd times. I whistle. There are now whistler organizations. They whistle parts to concertos, symphonies. But one of the best whistlers I ever heard was a woman who whistled pop tunes to herself as she cooked or cleaned house.

(Whistle is 2 octaves higher)

By Pete Seeger
© 1993 by Sanga Music Inc.

* A rhythmic punctuation, like a drummer's rim shot, a clap. I do it with a mouth click, as in Miriam Makeba's African songs. It's optional.

But one "whistler" I really couldn't get out of my head. I thought I'd swiped it from an old pop tune. Ended up putting a story to it and performing it on stage.

Whistling Past a Graveyard

`C60`

*mouth click

Eventually I found a way to perform this on stage. I pitch it in F because that's the best key for me to whistle it in. But guitarists will know it's easier to play in G, C or D. Use a capo! I play it first, then start talking:

For 20 years I've had this tune in my head. I can't find where I stole it from. I whistle it in the streets of New York. People look at me and grumble, "What you so happy about?" I finally decided what to do with it. It'll be a music video! The scene is a dirty city street. Trash in the gutter. Boarded up buildings. Down the sidewalk come two people whistling. A kid is sitting on the steps. "Joe, want to learn to whistle?" They take his hand.

Another kid is sitting on the curb. "Hey, Maria, want to learn to whistle?" So now there are four of them, dancing down the street. Kicking at the garbage cans! Suddenly they come to something you can see in an old city: a little graveyard between two buildings. The camera zooms in between the iron fence and you see a gravestone.

"Catherine Johnson, born 1890, died 1895." The kids grow silent, thinking of a little girl that only lived five years. But the grown-ups turn to the kids and sing:

C61...

Whis-tl-ing past a grave-yard   is not a

fool-ish thing,   When all o' the world ap-pears to be

com - ing a - part at the seams. And

who can tell for sure what - 'll be

next to go?—   Did you ev - er think that

Trick-y Dick* would leave like he did?

Whis-tl-ing past a grave-yard,   I'll keep on whis-tling.

And if you want, you can whis-tle a - long.— For

who knows just how man-y more— might

like to try the mel-o-dy and whis-tle

a sim-i-lar song?   (answer back)   and

whis - tle a si-mi-lar song.

*This refers to past President Richard Nixon and Watergate.

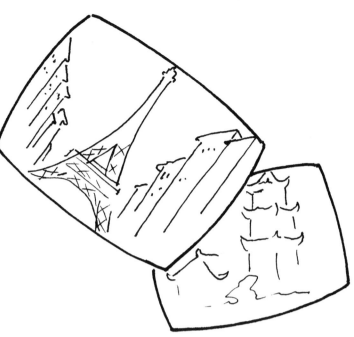

Now the kids are smiling again. The four start down the street once more, whistling. But in only a few seconds (this needs trick camera work) they see the Eiffel Tower in front of them.

Some French kids come out to join 'em. A few seconds later there's the pyramids of Egypt. Some Egyptian kids come out to join them. All of a sudden there's a pagoda, and some Chinese or Japanese kids come to join them. Suddenly there's the pueblos of New Mexico, and some Native American kids come out. All of a sudden there's palm trees, and Sugarloaf Mountain in Rio de Janeiro, some Brazilian kids come out, and everybody's on a beach, that famous beach. There's high surf, spray blowing. Whshhh…whshhhh!

The two grown-ups sing:

Whistling by the seashore
Upon a windy day.
Look at the breakers trying to
Drown out the song!
The seagulls laugh as they glide past
And sandcastles all around
Come tumbling down.
Whistling by the seashore —
We'll keep on whistling —
And if you want you can whistle along.
The ocean may be wide but on the other side
There lot's of people
Whistling a similar song.

C...61

All of a sudden on the screen is a woman in Japan, in ancient costume, kneeling on the floor playing the koto.

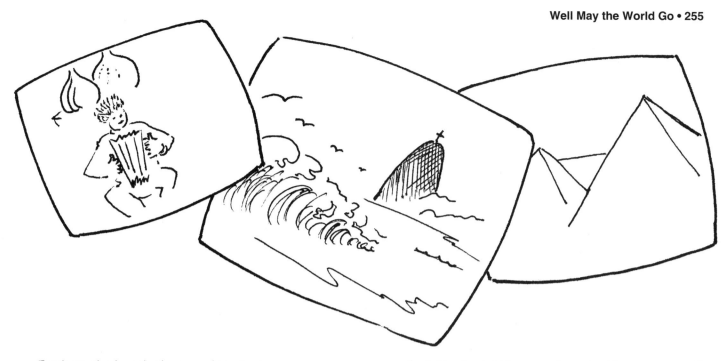

Back on the beach the crowd is singing

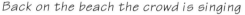

Whis - tling   a si - mi - lar song.

On the screen is a family from Guatemala, playing the xylophone.

(SING)   Whistling a similar song.

(ON STAGE I MIMIC EVERY INSTRUMENT PLAYING THE SAME SHORT PHRASE)

On the screen is the whole Vienna Symphony in white tie and tails, fiddling.

There's Mount Kilimanjaro in East Africa, and someone playing the thumb piano.

There's a rock band with an electric guitar. Ka-twee, ka-twee.

There's the Taj Mahal in India, and a fellow playing tuned teacups. Tinkle tinkle.

There's St. Basil's Cathedral in Moscow and an accordion player.

We end up with the birds in the tree overhanging the beach all whistling.

And the last thing you hear is the ocean surf: whshsh... whshsh...

That's the end of my music video.

But, now, if you'd like to try whistling that tune, it's not hard to get that flutter:

You don't raise your tongue. You should push your tongue forward till it suddenly touches all the lower teeth.

Try it.

AUDIENCE TRIES IT. I NOW WHISTLE THE WHOLE TUNE THROUGH ONCE, WITH THE AUDIENCE AND AT THE END GO BACK TO SINGING.

We're on the beach to - geth - er

We're on the beach together
Whistling a similar song.
Come on and pucker up now (SAME TUNE)
Whistling a similar song.
We won't be drowned out if we (SAME TUNE)
Whistle a similar song. Whshsh...whshsh...

Words (1984) & music (1965) by Pete Seeger   Second verse by Lorre Wyatt
TRO - © 1987 Melody Trails, Inc., New York, NY.

And right while this book was in preparation, came a song for a family birthday party. Strictly speaking, this song should have been in Chapter IV. If all goes well while the presses are printing this book, Toshi and I will celebrate 66 years of marriage.

Only in my sixties did I realize I was carrying on an old family tradition of living in a three-generation family. I was close to grandparents as a kid. Our own children knew grandparents well. Now Toshi and I live near our daughter Tinya's family. Modern industrial society has done many bad things, and one of them has been to take children too far from their grandparents. But I confess, in the old pre-penicillin days, there weren't so many of us grandparents still alive and kicking.

Photo by Wendy Carlson

PETE & GRANDDAUGHTER MORAYA JACKSON

A Little a' This 'n' That

C62...

1. My grand-ma, she can make a soup,— with a little a' this 'n' that.* She can feed— the whole sloop group, with a little a' this 'n' that.

Stone soup! You know the story. Stone soup! Who

needs the glo-ry? But with grand-ma cook-ing, no need to worry. Just a little a' this 'n' that. *Fine*

2. Grand-ma likes to make a gar-den grow,— with a little a' this 'n' that. But she likes to have the ground just so, with a little a' this 'n' that. Not too loose— and not too firm.— In the spring, the ground's all got to be turned. In the fall, lots of com-post, to feed the worms, with a lit-tle a' this 'n' that.

3. Grand-ma knows we can build a fu-ture, with a lit-tle a' this 'n' that. And a few ar-gu-ments nev-er ev-er hurt ya, with a lit-tle a' this 'n' that.

True, this world's in a hell-u-va fix, And some say oil and wa-ter don't mix. But they don't know a sal-ad-mak-er's tricks, with a lit-tle a' this 'n' that.

4. The world to come may be like a song, with a lit-tle a' this 'n' that. To make ev-'ry-bod-y want to sing a-long, with a lit-tle a' this 'n' that. A lit-tle dis-so-nance ain't no sin, A lit-tle sky-lark-ing to give us all a grin. Who knows but God's got a plan for the peo-ple to win, with a lit-tle a' this 'n' that.

Words & music by Pete Seeger (1991)
© 1991, 1993 by Sanga Music Inc.

1. My grandma, she can make a soup,
     with a little a' this 'n' that.
   She can feed the whole sloop group,
     with a little a' this 'n' that.
   Stone soup! You know the story.
   Stone soup! Who needs the glory?
   But with grandma cooking, no need to worry.
     Just a little a' this 'n' that.

2. Grandma likes to make a garden grow,
     with a little a' this 'n' that.
   But she likes to have the ground just so,
     with a little a' this 'n' that.
   Not too loose and not too firm.
   In the spring, the ground's all got to be turned.
   In the fall, lots of compost, to feed the worms,
     with a lit-tle a' this 'n' that.

3. Grandma knows we can build a future,
     with a little a' this 'n' that.
   And a few arguments never ever hurt ya,
     with a little a' this 'n' that.
   True, this world's in a helluva fix,
   And some say oil and water don't mix.
   But they don't know a salad-maker's tricks,
     with a little a' this 'n' that.

4. The world to come may be like a song,
     with a little a' this 'n' that.
   To make ev'rybody want to sing along,
     with a little a' this 'n' that.
   A little dissonance ain't no sin,
   A little skylarking to give us all a grin.
   Who knows but God's got a plan for the people to win,
     with a little a' this 'n' that.

A nice verse added by Molly Mason:

5. My grandma, she can make a quilt with a . . .
   She's got patience and skill with a needle and
       thread and a . . .
   With scraps of cloth that are worn and old
   She makes works of art that are bright and bold
   And they keep out the winter's nighttime cold . . .

*I know this measure would be easier:
But it isn't right.

The tempo is ♩ = **120**. Those six notes should be *fast*.

**I usually strike the most dissonant chord I can, at this point.
  Banjo tuning, GCGBD.

Sometimes I repeat the 1st verse. However you decide to end it, take advantage of the fact that your listeners now are comfortable with the little phrase, and with a bit of encouragement can repeat it several times before a nice abrupt ending, a bit like "All Mixed Up" in Chapter 1.

Melodies? #3

Continuing the discussion from p. 89, how *does* one learn to make up melodies? Inspiration surely has a part to play, but I think, as in any other field of endeavor, whether cooking or carpentry, one starts by imitating. Using recipes. Later one starts making small changes according to one's own personal likes and dislikes. Then with luck comes the wonderful discovery that there is no great crime in making bigger changes.

Keep in mind that one tradition's "good melody" is another tradition's pain-in-the-ear. A melody can be:

Short (3 seconds) or long (3 minutes)
Much repetition — or none
3 note range or 30 note range
Major, minor scales of several kinds
Many different kinds of rhythm — or none

Think of the wide varieties of melodies in one country – France, for example. Melodies with a range of five notes, like "Go Tell Aunt Rhody" (originally French):

And another famous French tune with a range of five notes — "A La Claire Fontaine."

Compare the above two conservative melodies to this adventurous one ("La Marseillaise").

Well, now I give you a melody with only one adventurous note. But it works. Elsewhere in the song are 17 notes in a row that don't change pitch, but changes in the accompaniment make them meaningful, just as on p. 123 changes in harmony give meaning to a Beethoven melody (12 notes the same).

I read the words in *The Nation* magazine, summer '92. Rearranged them slightly so people could join in more easily. And surprised myself with finding a tune which did justice to them. I think the ghosts of Gilbert and Sullivan would be amused.

I accompany it with guitar in Dropped D tuning. The chords are not that difficult. Check the Appendix.

The Politician's Guide to Answering Embarrassing Questions | C64

Words by Calvin Trillin   Music & adaptation of lyrics by Pete Seeger (June 19, 1992)
The poem originally appeared in *The Nation* as "The Ross Perot Guide to Answering Embarrassing Questions."
Words © 1992 by Calvin Trillin   Music © 1993 by Sanga Music. Inc.

1.   When something in my history is found,
     Which contradicts the views that I propound,
     Or shows that I perhaps am not the guy
     I claim to be, here's what I usually do:
        CHORUS (AFTER EACH VERSE):
        I lie.
        I simply, boldly falsify.
        I look the other feller in the eye,
        And just deny, deny, deny.
        I lie.

2.   I don't apologize. Not me. Instead,
     I say I never said the things I said.
     Nor did the things some people saw me do
     When confronted by some things they know are true,

3.   I hate the weasel words some slickies use
     To blur the past or muddy up their views.
     Not me. I'm blunt. One thing that makes me great
     Is that I'll never dodge, or obfuscate.

Admittedly, no music school teaches students how to write a good melody. To write a half-good melody is easy. But writing one that people cannot forget; that's something else.

I asked a number of musicologists how one could define a good melody; they all shrugged. "It depends upon the culture." I've always admired the slow Irish airs — the tradition that gave us "The Londonderry Air," "The Minstrel Boy," "My Lagan Love," (p. 87) "Hills of Glenshee" (p. 87) and countless others.

So when I found the next tune taking shape, I wrote it down. In the first edition of this book in 1993, I called it "The Autumn Wind."

The autumn wind
Whispered, don't be afraid
Though winter chills will still be here
If we work together, learn together,
Sing together now,
When spring comes 'round again
We will still be here

Nobody, not even me, sang it. But five years later I improved the tune by repeating the first two measures, and even found some better words. Here's some.

And Still I'm Searching

And still I'm search-ing, yes, I'm still search-ing for a way we all can learn. To build a world Where we all can share the work, the fun, the food, the space, the joy, the pain. And no one, no one will ev-er, ev-er want or need to be a mil-lion-aire

By Pete Seeger (1980)
© 1993 by Sanga Music Inc.

Later, I realized I'd swiped most of the second line from my brother-in-law, Ewan MacColl. See the second line of "The First Time Ever I Saw Your Face." When my sister Peggy heard me play this, she laughed to recognize an old folk tune Ewan borrowed from to write his famous song for her.

I thought the sun rose in your eyes

Then I found other lyrics for this same tune. I also found I prefer no accompaniment except a bass E — one note. If the song were sung in India, this would be the normal accompaniment — an E note droning on. Like a bagpipe.

Interesting thing about the tune: it only touches the first note of the scale, the "do" of "do-re-mi," briefly in passing. It lingers at times on the fourth note of the scale, or the third or the fifth, and especially on the seventh note of the scale, only a half-step below "do," while the bass is still sounding E, the "do" or first note of the scale.

The melody, first attempted in 1992, is fairly well set now, but I'm still looking for other words — most recently for good folks in Latin America trying to find a future free of Uncle Sam's domination but also free from violence from desperate poor people. All I have so far is "No Mas Violencia! No mas, no mas, no mas violencia en Colombia!" (We'll learn to talk though we disagree. And if we sing, or eat, or tolerate each other's company-y-y. Who knows, who knows, what changes yet our grandchildren will someday see.) See p. 262.

As a child I played a pennywhistle by ear, any tune that struck my fancy. Age 17, I switched to the English recorder, with greater range and slightly different fingering. Started discovering a wider range of melodies. Age 30, met an Israeli, Ilka Raveh. As I told you, he learned from Arab shepherds how to make and play an open end reed flute called "nai" in Arabic. Ilka adapted it to western scales and called it a "chalil."

Ilka is one of the world's greatest masters of this difficult instrument. I never became very good at playing it, but I found myself making up tunes on it which I would not have made on the recorder. The chalil has a smaller range — about 12 notes, for the average player — but you can make the high notes soft, the low notes louder. That's impossible on the recorder.

So on the next page is a free, rambling little tune composed for a bamboo flute, which I made up 55 years ago. On p. 43 I told you how it got its title. Every time I play it I think of Ilka Raveh and his Arab friends. If you have a blue pencil in the house, color the little globe bluish. The music notes could be all colors of the rainbow. The title is ...

How Soon?

Free — imperiodic rhythm

By Pete Seeger (1950)
© 1993 by Sanga Music Inc.

Extroduction

In May 1968 I got a phone call from poet John Beecher. "Pete, I'm down at Duke University, North Carolina. A thousand students are having a sit-down strike demanding some changes be made. Can you come down and sing them a few songs?"

It seems that in April, when Martin Luther King was assassinated, a group of white students at this conservative institution of the Solid South had visited the college president, demanding he give more scholarships to black students, also start negotiating in good faith with the union of maintenance employees, mostly black. And he should resign from his white-only country club. The President said, in effect, thank you for your advice, but I'm running this university. The president went to bed; in the morning the students were still in his living room.

"We don't think that's a good enough answer. We're staying here till we get a better one." After a week the president moved to the college infirmary. The students moved their protest to a large quadrangle and their numbers grew to over a thousand; I sang to them as they were sitting on the grass.

"You young folks are risking your scholarships, your college careers. This kind of thing has never happened at Duke. How come I haven't heard of it in the media? This is news."

"Oh, we called up the *New York Times*. They gave us a couple inches on the back pages. We called NBC and CBS, and they said they couldn't spare any cameramen. But they said, '*Let us know if there's any violence; we'll send somebody down.*'"

I felt the blood rushing to my head. This is how our country is misgoverned. I picked up a small stone the size of a golf ball, started shouting (unwise any time). "I've never thrown a stone at a person; I've had stones thrown at me and it's no fun. But I'm going to carry this in my banjo case; some day there could be some glass broken."

A stone's still in my case, 41 years later. The problem is still as big as ever. In a world of misinformation what do you do? It's like being at a noisy cocktail party, trying to get a sensible word in edgewise. In any given minute any day in 2005, nearly $2 million is spent on armaments in the world, and in that same minute some 15 children in the world die of malnutrition.

Back in the 1950s there was a tiny peace demonstration in Times Square. A young Quaker was carrying a sign. A passerby scoffed:

"Do you think you're going to change the world by standing here at midnight with that sign?"

"I suppose not," said the young man. "But I'm going to make sure the world doesn't change me."

★ ★ ★

I've been surprised by some good things happening in my lifetime. Sometimes quite suddenly.

Imagine a big seesaw, with a basket half full of rocks sitting on one end. That end is down on the ground. At the other end, up in the air, is a basket one quarter full of sand. Some of us are trying to fill it, using teaspoons. Most folks laugh at us. "Don't you know the sand is leaking out even as you put it in?"

We say, that's true, but we're getting more people with teaspoons all the time. One of these days that basket of sand will be more than half full and you'll see this whole see-saw go zzzip the opposite way. People will say, "Gee, how did it happen so suddenly?" Us, and our little teaspoons.

Will there be a human race here in another 200 years? Yes, it's a possibility. If so, it will be partly because songwriters and singers of many kinds used whatever talents they were born with or developed. And remember that even after that seesaw tips, the basket still leaks. It could tip back again. We have to keep using our teaspoons.

And use them to help our fellow humans get together. Their closer neighbors. Their distant cousins in the wider world. These pages show some of the mistakes made and some of the small successes of one songwriter and his friends over a long life.

Here's hoping that readers will find a few ideas worth stealing.

Still rockin' and reelin',

Pete Seeger

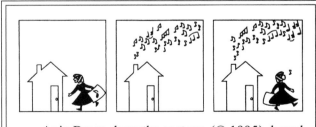

Axie Breen drew the cartoon (© 1995), based on an original idea by Susan Salidor, a children's songwriter and performer from Chicago. Susan uses it as the letterhead for her business stationary and cards. Thanks, Susan, for reminding me where I got it!

Illustration by Axie Breen

Postscript

First putting this book together 14 years ago, Peter Blood and I tried to squeeze in as many songs as we could without ever asking readers to turn a page in the middle of a song. The book was already more expensive than we wished. In the late '90s we spent two days trying to "repaginate" the book but realized the job would take more time than either of us had. Then Peter and his wife got busy putting out a sequel to the great book of 1,200 songs *Rise Up Singing* (the sequel will be called *Spread Your Wings*).

When I met Michael Miller and found he was willing to take time to help with the present volume, we made the decision not to repaginate. We knew that if we wanted to add something, we'd have to drop something.

So now I apologize to some songs, and to some good people, for what has had to be dropped. And then I realized that I'd helped put some things together that I still wanted to see in print, so we decided to put them in this Postscript.

The 1993 melody I put on p. 259 I added to by repeating the opening phrase. Behold! A better melody. Then I found I had four more sets of words to put to it which I think are better than the ones I thought of first.

Note that the melody hardly ever touches E, the first note of the scale, except briefly in passing. The note just below it, D♯ ("the leading tone"), is emphasized, giving a nice dissonance when the bass E string is sounded at the same time.

Here are some of the other lyrics that fit the melody — which sounds quite different when some notes are held longer or shorter, as you see (and hear).

For Mumia

Mumia Abu-Jamal has been on Pennsylvania's death row since 1982. A wide campaign in his support has built up. Maybe this song can help. For information on his case, see <www.refuseandresist.org>.

1. We say he's innocent!
   We say he's innocent
   And if still you disagree
   At least a new trial
   A new trial should be held
   With witnesses who 10 years ago
   Were never heard
   Let not this good man
   Be executed on just
   One policeman's word

2. We say he's a good man
   We say he's a good man
   And we challenge you to read
   What he has written
   Before and after that fateful night
   And if you say that right now
   You really just don't have the time
   Here's a petition. Do you
   Have time right now to sign?

I've tried two other sets of lyrics to this melody. They started off good, but I don't think much of the latter parts, so I cut 'em off hoping some reader will add something so good that listeners will murmur, "Let me hear that again."

All I know is, I have a usable melody that could carry, as you see above, quite different words.

If you are skimming this book (I skim books, don't you?), I assume you've checked out the first few pages and now skim the last few. Use the Index. If you're into politics for example, read Chapter 10 as well as Chapter 2. Religion? Read the Postscript as well as Chapter 8. Unions? UTI (Use The Index.) Race relations? UTI. The other arts, including cooking? UTI. War and peace? Chapter 7, but UTI. Hudson Valley? Chapter 9, but UTI. Banjo? Guitar? UTI. You get the idea.

The Ocean's Rising

The ocean's ris - ing.— The ocean's ris - ing and the on - ly question is: How much, how soon? And will we act in time?

★ ★ ★

No Mas Violencia

Freely

No más vio - len - cia! No más, no más vio-len-cia en Co-lom - bi - a, We'll learn to talk, although we— disagree.— And if we...

No Mas Violencia!
No mas, no mas, no mas violencia en Colombia!
We'll learn to talk though we disagree.
And if we sing, or eat, or tolerate each other's
    company-y-y.
Who knows, who knows, what changes yet our
    grandchildren will someday see.

★ ★ ★

The next song, written after 9/11, should have been in Chapter 8. I now sing it in some church every January when Martin Luther King's birthday is celebrated. I've laughed to think that I, who long thought of myself as an atheist, learned the most important political lessons of my life from a Baptist preacher.

What lessons? Consider: if you face an opponent over a broad front, you don't try to attack the opponent's strong points. You pick some outlying point that you can surround and *win*. Who would have said in 1955 that riding in the front of the bus was that important? Why didn't King concentrate on jobs, or voting, or housing, or education?

In the course of trying to write the song I read books by and about Martin Luther King Jr. He graduated from high school at age 15. After four years at Morehouse College in Atlanta he did three years in divinity school in Pennsylvania. He admired two professors of philosophy in Boston and did two more years of graduate study at Boston University. By that time his academic reputation had spread and he was offered good jobs in the philosophy departments of three separate northern universities. He turned down all three to take a lower-paying job in a small church in Alabama. He knew: that was *where* the job had to be done.

Illustration by Sibylle Pfaffenbichler

MARTIN LUTHER KING FROM A 24" X 28" COLOR POSTER BY SIBYLLE PFAFFENBICHLER. THE POSTER CAN BE VIEWED AND PURCHASED AT <WWW.NORTHLANDPOSTER.COM>.

Take It from Dr. King

C67

(Accompanists: see next page, column two)

Strict tempo ♩=104   (Accompanists: see p.265, col.2)

1. Down in Al-a-bam-a, nine-teen hundred fif-ty five, not many of us here to-day were then a-live. A young Bap-tist preach-er led a bus boy-cott. He showed a way for a brand new day with-out fi-r-ing a shot.

a single low note

REFRAIN
DON'T SAY IT CAN'T BE DONE.

THE BAT-TLE'S JUST BE-GUN.

Accompaniment just plays melody or bass here — see next page.

TAKE IT FROM DOC-TOR KING, YOU TOO CAN LEARN TO SING SO DROP THE GUN!

> "The ultimate weakness of violence is that ... instead of diminishing evil, it multiplies it. Through violence you may murder the hater but you do not murder hate. In fact violence merely increases hate. Darkness cannot drive out darkness; only light can do that. Hate cannot drive out hate; only love can do that."
>
> — Martin Luther King

C68   2. Ohh! Those mus-sta' been an ex-cit-ing thir-teen years! Young he-roes, young he-ro-ines, there was laughter, there were tears. Stu-dents sit-ting down at lunch count-ers, child-ren danc-ing in the streets. To think, it all start-ed with Ro-sa re-fus-ing to give up her seat.

tacit   *low note*

I have never failed to get *any* crowd singing this syncopated chorus. To teach it takes about 50 seconds. After you've sung two verses and sung the chorus after each verse, you now speak to the crowd. (Lines you speak are in quotes. Lines you sing alone are in italics. Lines you all sing together, unaccompanied now, are capitalized.)

"You can sing this!" *Don't say it can't be done.* DON'T SAY IT CAN'T BE DONE. "Good!" *The battle's just begun.* THE BATTLE'S JUST BEGUN. *Take it from Doctor King.* TAKE IT FROM DOCTOR KING.

"Let's sing all those three lines!" (Accompaniment now) ♩ ♩ ♩ DON'T SAY IT CAN'T BE DONE. "The battle!" THE BATTLE'S JUST BEGUN. "Take it!" TAKE IT FROM DOCTOR KING.

(Without pause, but singing slower, with no accompaniment) *You too can learn to sing.* YOU TOO CAN LEARN TO SING. *So drop the gun!* SO DROP THE GUN! "Now we know the whole chorus! ♩ ♩ ♩ DON'T SAY IT CAN'T BE DONE. THE BATTLE'S JUST...etc. The crowd sings the whole chorus with accompaniment.

Go right into the third verse. The crowd will sing the chorus whenever they hear the three cue notes (or three beats of a drum, perhaps?).

C69 3. Songs, songs,— songs— kept 'em go-ing and grow-ing.— They didn't know all the millions of seeds that they were sow-ing.— They were singing on marches, ev-en sing-ing in— jail.— Songs gave them courage to be-lieve— they would not fail.

tacit Accomp. *to Refrain*

(Now's a good time for an instrumental break or two. Harmonica? Trumpet? Fake it! Then keep improvising when the crowd sings the chorus!)

C70 4. We sang— 'bout Al-a-ba-ma, nine-teen hun-dred fif-ty-five.— But since Sep-tem-ber E-lev-enth, many won-der: will this world sur-vive?— But if the world learns the les-sons— from Doc-tor— King, we can— sur-vive,— we can,

(shout) — WE WILL!— And so we sing!

tacit Accomp. *to Refrain*

After the fourth refrain I like to get the crowd clapping on the offbeat for a final chorus, hands high in the

air. (The ⊕ shows the offbeat claps. If kids push their hands apart on the word "put" and bring them together after the word "'em" they'll be clapping on the offbeat.)

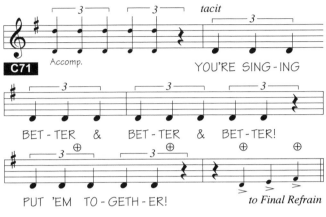

C71 Accomp. YOU'RE SING-ING BET-TER & BET-TER & BET-TER! PUT 'EM TO-GETH-ER!

to Final Refrain

Words & Music by Pete Seeger
© 2002 by Sanga Music, NYC

Accompanist:

G is too low a key for the average audience to sing this song. C is too high, I think. I propose that guitarists capo up two frets; play it in G and it comes out A. If you've never before tried it now's a good time to learn Dropped D tuning (DADGBE) (p. 287). No trouble about the first twelve measures. Here's chords. Then the next four measures, including a low D single note, tacit for a few beats, then the three important single bass notes to cue the crowd to sing the chorus ♩ ♩ ♩

First twelve measures:

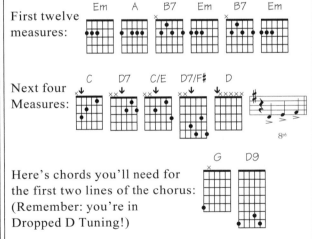

Next four Measures:

Here's chords you'll need for the first two lines of the chorus: (Remember: you're in Dropped D Tuning!)

For the last three measures of the chorus just play a syncopated scale on the lower strings.

It's not as hard as it looks. Just follow the melody of the chorus.

"Take..." "...too..." "...sing..." "...gun"
G   A   B   C   D   E   F#   G

English Is Cuh-ray-zee

This "talking" song was put together by Josh White Jr. after reading the book *Crazy English* by Richard Lederer. It has been slightly shortened, and I added a refrain.

You can tap on a wastebasket for rhythm or use a rattle. I used the pattern below on a banjo. No two people will declaim the words the exact same way. I give the first two lines just as a sample of how they might be done.

1. English! is the most widely used language in the history of the planet. / One out of every seven human beings can speak or read it. / Half the world's books are in English. / It has the largest vocabulary, perhaps two million words. / But face it, (SING:) English is Cuh-ray—zee!* "Next time help me out."

2. Just a few examples: / There's no egg in eggplant, no pine or apple in pineapple. / A writer writes, but do fingers fing? / Do grocers gross? / Quicksand works slowly. / Boxing rings are square. / English is Cuh-ray—zee! (AFTER EVERY VERSE)

3. If the plural of tooth is teeth, shouldn't the plural of booth be beeth? / We have one goose, two geese. / Why not one moose, two meese? / The plural of index is indices. / Should it be one Kleenex, two Kleenices?**

4. In what other language do you drive on a parkway and park on a driveway? / Recite at a play but play at a recital? / Ship by truck but send cargo by ship? / Have noses that run and feet that smell. / English is Cuh-ray—zee! (GET SOME HARMONY!) Cuh-ray—zee!***

5. You have to marvel at the lunacy of a language in which your house can burn up when it burns down. / You fill out a form when you fill it in. / Your alarm clock goes off when it goes on. / And if a vegetarian eats vegetables, what does a humanitarian eat? / English is Cuh-ray—zee!

6. Well, English was made up by people, not computers. / It reflects the creativity of the human race. / So that's why when I wind up my watch I start it. / When I wind up this rap I end it. / English is Cuh-ray—zee!

© 1998 by Richard Lederer, 10034 Mesa Madeira Dr., San Diego, CA 92131

★ ★ ★

Or Else! (One-a These Days)

In my old age, as my own voice collapsed, I got more skilled at getting audiences to singalong. Not just melodies, but high or low harmonies, and with this curious little song, a rich G major chord, and then a rich E minor. I point to my left. "You over here hum this note." I hum a G into the mike. "Keep humming." I point in front of me. "You in the center hum this note." I hum a B. "You over here hum this note." I point to my right and hum a high or low D. "Everyone: open your mouth." There is an expression of pleasure and surprise as a nice G major chord is heard by all.

"That's what musicians call a 'major chord.' Here's a second one." I point to the left, center, and right again and give them an E, a G, a B, sounding an E minor when they open their mouths. Right away I start singing the song, holding up an open hand as we repeat "One-a these days" and on the second response, closed hand. By the third verse, they know what to do, even the half-spoken "OR ELSE."

Eng-lish is cuh-ray-zee!___

** In India nobody knew what a Kleenex was, so I said, "If males are one sex, are male and female two 'cices' (see-sees)?"

get the mon-ey it needs for smaller class-es.

And the Na-vy will hold a

bake sale to build a battleship. *(to Chorus)*

VERSE

2. And Johnny will get the

money he needs for that op-er-a-tion.

And the Air Force will hold a

raf-fle to buy a bomb-er. *(to Chorus)*

VERSE

3. And ev'-ry vote will be counted in

every e-lec-tion. And the winners will

al-ways keep all of their promises. *(to Chorus)*

VERSE

4. A-round this world we'll start to learn each other's

lan-gua-ges.

(MUSIC STOPS ABRUPTLY.
SEE BELOW.)

CHORUS:
One-a these days (ONE-A THESE DAYS)
One-a these days (ONE-A THESE DAYS)
One-a these days, one-a these days,
OR ELSE! (REPEAT CHORUS AFTER EACH OF 3 VERSES)

1. Our school will get the money it needs for smaller classes,
   And the Navy will hold a bake sale to build a battleship. (CHORUS)

2. And Johnny will get the money he needs for that operation,
   And the Air Force will hold a raffle to buy a bomber. (CHORUS)

3. And every vote will be counted in every election,
   And the winners will always keep all of their promises. (CHORUS)

4. Around this world we'll start to learn each other's languages.

The music stops abruptly. I ask the crowd, whether 20 or 200, "Who knows the word for 'Hello' or 'Good Morning' in some other language? Raise your hand." In a classroom, it can go on for two or three minutes, singing the chorus after every two or three responses. If it's a large crowd, I pass a mike to whoever raises a hand. In 2006 at the Beacon Waterfront Corn Festival it went on for five minutes. I saw one family whispering to a five-year-old and pushing him toward the mike. He shyly faced it: "BON GIORNO!" A black girl of 8 or 10 came up and said a word that sounded like "Pel." "Where's that from?" says I. "Haiti!" said she and skipped back to her family, and we all sang the chorus.

But come February 2007, in a Westchester County church were 400 people. Earlier in the evening I'd got them humming a rich G chord (see page 266, column 2), then an E minor chord. They were primed for this song. As I went down the center aisle passing my radio mike to people on the right and the left ("Pass it to the little girl over there") I needed no accompaniment to get the crowd singing the chorus. I held the mike close to the banjo for one short strum (open G tuning) then raised the mike to my lips, sang only the first three words "One-a these days." From then on we had a 400-voice a-cappella chorus response in rich harmony. We kept it going eight or ten minutes.

Next day I found out why it went so well. Clearwater's Walkabout Chorus, which had sung a few songs early in the evening then took seats scattered from front to back, right and left, so no one in the audience was more than 6 or 7 feet from a bass, a tenor, an alto or a soprano. When I was finally back up front we did one more chorus slowly, with a final "OR ELSE."

Music by Pete Seeger
3rd verse by David Bernz
1st verse by A.N. Onymous

Tzena, Tzena, Tzena, Tzena
(Tsenna, Tzena, Zeina)

In 1939 two young men, composer Issachar Miron and lyricist Yehiel Hagiz, met in a Jewish brigade of the British army, which then controlled Palestine. They made up this great song. "Come out, come out, girls; see the soldier boys in the village. Let's sing and dance." It was sung through North Africa, and from the Normandy beachhead to the Holocaust camps.

In 1950 popular bandleader Gordon Jenkins heard the Weavers sing it and wrote English lyrics for it. We had a million-seller hit. In 1997 I got together with Issachar Miron, now living in New York, to see if, in the present world situation, the song could perhaps have a new career. Issachar got his friend Salman Natour, a leading Arab poet in Israel, to write a verse in Arabic with basically the same meaning, "Come, let's dance the Dabkeh (a Palestinian dance) and dance the Hora (an Israeli dance)." The word "Zeina" means "beautiful" in Arabic.

Remember Thoreau's advice "Simplify, Simplify!" We've changed a word here and there. This very rhythmical song is a 3-part round. You need at least three people to lead it, or a chorus divided into three parts. I suggest some women in your chorus sing the Arabic lyrics, other women sing the Hebrew. Then all the men sing the English. It's a 48-measure song. Although I print the English words first, I propose we let the *Arabic* words be heard first. After 32 bars, the other group of women start the song in Hebrew. *32* bars later all the men start the English version.

Now all three versions are being heard simultaneously. No handclaps. 48 bars later we'll have heard the exciting round three ways, at which point the singing and accompaniment come to a dead stop. In one second of silence a child or young woman spreads arms wide, palms down and shouts:

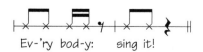

Ev-'ry bod-y: sing it!

Tze - na, Tze - na, when the band is play - ing
Tsen - na, Tsen - na, Tsen - na, Tsen - na, Tsen - na,
Zei - na, Zei - na, Zei - na, Zei - na, Zei - na,

my heart's say - ing "Tze - na, Tze - na, Tze - na." ("Everybody: Sing it!")
Tsen - na, Tsen - na, Tsen - na, Tsen - na, Tsen - na,
Zei - na, Zei - na, Zei - na, Zei - na, Zei - na.

Tze - na, Tze - na, CLAP! Tze - na, Tze - na, Tze - na,

tacit or single notes

Tze - na, Tze - na, Tze - na, Tze - na, Tze - na, Tze - na,

Tze - na, Tze - na, CLAP! Tze - na, Tze - na, Tze - na,

Tze - na, Tze - na, Tze - na, Tze - na. Tze - na!

* "ghr" is like the French "r" in "Paris" ("Paree"). The Arabic "h" is only slightly like "ch" in "Bach;" "a" is like our "ah" *except* the "a" in "ghrannu," which is more like the "a" in "hat." "Ei" is as in "weight." The "i" in "nidbek" is like "it" or "in."

Music by Issachar Miron
English lyrics by Gordon Jenkins
(One line altered by Pete Seeger)
Hebrew lyrics by Yehiel Haggiz
Arabic lyrics by Salman Natour
© 1998 Issachar Miron / EMI Music

Below, see my fast syncopated 4-measure introduction. I've tuned my banjo so both 1st string and 5th string are F. With thumb and two fingers you can get these very fast four measures. Tap your feet if you don't have an instrument. The same effect can be got by two drummers. The deeper drum keeps the main beat. Note the > over 1st and 3rd beats. The higher drum, using thumb and two sets of fingers, gets the same effect as the banjoist's two fingers and a thumb. FAST!! ♩ = 152 (standard march time is ♩ = 120).

Banjo intro.

I M T I M T I M T   I M T I M T I   M T   I M T I M T   I M T I M T I M

F
D
B♭
F
F

All the song leaders, whether three or thirty, now reach out their right hand, palm up, and raise it above their heads while they sing in full harmony, the two words "Tzena, tzena." On the third measure they make a loud CLAP by raising their left hands and slicing down on them with the right. This is repeated eight measures later; "Tzena, tzena," CLAP!

The audience probably will want to sing these 16 bars again. And again. You may decide to sing it in all three languages. My hope, of course, is for the song to become so well known that audiences will know how to sing it in harmony and get that fine augmented chord with the F♯ in the 3rd and 11th measures.

Who knows? Maybe the song could be sung in Serbian and Bosnian, or Hindi and Urdu, or Quechua and Spanish (in Peru), or Chechen and Russian. In Japan they could sing two short syllables "Hey wa" which means "Peace in the world." Eventually it could be a true victory song. World peace, prevailing over senseless hatred, will be the real victory for the human race. Then war, like cannibalism, will be something that children read about in history books.

A note on the harmony, at left. Until the crowd is invited to sing along with one word shouted, these harmony parts are not sung, nor is the augmented chord with the F♯ played by the accompaniment.

This is the old Weavers arrangement. Lee Hays, a baritone, and Ronnie Gilbert, an alto, sang the melody, the lowest of the three notes. Fred Hellerman sang two notes above the melody most of the time. I was a tenor then and sang the F, the F♯, and the G. If you want those notes louder, a few altos can help. The F♯s are important! If you have some frustrated sopranos let them sing an octave higher than Fred. I bet audiences will want to sing it twice. Maybe thrice!

Exactly what do the Hebrew and Arabic words mean? Turn to p. 270.

Zeina, Zeina, Zeina, Zeina
(Arabic)

زينة، زينة، زينة، زينة،
دبكة ندبك، نرقص هورا
بليلة تواعدنا، يالله معنا، معنا يالله
ردّوا يالله، ردّوا معنا غنّوا يا أحباب
زينة، زينة، دبكة ندبك يالله
نرقص هورا يا أصحاب
يالله معنا، يالله ردّوا معنا
أهلا بكم يا أصحاب
زينة، زينة، زينة، زينة، ــ ــ ــ

Zeina, zeina, zeina, zeina,
Dabkeh nihdbek nurkus hora
Bleilet twa adna.
Yalla ma'ana, ma'ana yalla
Rudu ma'ana, rudu ma'ana
Ghrannu ya ah-bab.
Zeina, zeina, dabkeh nihdbek yalla.
Nurkus hora ya as-ha-a-a-ab.
Yalla ma'ana, yalla rudu ma'ana
Ah-lan bikom ya as-hab!
Zeina, zeina, zeina, zeina _ _ _

Literal translation of the Arabic:

Beautiful, beautiful, beautiful, beautiful
We dance the dabkeh, dance the hora
One night we have a get-together
Come on, let's go, let's go, come on
Repeat with us, sing with us, oh beloved
Beautiful, beautiful, let us dance the dabkeh, dance
   the hora, oh friends.
Come on with us, repeat with us.
Welcome, oh friends.
Beautiful, beautiful, beautiful, beautiful _ _ _

Pronunciation Guide
(Hebrew and Arabic)

"a" as in "ah," except "ghrannu" as in "hat"
"e" as in "met" (the English "Tzena" as in "late")
"i" as in "magazine"
"ih" as in "it" ("nihdbek")
"o" as in "more"
"u" as in "flute"
"ei" as in "sleigh"
"kh" (Hebrew) as the "ch" as in "Bach"
"h" (Arabic) a lighter "ch" as in "Bach"
"ghr" (Arabic) a harder guttural, like the "r" in the French City of
Paris ("Paree")
"c" as in "cat"
"g" as in "dog"
"d, f, l, k, m, n, p, s, t, v, sh, z, y," all as in English pronunciation
"r" slightly rolled, as the Italian "rondo"

Tsenna, Tsenna, Tsenna, Tsenna
(Hebrew)

צֶאנָה, צֶאנָה, צֶאנָה, צֶאנָה.
הַבָּנוֹת וּרְאֶינָה חֲבֵרִים בָּאִים לָעִיר.
אַל נָה, אַל נָה, אַל נָה, אַל נָה.
אַל נָה תִּתְחַבֵּאנָה, וּמִזְמוֹר יַחְדָּו נָשִׁיר.
צֶאנָה, צֶאנָה, הַבָּנוֹת וּרְאֶנָה.
חֲבֵרִים בָּאִים לָעִיר.
אַל נָה, אַל נָה, אַל נָה תִּתְחַבֵּנָה.
וּמִזְמוֹר יַחְדָּו נָשִׁיר.
צֶאנָה, צֶאנָה, (CLAP) צֶאנָה, צֶאנָה,

Tsenna, Tsenna, Tsenna, Tsenna
Habanot urenna khaverim, Ba'im la'ir.
Alna, alna, alna, alna, Alna titkhabenna,
Umizmor yakhdav nashir.
Tsenna, tsenna, Habanot urenna, Khaverim ba'im la'ir.
Alna, alna, Alna titkhabenna, Umizmor yakhdav nashir.
Tsenna, Tsenna, Tsenna _ _ _

Literal translation of the Hebrew:

Come out, / come out, girls /
See friends / in the village. /
Don't be – / don't be shy! /
Let's sing / and dance, /
All of us / together! /
Come out, come out, come out _ _ _

Tzena, Tzena, Tzena, Tzena
(English)

Tzena, Tzena, Tzena, Tzena,
Can't you hear the music playing
In the city square?
Tzena, Tzena, Tzena, Tzena,
Come where all our friends will find us
With the dancers there.
   Tzena, Tzena! Join the celebration.
   There'll be people there from every nation.
   Dawn will find us laughing in the sunlight,
   Dancing in the city square.
Tzena, Tzena, (CLAP) Come and dance the hora.
Dance the dabkeh. All of us will dance together.
Tzena, Tzena, (CLAP) When the band is playing,
My heart's saying "Tzena, Tzena, Tzena!"

> This planet will eventually be at peace. With
> or without people. If the human race is still
> here, music will be one of the reasons why. If
> any reader finds a way songs in this book can
> be improved, I urge you try them out. Let the
> folk process roll on.

Didn't Ol' John

This song was recorded by Alan Lomax for the Library of Congress archives in 1937. It was a song of African American prisoners in South Carolina chopping logs on a state prison farm. The first verse is theirs. But I've sung it to myself, while chopping wood for 50 years, and done it on stage, too, chips flying out into the audience.

But sooner or later a chip was going to put someone's eye out, and now I use a 6-pound sledgehammer on a spike in a large log. The "spike," a splitting wedge, but put in at 90 degrees to the grain, so it *won't* split the log. I've drilled a wedge-shaped hole first, then hammered the steel wedge tight so it won't go further.

The asterisks and underlines show where the sledgehammer falls, always on the third beat of the measure.

1. Didn't ol' John * cross the water, <u>wa</u>ter on his knees *
   Didn't ol' John * cross the water * on his knees *
   Let us all * bow down * good Lord and face, *<u>face</u> the rising sun.
   Didn't ol' John * cross the water, <u>wa</u>ter on his knees. *

2. Now, don't let the Devil * get you believin' he'll <u>say</u> we can't learn to get along. *
   Don't let the Devil * get you to believin' * we can't learn to get along *
   He will try, * try to fool yuh, * try to divide, * divide and rule yuh *
   I do believe * we can put a rainbow, <u>rain</u>bow,[1] 'round this world. *

3. One a' these days * we gonna see big changes we ain't <u>never</u> didn't ever see before *
   One a' these days * we gonna see big changes * we didn't ever see before. *
   When all the world * sees the danger * and we learn to take the hand * of a cousin and a stranger. *
   I do believe * we can put a rainbow, <u>rain</u>bow 'round this world. *

4. Didn't we once * stop a damn fool war * over 40 years ago? *
   Didn't we once * stop a damn fool war * over 40 years ago? *
   So right now * ain't the time at hand * we all get to save * this precious land? *
   I do believe * we can put a rainbow, <u>rain</u>bow 'round this world. *

African American chopping song
Verses 2-3-4 by Pete Seeger, 1996

[1]This line from Randolphe Harris

During WWII Woody Guthrie had a sign on his guitar: "This machine kills fascists." When he was hospitalized in '52 I wrote on the head of my banjo: "This machine surrounds hate and forces it to surrender." As I start the 90th year of my life on this earth, I do believe it will be the women who will show how to get this warring world together. In millions of little organizations north and south, east and west, city and country, men and women will show how to accomplish things that big power-hungry organizations have been unable to do.

NOTE: * = the ax hitting wood, or hands hauling a rope, etc., on third beat of each measure

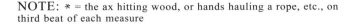

Arrange and Re-arrange

This is a true story. Early morning in February a few years ago, I went out to get some firewood and saw the sun peeking over Mt. Beacon. A verse and a tune came to me all at once.

HIGH HARMONY

Oh - wee,___ oh - wye,___ to ar -
range and re - ar-range and re - ar - range.

Oh - wee,___ oh - wye,___ to ar -
range and re - ar-range and re - ar - range.

1. Early in the morning, I first see the sun,
   I say a little prayer for the world.
   I hope all the little children live a long long time
   Yes, every little boy and little girl.
   I hope they learn to laugh at the way
   Some precious old words do seem to change,
   'Cause, that's what life is all about:
   To arrange and re-arrange and re-arrange.

   CHORUS:
   Oh-wee, oh-wye, to arrange and re-arrange and
   re-arrange.
   Oh-wee, oh-wye, to arrange and re-arrange and
   re-arrange.

I liked to sing it, but I couldn't think of a good second verse until the maple syrup season started a few weeks later:

2. Early in the mornin' I'm a-carrying the sap
   And I say a little prayer for the maple.
   Like old Mama Quad, on the northwest slope,
   I'll protect her 'long as I am able.
   She gives more sap year after year,
   Than any single other tree.
   So bring on the pancakes! Here's to Mama Quad!
   May she live for another century.

   CHORUS:
   Oh-wee, oh-wye, to arrange and rearrange and
   re-arrange.
   Oh-wee, oh-wye, to arrange and rearrange and
   re-arrange.

Now I had two singable verses. Where do I go from here? A change of pace is needed.

3. Sometimes I wake in the middle of the night
   And rub my achin' old eyes.
   Is that a voice from inside-a my head
   Or does it come down from the skies?
   "There's a time to laugh but there's a time to weep,
   And a time to make a big change.
   Wake-up-<u>you</u>-bum-the-<u>time</u>-has-come
   (Drop beats to indicate haste)
   To ar<u>range</u> and re-arrange and re-arrange"
   (REPEAT CHORUS)

C77...

...change.   Wake up you bum the time has come to re-ar -

Soon after this, a philosophical relative was visiting me and I sang her my new song. She said, "Peter, I don't think I approve of this song. We need a more stable world." I replied, "Maybe you're right!" And soon I had the prize verse. I thought.

C...77

4. Maybe the biggest change will come
   When we don't have to change much at all.
   When maniacs holler "GROW, GROW, GROW!"
   We can choose to stay small.
   The key word may be "little."
   We only have to change a little bit.
   So eat a little food; drink a little drink;
   And only have to shit a little shit.
     Oh-wee, oh-wye,
     And only have to shit a little shit.
     Oh-wee, oh-wye,
     And only have to shit a little shit.

And I followed with singing the first verse of the song, a little slower, and with the word "wicked" instead of the word "precious." I sang it once this way for three thousand Quakers.

And it led to some family discussions. I finally decided that in this crucial 21st Century, it's more important to concentrate on getting the world together to save the planet than to make a big thing out of trying to make the English language more honest. I don't sing it now.

'Way back then, though (1990s), I used to point to kids in the audience and say "Kids, I know you have been told: 'You will *not* say that word in this house.' But you're not in that house now. Besides, it's not words that are so bad, it's the things people *do* that are bad. And grown-ups are doing most of them. So sing it again!"

After a second chorus, I'd repeat the first verse at a slower tempo and as I said, substitute the word "wicked" instead of the word "precious."

★ ★ ★

In 1971 two young people painted this on the side of my barn:

I am done
with great things and big things,
great institutions and big success,
  and I am for
those tiny, invisible, molecular moral forces
that work from individual to individual,
creeping through the crannies of the world
like so many rootlets,
or like the capillary oozing of water,
yet which, if you give them time,
will rend the hardest monuments of man's
  pride.

— William James

In the 1980s I wrote to the *Harvard Magazine*, "Is this a correct quote?" They printed a reply that Israel Sheffler, who is Victor S. Thomas Professor of Education and Philosophy at Harvard, found this needle in a haystack. The text, in a letter from James to Mrs. Henry Whitman (June 7, 1899), actually reads:

As for me, my bed is made: I am against bigness and greatness in all their forms, and with the invisible molecular moral forces that work from individual to individual, stealing in through the crannies of the world like so many soft rootlets, or like the capillary oozing of water, and yet rending the hardest monuments of man's pride, if you give them time. The bigger the unit you deal with, the hollower, the more brutal, the more mendacious is the life displayed. So I am against all big organizations as such, national ones first and foremost; against all big successes and big results; and in favor of the eternal forces of truth which always work in the individual and immediately unsuccessful way, under-dogs always, till history comes, after they are long dead, and puts them on top.

The letter appears in *The Letters of William James*, volume 2, edited by his son Henry, p. 90 (published by the Atlantic Monthly Press).

The Hammers Are Bangin' Away

This curious tune in 5/4 time was made up back in the 1970s when Congresswoman Bella Abzug was running for mayor of New York City. I've never succeeded in getting long-lasting words, but the tune sticks with me. In '94, coming back from a trip to Paraguay, we stopped at Bluefields, a small English-speaking town on the east coast of Nicaragua. A hurricane had hit them a few weeks before, and from dawn to dark, people were sawing and hammering, repairing their homes.

C78

The ham-mers are bang-in' a -

way all o-ver Bluefields, the people o'

Bluefields are building up a-gain.__ The hammers are

bangin' a-way all o-ver Bluefields, the people o'

Bluefields are building up a-gain.__ The ver-y first

boat ar-rived just two days later with friends from

Cuba bringing med-i-cal supplies, And food and

wa-ter and then soon right af-ter the things we

needed were set down before our eyes.The hammers are

As you can see I never took time to finish the song. A day later we flew back to the States. But I print it here in case any rhymester would like to take up the challenge of writing verses of any sort for a melody in 5/4 time. Harry Belafonte wrote a great children's song in 5/4 time ("Turn the World Around"). The future world will not be all in 4/4 time. Write it for your home town or neighborhood.

Fellow editor Dave Bernz made up new words to this melody way back in 1990! He likes to sing it in 4/4 time, but I find I can still sing his words in 5/4 time.

One Percent Phosphorous

I've heard it said that all people are different.
I've heard it said all people are the same.
Scientists give us a wonderful answer.
For now we know precisely what we're made from.

One-percent phosphorus, one-point four percent calcium,
Carbon and nitrogen, twenty-six percent.
Then we are seventy-one percent water
And smaller amounts of forty other elements.

★ ★ ★

Trouble at the Bottom

You can see I like words that help give out rhythm. They need consonants like T, B, also K, D, G, P. This tune was written for steel drums many decades ago. Only recently I got these words with the help of grand-son Tao Rodriguez.

C79

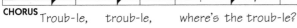

1. Some say the trouble's in the Pentagon
   Some say the trouble's in the street
   Some say the president's a paragon
   Where's the trouble at the bottom?
   Some say the trouble's the psychology
   Some say the trouble's in the head
   Some say the trouble's the anatomy
   There's the trouble at the bottom!

   CHORUS:
   Trouble, trouble, where's the trouble?
   Oh, Mama, where's the trouble?
   Got a headache, seeing double!
   Where's the trouble at the bottom?

2. Some say the trouble is the principal
   Some say the trouble is the kids
   Some say the trouble's the curriculum
   Where's the trouble at the bottom?
   Some say the trouble's with the textbook
   Some say the trouble's with the class
   Over all, the school board fuggin up
   Where's the trouble at the bottom!

(CHORUS)

3. Some say the trouble's in the family
   Some say the trouble's on the job
   Some say whatever the analogy
   Find the trouble at the bottom?
   Some say the trouble's in the system
   Some say the trouble's in the class
   Karl claimed the trouble was the upper one
   That is the upper not the bottom

(CHORUS)

You'll probably want to sing this in a lower key. The tune sounds good on a mandolin or keyboard. I fake the "rim shots" by pulling my tongue down from the roof of my mouth, giving a loud click, as in some South African songs.

★ ★ ★

As a kid I sang rounds at home and at school. My father, in 1934, persuaded some of his colleagues in the Composers Collective to write "rounds about the very rich." Three of them are printed in the book *Rise Up Singing* and others are in the Sing Out! library "SORCe."

But if you are really into rounds, look up the books from Sol Weber at <http://roundz.tripod.com/>

My lifetime favorite round is this one by William Boyce ca. 1750.

Alleluya

By William Boyce, 18th Century

Pronounced "ah-lay-loo-yah," this ancient Hebrew word (it means "Praise God") must now be the second most well-known word in the world. The first is "Okay."

William Boyce was a church organist. In 18th Century London, I think. Wrote some oratorios and an opera. This round of his has become justly famous. I print it in this book because I discovered a way to get large audiences singing it. I bought a large piece of unbleached muslin cloth (9' x 30') and in a day, with rolls of black masking tape and some brushes and paint, I put the 24 measures of Boyce's round on it on three staffs. For smaller audiences I made a 3' x 10' banner.

I need at least three people or a chorus up front to demonstrate how the round sounds. After 24 bars I stop them, turn to the audience and say, "Now we will *all* sing it." I hear a murmur of disbelief. "We have help from on high."

If we are in a theater, the 30-foot banner is now lowered from above or carried in on five or ten long bamboo poles. I point to the upper left of the banner and say: "See that letter O? It's a music note. There's four of them. Each one has four beats. See how the first one is on a space, the next one is on the line below it, and the next on the space below that line?"

I sing "*AH - - - LAY - - - LOO - - - YAH - - -*. Sing those four notes with me." The banjo plays four notes to each syllable. We sing (correct spelling) "*A - - - le - - - lu - - - ya - - -*. See, you're reading music already. When the notes get tails on them they move faster." (But I sing the melody slowly now.) "*One* two three four, *one* and two and three and four and *one* , two, *three* , four, *one*, two, three, four. You can see there's always four beats between the verti-

cal lines, no matter whether you have a lot of short notes or a few long notes. Let's sing the whole line together. One two three SING!" (slowly).

The whole crowd now sings *A - - - le - - - lu - - - ya - - -. A - - le luu uu uu uu u- u- ya - - -. "Good! Let's sing a little faster."* We repeat the whole first line of the round. "Those who know music sing out strong, so that others can take courage from your efforts. That's the way it is in life. Them that knows should lead. If we can only agree who knows."

"Now at the left of the next line is a red squiggle. That's called a 'rest' because the rhythm keeps going but you don't sing till you come to the second beat of the measure. So it's REST! *two, three, four*. Let's sing the words, and go on through the line. Here we go. … *A le lu ya A le* etc. through eight bars."

"Good! Let's sing this second line through a little faster." (We do that.) "I suppose you've noticed those blue curved lines. They tie together two or more notes, making them sound like one longer note. Now, at the

PETE SEEGER AND HIS 9' X 30' "ALLELUYA" BANNER.

right end of this second line is a note with two beats and a curved line connecting it with the first note of the third line. It's the longest note in the whole song! Two beats here" (I point) "and three beats here" (I point) "because the note has a dot after it. So let's sing slow, first. *A - - - - le luu uu ya-, A le lu - ya - -, A le - lu - ya - -, A le - lu - ya - - -!* Now we can sing the whole song!"

Now, the audience and I, and whoever is on the stage, we sing the whole 24 bars through two or three times, slower at first, and then faster. The first time through, the banjo can just play melody, or a few chords. The third time I give it a syncopated, almost Scruggs-type rhythm, you can hear on the CD. I give the tablature here.

Banjo Tuning—GCGBD

C84

"Now," I say, "let's make a round out of it." I point to my left. "All the women on this side start singing." I face my right. "When the women over there get to the end of the first line and start the second line, then you over here start singing the first high note. All the men stay silent until the second group of women get to the end of the first line, *then* ALL the men, left, right, back, front, high, low, fat, thin – all the men start.

"The first group of women sing the song three times."

"The second group of women" (I face them) "sing it two and two-thirds times through."

"All the men sing it two and one-third times – and we all end at the same time. Women high! Men low." I'm gesturing with my arms, pointing up, pointing down.

The banjo plays a high C up the neck.

"One, two, three, sing!"

I usually keep a steady tempo, then on the last eight bars a bit slower, with a ritard on the last measure – holding the last note.

And I end up applauding the audience and whoever is on stage with me for a good job well done. Is Boyce rolling over in his grave? I think not. He liked syncopation, as did Bach and Handel. Speaking of Handel, someone once said to Boyce, "Isn't it terrible the way Handel steals your best melodies?"

Boyce replied, "That's all right. Handel steals pebbles and gives back diamonds."

Anyone that generous deserves to be remembered.

★ ★ ★

Over the Rainbow

I assume everyone in the world knows the melody of "Over the Rainbow." I include it here because I invented a way for audiences to sing it, and I changed two words near the end to emphasize its timeliness.

The original words were written by lyricist Yip Harburg, whose son Ernie, with Harold Myerson, wrote a fine biography, *Who Put the Rainbow in* The Wizard of Oz? *Yip Harburg, Lyricist* (University of Michigan Press, 1993).

In 1938, Yip and composer Harold Arlen got the plum of a job to write songs for a musical film version of *The Wizard of Oz*. At their first meeting in Hollywood, Yip said, "Harold, get me a melody for the phrase 'Somewhere over the rainbow.'"

Harold said, "There's no rainbow in *The Wizard of Oz*."

"I'm putting it in," said Yip.

When they got the great song, the producer wanted to cut it out of the movie. "It slows up the opening," said he.

Yip and Harold went on a two-man strike. "This movie is *not* going to be made unless this song is in it."

Finally it took Arthur Freed, a musical associate of the film's producer at MGM, to break the impasse. He interceded with Louis B. Mayer, head of the studio, who finally gave in, saying, "Oh, let the boys have their song. Let's get rolling."

In the 1990's my voice got so bad I could only lead audiences in singing songs they already knew. Lee Hays taught me how to "line out" hymns, such as "Amazing Grace," but I get audiences singing "Over the Rainbow" when I play a guitar accompaniment.

If you do the song slowly, you can get all the words in without skipping a beat. First I play the opening seven notes of the famous melody. Then I say, "I'll give you the words so you can sing it! *Somewhere over the rainbow*." (The words I speak are in parentheses, while what the crowd is singing is outside the parentheses).

```
 A              C♯m
Some...Where...over the rainbow  ("way up high")

 D        A
way...up...high ("There's a land that I heard of once...")

 D/F♯  Dm/F  A         F♯7      Bm      E7 A
There's...a...land that I heard of...once in a lullaby

("Somewhere over the rainbow")

 A              C♯m
Some...where...over the rainbow ("skies are blue")

 D            A
skies...are...blue ("And the dreams that you dare to")

 D/F♯  Dm/F  A          F♯7      Bm        E7
And...the...dreams that you dare to dream really do

        A
come true
```

("Someday I'll wish upon a star and wake up where the clouds are far")

      A   E7
Someday I'll wish upon a star and wake up where the
                    A   E7   A
clouds are far behind ... me *("Where troubles melt like*

lemon drops 'way up above the chimney tops")

    A   G#7
Where troubles melt like lemon drops 'way up above the

chimney tops *("That's where you'll find me")*

         C#m   Bm E7
That's where...you'll...find...me *("Somewhere over the*

rainbow")

      A   C#m
Some...where...over the rainbow *("bluebirds fly")*

  D   A
blue...birds...fly *("Birds fly over the rainbow, why
    then oh why can't I")*

D/F# Dm/F A   F#7   Bm   E7   A
Birds...fly...over the rainbow...why then o why can't I?

I tell the crowd there are two more lines to the song, but I've changed two words, because if I'd been there when little Dorothy sings "Why oh why can't I?" I'd tell her, "You know why you can't, Dorothy? It's because you only ask for yourself. You've got to ask for everybody. Because either we're all going to make it over that rainbow, or nobody's going to make it. So sing 'If *plucky* little bluebirds fly beyond that rainbow, why can't *you* and I?'" And now the whole crowd sings:

    A   E7
If plucky little bluebirds fly beyond the rainbow

D   A/C# Bm E7   ⌢A
why...can't...you...and...I?

The final eyebrow (fermata) is held long. This encourages some sopranos to sing a high C#, and I add a high E in falsetto. Then we all repeat the 2nd half of the song from the words "Someday I'll wish ... ." I only need to prompt with one or two words or none. And we get harmony again!

Unless you play the song too fast, you can still keep a steady rhythm and not have to add a beat. Here I put the song in A, but of course you can capo up.

Here are the chords for a normal guitar in dropped D tuning (DADGBE). Capo up 2 frets puts you in B.

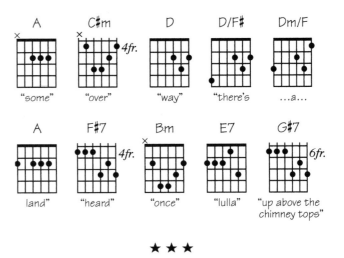

★ ★ ★

Yip Harburg was born on the Lower East Side of Manhattan in 1893. Yip got good marks in school and went on to City College. He got the nickname "Yip" as a kid because he was always climbing trees, and the family called him "Yipsel," meaning "squirrel" in Yiddish.

After college he went into business, but he hated business. A longtime friend in school and college was Ira Gershwin, brother of composer George Gershwin. Ira one day said, "Yip, you're always making up verses. I bet you could make a living writing words for songs."

As Yip said later, "I left the fantasies of business for the realities of songwriting." It was 1928. The Wall Street crash came in '29. In 1931 with musician Jay Gorney he wrote "Brother, Can You Spare a Dime?" In 1934 with Harold Arlen he wrote "It's Only a Paper Moon." Around 1969 he sent me and many others a little booklet, "Rhymes for the Irreverent," but I'm ashamed to say I didn't make up a tune for this till 1993, when his son Ernie gave me another copy of it and asked me to try and find a tune for it.

For what would have been Yip's 100th birthday in 1993, the next song was first sung in the auditorium of an elementary school in the Lower East Side neighborhood where he grew up. The renovation was paid for by royalties from his songs.

The Odds-On Favorite
(Long Story Terse)

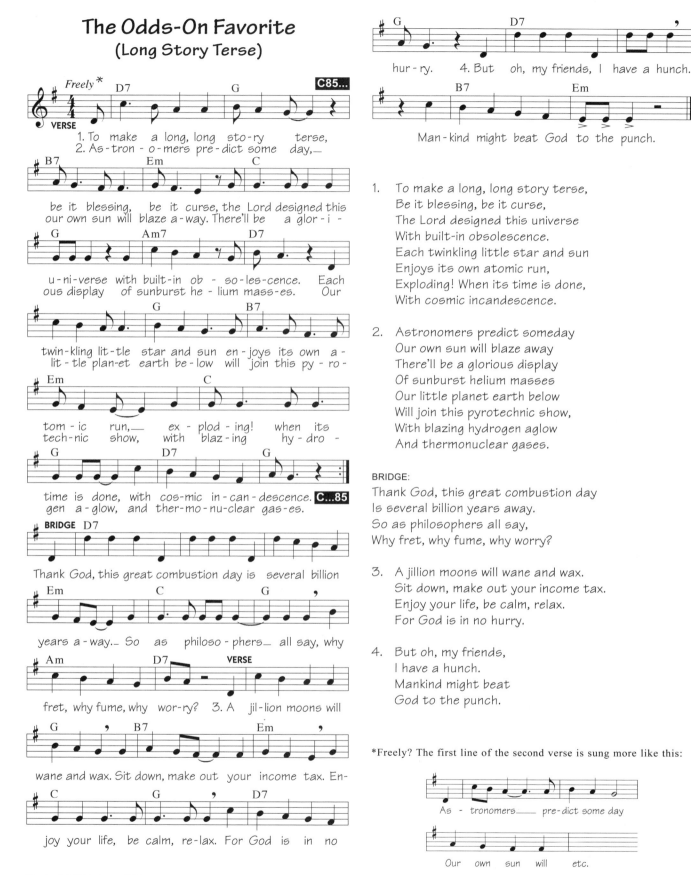

1. To make a long, long story terse,
   Be it blessing, be it curse,
   The Lord designed this universe
   With built-in obsolescence.
   Each twinkling little star and sun
   Enjoys its own atomic run,
   Exploding! When its time is done,
   With cosmic incandescence.

2. Astronomers predict someday
   Our own sun will blaze away
   There'll be a glorious display
   Of sunburst helium masses
   Our little planet earth below
   Will join this pyrotechnic show,
   With blazing hydrogen aglow
   And thermonuclear gases.

BRIDGE:

Thank God, this great combustion day
Is several billion years away.
So as philosophers all say,
Why fret, why fume, why worry?

3. A jillion moons will wane and wax.
   Sit down, make out your income tax.
   Enjoy your life, be calm, relax.
   For God is in no hurry.

4. But oh, my friends,
   I have a hunch.
   Mankind might beat
   God to the punch.

*Freely? The first line of the second verse is sung more like this:

As - tronomers____ pre-dict some day

Our own sun will etc.

Words © E.Y. Harburg, 1976
Tune by Pete Seeger, 1993

Lorre Wyatt wrote two of Clearwater's most popular songs. See p. 213. I've sung them hundreds of times. We collaborated on one 20 years ago (p. 132) and on this one, too.

Wonderful Friends

Words by Lorre Wyatt
Music by Lorre Wyatt and Pete Seeger
© Roots & Branches Music / BMI, P.O. Box 21, Amherst, MA 01004

CHORUS:
When I think of the ways that I've grown
I know I couldn't a' made it alone
I owe a lot to the sharing, caring, daring
Wonderful friends that I've known
I-owe-a-lot to the sharing, caring, daring
   wonderful friends that I've known

1. Here we are my trusted friends all gathered
     together
  We've helped each other down this road whatever
     the weather
  We have no need for pots of gold, for friends are a
     treasure
    So hold hands, and sing it again: O-when-I-
  (CHORUS)

2. Many years ago when I was feeling discouraged
  I found that singing with my friends would fill me
     with courage
  It's a rough and rocky road we're on, so when we
     get worried
    We'll hold hands, and sing it again: O-when-I-
  (CHORUS)

3. It looks like we might sing all night, but looks are
     deceiving
  That old <u>clock</u> upon the wall says, soon I got to be
     leaving
  And though we go our separate ways, there's no
     need for grieving
    Just hold hands, and sing it again: O-when-I-
  (CHORUS)

★ ★ ★

Just as we were going to press, I surprised myself working out a tune for a wonderful short poem which Malvina Reynolds (pp. 107-115) sent to friends as a New Year's greeting.

If this world survives
And every other day I think it might
In good part it will be
Because of the great souls
In our community.

There are a lot of them
I've seen them walk
In lonely thousands down a city's streets
Or hand out leaflets in the rain
Or turn the handle of a print machine
Or empty their pockets as the plate comes by
Or gaze into the camera's eye.

And answer the question:
"Will the world survive?"
And they have said
"We'll try. We'll try."

I've put the song in a key good for altos. Too low for the men? Capo up. It doesn't need much accompaniment; sometimes I just use a single bass note. In my old age I'm better at getting crowds to sing with me (see p. 266). In the last couple measures I only need to point to them and they sing in harmony, then richer harmony. I stop singing myself, cup one hand to an ear, and lift the other hand palm up, then in the last measure lift both hands palms up. I sing the short song through a second time, and at the end get even richer harmony.

I've tried making slight changes in Malvinas's words: "– stand in vigils in the rain, and pass out leaflets from a print machine." In the end, decided to print it just as she wrote it, except to repeat her last line.

Choral directors: For the very last measure, if the crowd is singing well, have your chorus stop singing, but you, facing the audience, hold hands, palms up, even higher. The crowd hears itself, in rich harmony. Then in the last few seconds, your chorus adds its high notes.

If This World Survives

Words by Malvina Reynolds 1972. Music by Pete Seeger 2007.
© 2007 Schroder Music Co., Berkley, CA. Used by permission.

(In Dropped D tuning: DADGBE the chords up-the-neck are not difficult – with a little practice! See p. 289.)

*When do we breathe? Answer: at different times!

★ ★ ★

My father, born in Mexico City in 1886 (his father was a Yankee businessman), was over-enthusiastic about many different things in his long life. In his teens he became enthusiastic about European "classical" music. He could read a symphony score with thousands of notes on it, and know what they were supposed to sound like. But in 1909 as a guest conductor of the Cologne opera in Germany he found he was growing deaf at an early age. Then he met the head of the University of California, and at age 24 found himself head of the Music Department at Berkeley.

Some of his fellow professors said, "Seeger, you know a lot about music, but you're an ignoramus when it comes to economics or history." He started auditing their classes and pretty soon was radicalized. During World War I he was making speeches against imperialist war and got fired.

He brought the family back east and said to my mother, "We can make good money playing for rich people in New York, but why don't we take our beautiful music out to the countryside and the small towns and play it for them?" Over the next year he built one of America's first automobile trailers. With four solid rubber tires and a canvas top like a covered wagon, it was pulled by a Model T Ford (see picture on p. 11). My older brothers had small bunks, and my cradle hung from the steamed hoops overhead.

But paved roads were only in cities then. My mother had to wash my diapers in an iron pot over an open fire. Once they all almost got drowned in a flood. My mother put her foot down. They returned to New York and got teaching jobs. My father kept his mouth shut until the Wall Street crash of 1929. It seemed to him (and millions of others) that this was the end of the free enterprise system.

He became enthusiastic about Soviet Communism. With Aaron Copland and other classical musicians he helped form "The Composers' Collective" in New York City, aiming to develop "new music for the new society." But the proletariat was not enthusiastic about what they were writing.

A Kentucky miner's wife, Aunt Molly Jackson, had written songs about a mine strike, and he brought her to their "collective." But they said, "Charlie, this is the music of the past. We're supposed to be creating the music of the future." He took Molly back to her little room on the Lower East Side. "Molly, I'm sorry they didn't understand you. But I know some young people who will want to learn your songs." And I guess I was one of them. My father got very enthusiastic about some kinds of folk music in America.

In his last few years my father became very pessimistic. "Peter, I can't persuade scientists that they have the most dangerous religious belief in the world. They

ON P. 11 WAS ANOTHER PICTURE OF OUR FAMILY'S "TRAILER TRIP" IN 1921. HERE WE'RE CAMPED IN ROCK CREEK PARK, WASHINGTON, D.C. I'M SITTING ON MY FATHER'S LAP WHILE HE PLAYS THE PUMP ORGAN. MY MOTHER IS PLAYING VIOLIN, WHILE MY BROTHERS CHARLES AND JOHN ARE DEEP IN STUDY.

say 'Charlie, I don't have a religious belief. I base all my actions on observation, double-checked around the world, as all science should be, and then draw logical conclusions.'

"'Oh no,' I tell them. 'Haven't you observed that there are insane, power-hungry people in the world, people like Hitler? Is it logical to put in their hands the ability to destroy the world?' They say to me, 'But Charlie, you're attacking all science. If I didn't discover these things someone else would.' 'Yes,' I tell them, 'I suppose if you didn't rape this woman someone else would, so why not?' They usually stagger away saying, 'You have no right to ask such questions.' I shout after them, 'Face it, it's a religious belief; you think that an infinite increase in empirical information is a good thing. Can you prove it?'"

My father turned to me with an ironic smile. "Of course, Peter, if I'm right, perhaps the committee that told Galileo to shut up was correct."

If he were alive, I'd argue with him. "Remember Hegel? He said there is always thesis, antithesis and synthesis.

Perhaps the synthesis is in the song 'Turn! Turn! Turn!' There's a time for this and a time for that. We are all descended from people who were good killers. The ones who were not good killers didn't have descendants. Now? Maybe we can all learn what FDR told us in the last year of his life: 'If civilization is to survive, we must cultivate the science of human relationships – the ability of all people, of all kinds, to live together in the same world, at peace.'"

★ ★ ★

Now I bring this book to a close. It is a record of many mistakes made as well as a few "successes" in getting songs put together. I hope, with the help of the three CDs (A, B and C) you've found a few you'd like to spend a little time with. Here's a few closing quotes:

"Music is an elegant art and fine amusement, but as an occupation it hath little dignity, having for its object nothing better than entertainment and pleasure."
— George Frederic Handel's father,
in a letter to his young son.

"That boy has absolutely no talent. You who are his friend please prevail upon him to refrain from painting."
— Manet to Monet, referring to Renoir

"This book was begun in depths of humility and ended likewise with the murmur, 'God be merciful unto me, a sinner.'"
— Carl Sandburg,
Apologia in *The American Songbag,* 1927.

"There are two infinite things. One is the universe. The other is human stupidity. I am not sure about the universe."
— Albert Einstein

Music Notation Is a Kind of Shorthand –
An Appendix

Can you carry a tune in your head? If your eyes can focus on a page, you can probably learn within a few weeks or months how to pick up average tunes out of a songbook.

You'll find it a handy skill. And you'll be able to write down new tunes when you think of them, before you forget them.

At right are two NOTES, the most common kind. The first one is called a QUARTER NOTE, and the one on its right is a HALF NOTE, and lasts twice as long. The STEMS can point up or down. Put a note on a line or a space of a STAFF.

Yan-kee Doo-dle went to town, a-rid-ing on a po-ny.

Between each vertical BAR LINE you can count 4 beats.

The spiral thingummy at left is called a TREBLE CLEF sign, or a G CLEF, because it's an ancient way of writing the letter "G." Yes, every line and space has a letter. Before long you'll have 'em memorized, just as you can memorize a typewriter keyboard or the calendar.

To memorize the spaces try "FACE." For the lines, try "Elsa Gobbles Butter Down Fast," or "Even Government Bureaucrats Deserve Food."

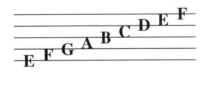

Seven letters, and with short LEDGER LINES you can repeat them below or above the staff:

D C B A G F E D G A B C D E

The PITCH of a note can be raised a HALF STEP (or HALF TONE) by putting a SHARP SIGN ♯ in front of it. Pitch can be lowered a half step by putting a FLAT SIGN ♭ in front of the note. To get back to the regular pitch in the same measure, use a NATURAL SIGN ♮ before the note. (After a bar line, the pitch reverts to what it was anyway.) Next time you're in a music store check out Irving Berlin's famous song "White Christmas." You'll see sharps, flats, naturals in the very first line, such as:

...dream-ing ♭ of ♮ a... white ♯ Christ-mas

All this is why pianos have black keys. You'll find out later why each black key can be called either a flat or a sharp.

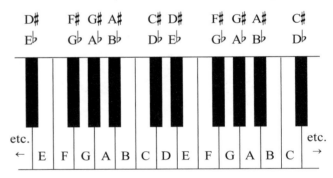

Here's a more complete list of notes:

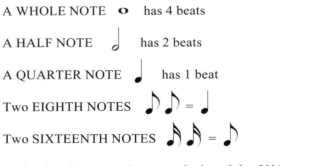

A WHOLE NOTE ○ has 4 beats

A HALF NOTE ♩ has 2 beats

A QUARTER NOTE ♩ has 1 beat

Two EIGHTH NOTES ♪ ♪ = ♩

Two SIXTEENTH NOTES ♬ = ♪

And a dot after a note increases its length by 50%.

Thus: ♩. = ♩ + ♪   ♩. = ♩ + ♪   ♪. = ♪ + ♪

Short notes can have BEAMS instead of FLAGS, thus:

(A "BEAT" is like one tap of a foot, or one bang of a drum when you're marching, or one step when you're dancing.)

Sometimes there's a moment of silence, so you put a REST on the staff:

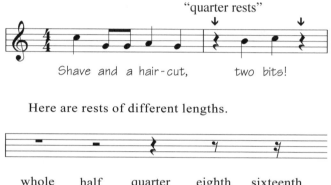

Shave and a hair-cut, two bits!

Here are rests of different lengths.

whole rest	half rest	quarter rest	eighth rest	sixteenth rest
4 beats	2 beats	1 beat	½ beat	¼ beat, etc.

(And each rest can also be made 50% longer by adding a dot to it.)

You may have wondered what the $\frac{4}{4}$ next to the clef sign meant.

It's a TIME SIGNATURE. As written here, both "Yankee Doodle" and "Shave and a Haircut" have four beats in each MEASURE. The space between bar lines is called a "measure." Most of our songs are like this, in "four-four" (4/4) time. Four quarter notes.

There's other TIME SIGNATURES, like 2/4 ("two-four") or 3/4 ("three-four" — that's like a waltz), 6/8 ("six-eight" — like an Irish jig) and 12/8 ("twelve-eight"). In the last two rhythms *three* eighth notes add up to *one* beat.

4/4 time is sometimes written as 𝄴 ("common time") but if it's fast it might be written as 𝄵 ("cut time") or as 2/2 ("two-two"). And there's other less common rhythms and time signatures.

Now would be a good time to go through any songbook that has in it songs that you know. Follow the notes up and down on the staff. Note the time signature of each song, and see how each measure has the correct number of beats in it, whether of notes or rests.

But before you can read unfamiliar melodies, you need to know what KEY it's in. The same tune can be written high or low on a staff, that is, in different keys. If you're a guitar picker, the chords will help you find the key. But between the clef sign and the time signature you'll often see one or more sharps or flats on the staff. These are known as the KEY SIGNATURE. Here's old "Shave and a Haircut" in six common "keys" (there's six more, less commonly used). And a faster speed, 2/4.

When will you *not* see a key signature next to the clef sign? Answer: when you're singing a song in the key of C. On a piano, you can play in C major without having to play any of the black notes.

And if a song is in A minor (Am) you also don't need a key signature. Minor scales have a flatted 3rd, and usually flatted 6th and 7th notes of the scale. Do you know any of the following songs? They're all in minor:

Volga Boatmen
God Rest Ye Merry, Gentlemen
Greensleeves
Hey, Ho, Nobody's At Home
Hatikva
House Of The Rising Sun
Bei Mir Bist Du Shayn
Go Down Moses
What Shall We Do With The Drunken Sailor?

Here's the first line of "Drunken Sailor" written out for several common minor keys:

But for reference only, here's most of the possible key signatures:

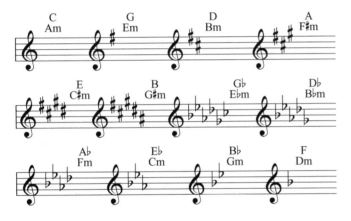

Sharpening or flattening a note becomes more complicated when you're in some other key than C. Here's "Down By The Old Mill Stream" in the key of C and then the key of F. The FERMATA ⌢ ("eyebrow") means "hold this note longer."

Down by the old mill stream where I first met you,

With your eyes of blue, dressed in gingham too. It was...

By Tell Taylor, 1910

Down by the old mill stream where I first...

At last! Test your knowledge. Open some of those songbooks again. Before you try reading the melody of any song, check the key signature as well as the time signature. But you may be wondering about some curved lines:

I - rene, good - night,_____

I - rene, good - night,_____

By Huddie Ledbetter & John A. Lomax TRO © 1936 (renewed) & 1950 (renewed) Ludlow Music, Inc.

Those curved lines are called SLURS (where a voice slurs from one note to another) and TIES (which makes two notes into one longer note).

In general, it helps to learn to recognize the 1st, 3rd, and 5th notes of any scale. They make a bugle call. Here's "Taps" in G:

5 5   1   5 1   3   5 1   3 5 1 3 5 1

3   1 3   5   3 1   5   5 5   1

An assignment: write down "Taps" in all the keys you can think of.

When a melody takes a big jump, you may be uncertain what note it's jumping to. So try counting up or down one step at a time.

1   2   3   4   5

Now you'll recognize this tune:

Twinkle, twinkle, little star ← answer

In time you'll get to recognize and hear in your head how far apart any two notes are. And if you want to study music further, you'll learn that the different INTERVALS between any two notes all have names. But for now, if you can find what key a song is in, and you can sing the scale to yourself, major or minor, you can feel your way up or down the staff to any note in the song you're trying to learn. Just make sure you know where the first note of the scale is on the staff.

I first learned how to read music better by whistling my way through a book of fiddle tunes.

Getting used to hearing the pitch of a note in your head is usually easier than getting to hear the rhythm in your head. It's especially hard when it comes to blues and gospel songs, which have such a liquid flow, such a syncopated rhythm. "Syncopated" means that the note is advanced or delayed, not right on the beat. In learning to read music, RHYTHM IS USUALLY A STUMBLING BLOCK.

On the next few songs, try tapping your foot regularly, four beats to the measure. Note the arrows. But sing the melody like you remember hearing it. Remember, a tie makes two notes into a longer one.

He's got the whole world— in his hands,— He's got the...

Note that each of the two words "his hands" started *before* the foot-tap came down: "his__↓__hands__↓__." Try reading the two well-known songs below:

We come on the Sloop John B., my grand-fa-ther and me. Round Nas-sau town...

Words and music adapted by Lee Hays
TRO © 1951 (renewed 1979) Folkways music Publishers, Inc., NY, NY.

And I hope you know this one:

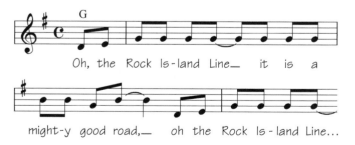

Oh, the Rock Is-land Line— it is a might-y good road,— oh the Rock Is-land Line...

New words and music arrangement by Huddie Ledbetter Edited with new additional material by Alan Lomax
TRO © 1959 (renewed 1987) Folkways music Publishers, Inc., NY, NY.

And you can try looking at some of the songs in this book, such as "Kisses Sweeter Than Wine," (p. 64), or "Both Sides Now," (p. 139), or "Proud Mary," (p. 138).

If by now you say, "This is an awfully complicated way of writing down a simple tune," I agree with you. This kind of music notation was first put together by European church musicians in the Middle Ages. It's not as good for writing down the music of Africa, Asia, or Latin America. And a good opera singer wouldn't think of sticking to the bare bones of a melody. Yes, a tune on paper, compared to a recording of it, is like the stick figure at left, compared to the silhouette at right.

It's a shorthand; it can't really show the liquid flow of a human voice. It tends to put everything into steps, as on a keyboard instrument. But it's the main system of writing music we have right now. Any music store can sell you books about it. I even wrote one years ago (see Bibliography). But no matter what instruction book you get, the best way to learn to transfer the music from the page to your throat or your hands is this:

> GET A SONGBOOK WITH SONGS YOU KNOW AND LOVE TO SING. FOLLOW THE NOTES UP AND DOWN ON THE STAFF. GET TO RECOGNIZE DIFFERENT KEYS, DIFFERENT RHYTHMS.

Like anything else in the world, you do it over and over and you get better at it. I'll close by giving a few more musical terms you may run into:

RITARD (or "rit.") means "slow down."

—————————— means to get softer.

—————————— means to get louder.

8va (8va) means "sing or play these notes an octave higher."

8vb (8vb) means "sing or play these notes an octave lower."

Dots under or over a row of notes mean to cut the notes very short ("staccato").

At the end of a song is always a double barline. A double barline with dots is a REPEAT sign. Two of these bracket the section to be repeated:

D.C. means "Repeat from the beginning," and D.S. means "Repeat from the sign." Rove your eye over the song till you see a fancy cross: 𝄋
That's where you repeat from.

Repeat signs are used to save space, but often there's a different ending the second time through. So above the staff you'll sometimes see a horizontal line with a number. This means to repeat the chorus, or whatever it is, and on the second time through you have the final ending:

The sign 𝄎 means "Repeat the previous measure." A number over it tells you how many times to repeat it.

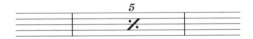

In this book you'll often see the number 3 over three notes. They're called TRIPLETS. The three notes take up the same amount of time as two notes normally would.

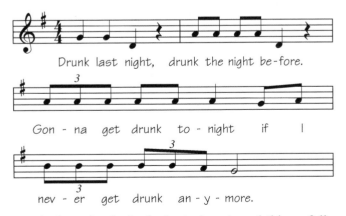

And maybe that's the best place to end this awfully incomplete discussion on how to read music.

Tablature...

...is a form of writing for stringed instruments first developed by lute players in 16th Century Europe. The horizontal lines stand for the strings of the instrument, six for a guitar (even a twelve-stringer with its double strings), five for a banjo.

I give the tuning for the instrument at left of the letters "TAB." The numbers on the lines tell at which fret the fingers of the left hand stop the string. "O" means to sound the open string, not fretted at all. Here's tablature for two scales in E:

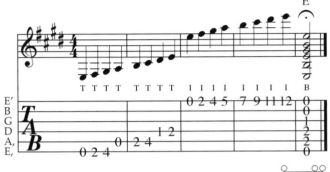

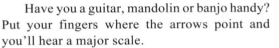

Have you a guitar, mandolin or banjo handy? Put your fingers where the arrows point and you'll hear a major scale.

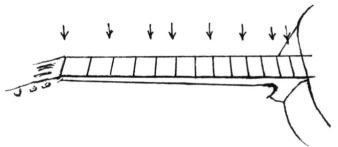

Put your fingers where the arrows point and you'll have a natural minor scale (there's other minor scales, too).

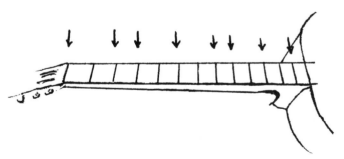

Above the TAB, but below the music, sometimes is indicated how the string is sounded:

T - right thumb, plucking down
I - right index finger, plucking up
M - right middle finger, plucking up
R - right ring finger, plucking up

L - right little finger, plucking up

B - brushing *down* across the strings, with thumb for a guitar, with back of fingernails for banjo.

ST - the index finger strums *up* across the strings

H - "hammering on" – a finger of the left hand frets a string so forcefully that it sounds

P - "pulling off" – a finger of the left hand plucks a string, or several strings. I'm quite proud that the last two terms, which I invented in the 1940s for my banjo book, are now in general use. Violinists call pulling off "left hand pizzicato."

SL - the left hand slides from one fret to another, the instant after the string is plucked, keeping the pressure on the string

CH - the fretted string is plucked, and immediately the finger fretting it pushes it to one side, stretching it and raising its pitch. It's a tradition when playing blues or rock. Sitar players in India do it too.

Dropped D Tuning

If any guitar picker has struggled through this book, he or she will have learned about the Dropped D tuning, D A D G B E. I use it to play mostly in D, G, or A, capoed up or down. My 12-string guitar has very heavy strings, tuned lower than normal. Without a capo my strings sound C F B♭ E♭ G C. No buzzing. LaBella in Newburgh, New York, makes strings for me – a wonderful family business. The gauges I use are as follows, in inches/millimeters: 1st pair, .011/0.279 and .010/0.254; 2nd pair, both .018/0.457; 3rd pair, .024/0.610 and .010/0.254; 4th pair, .034/0.864 and .017/0.432; 5th pair, .046/1.168 and .023/0.584; 6th pair, .067/1.702 and .032/0.813. (Thanks, Bruce Taylor!) 90% of the time my capo is at the 4th fret — concert pitch.

If I play in E or C, and sometimes A, I'll use standard tuning. To play in F, B♭, A♭, or B or F♯, I always capo up or down. I like the ring of open strings; you tend to lose that when you use a lot of barred chords.

I got into using Dropped D in the mid-1950s when I visited the great folk guitarist Joseph Spence, carpenter, in Nassau, Bahamas. Before then I'd only used it occasionally.

Some chords become difficult to play in Dropped D. But a batch of new ones become possible. Here's a lot of chords for you to try out. Use a left thumb when necessary to fret the 6th string.

Well, after all this technical talk, I guess we need to remind ourselves that to make good music you have to put the paper down, and let the melodies, rhythms, harmonies flow out from your heart, to your throat, to your hands. May the muse smile on you.

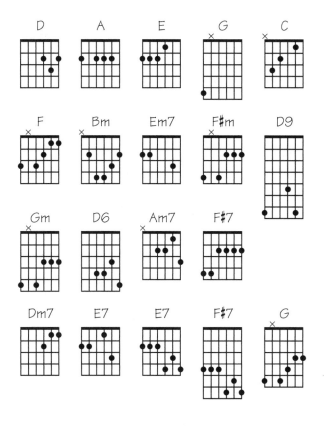

"Can you read music?"
"Not enough to hurt my playing."

— Overheard in Nashville

Bibliography

Songbooks and instructional guides by Pete Seeger

How to Play the Five-String Banjo. Self-published, 1948. Oak, 1962, 1998.

How to Make and Play a Chalil. Self-published, 1955.

Bantu Choral Folk Songs. G. Schirmer, 1959.

American Favorite Ballads, Tunes and Songs as Sung by Pete Seeger (ed. by Irwin Silber & Ethel Raim). Oak, 1961.

The Goofing Off Suite. Hargail, 1961.

The Bells of Rhymney and Other Songs and Stories. Oak, 1964.

Bits and Pieces. Ludlow Music, 1965.

The Twelve-String Guitar as Played by Leadbelly, (with Julius Lester). Oak, 1965.

Pete Seeger Sings Popular American Songs, compiled by Grigory Schneerson, translated into Russian by Samuel Bolotin & Tatyana Sikorskaya. Moscow: State Publishers Music, 1965.

Songs for Peace (ed. with Jeff Marris & Cliff Metzler). Oak, 1966.

The Folksinger's Guitar Guide (with Jerry Silverman). Oak, 1967. [originally published as booklet accompanying Seeger's 1956 guitar instruction album on Folkways]

Hard Hitting Songs for Hard Hit People, compiled by Alan Lomax, notes on the songs by Woody Guthrie, music transcribed & edited by Pete Seeger. Oak, 1967. University of Nebraska Press, 1999, with new forward by Seeger.

Oh Had I a Golden Thread. Sanga Music, 1968.

Henscratches and Flyspecks: How to Read Melodies from Songbooks in Twelve Confusing Lessons. Berkeley Books, 1973. [watch for forthcoming reprint]

Carry It On; The Story of America's Working People in Song and Picture (with Bob Reiser). Simon & Schuster, 1985. Sing Out, 1991.

Everybody Says Freedom (with Bob Reiser). W.W. Norton, 1991.

Other books by or about Pete Seeger:

The Steel Drums of Kim Loy Wong, by Pete Seeger. Oak, 1961.

Pete Seeger on Record. Ludlow Music, 1971.

The Incompleat Folksinger, by Pete Seeger, edited by Jo Metcalf Schwartz. Simon & Schuster, 1972. [collection of autobiographical writings & essays]

The Foolish Frog, by Charles Louis Seeger and Pete Seeger. Macmillan, 1973.

How Can I Keep from Singing: The Ballad of Pete Seeger, by David King Dunaway. McGraw-Hill, 1981. Villard Press/Random House, 2008. [biography – new edition includes many corrections by Pete Seeger]

Abiyoyo, by Pete Seeger, illustrated by Michael Mays. Macmillan, 1985 (paper & hardback). Alladin, 2005 ("Stories to Go!" series)

Pete Seeger's Storytelling Book, by Pete Seeger and Paul DuBois Jacobs. Harcourt, 2000. Harvest paperback, 2001

Abiyoyo Returns, by Pete Seeger & Paul DeBois Jacobs, illustrated by Michael Mays. Simon & Shuster, 2001.

One Grain of Sand: A Lullaby. Song by Pete Seeger, illustrated by Linda Wingerter. Meagan Tingley Publications. 2003.

Turn! Turn! Turn!, illustrated by Wendy Anderson Halperin, Simon & Schuster, 2003.

The Deaf Musicians, story by Pete Seeger & Paul DuBois Jacobs. Illustrated by R. Gregory, Christie, G.P. Putnam & Sons, 2006.

Books by & about other Seegers:

Poems, by Alan Seeger (author's uncle). Published posthumously after WWI. Available as a free e-book download from <www.gutenberg.org>

American Folksongs for Children, by Ruth Crawford Seeger. Doubleday, 1948.

Animal Folksongs for Children, by Ruth Crawford Seeger. Doubleday, 1950. Linnet, 1993.

American Folksongs for Christmas, by Ruth Crawford Seeger. Doubleday, 1953. Oak, 1990.

The Ewan MacColl-Peggy Seeger Songbook. Oak 1964.

The Folk Songs of Peggy Seeger. Oak, 1964.

Old-Time String Band Songbook, ed. by Mike Seeger & John Cohen. Oak, 1964 (as *The New Lost City Ramblers Songbook*), 1976.

Studies in Musicology, by Charles Louis Seeger. University of California Press, 1977.

Why Suyá Sing: A Musical Anthropology of an Amazonian People, by Tony Seeger. Cambridge University Press, 1987 [Tony is author's nephew and former curator of Smithsonian Archive of Folk Culture from 1988-2000]

Charles Seeger: A Life in American Music, by Ann M. Pescatello. University of Pittsburgh Press, 1992 [biography of author's father]

Nineteen Folk Songs, by Ruth Crawford Seeger. G. Schirmer Inc., 1995.

The Peggy Seeger Songbook, Warts & All. Oak, 2001.

The Weavers

The Weavers Sing, by Ronnie Gilbert, Fred Hellerman, Lee Hays, and Pete Seeger. Folkways, 1951.

The Carolers Songbag, by Pete Seeger (with the Weavers). Folkways, 1952.

Weavers Songbook. Harper, 1960.

Traveling On with The Weavers. Harper, 1966.

Lee Hays: Lonesome Traveler, by Doris K. Willens. University of Nebraska Press, 1988. [biography]

Clearwater / Environmental songs

Songs and Sketches of the First Clearwater Crew, edited by Don McLean, with forward by Pete Seeger. North River Press, 1970.

The Clearwater Songbook, edited by Ed Renehan, introduction by Pete Seeger. G. Schirmer, 1980.

For the Beauty of the Earth: An Environmental Songbook to Benefit the Hudson River Sloop Clearwater, by Liza DiSavino. Mendham NJ: The Folk Project, 1993.

Web resources:

Pete Seeger appreciation website: <www.peteseeger.net>, managed by Jim Capaldi.

Peggy Seeger: <www.pegseeger.com>

Mike Seeger: <http://mikeseeger.info>

Tao Rodriguez-Seeger (author's grandson) <www.themammals.net>, <www.myspace.com/taorodriguezseeger>

Woody Guthrie Foundation & Archive <http://woodyguthrie.org>

Clearwater (sloop, campaign) <http://clearwater.org/>

Great Hudson River Revival (folk festival) <http://clearwater.org/festival/>

Sing Out! (publisher of *Sing Out! Magazine*, which was founded by Pete Seeger and others, also publisher of this book & forthcoming accompanying teaching discs) <www.singout.org>

Smithsonian Folkways (all of Pete Seeger's Folkways LPs can now be purchased as special order CDs) <www.folkways.si.edu>

Appleseed Recordings (includes the "Songs of Pete Seeger" series of CDs) <www.appleseedmusic.com>

Information on Pete Seeger's life & work, books & CDs & supplementary materials related to this book. <www.quakersong.org/pete_seeger> (website of this book's editor, Peter Blood)

Discography

The following list indicates where specific songs in this book can be found on the author's recordings, as well as on selective recordings by other artists. Songs not listed have not been released on any recordings to date to our knowledge.

A listing of Pete Seeger's recordings that include more than one song in this collection with catalog information can be found at the end of this discography. A more complete Pete Seeger discography can be found in David Dunaway's recently revised and re-issued biography, *How Can I Keep from Singing* (see Bibliography).

Over 80 of the songs in this book are available from Appleseed Recordings on a 3 volume series called the *Songs of Pete Seeger* and a new Pete Seeger CD, called *At 89*. The Songs of Pete Seeger CDs consist mainly of other artists recording songs that Seeger has written or been closely identified with. These volumes recordings are abbreviated in this Discography as follows:

S of PS V.1 = *Where Have All the Flowers Gone: The Songs of Pete Seeger*, Volume 1 (2 CD set)

S of PS V.2 = *If I Had a Song: The Songs of Pete Seeger*, Volume 2

S of PS V.3 = *Seeds: The Songs of Pete Seeger*, Volume 3 (2 CD set) Note: The first disc includes tracks of Seeger singing himself along with his grandson Tao Rodriguez-Seeger.

At 89 is the 2008 release of new Pete Seeger recordings and includes many songs from this book never before recorded. A number of tracks from the *Songs of Pete Seeger* series have been re-released with additional new original recordings on *Sowing the Seeds*. Contact Appleseed Recordings at P.O. Box 2593, West Chester PA 19380. <www.appleseedmusic.com> or e-mail: <folkradicl@aol.com>.

Although many of the Seeger recordings included in this discography are out of print, a number have recently been reissued on compact disc by Folkways, Columbia, Vanguard, and other labels. Bear Family Records has issued a 10-CD set, *Songs for Political Action*, that includes much of the early material found in Chapter 2 (see below under Almanac Singers recordings). In addition, *all* LPs on the Folkways label can be purchased as custom CDs with the original cover art and liner notes directly from Smithsonian Folkways. For ordering information and a catalog, contact: Smithsonian Folkways Records, 600 Maryland Ave. SW, Suite 2001, Washington, DC 20024 . Phone: 1-888-FOLKWAYS (365-5929) or 1-202-633-6450, Fax 202-633-6477. Website: <www.folkways.si.edu>.

Nearly 1200 mp3 tracks for Pete Seeger are listed on <www.rhapsody.com/peteseeger>.

Finally, a wide variety of Pete Seeger CDs as well as the *Power of Song* DVD can also be ordered from Peter Blood's website at <www.quakersong.org>.

(Titles in bold had been released on CD as of 2008. Others may be as well.)

Abiyoyo
PS: **Abiyoyo, Greatest Hits, Sing-a-long Demonstration Concert,** Bantu Choral Folksongs, Children's Concert, Family Concert (video), If a Revolution Comes, Sleep-time, on Folk Festival at Newport V.1
Bill Harley: **Monsters in the Bathroom**

Aircraft Mechanic Song
tune: (Lincoln & Liberty Too) Songs of the Civil War (Folkways 5717)

Alleluya (William Boyce round)
PS: **At 89**

All Mixed Up
PS: **Pete,** Strangers & Cousins
Peter, Paul & Mary: **S of PS V.1, Flowers & Stones, Peter, Paul & Mommy Too** (video & CD)

All My Children of the Sun
PS: Young vs. Old
Tim Robbins: **S of PS V.1, Sowing the Seeds**

And Still I Am Searching (poem)
PS: S of PS V.1

Andorra
PS: The Bitter & the Sweet
Annie Patterson: **Rise Up Singing/Teaching Disc P** (Peace/Creativity)

Arrange and Re-arrange
PS: **At 89**

Bach at Treblinka
PS: **At 89**

Ballad of Harry Bridges
PS: **First Rays of Protest**
Almanac Singers: Ballad of Harry Bridges (78rpm single: Keynote 304)

Ballad of October 16th
PS: **First Rays of Protest**
Almanac Singers: Songs for John Doe , **Songs for Political Action**

Ballad of the Sloop Clearwater
PS: Rainbow Race

Barbara Allen
PS: **Amer. Fav. Ballads V.2,** The Bitter & the Sweet, God Bless the Grass, Sings American Ballads, World of
Joan Baez: Ballad Book
Ewan MacColl & Peggy Seeger: Cold Snap (Folkways), Long Harvest V.4 (Argo)
New Lost City Ramblers: Old Timey Songs for Children, 20th Anniversary Concert
John Jacob Niles: Folk Balladeer
Jean Ritchie: British Traditional Ballads

Bells of Rhymney
PS: **Essential** (Vanguard), **Greatest Hits, Hard Travelin',** I Can See a New Day, Sings & Answers Questions, World Of, PS & Sonny Terry, 12 String Guitar, The Essential (Sony), on Folk Festival at Newport V.1, on Live Hootenanny
Roger McGuinn: **S of PS V.1**
Dick Gaughan: **S of PS V.3**
The Byrds: **The Byrds, Greatest Hits**
Judy Collins: **#3**
Also recordings by Chad Mitchell Trio, Cher, John Denver, Ian Campbell Group, Phil Ochs, The Oyster Band, Gram Parsons, Serendipity Singers, The Spinners, others

Blessed Be the Nation (poem)
Studs Terkel: **S of PS V.1**

Both Sides Now
PS: Young vs. Old, World of
Joni Mitchell: **Clouds, Miles of Aisles**
Judy Collins: **Wildflowers**, First 15 Years
Dave Van Ronk: and the Hudson Dusters, A Chrestomathy

Bright Yellow Forsythias
tune ("Midnight Special") on PS: **Amer. Fav. Ballads V.2**

Bring 'Em Home
PS: **S of PS V.3, Sowing the Seeds** (both with Billy Bragg, Ani DiFranco & Steve Earle), Young vs. Old
Bruce Springsteen: **Seeger Sessions Expanded Edition**
Barbara Dane: Songs of the GI Movement (Paredon)

Broad Old River
PS: With Hudson River Singers (Clearwater Records 300CR)

Business
Broadside Ballads V.2 (Broadside302)

C for Conscription
PS: **First Rays of Protest,** Pioneer of Folk, **Which Side Are You On?**
Almanac Singers: Songs for John Doe, **Songs for Political Action**
tune ("T for Texas") on PS: Almanac (Folkways)

The Calendar
Short Sisters: A Planet Dancing Slow (Black Socks Press 8654-12) [Black Socks Press, Box 208, Harrisville NH 03450]

Come All Ye Fair & Tender Ladies
PS: Essential, Sing Out! Hootenanny
Odetta: **One Grain of Sand**

Dear Mr. President
PS: **First Rays of Protest,** Pioneer of Folk, **Which Side Are You On?**
Almanac Singers: Dear Mr. President, **Songs for Political Action**

Deck the Halls
PS: Indian Summer (listed as "Many Colored Paper")

Deliver the Goods
PS: **First Rays of Protest,** Talking Union
Almanac Singers: Dear Mr. President, **Songs for Political Action**

Djankoye ("Zhonkoye," "Hey Zhankoye")
PS: Zhonkoye (1948 78rpm single Charter 30A), We Sing V.1, **Songs for Political Action** (on Disc 8)

Annie Patterson: **Rise Up Singing/Teaching Disc M** (Mountain Voices, Farm & Prairie)

The D Minor Flourish
PS: **At 89**

The Emperor Is Naked Today-o ("As the Sun")
PS: on **Sowing the Seeds** (Appleseed)
Dave Carter & Tracy Grammer: **S of PS V.2**
Circles & Seasons (as "As the Sun"), on What Now People? V.3 (Paredon 2003)

Empty Pocket Blues
PS: Goofing-Off Suite (as "Barrel of Money Blues"), **Darling Corey** (CD re-issue)
Ronnie Gilbert (with Robin Flower & Libby Mclaren): **S of PS V.1**
Weavers: At Home
Also recordings by Esther & Abi Ofarim, The Incredible String Band, Odetta, Rod McKuen

English Is Cuh-ray-zee
PS: **S of PS V.3**
Peggy Seeger: **Three Score and Ten** (with PS)

Estadio Chile
PS: **S of PS V.3, HARP,** Banks of Marble, If a Revolution, Together

Everybody Loves Saturday Night
Annie Patterson: **Rise Up Singing/Teaching Disc S** (Seas, Good Times)
Alex Campbell: on Tonder Musik Festival 1976 (Rica 4511)
The Spinners: Carribean Sunshine Hits (One Up 2235)
Also recorded by The Wayfarers, Percy Faith Orchestra, others

False from True
PS: **At 89**
PS: Pete Seeger Now
Guy Davis: **S of PS V.1**

Festival of Flowers
Tish Hinojosa: **S of PS V.1**

The Foolish Frog
PS: **Birds Beasts Bugs & Fishes,** Live at Newport, Story Songs, Three Saints
Dave Van Ronk: Peter & the Wolf (Alacazam 1004)

Frank's Yodel
PS: Banks of Marble (as "Yodel"), Together (as "Yodelling")

Franklin D.
Almanac Singers: Songs for John Doe, **Songs for Political Action**
tune ("Ida Red") on PS: Amer. Fav. Ballads V.5, Darling Corey, Essential

From Way Up Here
PS: Broadsides, God Bless the Grass, We Shall Overcome
Malvina Reynolds: Malvina Reynolds (Cassandra 5100) [available from Schroder Music, 1450 6th St, Berkeley CA 94710]
Michele Greene: **S of PS V.3**
Also recorded by Glen Yarborough

Full Fathom Five
PS: Dangerous Songs
Garbage
PS: **Pete,** Banks of Marble, Circles & Seasons, PS & Bro. Kirk Visit Sesame Street

Bill Steele: Garbage (Bay 202)
Peter Alsop: **Peter Alsop**
Guy Carawan: My Rhinoceros, Songs of Struggle & Celebration

Get Up and Go
PS: **Link in the Chain,** Broadsides, Together, Young vs. Old
The Weavers: **Together Again,** Wasn't That a Time (video)
Tom Paxton **S of PS V.1**

Give Peace a Chance
John Lennon: **Imagine**
Plastic Ono Band: **Live Peace in Toronto**

Guantanamera
PS: **HARP, Greatest Hits, The Essential** (Sony), If a Revolution, PS &
    Bro. Kirk Visit Sesame Street, Together, We Shall Overcome, World
    of, Canto Obrero (Americanto 1004), Family Concert (video)
The Weavers: **Greatest Hits, Reunion at Carnegie Hall** (1963),
    Traveling On, **Wasn't That a Time** (box set, video)
Jackson Browne & Joan Baez: **S of PS V.2,** on **Sowing the Seeds** (Appleseed)
Joan Baez: **Gracias a la Vida**
Also recorded by Eddie Albert, Celia Cruz, Jose Feliciano, Julio Iglesias,
    Trini Lopez, Tony Martin, Andy Russell, The Sandpipers, Roger
    Williams & many other artists.

Haul, Make Her Go High
Hudson River Sloop Singers (includes PS – Clearwater Records 300)

He Lies in the American Land
PS: **Amer. Industrial Ballads, If I Had a Hammer,** Amer. History in
    Ballad & Song V.1&2, Carry It On, on Live Hootenanny, PS in
    Concert V.1&2

Here We Are in Madison Square
tune ("New York City" by Lead Belly) on PS: At the Village Gate V.1

Here's to the Couple
PS: Bantu Choral Folk Songs

Hold the Line
PS: Gazette V.1
Weavers: Almanac (Fontana/Topic 6028), also as "The Peekskill Story"
    (1949 78rpm single Charter 502), on **Songs for Political Action**
    (Bear Records)

Hole in the Bucket – see There's a Hole in the Bucket

How Soon? ("Chalil Melody," "Hillel Melody," "Ilka's Bedoin Melody")
PS: **At 89, Children's Concert at Town Hall,** Big Bill Broonzy & PS

Huddie Ledbetter Was a Helluva Man
PS & Friends: **Pete**

I Come and Stand at Every Door ("Girl of Hiroshima")
PS: Gazette V.2, I Can See a New Day, on Swords Into Ploushares (Folk
    Tradition S005,006)
Anne Hills: **S of PS V.1**
Annie Patterson: **Rise Up Singing/The Teaching Disc P** (Peace/Creativity)
The Byrds: **Fifth Dimension**
Sally Rogers: **Generations**
Sands Family: Now & Then (Spring 1008)

I Had a Rooster
PS: Amer. Fav. Ballads V.2; Birds Beasts Bugs & Fishes

I Wonder What Tinya Is Doing?
PS: **Song & Play Time**

If a Revolution Comes to My Country
PS: If a Revolution, on What Now People? V.2 (Paredon 2002)

If I Had a Hammer ("The Hammer Song")
PS: **The Essential** (Sony), **Hard Travelin', If I Had a Hammer,** Love Songs
    for Friends & Foes, **Precious Friend,** Sing Out with Pete, **Sing-a-long
    Demonstration Concert,** Strangers & Cousins, Wimoweh, World of, on
    Peace Is the World Smiling (Music for Little People D-2104)
Weavers: The Hammer Song (1949 single Hootennany H-101), **Reunion
    at Carnegie Hall, Wasn't That a Time** (box set & the video)
Nancy Griffith & Friends: **S of PS V.1**
Billy Bragg with Eliza Carthy: **S of PS V.2**
Peter, Paul & Mary: **Peter Paul & Mary**
Aretha Franklin: **Yeah!!!**
Also recorded by: Eddy Arnold, Anita Bryant, Ray Coniff, Sen. Sam
    Ervin, Percy Faith, Waylon Jennings, and many other artists.

If This World Survives
PS: **At 89**

I'm Gonna Sing Me a Love Song
PS: Love Songs for Friends & Foes

I Wonder, I Wonder, I Wonder
PS: **Song & Play Time**

In Dead Earnest ("Lee's Compost Song")
PS: **Precious Friend**

In the Evening
PS: **Pete, Folk Music of the World,** At the Village Gate V.2, (with
    Memphis Slim & Willie Dixon), Bawdy Songs & Real Sad Songs,
    Folkpeople (Time Wind F 5000), If a Revolution Comes, PS Concert
Roger McGuinn: **Treasures from the Folk Den** (with PS, Appleseed)

It's a Long Haul ("Long Haul")
PS: **At 89**

Jacob's Ladder
PS: **HARP, Sing-a-long Demonstration Concert,** Hootenanny at
    Carnegie Hall
Bruce Springsteen: **Seeger Sessions**
Bernice Reagon: **River of Life**
Paul Robeson: The Essential

Jesu, Joy of Man's Desiring ("We Will Love or We Will Perish")
PS: **At 89, Darling Corey,** Goofing-Off Suite, Folk Music Blues, Live
    Hootenanny, PS in Concert V.1-2, on Studs Terkel's Weekly Almanac
Tony Trischka & Jennifer Kimball: **S of PS V.3**

Kayowajineh ("Seneca Canoe Song")
PS: Champlain Valley Songs, Circles & Seasons, Family Concert (video),
    Fifty Sail on Newburgh Bay

King Henry
PS: Dangerous Songs
Steeleye Span: **Below the Salt**

Kisses Sweeter Than Wine
PS: **Pete, Folk Music of the World, Hard Travelin',** Love Songs for
    Friends & Foes, On Campus, **Precious Friend,** on A Tribute to
    Leadbelly (Tomato R2-70665)

Jackson Browne & Bonnie Raitt: **S of PS V.1**
Weavers: orig. 1951 single (Decca 27670), At Carnegie Hall, Best of,
    Greatest Hits, Reunion at Carnegie Hall Part 2, Together Again,
    Wasn't That a Time (CD set & video)
Jimmie Rodgers: The Best of
Peter, Paul & Mary: **Album**
Kate Smith: The Golden Voice of
Aoife Clancy: **Silvery Moon**
Also recorded by Ray Coniff, Marlene Dietrich, The Lennon Sisters, Rod
    McKuen, Piano Roll, Andy Williams, and many others
Also recordings in French ("Ses Baisers Me Grisaient") by Zack Matalon,
    in Swedish ("Vuddet Elamaa On") by Reijo Taipale

Kuroda Bushi
Myrdhin & Pol Huellou: Harp & Shakuhachi (Goasco 027)

Last Train to Nuremburg
PS: Rainbow Race, World of
Joel Rafael Band: **S of PS V.2**

The Leatherwing Bat
PS: **Birds Beasts Bugs & Fishes, Amer. Fav. Ballads V.4** (CD)**,** Amer.
    Fav. Ballads V.5 (LP)

Letter to Eve
PS: Pete Seeger Now
Indigo Girls: **S of PS V.1**
Magpie: **Living Planet** (Collector 1948)

Lisa Kalvelage ("My Name Is...")
PS: Sings & Answers Questions, Waist Deep in the Big Muddy
Ani Difranco; **S of PS V.1**
Charlie King: **Food Phone Gas Lodging**

A Little a' This 'n' That
PS & Tao Rodriguez-Seeger: **S of PS V.3**

Little Boxes
PS: Broadside, Little Boxes & Other Broadsides, We Shall Overcome
Malvina Reynolds: **Ear to the Ground** (Folkways), Malvina (Cassandra),
    Sings the Truth (Columbia) [for ordering information see p.107]
Kate & Anna McGarrigle: **S of PS V.2** (French translation)

Little Fat Baby
PS: **At 89**

Little Girl See Through My Window
PS: Love Songs for Friends & Foes
Magpie: [forthcoming recording of their version]
tune ("Fly Through My Window") on PS: **Birds Beasts Bugs & Fishes,**
    Children's Concert

Living in the Country ("Singing in the Country")
PS: **Pete,** Bitter & the Sweet, Family Concert (video), Greatest Hits, If a
    Revolution Comes, Nonesuch (as "Singing in the Country")
Martin Simpson: **S of PS V.1**
Arlo Guthrie: **Running Down the Road**
Leo Kottke: **My Feet Are Smiling**
Kevin Roth: Mountain Dulcimer Instrumental Album (Folkways)
George Winston: **Summer**

Lonesome Valley (Guthrie version)
PS: Sing-a-long Demonstration Concert, Together, Family Concert
    (video), on **Hard Travelin'** (soundtrack CD, video)

Woody Guthrie: Library of Congress
[cf. original version on Joan Baez: **Very Early**; Carter Family: The Famous]

Lulloo Lullay (Coventry Carol)
Weavers – We Wish You a Merry Christmas

Maple Syrup Time
PS: **S of PS V.3,** on Christine Lavin: **One Meal Ball** (both with Tao
    Rodriguez-Seeger), Circles & Seasons
Moxy Fruvous: **S of PS V.2**
Track on Lavin's album IS THE SAME VERSION AS ON S of PS V.3 –
    recorded by Pete and Tao, not Christine

Mbube ("Wimoweh," "Lion Sleeps Tonight")
PS: **Amer. Fav. Ballads V.2** (CD), Amer. Fav. Ballads V.3 (LP), **Essential**
    (Sony), **Essential** (Vanguard), **Greatest Hits, HARP, Hard**
    Travelin', Hootenanny at Carnegie Hall, Hootenanny Tonight!,
    Precious Friend, Sing Out with Pete, With Voices Together
Weavers: **S of PS V.1,** orig. 1952 single (Decca 2792), At Carnegie Hall,
    Best of, Greatest Hits, **Reunion at Carnegie Hall,** on Dogfight
    (soundtrack from the film – Nouveau 10082), Together Again,
    Wasn't That a Time (video)
Nanci Griffith (with Odetta): **Other Voices/Other Rooms**
Hugh Masakela: **Tseposhola – A New Dawn**
Miriam Makeba: **Africa, The Click Song, Country Girl, Meet Me at**
    the River, Miriam Makeba
The Tokens: **Lion Sleeps Tonight**
"The Lion King" (soundtrack CD & DVD)
Other recordings by Soweto Gospel Choir, Chad Mitchell Trio, New
    Christy Minstrels, Kingston Trio, Chet Atkins & many others

Melodie d'Amour
PS: Waist Deep in the Big Muddy
Original single by the Ames Brothers (1957)

Mexican Blues
PS: Circles & Seasons, The Folksingers Guitar Guide

Mrs. Clara Sullivan's Letter
PS: I Can See a New Day, We Shall Overcome
John McCutcheon: **S of PS V.3**

My Father's Mansion
PS: Banks of Marble, **Essential** (Vanguard), Waist Deep in the Big Muddy
Billy Bragg & Eliza Carthy: **S of PS V.1**

My Rainbow Race
PS: **Pete,** Family Concert (video), Rainbow Race, World of
Donovan: **S of PS V.1**
Nana Mouskouri: **Alone,** on **The American Mall** (original soundtrack
    CD & DVD)
Annie Patterson: **Rise Up Singing/Teaching Disc E** (Ecology, Outdoors)
The Bergerfolk: Sing of Sunshine & Rainbows (Folkways)
Peter La Farge: Sing Women Blues (Folkways)

Now We Sit Us Down ("Old Father Hudson")
PS: **At 89**
Casey Neill: **S of PS V.1**

O Sacred World Now Wounded
PS: **S of PS V. 3, Sowing the Seeds**
Studs Terkel: **S of PS V.1**
tune ("Chorale from Beethoven's 9th Symphony") on PS: Goofing-Off
    Suite, **Darlin' Corey**

Odds On Favorite ("Long Story Terse")
PS: **S of PS V.3**

Ode to Joy
PS: **Pete**
Ed Sweeney: The Times They Are Something Like They Used to Be (Old
 Harbour 001)

Of Time and Rivers Flowing
PS: **Pete,** Fifty Sail on Newburgh Bay
Richie Havens: **S of PS V.1**
tune ("Lo How a Rose E'er Blooming") on PS: The Nativity

Oh Had I a Golden Thread ("Golden Thread")
PS: **Essential** (Vanguard), **If I Had a Hammer,** Live at Newport!,
 Rainbow Quest, Strangers & Cousins
Judy Collins: **Whales & Nightengales,** on **S of PS V.1,** Sowing the Seeds
Dar Williams & Toshi Reagon: **S of PS V.2**
Also recorded by Nana Mouskouri.

Oh How He Lied
PS: **Amer. Fav. Ballads V.4**

Old Devil Time
PS: **Pete, Sing-a-long Demonstration Concert,** Rainbow Race
"Tell Me that You Love Me Junie Moon" (1969 soundtrack album,
 Columbia 3540)
Kim & Reggie Harris & Magpie: **S of PS V.2, Guide My Feet**
Pat Humpries: **S of PS V.3**
Claudia Schmidt: **New Goodbyes Old Helloes**
Rosalie Sorrels: **Report from Grimes Creek**

Old Time Religion (parody)
PS: **Sing-a-long Demonstration Concert, Precious Friend,** Together
Annie Patterson: **Rise Up Singing/Teaching Disc D** (Dreams/Funny
 Songs)

Oleanna
PS: Folksongs of 4 Continents, With Voices Together
In orig. Norwegian recording by Lille Bjorn Nilsen (Scandisk Music)
 [7616 Lyndale Ave. S, Minneapolis MN 55423]
Annie Patterson: **Rise Up Singing/Teaching Disc D** (Dreams/Funny Songs)
Kingston Trio: **At Large/Here We Go Again** (2 CD set)
Theodore Bikel: Folk Songs from Just About Everywhere

One Dime Blues
Blind Lemon Jefferson: **Best of, Classic Sides, Complete Recordings,
 King of the Country Blues**

One Grain of Sand
PS: **Abiyoyo,** Dangerous Songs, Folk Festival at Newport V.1, Sleep-time,
 on Equilibrium (Audobon's Album of Nature & Humanity – Folkways
 37305)
Odetta: **S of PS V.1, One Grain of Sand**
Carolyn Hester: on Kerrville Folk Festival 1977

One Man's Hands
Carolyn Hester: **S of PS V.3,** on Kerrville Folk Festival 1977 (PSG 77)
Annie Patterson: **Rise Up Singing/Teaching Disc U** (Unity/Women)
Odetta: In Japan, It's a Mighty World
The Womenfolk: **Volume 2** (1964)
Chad Mitchell Trio: **Slightly Irrelevant**
Jackie Washington: on **Newport Folk Festival Evening Concerts 1963**
The Highwaymen: March On Brothers

Only Remembered
Bill Shute & Lisa Null: American Primitive (SIF 1025 c/o Green Linnet)

Or Else ("One-a These Days")
PS: **At 89**

Our Generation
PS: Rainbow Race

Over the Hills
PS: Love Songs for Friends & Foes, Waist Deep in the Big Muddy
Tommy Makem: **S of PS V.1**
Weavers: On Tour

Over the Rainbow
PS: **S of PS V.3**

People Are Scratching, The
PS: God Bless the Grass
Annie Patterson: **Rise Up Singing/Teaching Disc E** (Ecology, Outdoors)

Plow Under
PS: **First Rays of Protest**
Almanac Singers; Songs for John Doe, **Songs of Political Action**

**The Politican's Guide to Answering Embarrassing
 Questions (Ross Perot Guide…)**
PS with Tao Rodriguez-Seeger: on **Sowing the Seeds**

Precious Friend
PS: Banks of Marble, **Precious Friend**
Annie Patterson: **Rise Up Singing/Teaching Disc K** (Friendship, Play)
Holly Near and Ronnie Gilbert **S of PS V.3**
Bright Morning Star: Live in the USA

Proud Mary
Creedence Clearwater Revival: **Bayou Country, Chronicle, Concert,
 Gold, Live in Europe, 1968-69**
Elvis Presley: **On Stage, As Recorded at Madison Square Garden**
Ike & Tina Turner: **Ike & Tina Turner**
Tina Turner: **Alone**

Quite Early Morning
PS: on **Sowing the Seeds,** Banks of Marble, **Essential** (Vanguard),
 Together, on Feeding the Flame (gay liberation album – Flying Fish
 70541), on Songs for Peace (Rounder 4015)
Holly Near: **S of PS V.1, Early Warnings**
Guy Carawan: The Land Knows You're There
Annie Patterson: Deep Roots

Reuben James ("The Sinking of the Reuben James")
PS: **First Rays of Protest,** Folk Music, Gazette V.1, Sing with Seeger,
 Sings Woody Guthrie, World of, on **Hard Travelin'** (box set, video)
Woody Guthrie: **Greatest Songs of**
Almanac Singers: Dear Mr. President, **Songs of Political Action**

River of My People
PS: **If I Had a Hammer, Pete,** Love Songs for Friends & Foes
Priscilla Herman, Anne Hills & Cindy Mangsen: **S of PS V.3**

Rockin' Solidarity
Dave Welsh & the Rockin' Solidarity Band: Rockin' Solidarity [write
 P.O. Box 26581, San Francisco CA 94126]
Also on: This Line Is Singin' (Freedom Song Network)

Original version on PS/The Union Boys: Solidarity Forever (1945 single with Tom Glazer & Burl Ives – Stinson 622)

Round and Round Hitler's Grave
PS: **Brothers & Sisters,** Pioneer of Folk, **First Rays of Protest, Which Side Are You On?**
Almanac Singers: Dear Mr. President, **Songs for Political Action**
The Unforgotten Men (National Guardian album from early 1950's)
tune ("Old Joe Clark") on PS: Bitter & the Sweet, Darling Corey, **Essential,** Folk Music Blues

Sacco's Letter to His Son
PS: on Ballads of Sacco & Vanzetti, on Folk Song America V.4 (Smithsonian Collection 0464)
Magpie: **S of PS V.3,** If It Ain't Love (Philo 1112 cassette)

Sag Mir Wo Die Blumen Sind
Marlene Dietrich: **Marlene, Der Grosse Erfloge,** also 2 videos on YouTube
Joan Baez: **Farewell Angelina**

Sailing Down My Golden River
PS: **S of PS V.3, Pete,** Circles & Seasons, Rainbow Race, on Bread & Roses Festival of Acoustic Music V.1 (Fantasy79009)
Greg Brown: **S of PS V.1**
Arlo Guthrie: **Outlasting the Blues** (as "Golden River")

Sailing Up My Dirty Stream ("My Dirty Stream")
PS: God Bless the Grass, on Clearwater II (Sound House 1022)
Casey Neill: **S of PS V.1**

Seek and You Shall Find
PS: Rainbow Quest, Waist Deep
Annie Patterson: **Rise Up Singing/Teaching Disc R** (Rounds, Spirituals)

Seventy Miles
PS: God Bless the Grass
The Coachmen: The Coachmen (Fantasy2482)

66 Highway Blues
PS and Arlo Guthrie: **S of PS V.2**

Snow, Snow
PS: Rainbow Race
Eric Anderson: **S of PS V.2**
The Short Sisters: A Planet Dancing Slow (Black Socks Press 8654-12 - write: Box 208, Harrisville NH 03450)

Sour Cream
PS: Circles & Seasons

Sower of Seeds
PS (with chorus): **S of PS V.3**
Original version ("Minuit") Paul Winter Consort: Common Ground, **Icarus, Wolf Eyes.**

Spider's Web ("Natural History")
PS & Friends: **Pete**
Peggy Seeger: **S of PS V.3**

Spring Fever
PS: **At 89**
Strange Death of John Doe
PS: **First Rays of Protest**

Almanac Singers: Songs for John Doe, **Songs of Political Action**
tune ("Young Man Who Wouldn't Hoe Corn") on PS: Frontier Ballads, Songs to Grow On V.3

Step by Step
PS: **If I Had a Hammer, Carry It On,** Rainbow Quest, Songs of Struggle & Protest, on Can't You See the System Isn't Working (Paredon)
Sweet Honey in the Rock: **S of PS V.1, The Other Side**
John McCutcheon: **Step by Step**
Ronnie Gilbert, Earl Robinson & Chet Washington: Songs of the Working People from the American Revolution to the Civil War (Flying Fish 483)

Sweepy, Sweepy, Sweepy
PS: **Abiyoyo,** Sleep-Time

Sweet-a-Little Baby
PS: **Abiyoyo,** Sleep-time

Take It from Dr. King
PS: **S of PS V.3**
Peggy Seeger: **Three Score and Ten** (with PS, Appleseed)

Talking Blues (original version)
PS: **Amer. Fav. Ballads V.4,** Amer. Fav. Ballads V. 5
Weavers: On Tour
Talking Union
PS: Carry It On, **The Essential** (Sony), **First Rays of Protest, Greatest Hits,** Hootenanny NYC (Topic 37), Hootenanny Tonight!, Pioneer of Folk, Songs of Struggle & Protest, **Talking Union, Which Side Are You On?,** on The Unforgotten Men (National Guardian album in early 1950's)
Almanac Singers: Talking Union, **Songs for Political Action**
John McCutcheon & Corey Harris: **S of PS V.2**

Teacher Uncle Ho
PS: If a Revolution Comes, Rainbow Race
Theme from the "Goofing-Off Suite"
PS: **Darling Corey,** Goofing-Off Suite, Big Bill Broonzy & PS in Concert, PS & Sonny Terry, on Raising Arizona (original soundtrack album)
Tony Trischka Band: **S of PS V.1**

There's a Hole in the Bucket ("Hole in the Bucket")
PS: **Sing-a-long Demonstration Concert,** Amer. Fav. Ballads V.4
Oscar Brand: Laughing America
Burl Ives: Cheers
Faith Petric: Sing a Song / Sing Along (Gentle Winds)

This Is a Land
PS: Banks of Marble, Fifty Sail on Newburgh Bay

This Land Is Your Land
PS: **Amer. Fav. Ballads V.1, If I Had a Hammer,** Children's Concert, Family Concert (video), Folk Music, I Can See a New Day, Live at Newport!, PS & Bro. Kirk Visit Sesame Street, Sing with Seeger, Sings Woody Guthrie, Songs to Grow On V.3, World of, on **Hard Travelin'** (box set, video).
Weavers: **Greatest Hits,** At Home, Songbag, **Wasn't That a Time** (CD set, video)
On Folkways' **A Vision Shared / A Tribute to Woody Guthrie & Leadbelly** (CD, video)
Woody Guthrie: **Greatest Hits**
Flatt & Scruggs: Changing Times
Peter, Paul & Mary: **Moving**

This Old Car
PS: **S of PS V.2** (with Arlo Guthrie), Young vs. Old

Times A-Gettin' Hard, Boys
PS: **Darling Corey**, Goofing-Off Suite, At the Village Gate V.1
Tom Paxton: **S of PS V.3**
Harry Belafonte: Scarlet Ribbons
Kevin Roth: Somebody Give Me Directions (Folkways)

Throw Away That Shad Net
PS: **At 89**
To Everyone in All the World
PS: Rainbow Quest
Cathy Fink & Marcy Marxer: **S of PS V.1**
Raffi: **Baby Beluga**
To My Old Brown Earth
PS: **Pete**, Broadsides
Pat Humpries: **S of PS V.3**
Tomorrow Is a Highway
PS: Gazette V.2, **Hard Travelin'**
Magpie with Kim & Reggie Harris: **S of PS V.3, If I Had a Hammer**
Tomorrow's Children
PS: Broadsides

The Torn Flag (poem)
PS: Pete Seeger Now
John Trudell: **S of PS V.1**

Trouble at the Bottom
PS: **S of PS V.3** (with Tao Rodriguez-Seeger & Arlo Guthrie)

Turn, Turn, Turn
PS: Bitter & the Sweet, **The Essential** (Sony), **Greatest Hits, If I Had a Hammer**, World of, on Troubadours of the Folk Era V.2 (Rhino 70263)
Bruce Cockburn: **S of PS V.1, Sowing the Seeds**
Martin Simpson & Jessica Radcliffe: **S of PS V.3**
Dick Gaughan: **Redwood Cathedral**
The Byrds: **The Byrds, Greatest Hits, Essential, Original Singles V.1** (1965-1967), **Turn Turn Turn**
Judy Collins: **#3, Recollections**
Nina Simone: **To Love Somebody**
Also recorded by Theodore Bikel, Ed Sullivan Singers, Ronnie Gilbert, The Lettermen, Gordon Lightfoot, Mitch Miller, Dolly Parton, The Seekers, and many others
Recorded in French ("Tourne le Temps") by Gerard Melet, in Spanish ("Todo A Su Tiempo") by Las Cerezas

Tzena, Tzena, Tzena
PS: **At 89, Brothers & Sisters**

Visions of Children
PS: **S of PS V.3, At 89** – At 89 version is with chorus but not Anna Crusis Women's Choir
tune on PS: Goofing-Off Suite (as "Duet from Beethoven's 7th Symphony") and **Darlin' Corey**

Waist Deep in the Big Muddy
PS: **At 89**, The Essential (Sony), Sings & Answers Questions, Waist Deep, original 1967 single on Columbia,
Dick Gaughan: **S of PS V.1, Sail On**
Ani DiFranco: **Sowing the Seeds** (Appleseed)

Water Is Wide, The
PS: **Amer. Fav. Ballads V.2, At 89, HARP, Pete, Sing-a-long Demonstration Concert**, On Campus, PS Now, Twelve String Guitar
John Gorka: **S of PS V.1**
Joan Baez: **Very Early**
Indigo Girls, Jewel & Sarah McLachlan: on **Lilith Fair** (orig. volume), video on YouTube
Buffy Sainte-Marie: **Little Wheel Spin & Spin**
Ronnie Gilbert: The Spirit Is Free, video on YouTube

We Shall Overcome
PS: Bitter & the Sweet, Broadsides, Carry It On, Complete Carnegie Hall Concert, **Greatest Hits**, Sing Out! Hootenanny, We Shall Overcome, on Dogfight (original soundtrack - Nouveau 10082)
Bruce Springsteen: **S of PS V.1, If I Had a Hammer**
Louis Armstrong: **What a Wonderful World**
Joan Baez: **In Concert**
Guy Carawan: Songs of Struggle & Celebration
Kim & Reggie Harris & Rabbi Jonathan Kligler: **Let My People Go! A Jewish & African American Celebration of Freedom**
SNCC Freedom Singers: on Evening Concert/Newport Folk Festival 1963 (Vanguard 77002), on Sing for Freedom/The Story of the Civil Rights Movement through Its Songs (Folkways 40032)
On Voices of the Civil Rights Movement: Black American Freedom Songs 1960-66 (Folkways SFW40084)
Also recorded by: James Cleveland & the Troubadours, Eileen Farrell, Roberta Flack, Huntley & Brinkley, Mahalia Jackson, Odetta, Bernie Sanders (senator from Vermont), and many others including recordings in many different languages
Videos: We Shall Overcome (1989 PBS special on the history of the song)
Eyes on the Prize (6 part PBS series on the history of the Civil Rights Movement, Blackside Productions, 1986)

We Wish You a Merry Christmas
Weavers: We Wish You a Merry Christmas (1951 single Decca 27783, 1952 Decca LP), **At Carnegie Hall, Best of, Greatest Hits**
Kingston Trio: The Last Month of the Year (Capitol 93116)
Peter, Paul & Mary: **A Holiday Celebration**, A Holiday Concert (video)

We'll All Be a-Doublin'
PS: **If I Had a Hammer**
Si Kahn with the Freighthoppers: **S of PS V.1** (as "Doublin")

Well May the World Go
PS: **Banks of Marble, If I Had a Hammer, Pete, S of PS V.2** (with Larry Long), Together
New Lost City Ramblers: Second Annual Farewell Reunion (PS plays & sings – Mercury 1-685), 20th Anniversary Concert (Flying Fish 090)

When I Was Most Beautiful
PS: **At 89**, Young vs. Old
Last Forever: **S of PS V.3**

Where Have All the Flowers Gone
PS: 1963 single (Columbia), Bitter & the Sweet, **Essential** (Vanguard), **The Essential** (Sony), **Greatest Hits, Hard Travelin', If I Had a Hammer, Live at Newport!,** Rainbow Quest, World of
Tommy Sands with Dolores Keane & Vedran Smailovic: **S of PS V.1, Sarajevo & Belfast, Sowing the Seeds**
Peggy Seeger (with PS): **Three Score & Ten**
Joan Baez: **Very Early**
Kingston Trio: **Best of, College Concert, 25 Years**
Peter Paul & Mary: **Peter Paul & Mary**

Also recorded by: Bobby Darin, Earth Wind & Fire, Flatt & Scruggs, Richie Havens, Huntley & Brinkley, The Lennon Sisters, Gordon Lightfoot, and many others

For German see above under "Sag mir wo die Blumen sind"

Where's My Pajamas

PS: **Abiyoyo**, Sleep-time, Stoney Plain (Smithsonian Folkways 45001)

Joanne Olshansky: Pizza Boogie (JHO 101)

Whistling Past the Graveyard

PS: Love Songs for Friends & Foes

Who Killed Norma Jean?

PS: Little Boxes, We Shall Overcome

Janis Ian: **S of PS V.3**

Whole Wide World Around, The ("Because All Men Are Brothers")

PS (with Tom Glazer, Hally Wood Faulk & Ronnie Gilbert): On People's Songs for National Maritime Union (soundtrack for filmstrip, People's Songs, 1947), on **Songs for Political Action**

Peter, Paul & Mary: **See What Tomorrow Brings**

Annie Patterson: **Rise Up Singing/Teaching Disc U** (Unity/Women)

Wimoweh – see under Mbube

Wonderful Friends

PS: **At 89**

Words, Words, Words

PS: Rainbow Race

John Wesley Harding & the Minus 5: **S of PS V.2**

You'll Sing to Me Too

Guardabarranco: **S of PS V.2**

The following lists catalog numbers for Pete Seeger albums that include one or more songs from this collection: (* = available as of 2008 on CD and/or online downloads. Others may be as well.)

* Abiyoyo & Other Stories and Songs for Children - Folkways 45001 (CD & cassette), 1500, 7525 (LPs)

Almanac – Folkways (early 1950's)

American Ballads – Folkways 2320 (1957)

* American Favorite Ballads, V.1 – Folkways 40150 (2002)
* American Favorite Ballads, V.2 – Folkways 40151 (2003)
* American Favorite Ballads, V.3 – Folkways 40152 (2004)
* American Favorite Ballads, V.4 – Folkways 40153 (2006)

American Favorite Ballads, V.2 – Folkways 2321 (1959)

American Favorite Ballads, V.3 – Folkways 2322 (1960)

American Favorite Ballads, V.4 – Folkways 2323 (1961)

American Favorite Ballads, V. 5 – Folkways 2445 (1962)

American History in Ballad and Song, Vols. 1,2 – Folkways 5801, 5802 (1961)

* American Industrial Ballads – Folkways 40058 (CD), 5251 (LP - 1956)

* At 89 – Appleseed Recordings APR 1113 (2008)

At the Village Gate, V.1 (with Memphis Slim & Willie Dixon) – Folkways 2450 (1960)

At the Village Gate, V.2 (with Memphis Slim & Willie Dixon)1 – Folkways 2451 (1962)

Ballads of Sacco and Vanzetti (with Woody Guthrie) – Folkways 5485 (1963)

Banks of Marble - Folkways 31040 (1974)

Bantu Choral Folk Songs (with chorus) – Folkways 6912 (1955)

Bawdy Songs & Real Sad Songs (with Betty Sanders) – Charter (1947)

Big Bill Broonzy & Pete Seeger in Concert – Verve Folkways 9008 (1965)

* Birds, Beasts, Bugs and Fishes (Little & Big) – Folkways 45029 (CD reissue of 2 LPs including 7610 - 1954)

The Bitter and the Sweet – Columbia 8716 / mono: 1916 (1963)

Broadside Ballads, V.2 – Broadside Records 302 (1965)

Broadsides - Folkways 2456 (1964)

* Brothers & Sisters – Discmedia (2006)

Carry It On (with others) – Flying Fish (LP & CD but out of print)

Champlain Valley Songs – Folkways 5210

* Carry It On (with Si Kahn & Jane Sapp) – Flying Fish 104, CD [companion recording for Seeger's book of labor songs, see Bibliography]

* Children's Concert at Town Hall – Columbia 8747/mono: 1947 (1963) [reissued as Harmony 30399], Sbme Special (2008 CD)

Circle and Seasons – Warner 3329 (1979)

Clearwater II – Sound House Records 1022 (1977)

* Collection, The – EMI Plus

Complete Carnegie Hall Concert (June 1963 – 2 CD set, Columbia 45312) Dangerous Songs – Columbia 9303 / mono: 2503 (1966)

Dangerous Songs – Columbia LP, Sony CD (1998 – unavailable)

* Darling Corey and the Goofing – Off Suite, Folkways 40018 (CD reissue of 2 LPs)

* The Essential Pete Seeger – Vanguard 97/98 (1978, on CD 1990)

The Essential Pete Seeger – Sony (2005 CD not currently available)

Fifty Sail on Newburgh Bay (with Ed Reneham) – Folkways 5257 (1976)

* First Rays of Protest in the 20th Century (with Woody Guthrie) – Primo (2006 – 2 CD set)

Folk Festival at Newport, V.1 (various artists) – Vanguard 9062 (1959)

Folk Music – Folkways 9013

Folk Music Blues – Folkways 3864

*Folk Music of the World – Legacy (1994) & Collectables (2007)

Folksongs of Four Continents – Folkways 6911 (1955)

Frontier Ballads, V.1 – Folkways 2176 (1954)

Gazette, V.1 – Folkways 2501

Gazette, V.2 – Folkways 2502 (1961)

God Bless the Grass – Columbia 9232 / mono: 2432 (1966), Folkways 37232

* Goofing-Off Suite – Folkways 2045 (1954), reissued in 1993 on CD as Folkways 10018 with Darling Corey

* Greatest Hits – Columbia 9416 / mono (1967) & Sony CD 2616

* HARP (with Holly Near, Arlo Guthrie & Ronnie Gilbert) - Redwood 409 (1985 live concert recording at Universal Ampitheater, Los Angeles). Re-issued with additional material on a 2 CD set as Appleseed 1054

* Hard Travelin' (with Arlo Guthrie, others) – Arloco 284, MCI (2003 CD) [original soundtrack recording from the film on Woody Guthrie's life and work]

Hootenanny at Carnegie Hall – Folkways 2512 (1960)

Hootenanny Tonight! – Folkways 2511 (1959)

I Can See a New Day – Columbia 9057 / mono: 2252 (1965)

If a Revolution Comes – Oktober 508

* If I Had a Hammer – Folkways SFW40096 (1998)

* If I Had a Song: The Songs of Pete Seeger, Volume 2 – Appleseed 1055

In Concert, Volumes 1 & 2 – Folklore/Topic F-LAUT-1, VOX 1.580

Indian Summer (soundtrack of the film) – Folkways 3851 (1961)

* Link in the Chain (Sony)

Little Boxes & Other Broadsides – Verve/Folkways 9020 (1963)

* Live at Newport! – Vanguard 77008 (1993)

Live Hootenanny – Aravel 1006

Love Songs for Friends and Foes – Folkways 2453 (1956)

The Nativity – Folkways 35001 (1964)

Nonesuch (with Frank Hamilton) – Folkways 2439 (1959)

* Odds and Ends – Appleseed (2008)

On Campus – Verve/Folkways 9009 (1965)

* Pete – Living Music 1048 (Produced by Paul Winter. Pete sings with choruses on many tracks. Won a Grammy.)

Pete Seeger & Bróther Kirk Visit Sesame Street – Children's Records of America 22062 (1974)

Pete Seeger & Sonny Terry – Folkways 2412 (1958)

A Pete Seeger Concert – Stinson 57 (1954)

Pete Seeger Now – Columbia 9717 (1969)

Pioneer of Folk – see below under Almanac Singers

* Precious Friend (with Arlo Guthrie) – Warner Bros. 2-3644, (2CD set 1990)

The Rainbow Quest – Folkways 2454 (1960)

Rainbow Race – Columbia 30739 (1973)

* Seeds: The Songs of Pete Seeger, Volume 3 – Appleseed (2 CD set – 2003)

Sing Out! Hootenanny (with "The Hooteneers") – Folkways 2513 (1959)

Sing Out with Pete! (with group) – Folkways 2455 (1961)

* Sing-a-long Demonstration Concert – Folkways 40027/8 (2 CDs), 36055 (LP – 1980) [live concert recording includes Pete teaching and coaching the audience]

Sings and Answers Questions at the Ford Hall Forum in Boston – Broadside 502 (1968)

Sing with Seeger – Disc 1101

Sings Leadbelly – Folkways 31022 (1968)

Sings Woody Guthrie – Folkways 31002 (1967)

Sleep Time: Songs & Stories by Pete Seeger – Folkways 7525 (1958)

* Song and Play Time with Pete Seeger – Folkways 45023 (CD) 7526 (LP – 1958)

Songs of Struggle and Protest – Folkways 5233 (1965)

Songs of the Civil War – Folkways 5717 (1960)

Songs to Grow On, V.3 – Folkways 7027 (1951)

* Sowing the Seeds: The 10th Anniversary – Appleseed Recordings (2 CD set – 2007, includes other artists)

Story Songs - Columbia 8468 / mono: 1668 (1961) Strangers & Cousins – Columbia 9134 / mono: 2334 (1965)

Studs Terkel's Weekly Almanac on Folk Music Blues on WFMT (with Big Bill Broonzy) – Folkways – 3864 (1956)

* Talking Union – Xtra (2007 – UK import but widely available in US)

Three Saints, Four Sinners & Six Others – Columbia 160266

* Three Score and Ten (Peggy Seeger – 3 tracks feature Pete) - Appleseed

* Together in Concert (with Arlo Guthrie) – Warner / Reprise 2R5-2214 (1975), Rising Son (2005)

* Traditional Christmas Carols – Folkways SFW40024 (CD), 32311 (LP – 1967)

The Twelve-String Guitar As Played by Leadbelly – Folkways 8371 (1962)

Waist Deep in the Big Muddy – Columbia 9505 / mono: 2705 (1967), Sony CD (1994 discontinued)

We Sing, V.1 – MDH records ("bootleg" album recorded live at Reed College, 1950)

We Shall Overcome (1963 Carnegie Hall concert – Columbia 8901 / mono: 2101

* We Shall Overcome: The Complete Carnegie Hall Concert – Sony 2 CD set (1989)

* Where Have All the Flowers Gone: The Songs of Pete Seeger, Volume 1 – Appleseed 1024 (2 CD set).

* Which Side Are You On? – see below under Almanac Singers

With Voices Together We Sing – Folkways 2452 (1956)

The World of Pete Seeger – Columbia 31949 (1974)

Young vs. Old – Columbia 9873 (1971)

Seeger recordings with the Almanac Singers: *(Note: some recently CDs listed as being a Pete Seeger album are actually re-issues of Almanac Singers material.)*

3 original recordings in vinyl:

Dear Mr. President – Keynote 111 (1942)

Songs for John Doe – Keynote 102 (1941)

Talking Union and Other Union Songs – Keynote 106 (1941), Folkways 5285 (1955)

Re-issues:

* Songs for Political Action: Folk Music, Topical Songs and the American Left, Disc 3 & 4 – Bear Family Records (2000). All tracks on the 3 original Almanac Singers recordings listed above have been reissued with lots of other topical material from the period on a 10 CD set. See <www.bear-family.de>. (Sound clips of all tracks are available at Yahoo shopping.)

* Which Side Are You On? – Acrobat Music (2003 CD is out of print but available from several site as mp3 downloads. Issued as a Pete Seeger album.)

Pioneer of Folk – Prism Leisure (UK 2001 – discontinued. Also labeled as Seeger.)

Seeger recordings with The Weavers:

* At Carnegie Hall – Vanguard 6533 / reissued as CD: 73101 (1957)

At Home – Vanguard 2030 / mono: 9024 (1958)

* Best Of – Decca 7173 / mono: 8893 (1959), MCA 4052

* Greatest Hits – Vanguard 15/16

On Tour - Vanguard 6537 / mono: 9013 (1958)

* Pete Seeger: The Weavers – Goldie Records (3 CD box set, 2006)

* Reunion at Carnegie Hall – Vanguard 2150 (1963)

* Reunion at Carnegie Hall, Part 2 – Vanguard 79161 (1965)

Songbag – Vanguard 73001 (1967, from earlier albums)

* Together Again – Loom 10681 ["lost cache" is available from CD baby]

We Wish You a Merry Christmas – Decca 5373 (1952)

Videos which relate to content of this book: (*commercially available on DVD in 2008)

* Pete Seeger: The Power of Song – Jim Brown Productions (2007 documentary on Seeger's life and work)

* Love It Like a Fool (New Day Films) Seeger appears in Susan Wengraf's beautiful 1977 half-hour documentary on Malvina Reynolds. Originally produced in 35mm it is now again available on DVD, in time for the hundredth anniversary of Malvina's birth. Order from Susan at Red Hen Films, 1404 LeRoy Ave., Berkeley, CA 94708 – 510-843-3214 or loveitlikeafool@comcast.net.

Isn't This a Time! A Tribute Concert for Harold Leventhal – Jim Brown Productions (2005 documentary of a 2003 Carnegie Hall concert celebrating Pete Seeger's manager at which all the surviving members of the Weavers sang together – scheduled to be re-released on DVD early in 2009)

The Weavers: Wasn't That a Time – Warner Reprise Video 38304 (1981)

Pete Seeger's Family Concert – Sony Kids Video 49550 (1992)

The Rainbow Quest – Central Sun Video [10 videos of Seeger's television series, each featuring a guest artist including Doc Watson, Woody Guthrie, Leadbelly, Donovan, Judy Collins, Sonny Terry & Brownie McGhee, etc. – write: Box 3135, Reston VA 22090]

A Tribute to Woody Guthrie & Leadbelly: A Vision Shared (various artists) – CBS Music Video (1988)

Woody Guthrie: Hard Travelin' (with Arlo Guthrie) – MGM/UA Video 600884 [soundtrack from the film]

INDEX

Entries in **boldface** are used for titles of poems and songs included in this book with music & lyrics. Entries in *italics* are for first lines of such songs. When an alternative or former title of a song is listed, the main title used in this book follows in boldface. Titles in quotes indicate references to songs in the text. (Text references to songs that appear elsewhere in this book with music & lyrics are indicated by "refs." after the main page entry.) Where songs appear here only as excerpts or where the song title refers to the tune of a new song, this is indicated in parenthesis after the song title. The same is true for titles of books, recordings, films, and periodicals. "t.:" = tune. "tr." = translation.

66 Highway Blues 18
9/11-265

A
Abernathy, Ralph 32, 34
Abiyoyo 60 (refs. 15, 16, 56, 122, 124, 209)
Abu-Jamal, Mumia 262
Abzug, Bella 274
a capella 45-6, 68
Adam & Eve 171
African-American musical styles & traditions
    Afro-Cuban rhythm in **Guantanamera** 130
    churches/religious songs 16, 174, 219
    feeling "pulse" under some notes 186
    nonsense words in 153
    see also blues, gospel, jazz, spirituals
African American songs
    Didn't Old John 271
    Little Bird (t: **Little Girl See Through My Window**) 51
    Long John (t: **It's a Long Haul**) 216
    Old Reuben (t: **Lord Ha' Mercy**) 235
    Pay Me My Money Down (excerpt) 77
    Talking Blues 24
    see also blues, gospel, jazz, spirituals
African American musicians
    Brown, James 130
    Collier, Jimmy 144
    Kirkpatrick, Fred 144, 156, 236
    Robeson, Paul 36
    Slim & Slam 221
    see also Lead Belly
African Americans – see also Civil Rights, Martin Luther King Jr., race, slavery
    Davis, Ben 43
    Dubois, W.E.B. 15
African songs 58, 287
    Abiyoyo 60
    Everybody Loves Saturday Night 126
    Mbube (Wimoweh) 180-3
    vocal clicks in 253
    see also West Africa, South Africa
aging 107, 246, see also generational issues
    A Little a' This 'n' That 256
    Arrange & Re-arrange 272
    Get Up & Go 246
Agranoff, Mike 141
Ah my God! What is this land 118

"Aiken Drum" 62
Aims of Education, The (book) 184
Aircraft Mechanic Song 31
Air Force, The 267 see also Vietnam
"A La Claire Fontaine" 258
Albany, NY 216
All, all together 50
allegory 153
Alleluya 276
Allende, Salvador 102
All God's Critters (excerpt) 213
All Mixed Up 14 (refs. 88, 177, 258)
All My Children of the Sun 153
All people that on Earth do dwell 194
All we are saying is give peace a chance 156
Almanac House 26
Almanac Singers 19-29, 37, 43, 86, photo 29
    Ballad of Harry Bridges 25
    Ballad of October 16th 21
    Dear Mr. President 27
    Franklin D 22
    Plow Under 22
    Reuben James 26
    Round & Round Hitler's Grave 28
    Strange Death of John Doe 21
    Talking Union 23-4
    Why Do You Stand There in the Rain? 20
America First rallies 19
American Tobacco strike 32
answer back songs 152
"Amanece" 117
"Amazing Grace" 176
Ambellan, Harold 17
American Favorite Ballads (book) 134
American Folk Songs for Chidren (book) 49, 56
American Folk Songs for Christmas (book) 56
American Songbag, The (book) 76, 283
American Youth Congress 19
Ames Brothers 242
anarchism 84, 88, 92
Andorra 111-3
And still I choke on the smoke of Treblinka 237
And Still I'm Searching 259
Angulo, Hector 128, 128-30
Animal Folk Songs (book) 56

"Animals Need Water" 213
animals, songs about 45-6, 51, 56-8, 74, 79, 204, 243
Anonymous 136, 145
anticommunism
    Churchill's 26
    HUAC (author before) 54
    lyrics about 23, 25, 216
    Peekskill Riot (at Robeson concert) 36
    "This Land is Your Land" as Communist plot 143
    unions' 32, 43
    see also blacklisting, censorship, Communism
anti-Semitism 27, 121
    see also Holocaust, Judaism
Apartheid 91-2
Appalachian trad. songs 155, 195, 230
Appendix (on reading music notation) 284-8
Arab-Israeli Relations 122, 171-2, 193-4, 259, 268
Arabic
    How Soon (flute melody) 43, 259
    proverbs & stories 8, 207
    Zeina, Zeina (tr. Tzena) 268-70
Arana, Sylvia 35
Archive of Folk Culture (orig. of Folk Song) 50, 176
Arlen, Harold 277
Armstrong, Louie 45, 289
arpeggios 135
Arrange and Re-arrange 272
Artzner, Greg (of Magpie) 51, 92, 240
Asch, Moses 45, 53, 92
As I went through Sandgate 249
Ask not for whom the bell tolls 116
As the Sun (**The Emperor Is Naked Today-o!**) 192
astronomy 175, 198-20, 223, 279
Atlantic Monthly (magazine) 273
At midnight in a flaming angry town 153
A tous et chacun dans le monde 50
Augustus, Wilhelm 191
"Auld Lang Syne" 117
Australia 25
automobiles, song about 69
"Autumn Wind, The" 259
Avon Old Farms (author's H.S.) 101
Az men fort kain Sevastopol 121

B
babies, songs about 54
Bach, Johann Sebastian 11, 189-92, 205, 219, 277
   Bach at Treblinka 191
   Jesu Joy of Man's Desiring 190
   O Sacred World Now Wounded 192
   The Whole Wide World Around 192
Baez, Joan 67, 163
Baird, Fay 152
Baird, Peter 35
"Ballad of Billy the Kid" 86
Ballad of Harry Bridges, The 25
Ballad of John Doe 21
Ballad of October 16th 21
Ballad of the Sloop Clearwater 208
ballads – see English, Scottish trad.
Ballet Africains 180
banjo instrumentals
   D Minor Flourish 80
   Goofing Off Suite 10
   Jesu Joy of My Desiring 190
   Melodie d'Amour 242
   Ode to Joy 122
banjo accompaniment 24, 155, 269, 274, 277
   Hammers Are Banging Away 274
   Quite Early Morning 240
   Well May the World Go 249
Barbara Allen 230 (refs. 76, 90)
bar line 284
Barnwell, Ysaye 172
Barrel of Money Blues (**Empty Pocket Blues**) 72
"Battle Hymn of the Republic" 251
Beacon, NY 215, 267, 272
"Bear Hunt, The" 56
Beatles, The (Lennon-McCartney song) 156
Because All Men Are Brothers 192
Beethoven, Ludwig van 11
   author's parents' love of 11-2, 205
   The Beethoven Phenomenon (story) 197 (ref. 175)
   melodic line 258
   Ode to Joy 122
   use of traditional material by 12-3, 88
   Vision of Children 123
"Bei Mir Bist Du Shayn" 285
Belafonte, Harry 274
Bells of Rhymney 98-101 (ref. 173)
Belsey, Paula (verses by) 67
"Belt Line Girl" 28
Bennett, Louise 13-6
Berkeley, University of California at 11, 282
Berlin, Irving 222-3, 284
Bernz, David 9, 65, 274
Better late than never 116
Bevel, James 33
Bibb, Leon & Eric 67
Bible, The Ch 8 The Great Book (171-200) 19, 61, 154
biblical passages, songs based on
   Jacob's Ladder (Gen. 28:10) 199
   Letter to Eve (Gen. 1) 171
   My Father's Mansion (John 14:2) 178
   Seek & Ye Shall Find (Matt. 7:7) 184

   Sower of Seeds (Mark 4:1-20) 180
   Turn, Turn, Turn (Eccles. 3:1-8) 172
Big Bang, The (theory) 198
Big fool said to push on, The 150
Big Muddy, The 150
Big wheel keep on turnin' 138
"Bile Them Cabbage Down" 249
Bill of Rights, The 144
Birnbaum, Martin (trans.) 237
blacklisting 38, 45, 63 – see also anticommunism
Blind Lemon Jefferson 86
Blood, Peter 9, 262
Bloody Thursday 25
Bloom, Harry 92
"Blow the Man Down" 77
"blues", about the
   chord progression 64, 68
   folk music as 16
   talking blues genre 23-4
   see also Lead Belly
blues melodies 116, 213
   C for Conscription 12
   Empty Pocket Blues 72
   False from True 151
   Here We Are in New York City 43
   I'm Gonna Sing Me a Love Song 68
   In the Evening 137
   Mexican Blues 30
   New York Town 86
   Rockin' Solidarity ('blues stomp') 250
   Rock Island Line 287
   see also talking blues
Blue Skies 222
Blue Tailed Fly, The (excerpt) 86
Boardman, John 136
Bonar, Rev. Horatio 176
Bonneville Power Administration 26
Borman, Frank (astronaut) 130
Bossom-Seeger, Isabelle & Penny (author's grandchildren) 51
Both Sides Now 139 (ref. 287)
Bourgeois, Louis 194
Bows & flows of angel hair 139
Boyce, William 276, 277
Boyle, Robert 206
Bragg, Billy 149
Brand, Oscar 28, 46
Brandow, Karen 92
Brawley, Tawana 216
breathing breaks while singing 188
Brecht, Bertolt 198
Breen, Axie (cartoon by) 261
Bridges, Harry 24, 25
Bright Yellow Forsythias 227
Bring 'Em Home 149 (ref. 156)
Broad Old River 214
"Brother Can You Spare a Dime?" 278
Brown, James 130
Bruderhof, The (Christian commune) 238
Build the road of peace before us 122
Bül- Bül (cartoons by) 45, 171, 227
Bull, Ole 119
Burris, J.C. 58
"Bury Me Beneath the Willow" 249

Business 95
Butcher, the baker, the tinker &...tailor 28
But you who know days of a diff. kind. 228
But we are here 237
Byer, Sandy 62
Byrds, The 105, 171-3

C
Calendar, The 152
Calley, Lt. William 159
Calvin, John 194
calypso 134
Campaign for Nuclear Disarmament 88
campaign for public domain reform 61, 64, 76
Campbell, Rev. Will 199
Camp Woodland 128
Canada!, O 131
Capaldi, Jim 7, 8
capital punishment – see death penalty
capitalism – see also Communist Party
   author's teen attitude re 201
   Business 95
   Garbage 140
   I Want to Go to Azoty 113
   joke about 185
   songs about 141-44
   This Land Is Your Land 141-6
   US corporations' support of Franco 43
   wealth disparities under 175, 207, 210
capo, use of 281
Carawan, Guy 33, 34
Carmichael, Hoagy 230
Carnegie Hall 33, 57
carols
   Deck the Halls 187
   Lo How a Rose (t: **Of Time & Rivers Flowing**) 223
   Lulloo Lulay 188
   We Wish You a Merry Christmas 189
Carr, Leroy 137
Carson, Rachel 201
Carter, Gladys Burnette 33
Carter, Joseph 33
Carter Family 86
Carribean-influenced melodies
   All Mixed Up 13
   Clean Up the Hudson 216
   Guantanamera 128
   John B Sails (t: **Load Up the Moving Van**) 56
   Maple Sugar Thyme 231
   Trouble at the Bottom 275
   Uncle Ho (steel drum) 161
Carribean music, about 117, 289
Carthy, Martin 67
Cassidy, Eva 67
Castro, Fidel 130
Catskill Mountain 129, 131, 166, 210
Cavett, Dick 130
Cecil Sharp House 76
celebration 124, 126, 180, 209, 216
censorship 22, 28, 149, 157
C for Conscription 12
Chairborne Infantry 32
chalil (musical instrument) 43, 259

"Chanukah Chase, The" 236
"Chanukah, Oh Chanukah" 236
Chaplin, Charlie 131
Chaplin, Ralph 251
Charter Records 38
Chicago 242
childhood, author's
    family life 11, 46, 256, 282
    musical experiences 11-2, 62, 206, 253, 259
    political values 201, 227
    see also Seeger: Charles, Constance
children Ch. 3 Kids (45-62)
    author's children & grandchildren 45-9, 51, 53-6, 256
    choruses, song for children's 237
    Guthrie, Woody's songs for 86
    political rallies, attending with parents 156
    songwriting with 62, 101
    writing songs for 53, 62
    see also generational issues, schools, Seeger: Danny, Mika, Tao, Tinya
children, lyrics about Ch. 3 (45-62)
    Clearwater songs
        Ballad of the Sloop Clearwater 209
        Clean Up the Hudson 216
        It's a Long Haul 217
    death of in war
        Calendar, The 152
        I Come & Stand 106
    having a family
        Here's to the Couple 124
        Kisses Sweeter than Wine 64
    hope for
        All My Children of the Sun 154
        Arrange and Re-arrange 272
        One Blue Sky 83
        Sailing Down My Golden River 202
        Tomorrow's Children 228
        Visions of Children 123
        Walking Down Death Row 239
Children's Music Network 62
Chile 102
China 50
Choctaw language 88
choral arrangements of songs 82, 194
    Haul, Make Her Go High 218
    Here's to the Couple 124
    Jesu, Joy of Man's Desiring 191
    Old Hundred 194
    Of Time & Rivers Flowing 224
    Precious Friend 244
    Rainbow Race 82
    Rockin' Solidarity 250
    Sacco's Letter to His Son 93
    Visions of Children 123
choral patterns, African 182
Christianity 22, 186, 208, 210, 238, 239
    see also Bible, religion
Christmas 244, see also carols
Christmas Poem 175
Chucho, Mungo 64, 65
Churchill, Winston 19, 26
CIA (Central Intelligence Agency) 102

CIO (Congress of Industrial Organizations) 25
Civil Rights Movement 8, 32-5, 144, 147, 151, 238, 261
    South African 92
    see also Martin Luther King, Fred Kirkpatrick, Bernice Reagon
Clapton, Eric 76
Clara Sullivan's Letter, Mrs. 110
Clarke, Septima 35
classical music 108, 282, see also Bach, Beethoven, Constance Seeger
Clean Up the Hudson 216
Clean Water Act 210
Clearwater (Sloop & organization) Ch. 9 (201-25)
    Ballad of the Sloop... 208
    Clearwater's on the river 218
        Festival 205, photos 60, 245
    Hudson River cleanup campaign 207, 210-6, 219, 223-5
    organization 9, 12, 45, 148, 164
    Sloop 205, 208-9, 216-9, 223-5
    songs re 138, 146, 172, 205-6, 208-20, 222-5
    Walkabout Chorus 191, 223-4, 267
clicks, vocal 275
Clifford, Clark 143
Clockback Song (**The New Hamburg...**) 212
Clouds (**Both Sides Now**) 138-9
coalition-building 248
Cohan, George M. 74
Collier, Jimmy 144-5
Collier, Sam 33
Collins, Judy 67, 138
colonialism 125, 160
Colpet, Max 117, 169
Columbia Records 76, 90, 96, 149
    see also Discography
Columbus, Christopher 16
Come All Ye Fair & Tender Ladies 230
Come along with me upon this... 214
"Come By Here" 119
Come fill up your glasses & set... 204
Comfort, Alex 88
Commoner, Barry 201
Commonwealth College 94
Communist Party Ch. 2 Politics 19-43
    author's relationship with 12, 17, 28, 56, 117, 238
    Bridges, Harry 244-5
    Davis, Ben 67
    father's relationship with 282
    Guthrie, Woody's relationship with 144
    Ho Chi Minh 160
    Hikmet, Nazim 105
    Jesus as a Communist 144
    Lowenfels, Walter 65, 95, 228
    MacColl, Ewan 75
    Nearing, Helen & Scott 231
    publishing "Negro Songs of Protest" 236
    Quin, Mike 43
    Reynolds, Bob (husband of Malvina) 107
    World War II, shifting position re 22, 26
    unions, role in 27

    see also anticommunism, blacklisting, capitalism, "Daily Worker", Soviet Union, Stalin
community 175
    see also utopian communities
Composers' Collective, The 276, 282
conscription – see military service
Conscription, C for 12
consonants in lyrics 101, 123, 247, 275
Cook, Harold Lewis 101
Cooke, Sam 38, 41
cooking 14, 45, 82, 117, 256
Copland, Aaron 282
copyrights – see also public domain reform, royalties
    alterations to lyrics 146, 165
    authorship, publisher concerns re 64, 167
    commercial use of songs, preventing 15
        Guthrie's ideas re 9
        Mbube (Wimoweh), issues re 92
        We Shall Overcome, issues re 33
corruption 170
Cossacks 120, 166
counter-culture 162
Country Joe McDonald 145
country music 17
Coventry Carol, The (**Lulloo Lullay**) 188
Cowboys, songs about 50
Cowell, Henry 11
Crane, Andrew 08
Crawly Creepy Little Mousie 45 (ref. 56)
Crawly Creepy Little Viney 46
Crazy English (book) 266
Crazy Horse 209
Creedence Clearwater Revival 138
Crimea 121
"Cristo Ya Nacio" 8
Crowdog, Henry 144
Cuba 128-30
cummings, e.e.. 95
Cunnigham, Sis 28-9, 172
    see also Almanac Singers
Cursed Be the Nation (poem) 205

D
dabkeh (dance) 270
Daily Worker, The (newspaper) 95, 144, 147
dancing 268, 270
Dane, Barbara 192
Danish, songs in 126
Davies, Idris 98-9
Davis, Ben 43
"D-Day Dodgers, The" 149
Dead Little Girl of Hiroshima (**I Come & Stand**) 106
Dear Mr. Editor, if you choose 110
Dear Mr. President 27
Dear Mr. President (recording) 28
"Dear Willie" 126
death & dying, songs about
    Estadio Chile (murder of Victor Jara) 102
    Full Fathom Five 101
    Get Up & Go 246
    In Dead Ernest (Lee's Compost Song) 94

In the Evening 137
Lord Ha' Mercy on Me 235
No Closing Chord 115
Only Remembered 176
Sailing Down My Golden River 203
These Bones You See (poem) 228
To Know Good Will (poem) 94
To My Old Brown Earth 247
Whistling Past a Graveyard 253
Who Killed Norma Jean? (suicide) 104
death in war Ch. 7 Vietnam (147-170)
    Ballad of October 16th 21
    I Come & Stand at Every Door 106
    I Have a Rendezvous with Death (poem)
      153
    Plow Under 22
    Strange Death of John Doe 21
    Where Have All the Flowers Gone 166
death penalty 92, 183
    For Mumia 262
    Sacco's Letter to His Son 93
    Walking Down Death Row 238
"Death of Harry Simms" 13
Decca Records 43, 64, 90, 299
Deck the Halls 187, tune 202
Declaration of Independence, The 174
"De Colores" 117
DeCormier, Robert 143
degenderizing lyrics 24, 39, 43, 88, 192
Deliver the Goods 28-9
Dellinger, Dave 22
democracy 20, 84, 160, 212, 267
demonstrations, political Ch. 2 (17-43) 151
    lyrics re 20, 159, 281
    media attitudes re 261
    photos 19, 21, 163
    singing at 8, 19, 68-9, 123, 156, 159, 163
    union meetings 33
Dennis the Menace (comic strip) 39
"Deportee" 8, 111
Depression, The Great 17
de Tocqueville, Alexis 238
Devil, The 186, 194, 229
dialect 117
Dias, José Fernandez 128
"Didn't My Lord Deliver Daniel" 123
Didn't Ol' John 271
Dietrich, Marlene 169
DiFranco, Ani 149
Diggit, Roy 215
Dirty Stream, Sailing Up My 202
disabilities 229
DiSavino, Liza 213
Disc Records 143
Disney Corporation 92
diversity – see multiculturalism
Djankoye 121
D-Minor Flourish 80
Do I see Lieutenant Calley 159
"Dona Nobis Pacem" 176
Donne, John 116
Don't play that closing chord for me 115
Don't you know it's darkest before... 240
Don't you know life is an onion 116
Doodle Dandy 46

Doubling Song, The (**We'll All Be a...**) 207
Down by the Old Mill Stream (excerpt) 286
Down in Alabama, 1955 264
Doxology, The (tune) 194
Dozier, Mary Ethel 33
drawings by author 6, 9, 57, 58, 125, 154-5,
    231, 254-5, 247, 261
"Drimmin Down" 63
drone notes 122
dropped D tuning on guitar 289
    Bells of Rhymney 100
    Deck the Halls (instrumental) 187
    Emperor Is Naked Today-o!, The 192
    Estadio Chile 102
    Guantanamera 130
    Living in the Country (instrumental) 78
    Old Hundred 195
    Times a' Gettin' Hard 76
    Water Is Wide 135
    misc. songs 39, 97, 133, 161, 180, 198,
      244, 258, 265, 278, 281
Drowned in Paper 205
Drunken Sailor, The (excerpt) 286 (ref. 213)
Drunk Last Night (excerpt) 288
Dubois, W.E.B. 15
Duke University 261
Dutch, poem in (as source of song) 206
Dylan, Bob 68, 147, 155, 172

E
Earle, Steve 149
Early in the morning I first see the sun 272
Earthly nouris sits and sings, An 106
Easter Rebellion 63
Eastman, Max (poet) 101
Easy come, easy go 116
Ecclesiastes, Book of 13, 172-3
economic issues – see capitalism,
    Communism, poverty, unemployment
Ecuador 195
Edison, Thomas 68, 89
editing of songs 197, 210
editors, this book's 9
Edson, Constance DeClyvver – see Seeger,
    Constance
education 8, 184 – see also schools
"Eensy, Weensy Spider, The" 56
Ehrlich, Paul 201, 206
Eiffel Tower 254
Einbender, Dan 213-4
Einstein, Albert 283
Eisenhower, Dwight David 9, 147
Ej Bozemoj cotej Amerki! 118
Elisabeth, Sarah A. 9
El Martillito (Sp. tr. If I Had a Hammer)
    39
Embers of the Martyrs 237
Emperor Is Naked Today-O!, The 192
Empty Pocket Blues 72
English Folk Song and Dance Society 76
English Is Cuh-ray-zee 266 (ref. 183)
English trad. songs 17, 148, 152, 188, 230,
    249
environmental issues Ch. 9 (espec. 201-7,
    223-5) 123

Little Bird (Magpie's version) 51
My Rainbow Race 82
From Way Up Here 108
Seventy Miles 109
Here We Are Knee Deep in Garbage
    130
O Canada 136
Garbage 140
This Land Is Your Land (new v.) 144-6
Old Hundred 194, 197 (additional v.)
To My Old Brown Earth 247
Well May the World Go 248
EPA (Environmental Protection Agency) 211
Es ist ein Ros entsprungen 223
"Establishment", the 170, 175
Estadio Chile 102
Esta Es Mi Tierra 145
ethnocentricity – see multiculturalism
Europeanization of melodies 130
Evanson, Jacob 117-8
Eve, Letter to 171
Evening Birds 90-1
"Evening Shade" 176
Everybody Loves Saturday Night 126
"Everybody's Got a Right to Live" 156
Everybody, Sit Down! 220

F
Fadden, Ray 87
False From True 151 (ref. 82)
falsetto 91, 252
family life, author's 10
    see also children, marriage
"Farmer Is the Man, The" 17
farming, songs about
    Djankoye 121
    Times a' Gettin' Hard 76
Fascism 36, 102, 271, see also Nazism
Fat Little Baby 54
FBI (Federal Bureau of Investigation) 25
feminism – see gender issues
Feria de las Flores, La 66
fermata 286
Festival de la Nueva Cancion 195
Festival of Flowers 66
fiddle music 249, 286
Fiddler on the Roof (musical) 85
Filk Song Ole Time Religion 136 (ref. 113)
films 166, 229
"First Noel, The" 187
"First Time Ever I Saw Your Face, The" 259
First you get the buckets ready 231
fishing, commercial 206, 210, 223
Fitzgerald, Edward 117
Five-Part Handslap, A 59
"Fixin' to Die Rag" 166
flag, poem about the U.S. 153
"Flat Foot Floogie with a Floy, Floy" 221
flowers, songs about 206, 227
    Flower in the Crannied Wall 74
    Feria de las Flores, La 66
Fodeba, Keita 180-3, 220
Fogerty, John 138
Foggy Dew, The (tune) 63
folk music 282, definitions of 16, 84, 146

folk process 12, 76, 85, 88, 165, 248
  Charles Seeger's coining of term 15
  Guantanamera 128-30
  If I Had a Hammer 38-42
  Kisses Sweeter than Wine 64
  Mbube (Wimoweh) 90-2
  This Land Is Your Land 143-6
  We Shall Overcome 33-6
  Where Have All the Flowers Gone 166-9
  in other specific songs 67, 72, 180, 221
folk rock 172
Folkways Records 10, 23, 45, 53, 79, 92, 142-3, 166, see also Discography
Foner, Philip 236
Fong, Hiram (senator of Hawaii) 82
food 235, see also cooking
Foolish Frog, The 46
Foote, Bud 208
For Mumia 262
For the Beauty of the Earth (book) 213
Fox-Przeworski, Joanne (trans.) 102
France 149, 160, 183
  see also French language
Franco, Francisco 19, 22, 43, 162
Frank, Libby 39
Franklin D. 22
Franklin Roosevelt told the people 21
Frank's Yodel 252
Freed, Arthur 277
freedom of speech & press 148, 166-7, 175
  see also censorship
freedom songs – see Civil Rights, race
free rhythm 260
French poetry (Guillevic) 228
French tunes 194, 258
French language, songs in
  Everybody Loves Saturday Night 126
  Melodie d'Amour 243
  Minuit **(Sower of Seeds)** 180
  O Canada 131
  Que Sont Devenues les Fleurs 169
  To Everyone in All the World 50
Friends (Quakers) 107, 261, 273
friendship, 107, 226, 229, 244
  Old Devil Time 229
  Precious Friend 244
  Wonderful Friends 280
From Yale to Jail (book) 22
From Way Up Here 108
Frost, Robert 117, 186
Full Fathom Five 101
funny songs and stories – see humor

G
Gaillard, Slim 221-3
Gainin' Ground, The 236
Galbraith, John Kenneth 201
Galileo, Galilei 282
Gallo Records 90
Galvin, Patrick 81
Gandhi, Mahatma 174
Garbage 140
gardening 123, 131, songs about 94, 256
Garland, Jim 12, 13

Geiss, Theodore (Dr. Seuss – quote) 131
Gelders, Joe 18
Gellert, Lawrence 236
gender issues 8, 82, 98, 121, 136, 170, 172, 187
  Jacob's Ladder 199
  Letter to Eve 171
  My Body Was Made for Nurturing 170
  Old Hundred 194
  There's a Hole in the Bucket 127
  Talking Union 24
  Rockin' Solidarity 251
  see also degenderizing lyrics
generational issues 164
  Both Sides Now (new v.) 139
  Our Generation 162
  Old Hundred 194
  Well May the World Go 248
  see also aging, children
Genesis, Book of 171
Genghis Khan 22, 88
Georgia (state) 208
geritocracy 170
Germany 158, see also Hitler, The Holocaust, World War II
German music 85, 223
  see also Bach, Beethoven
German, songs in 126, 169, 190
Gershwin, Ira & George 278
Get Up and Go 246
Gibran, Kahlil 48
Gilbert and Sullivan 107, 258
Gilbert, Ronnie – see Weavers
Girl of Hiroshima (**I Come & Stand**) 106
Giuliani, Rudy 123
Give me that old time religion 136
Give Peace a Chance 156
Glazer, Tom 192
Glick, Hirsh 236
God 175-7, 186, 208, 279, 283
  see also religion
"God Bless America" 143
"Go Down Hannah" 08
"Go Down Moses" 285
"God Rest Ye Merry Gentlemen" 285
Golden Gate Quartet 235
Golden Thread, Oh Had I a 67
Goldwater, Barry 148
"Good King Wenceslas" 187
Goodman, Bill (verse by) 67
Goodnight Irene (excerpt) 85 (refs. 8, 64, 90, 172, 286)
Goofing Off Suite, Theme from 10
Gorman, Judy 136
gospel music 85, 153, 287, see also spirituals
  I'll Be All Right 32
  Only Remembered 176
  Seek and Ye Shall Find 184
"Go Tell Aunt Rhody" 258
Grand Ole Opry 24
"Great American Folk Melody, The" 25, 208
Great Peace March 180
Great Silkie, The 105-6
"Green and Yeller" 56
Green, Ber 237

"Green Grass Grows All Around, The" 56
Green Guerillas, The 123
"Greensleeves" 223, 285
Grose, Peter 147
group singing 12, 32-3
  see also choral arrangements, Rise Up Singing, songleading
growth, out of control 207
Grupo Monocotal 195
Guantanamera 128-30 (refs. 15, 102, 117)
Guard, David 167
Guardian, The (newspaper) 246
Guillevic, Eugene (French poet) 228
Guinea 180, 183
guitar, 12 string 133, 198
guitar instrumentals (regular tuning) 15, 157
  Deck the Halls 187
  Living in the Country 78
  Maple Sugar Time 232
  Mexican Blues 30
  Snow, Snow 164
  Spring Fever 234
  Who'd Believe I'd Feel So Good (Irish Air) 81
  see also dropped D tuning
Gunning, Sarah Ogan 12, 13
Gurney, Jay 278
Guth, John 183
Guthrie, Arlo 68, 142-3, 197, 198, 203, 245
Guthrie, Marjorie Mazia 143
Guthrie, Mary 17
Guthrie, Sarah Lee (daughter of Arlo) 203
Guthrie, Woody – see also Almanac Singers
  author's relationship with 8, 12, 17, 24, 201
  copyrights, attitude towards 9
  Communist Party, relation to 144
  folksinger, impact on definition of 16
  letter to Lead Belly 226
  mimeographing his songs 107
  photos 13, 18, 29, 143
  Sacco & Vanzetti project 92
  sign on guitar case re Fascism 271
  songwriting techniques 30, 85-6, 111, 115, 248
  tempo utilized by 159
  Woody Guthrie Trust Fund 144
Guthrie, Woody, songs by
  66 Highway Blues 18
  Lonesome Valley 134
  Reuben James 26
  Round & Round Hitler's Grave 28
  This Land Is Your Land 142-6
  Why Do You Stand There in the Rain? 19-20

H
Hagiz, Yehiel 268
Hair (musical) 68
Hall, Mrs. Francis (Ozark singer) 176
Hambone Lesson, The 58
Hamburg Clockback, The New 212
Hamilton, Frank 34, 79
Hammers Are Bangin' Away, The 274
Hammer Song, The 38-42

Hammond, John 149
Handel, George Frederic 277, 283
Hanoi 160
Happy Ploughman, The (excerpt) 85
Harburg, E.Y. ("Yip") & Ernie 277-9
"Hard, Ain't It Hard" 249
Hard Hitting Songs for Hard Hit People
	(book) 17, 19
harmonization – see also choral
		arrangements, songleading
	African American choral music use of 219
	leading audiences in 136, 198, 219
	politics, relationship with 198
	specific songs, use in 90, 184
Harris, Randolphe 151, 248, 271
Harvard University 7, 273
Hassler, Leo 192
hate crimes 229
"Hatikvah" 119, 285
Haul, Make Her Go High 218
Have you heard of a ship called the... 26
Hawes, Bess 29 – see also Almanac Singers
Haydn, Franz Joseph 12
Hays, Lee 18, 32, 39, 62, 64, 94-5, 244, 248
	photos of 19, 21, 37, 73, 94, 125
	Empty Pocket Blues 72
	Hold the Line 36
	If I Had a Hammer 38
	In Dead Ernest (Lee's Compost Song) 94
	Times a' Gettin' Hard 76
	To Know Good Will (poem) 94
	Tomorrow Is a Highway 37
	see also Almanac Singers, Weavers
Hear the Thunder! 162
Hebrew 43
He educated all the people 160
Hegel, Georg Wilhelm Frederich 282
He Lies in the American Land 118
Hellerman, Fred 27, 144, see also Weavers
Hellman, Lillian 35
hemiola (metrical pattern) 156-7
Hendrick, Minnie 33
Hennacy, Ammon 84
Henscratches and Flyspecks (book) 287
Here's to the Couple 124
Here We Are in Madison Square 43
Here We Are Knee Deep in Garbage 130
He's a long time gone 132
He's Got the Whole World (excerpt) 287
He told her he loved her, but oh how... 62
"Hey, Ho, Nobody Home" 285
Hey yup boy! Wimoweh 90
Hey Zhankoye (Djankoye) 121
Hickerson, Joe 166, 176
Higgins, Elizabeth 17
Highlander Center 18, 32-5
Hikmet, Nazim 105
Hill, Joe 84, 198
Hillel & Aviva 43
Hillel, Rabbi 197
Hille, Waldemar 35
Hills, Anne 149
Hills of Glenshee, The 87 (ref. 259)
Hiroshima 106
Hi, said the little leatherwing bat 79

hitchhiking 18
Hitler, Adolf 19, 22, 26-8, 282
Ho Chi Minh 160
Hold the Line 36
Hole in the Bucket 127
Holocaust, The Jewish 268
	Embers of the Martyrs 237
	Bach at Treblinka 191
home, author's 46
"Home on the Range" 50
homosexuality 229
Hoover, Herbert 17
Hopkinson, Francis 153
hora (dance) 270
Horton, Zilphia 32-5
housecleaning, songs about 48
"House of the Rising Sun" 8, 50, 286
How Are We Gonna Save Tomorrow? 210
How do I know my youth is all spent 246
How Much for Spain? (poem) 43
How Soon? 260 (ref. 44)
How to Play the 5-String Banjo (book) 167
HUAC (House Un-American Activities
		Committee) 54, 227
Huck, Gary (cartoon by) 24
Huddie Ledbetter Was a Helluva Man 132
Hudson River 45, 120, 129, map 16
	campaign to cleanup – see Clearwater
	Hudson River Sloops (poem) 206
	Hudson River Song, The (Sailing Up My
		Dirty Stream) 202
Hudson, William Elliot 81
humor 48, 119, 131, 160, 165, 248
	Oh How He Lied 60
	Politician's Guide 258
	Seek & Ye Shall Find (stories) 184-6
	There's a Hole in the Bucket 127
	see also parody, satire
"Humoresque" 245
Humphries, Pat 172, 213
Huntington's Disease 143
Hush Little Baby 58
hymns & religious songs – see also Bach,
		Beethoven, gospel, spirituals
	Only Rememberd 176
	Rock of Ages 85
	Seek & Ye Shall Find 184

I
Ibaragi, Noriko 96-8
I been many a mile in this old car 69
I can see them now, said old... 206
I Come and Stand at Every Door 106
"Ida Red" 22
I don't know where I'll go 55
"I Don't Want Your Millions Mister" 13
If a Revolution Comes to My Country 162
"I Feel Like I'm Fixin' to Die Rag" 166
If I could ring like a bell! 114
If I Had a Hammer 38-42 (refs. 13, 134)
If I should die before I wake 94
If I should one day die by violence 94
If it ain't one thing 116
If nothing happens, they will electrocute me
	93

If This World Survives 281
If you love your Uncle Sam 149
If you want higher wages let me tell... 23
If you would be patient & teach me 79
I Had a Rooster 56
I Have a Rendezvous with Death (poem)
	153
"I Know an Old Lady Who Swallowed a
	Fly" 56, 76
I'll Be All Right 32
I'll sing you a song & it's not very long 21
"I'm a Little Cookie" 56
I'm Doing Quite Well for the Shape I'm In
	(Get Up and Go) 245
I'm Gonna Sing Me a Love Song 68
"I'm Gonna Tell" 62
immigration 118-9, 248
"imperiodic rhythm" 247, 260
improvisation 65, 230
In Dead Earnest (Lee's Compost Song) 94
India 172
Industrial Revolution, The 146
I never had a pocket full of money 72
"In My Window" 236
In Scarlet Town where I was born 230
International Copyright Convention 15
International Workers Order 117
In the Evening 137
In the jungle, the mighty jungle 91
"In Them Long Hot Summer Days" 218
In the Stillness of My Heart 75
I Oleana der er det godt at være 119
"I Once Loved a Lass" 148
Iraq War 149
Irion, Johnny 203
Irish Air, An (Who'd Believe I'd Feel...) 81
Irish-American song 79
Irish Songs of Resistance (book) 81
Irish trad. songs 117, 152, 259
	Foggy Dew, The (t: Over the Hills) 63
	Leatherwing Bat 79-80
	Memory of the Dead, The (t: Who'd
		Believe I'd Feel So Good) 81
	My Lagan Love 87
	Praties They Grown Small, The (t: Step
		by Step) 35
"Irish Washerwoman, The" 230
Irwin, May 46-7
Isaac Woodward 111
Israel 43, 119-20, 194, 238
Israel, Cappy 144
Italy 92
I think that this whole world 14
It rained all night & I'm feelin'... 222
"It Really Isn't Garbage" 213
It's a Long Haul 216
It's gonna take everybody to win... 28
"It's Only a Paper Moon" 278
It's only a shanty in old shanty town 221
It was raining mighty hard 20
"I've Been Working on the Railroad" 245
I've Committed Crimes Against Nature 227
Ives, Burl 76, 86
I want to go to Andorra 112
I Want to Go to Azoty 113

I wish I had a bushel 28
I Wonder, I Wonder, I Wonder 49

J
Jackson, Andrew 88
Jackson, Aunt Molly 12, 13, 282
Jackson, Kitama (author's grandson) 54
Jackson, Mahalia 174-5
Jackson, Moraya (granddaughter) 22, 54, 256
Jacobs, Judy Gorman 136
Jacob's Ladder 198 (refs. 13, 34)
Jacobs, Mai 65
jail – see prison
James, William 273
Japan 82, 117, 153-4
    I Come & Stand at Every Door 106
    Kuroda Bushi 88
    When I Was Most Beautiful 96
Japanese-Americans 22, 32
    see also Toshi Seeger
Jara, Victor 39, 102-3
jazz 12, 97, 212, 221, 251-2
Jefferson, Blind Lemon 86
Jefferson, Thomas 174
Jeffrey, Travis (Clearwater captain) 214-7
Jenkins, Ella 62
Jenkins, Gordon 43, 64, 90, 268-9
Jesu, Joy of Man's Desiring 190
Jesus 144, 174, 176, 178
Jesus bleibet meine Freude 190
Jig Along Home (excerpt) 86
Jewish Currents (magazine) 237
Jingle Bells (excerpt) 288
John Birch Society 148
"John Brown's Body" 149
"John B. Sails" 56, 287
John Doe, Strange Death of 21
"John Henry" 45, 89, 132
Johnny Long's Orchestra 221
Johns, Leo 243
Johnson, David 08
Johnson, Lyndon 147, 150
"Johnson Says He'll Load More Hay" 169
Jones, Mother 116
Joseito (José Fernandez Dias) 128-30
Joy of Sex, The (book) 88
Juarez, Benito 197
Judaism 22, 120-2, 143, 227
    see also Arab-Israeli conflict, Hebrew,
        Holocaust, Yiddish
Juilliard Institute 11
Just my hands can't tear a prison down 89
Just when I thought all was lost 244
justice, economic – see also capitalism,
    Communist Party, unions
    Bells of Rhymney 98
    If I Had a Hammer 38-42

K
Kalvelage, Lisa 158
Kamtrovitch family 227
Kayowajineh 87
Keegan, Judge (of Albany) 216
Keel Row, The 249
"Keep Your Eyes on the Prize" 235

Keesler Field 31-2
Kennedy, John Fitzgerald 09
Kennedy, Robert 151
Kennedy, Sam 63-4
Ken, Thomas (composer) 195
Kent, Rockwell 117
key (in music) 9, 285
Khayyam, Omar 117
kibbutz (Israeli commune) 238
Killian, Bob 213
King, Charlie 92, 113
King Henry 146
King, Martin Luther, Jr. 32, 201, 263-5
    assassination, aftermath of 151, 261
    photos 34, 263
    Take It from Dr. King 264
    see also Civil Rights, race
King James Bible 172, 178
King Kong 92
Kingston Trio, The 167
Kirkpatrick, (Bro.) Fred 144, 156, 236
Kisses Sweeter Than Wine 63-4 (refs. 86,
    287)
Koheleth (Ecclesiastes) 172-3
Koloda Duda 168 (ref. 13)
Kottke, Leo 77
Kovaly, Andrew 117-8
Ku Klux Klan 35, 95
"Kumbaya" 119
Kuroda Bushi 88

L
Labor Songs of the 19th Century (book)
    236
labor unions & songs – see unions
Ladysmith Black Mambazo 72, 90
Lafayette, Bernard 33
La Feria de las Flores 65-6
Lagan Love, My 87
Lampell, Millard 19-29, 29
    see also Almanac Singers
Land, Robert 24
language, scatological ("bad words") 273
Lanjean, Marc 243
Larger the island of knowledge, The 116
"Last Night I Had the Strangest Dream" 87
Last Train to Nuremburg 159
Latin America 259, music 156
    see also Caribbean, Chile, Cuba
Lavalle, Calixa 131
League of Nations 22
Leatherwing Bat, The 79-80
Lead Belly 8, 12, 63-5, 85-86, 90, 132, 201
    Huddie Ledbetter Was a Helluva Man
        132
    letter from Woody Guthrie to 226
    photos 13, 132
Lead Belly, songs by
    Kisses Sweeter Than Wine 64
    Midnight Special (t: **Bright Yellow
        Forsythias**) 227
    New York City (t: **Here We Are in
        Madison Square**) 43
    Old Riley (t: **Haul Make Her Go High**)
        218

Ledbetter, Huddie – see Lead Belly
Ledbetter, Martha 132
Lederer, Richard 266
Led Zeppelin 88
Lee's Compost Song (**In Dead Ernest**) 94
Left a good job in the city 138
"Leiber Heinrich" 126
LeMay, Curtis (general) 9
Lennon & McCartney 156
Leonino, Terry (of Magpie) 51, 92, 240
Leopold, Prince of Anhalt-Cothen 191
"Let him go to jail." (Toshi Seeger quote) 54
Let me tell you of a sailor 25
Let me tell you the story of a line 36
"Let's Go on a Bear Hunt" 8, 56
Letter to Eve 171
"Let the Sun Shine In" 68
Leventhal, Harold 33, 144, 167
Leviticus, Book of 194
Levin, Joe 71
Lewis, John L. (of UMW & CIO) 20
Liberation Theology 8
Life (magazine) 104
Lilo, lullo, lilo 152
"Lincoln & Liberty Too" 31
Linda, Solomon 90-2
"lingocentric predicament" (expression) 183
Lion King, The (film) 91
"Lion Sleeps Tonight, The" 91
Lisa Kalvelage 158
Little a' This 'n' That, A 256 (refs. 45, 82)
Little Bird, Fly Through My Window 51
Little Boxes (excerpt) 107, ref. 206
Little Fat Baby 54
Little Girl of Hiroshima (**I Come & Stand**)
    106
Little Girl See Through My Window 51
Little, Jack 221
Litvinov, Maxim 22
Living in the Country 77-8
Lloyd, A.L. 168
Load Up the Moving Van 56
local focus in organizing Ch. 9 Think
    Globally, Sing Locally (201-25)
Lo How a Rose (t: **Of Time & Rivers
    Flowing**) 223
Lomax, Alan 8, 12, 17, 50 (photo), 56, 86,
    89-90, 184, 235
Lomax, John 8, 16, 50 (photo), 133
Lomax, John and/or Alan, songs collected by
    51, 59, 79, 85, 216, 218, 227, 271
Lo Mfan Unesongota (**Here's to the
    Couple**) 124
"Londonderry Air, The" 259
Lonesome Traveler (book) 95
Lonesome Valley (Guthrie v.) 134
Long Collection Speech, The (poem) 43
Long-Fong-Spong Song Bill 82
Long Haul, A 216
Long, Russell (Louisiana senator) 82
Long John (tune) 8, 216
Long March, The 170
Long Story Terse (**Odds On Favorite**) 279
Lord Ha' Mercy On Me 235
Louis, Joe 27

love Ch. 4 (63-84), 177, 184, 198, 243
   Both Sides Now 139
   Christmas Poem 175
   False from True 151
   Little a' This 'n' That, A 256
   Melodie d'Amour 242
   My Lagan Love 87
   Oh How He Lied 62
   Old Devil Time 229
   Water Is Wide 134
   Well May the World Turn 248
   When I Was Most Beautiful 96
   see also weddings
Love It Like a Fool (film) 107
Love Songs for Friends & Foes (LP) 63
Lowenfels, Walter (& Lillian) 65, 95, 228
lullabies 8, 75, 123, 236
   Abiyoyo 60
   One Grain of Sand 52
   Sweet-a Little Baby 53
Lulloo Lullay 188
Lynd, Staughton 89
lyrics – see also songwriting
   fit with melody 123
   omitting controversial 143

M
MacColl, Ewan (author's brother-in-law) 75, 259
MacDonald, Country Joe 145, 166
MacKenzie, Marion 67
MacLeish, Archibald 22
"Maggie's Farm" 173
Magpie 51, 92, 240
Makeba, Miriam 92, 253
Maladie D'Amour 243
Mammals, The (band) 240
Manet, Edouard 283
Manhattan School of Music 128
Mao Tse-tung 207
maple syrup 231, 272
Maple Syrup Time 231
Marcantonio, Vito 22, 43
"Marche Militaire" 156
Mariachi music 65
marriage 69, 120, see also weddings
   Toshi Seeger & author's 256
Marrs, Ernie 81, 169, 204
"Marseillaise, La" 258
Marti, Jose 15, 128-30
Martillito, El (Sp. If I Had a Hammer) 39
Martinez, Alberto O. 145
Martin, Harold 204
Maruga, Paloma (trans.) 35
Marx, Karl 206, 275
Masakela, Hugh 92
Maselwa, J.N. 60, 124
Mason, Molly 257
mathematics 175, 185
"Matilda" 216
Mayer, Louis B. 277
May Irwin's Frog Song **(Foolish Frog)** 46
May, May, the flowers bloom 152
May, Tim 145
Mbube (Wimoweh) 90-2

McCarthy, Joseph 43
McCrackin, Rev. Maurice 179
McCurdy, Ed 87
McGhee, Brownie 85, 137
McLean, Don 206
McManus, John T. (funeral for) 246
McNamara, Robert 112
meetings, songs for beginning 219-20
Me gusta cantarle al viento 66
Meidel, Ditmar 119
Melodie D'Amour 242
melodies, composition of Ch. 5 New Tunes
   to Others' Words (85-116), 68, 89, 173,
   188, 219, 258-9
   see also rhythm, songwriting
Memory of the Dead, The (tune) 81
Memphis Slim 137
Mexican-Americans 145
Mexican Blues 30 (ref. 230)
Mexican music 30, 65
Mexico City 282
MGM Studios 277
Midler, Bette 123
Midnight Special (new v.) 133, tune 227,
   ref. 8
military, share of budget 152, 159, 267
military service, author's 12, 27, 31
Milky Way, The 199
Millay, Edna St. Vincent 101
Miller, Michael 9, 262
Miller, Mitch 156
Mills, Alan 76
Minelli, Liza 230
miners 13, 18, 20, 98, 110, 282
minor mode 89, 153, 258, 285, 286
"Minstrel Boy, The" 259
Minuit **(Sower of Seeds)** 180, 220
Miron, Issachar 268
"Mister Farmer" 17
Mister Thompson calls the waiter 140
Mitchell, Joni 138, 172
Mockingbird Song, The **(Hush Little Baby)** 58
Model T Ford 11, 282
Monet, Claude 283
Money Is King (new v.) 134
Monroe, Marilyn 104-5
Montgomery Trio 33
morality 227, 273
Morehouse College 263
"More We Get Together, The" 62
Moving, songs about 56
Mozart, Wolfgang Amadeus 12
Mrs. Clara Sullivan's Letter 110
multiculturalism 88, 122, 177-8, 261, 267, 282
   A Little a' This n' That 256
   All Mixed Up 14
   Everybody Loves Saturday Night 126
   My Father's Mansion 178
   Old Hundred 194
   Tzena, Tzena 268
   Whistling Past a Graveyard 253
multilingualism 122, 126, 267-70, 269
Mumia (Abu Jamal) 262
Mungo, Chucho 65-6

Munnik, Len (cartoons by) 20, 117, 147,
   178, 188, 193, 213, 238, 239
Murphy, Luci 172
music notation, limitations of 132, 186, 287
music notation, reading 16, 284-8
Musselman, Jim 149
Mussolini, Benito 28
My Body Was Made For Nurturing 170
My Dirty Stream, Sailing Up 202
My Father's Mansion 178
My Golden River, Sailing Down 202
My grandma she can make a soup 256
My Lagan Love 87, (ref. 259)
My Lai massacre 159
My Name Is Lisa Kalvelage 158
My name is Patrick Spudnut 235
My Old Brown Earth, To 247
My Rainbow Race 82

N
Nashville 289
Nashville Quartet 33
national anthem, U.S. 144, 161
National Enquirer, The (tabloid) 175
Native Americans 16, 22, 87-8, 144, 152,
   209, 238
   Kayowajineh 87
   lyrics referencing 14, 144, 209
Natour, Salman (Arab poet) 268-9
Nat Turner **(Gainin' Ground)** 236
Natural History (poem put to music) 74
Navigator said to the engineer, The 153
Nazism 169, 192, see also Hitler, Adolf
"Nearer My God to Thee" 67
Near, Holly 172
Nearing, Scott & Helen 231
Negro Songs of Protest (book) 236
Nejmeh, Al 215
Nestler, Rick 213
New Deal, The 32
New Hamburg Clockback, The 212
new words to old tunes Chap 6 (117-46)
   see also list of other songs on p.146
Newport Folk Festival 76, 90, 172, 208
news media 147, 159, 175, 261
   lyrics' references to 104, 110
   using news stories as material for songs
   110-3, 158
   see also radio, television
New York City 278, 282
New York City (tune) 43
New York Times (newspaper) 92, 113, 147,
   261
New York Town (excerpt) 86
Nicaragua 195, 274
Nigeria (song in Yoruba) 126
nightclubs, Weavers singing at 64
Niles, John Jacob 188
Nixon, Richard 151, 159, 254
No Closing Chord 115
No fool like an old fool 116
No Mas Violencia 263 (ref. 259)
No news is good news 116
Nonsense words in songs 152

Norma Jean, Who Killed 104
Norwegian Emigrant Songs & Ballads
    (book) 119
Norwegian, songs in 119, 126
notation, musical 284-8
Now We Sit Us Down 219
nueva cancion 195
Nuremberg trials 158-9
nursery rhymes 45

O
Oberlin College 166, 248
O Canada! 131
Ocean's Rising, The 263
Ochs, Phil 147
Odds-on Favorite 279
Ode to a Composer (poem) 191
Ode to Joy 122
Of Time and Rivers Flowing 223
Ogan, Sarah 12, 13
Oh Eve, where is Adam? 171
Oh Franklin Roosevelt told the people 21
Oh, Had I a Golden Thread 67 (ref. 15)
Oh How He Lied 62
Oh if I could ring like a bell! 114
Ohio 166
Oh My Loving Brother (excerpt) 85
Oh pacem in terris 171
Ohta, Toshi-Aline – see Seeger, Toshi
Oh to be in Oleanna 119
Oh what will you give me? 98
Old Ark's A-Moverin' (tune) 206
Old Brown Earth, To My 247
Old Devil Time 229
Old Father Hudson, now we sit us... 219
Old Huddie Ledbetter he was a... 133
Old Hundred 194
"Old Joe Clark" 28
"Old Lady that Swallowed a Fly" 56, 76
Old Reuben 235
Old Riley (tune) 218
Old Shantytown 221
Old Time Religion 136 (ref. 113)
Oleanna 119
Once in the year it is not thought... 189
One-a These Days 266
One Blue Sky 82
One day, one day, I was walking... 216
One Dime Blues (excerpt) 86
"One Dollar Milk & Forty Cent Meat" 17
One Grain of Sand 52
One Man's Hands 88-9
One Percent Phosphorus 274
One sudden warm day in June 66
Only Remembered 176-7
Ono, Yoko 156
Opening **Theme from "The Goofing Off**
    Suite" 10
Orbon, Julian 128-30
Or Else 266
O Sacred Head Now Wounded (tune) 192
O Sacred World Now Wounded 192
Osborn, Susan 183
O'Sheel, Shaemas 88
Ottinger, Richard 210

Our Generation 162
outdoors, songs re 66, 152, 164, 206, 227,
    231
Out of sight, out of mind 116
Over the Hills 63
Over the Rainbow 278
Oyey, oyey 180
"Oyfn Pripichik" 236
Ozark Mountains 176

P
Pacheco, Tom 149
paganism 136, 187
Pacem in Terris 172-3
Page, Jimmy 88
parables 180, 184
Paragraph Troops, The 32
Parks, Rosa 34-5
parodies
    I Want to Go to Azoty (Andorra) 113
    Old Time Religion 136
    This Land Is Your Land 144-6
Partlow, Vern 24
patriotism 82, 142-6, 144, 147-8, 153
Patterson, Annie 9
Paul Winter Consort 180
"Pay Me My Money Down" 77
PCB Song, The 210
peace 9, 44, 269, see also Vietnam, World
    War I, World War II
    I Come and Stand at Every Door 106
    Letter to Eve 171
    Malvina Reynolds songs 108, 112, 114,
    281
    misc. lyric references 75, 189, 209, 248
    Oh Had I a Golden Thread 67
    Old Hundred 194
    One Man's Hands 89
    Quite Early Morning 240
    religious songs about 188-94, 199
    River of My People 120
    role of music in building 270
    Visions of Children 123
Peanuts (comic strip) 107
"Peanut Vendor, The" 15
Peekskill Riot (at Paul Robeson concert) 36
Pelham, Ruth 172
Penn, Larry 56
Pennsylvania 127
Pennsylvania Songs & Legends (book) 118
Pentagon, The 275
People Are Scratching, The 204
People's Music Network 92, 172
People's Songs (magazine & nonprofit) 32,
    34-5, 37, 45, 107
Perot, Ross 258
Pete (CD) 122
Peter, Paul & Mary 13, 38-41, 67, 156, 167
Petric, Faith 251
piano accompaniment 73
    Rockin' Solidarity 252
    This Old Car 70
Pinochet, Augusto (dictator) 102
pitch 284, 287
pitching songs – see key

plagiarism 248, 277, see also copyrights,
    folk process, songwriting
Plato 8
Platt, Dave 191
Plow Under 22
poems
    Christmas Poem 175
    Cursed Be the Nation 205
    I Have a Rendezvous with Death 153
    Long Collection Speech 43
    These Bones You See 228
    Torn Flag, The 153
    To Know Good Will 94
poems put to music Ch. 5 New Tunes to
    Others' Words (94-106), 205
    Embers of the Martyrs 237
    Flower in the Crannied Wall 74
    Hudson River Sloops 206
    If This World Survives 281
    I'm Doing Quite Well for the Shape that
    I'm In 246
    Natural History 74
    Odds-on Favorite 279
    Ode to a Composer 191
    Ross Perot Guide to Answering
    Embarrassing Questions 258
    Starlight, Starbright 75
    This Is a Land 206
    Versos Sencillos 128
poetry 95, 117, 160
Poland 113, 237
politicians 258
Politician's Guide to Answering
    Embarrassing Questions 258
pollution – see environmental issues
Polo, Marco 14, 88
polychlorinated biphenyls (PCBs) 210-1
"Poor Howard" 8
Poor Peoples' Campaign 144
popular music 221, 223, 253
population issues 65, 193, 206-7
Porter, Cole 130
Porter, Marjorie 169
Poussaint, Alvin 8
poverty 74, 221, see also capitalism,
    unemployment
Praetorius, Michael 224
Prague, Soviet invasion of 151
"Praties They Grow Small, The" 35
Pray for the dead 116
Precious Friend 244
Preminger, Otto (film director) 229
"Pretty Polly" 17
prison 54, 133, 170, 216, 271
progress 212
protest songs (inability to market) 172
Proud Mary 138 (ref. 287)
Proverbs (put to music) 116
Psalms, Book of 179, 194
public domain reform, campaign for 61, 64,
    76
purposes of music, the 168, essay on 84
Put Your Finger in the Air (excerpt) 86

Q
Quakers 107, 261, 273

Que Sont Devenues les Fleurs 169
Quin, Mike 43
Quite Early Morning 240

R
race & racism 16, 82, 122
  lyrics re 14, 27, 192, 196, 216
    see also African-Americans, Civil Rights,
      multiculturalism, slavery, South Africa
radio 28, 128, 169
Raffi 50
railroads 212, 234
Rainbow Race, My 82
Randolph, Vance 176
"rap" music 23
Raveh, Ilka 43-4, 259
Reader's Digest, The (magazine) 116
Reagan, Ronald 143
Reagon, Bernice Johnson 15, 33-5, 67, 172,
  248
Reagon, Toshi 67
recorder (instrument) 87, 105, 188, 236, 259
record industry 53, 76, 166-7
"Red Wing" 85
Reed, Gretchen 172
Reed, Jimmy 213
Reid, Bob 62, 213
religion Ch. 8 The Great Old Book (171-200)
  author's family's ideas about 56, 282
  creativity, divine inspiration and 89
  Didn't Old John 271
  "folk process" in 88
  Guthrie, Woody's beliefs about 144
  Hayes, Lee as preacher's son 94
  Lord Ha' Mercy 235
  lyrics in other songs re 74, 162
  Odds-On Favorite 279
  Ole Time Religion 136
  quotes about 43, 279, 283
  union rallies, prayer at 32
  see also Bible, Christianity, gospel,
    Judaism, spirituals
Remember when the AAA killed a... 22
Remembrance Rock (novel) 116
Renoir, Pierre-Auguste 283
repetition, in songs 68, 120, 152, 258
Resettlement Administration music project
  84
residence, author's 56, 77
Reuben James 26 (refs. 8, 22, 27, 28, 86,
  111)
revolution, political 146, 162 (song re), 231
Reynolds, Bud 107
Reynolds, Malvina 68, 107-15, 175, 281
  Andorra 112
  Christmas Poem 175
  From Way Up Here 108
  If This World Survives 281
  Mrs. Clara Sullivan's Letter 110
  No Closing Chord 115
  Ring Like a Bell 114
  Seventy Miles 109
rhyming in song lyrics 81, 117
rhythm
  5:4 - 51, 274

altering songs' original 64-7, 86-7, 134,
  167, 250
axe-chopping songs 218, 271
Bach's love of 189
"imperiodic" (free) 87, 247, 260
irregularities, respecting song's 86, 130, 173
music notation of 284-8
performance issues re 100, 164, 203
songwriting issues re 123, 155, 258
sustaining notes 186, 195
syncopation 250, 264, 287
see also Caribbean melodies, tempo
rhythm exercises
  Five-Part Handslap, A 59
  Hush Little Baby (hambone lesson) 59
  Two Against Three: A Rhythm Skill
    156
Richmond, Howie 90
Richmond Organization, The (TRO) 64, 146,
  188
riding the rails 18
"Riflemen of Bennington, The" 149
"rim shots" (vocal clicks) 275
Ring Like a Bell 114
Rio de Janeiro 254
Rise Up Singing (book) 9, 262, 276
ritard 287
"River" 213
River of My People 120
"River That Flows Both Ways, The" 213
Rivers and Harbors Act (1899) 210
Roberts, John 240-1
Robeson, Paul 36
Robinson, Carson 86
Rock Creek Park (Wash. D.C.) 282
Rockefeller, John D. 244
Rockin' Solidarity 250
Rock Island Line (excerpt) 287
Rodgers, Jimmie (pop singer) 64
Rodriguez-Seeger, Tao (author's grandson)
  55, 275
Rogers, Jimmie (yodeling brakeman) 12
Rolling on the River (**Proud Mary**) 138
Rolling Stone (magazine) 92
Roll On Columbia (excerpt) 85, ref. 26
"Roll the Old Chariot Along" 213
Roosevelt, Eleanor 21, 31
Roosevelt, Franklin Delano 19-22, 27, 32, 282
Roosevelt, Theodore 50, 170 (quote)
rope-hauling, song for 216
"Rosin the Beau" 31
Ross, Betsy 153
Rosselson, Leon 67
Ross Perot Guide 258
Rosten, Norman 104-5
Rouault, Georges (French painter) 96
Round and Round Hitler's Grave 28
rounds 276
Routhier, A.B. 131
Rows & flows of angel hair 139
royalties 34, 72, 92, 125, 130, 143, 146,
  183, 220
  see also copyrights, public domain reform
"Rozhinkes Mit Mandeln" 236
Rubaiyat of Omar Khayyam (book) 117

Rubin, Ruth 120-1
Russell, Bertrand 88
Russian trad. songs 120, 168
Russia – see Soviet Union

S
Sacco and Vanzetti 92-3
Sacred Harp, The (book) 176
Sacred World Now Wounded, O 192
Sag' mir, wo die Blumen Sind 169 (ref. 117)
sailing 101, 138, 201-26
  Sailing Down My Golden River 202
  Sailing 'round the bend 208
  Sailing Up My Dirty Stream 202
  "Sailing Up, Sailing Down" 132, 213
Salidor, Susan 261
Salvador, Henri 243
Sandburg, Carl 56, 76, 116, 283
Sandpipers, The 128
San Francisco 250
satire 119, 150
"scat" (musical style) 221
Scherker, Michael 223
Schimmel, Nancy 175
Schmidt, Eric von 13
schools – see also children
  challenges facing 130 266, 275
  Folkways records and 53
  sanitizing lyrics in 143
  schoolchildren & Clearwater 205, 216
  singing in 227, 278
Schumann, Robert 85
Schwartz, Vic 205
science 175, 198, 282
  see also astronomy, mathematics
Scottish songs – see also Ewan MacColl
  Great Silkie (t: **I Come & Stand**) 106
  The Hills of Glenshee 87
  I Once Loved a Lass (t: **King Henry**) 148
  pronunciation challenges 117
  vocables (nonsense words) in 152
  Water Is Wide, The 134
Scott, Jim 180
sea chanteys 77
Seeger, Alan (uncle) 153
Seeger, Cassie (granddaughter) 55
Seeger, Charles (brother) 11, 175, 282
Seeger, Charles Louis (father) 11, 45-7, 194,
  276, 282
  photos 11, 12, 84, 282
  political ideas 153, 276, 282
  Purposes of Music, The (essay) 84
  quotes & sayings 12, 15, 84, 87, 143, 183,
    248
Seeger, Constance (mother) 11, 227, 282
  "3 B's" of (vs. author's) 205
  father of 175
  sexism faced by grandmother of 187
  photos 11, 282
Seeger, Danny (son) 45, 49
Seeger, Elizabeth (aunt) 45
Seeger, Isabelle & Penny – see under
  Bossom-Seeger
Seeger, John (brother) 11, 46, 189, 282
Seeger, Kate (niece) 152, 236

Seeger, Kitama & Moraya – see under Jackson
Seeger, Mika (daughter) 45, 48, 49
Seeger, Mike (half-brother) 245, 252
Seeger, Peggy (half-sister) 75, 77, 134, 245, 259
Seeger, Ruth Crawford (stepmother) 49, 56
Seeger, Tao Rodriguez (grandson) 55, 275
Seeger, Tinya (daughter) 45, 49, 54, 204, 209, 256
Seeger, Tony (nephew) 290
Seeger, Toshi-Aline Ohta (wife)
   author's marriage to 32, 54, 68, 226, 256
   family life with 45, 256
   gardener, as 94, 131
   mother's religious beliefs 56, 177
   organizer for Clearwater 45
   photos of 68, 69, 82, 157, 256
   quote "Let him go to jail!" 54
   Selma march 35
   song re (**A Little a' This 'n' That**) 256
   travels with author 98, 147, 157, 160, 229
   see also Ch. 4 Love Songs (author calls 82 "best" for her)
Seek and You Shall Find 184
Selma to Montgomery March 35
Seneca Canoe Song (**Kayowajineh**) 87
sentimentality, risks of 84
September 11th, 2001 – 265
Sermon on the Mount 210
Serviceman's Club (photo) 31
Seton, Ernest Thompson 227
Seuss, Dr. (Theodor Geisel quote) 131
"Seven Cent Cotton & 40 Cent Meat" 18
Seventy Miles 109
sexism – see gender
Shabalala, Joseph 72
Shakers (religion) 68
Shakespeare, William 13, 101, 178-9
Shantytown 221
shape note singing 176
Shappes, Morris U. 237
Sharp, Cecil 134
Sharpton, Rev. Al 216
Shave and a Haircut (excerpt) 285
Shaw, George Bernard 178
"She'll Be Comin' 'Round the Mountain" 8, 56, 62
"She Moved Through the Fair" 88
"Shenandoah" 213
Shetland Islands 105
Shoals of Herring, The (tune) 75
Sholokhov, Mikhail 166
Short Sisters, The 152
short songs 130
"Shtille Di Nacht" 236
Silent Spring (book) 201
Silkie, The Great 106
Simmons, Lucille 32, 33
Simone, Nina 88
Simon, Helen Travis 22
sing-alongs – see group singing, songleading
Singing in the Country (**Living in the...**) 78
Sing Out (magazine & nonprofit)
   "alive & kicking" 9
   articles from 62, 131

author's membership in 12
contests in 126, 168
founding of 37-8, 45
learning songs from 172
ordering CDs for this book from 16
Resource Center of (SORCe) 125, 276
songs appearing in 134, 176
support for folk music projects 72
Sinking of the Reuben James, The 26
Sioux 144
Siras, John 221
Si tu viera un martillo 39
Sixty-six Highway Blues 18
"Skip to My Lou" 45, 56
slavery 22, 193 (lyric), 206, 236
Slavic melodies 123
Slim and Slam 221-3
Sloop Clearwater – see Clearwater
Sloop Clearwater, Ballad of the 208
Sloop John B. tune 56, ref. 287
Slovakian, songs in 118
Smith, Jerry J. 145
Smithsonian Folkways Recordings – see Folkways Records
Smoke of Treblinka, The 237
Smothers Brothers (Dick & Tommy) 149
SNCC (Student Nonviolent Coordinating Committee) 33-4
Snow, Snow 164
Solidarity Forever (**Rockin' Solidarity**) 250
So load up the moving van 56
So Long It's Been Good to Know You (excerpt) 86
Someday you'll be able to walk 54
Some Proverbs 116
Some say the trouble's in the Pentagon 275
Some seeds fall on fallow ground 180
Somewhere over the rainbow 277
Somos cinco mil 102
Somos El Barco (excerpt) 213, ref. 132
Somoza, Anastasio 22
songleading, about 39, 120, 218, 276, see also group singing
songleading technique – see technique suggestions re specific songs through out the book
   If I Had a Hammer (songleader's version) 42
songs for all purposes 168
Songs for John Doe (recording) 22
songwriting Ch. 6 New Words to Others' Tunes (117-46)
   altering original lyrics 82
   as gambling, joining, matchmaking 8, 12, 238
   by children 62, 101
   contest, author entering a 82
   deadline, writing under 230
   for children 45, 53
   Guthrie, Woody 12, 113, 248
   Dylan, Bob 68
   Harburg, Yip 278
   poems, writing tunes for 205
   Reynolds, Malvina 107, 114
   rhyming, use of 123

women songwriters 172
   see also folk process, melody composition, plagarism
Sorrels, Rosalie 62
Sour Cream 235
Sousa, John Phillip 08
South Africa 90-3, 124, 275
"South Australia" 213
Soviet Union – see also Communist Party, Russia, Stalin
   Djankoye 120
   father's enthusiasm for 282
   German invasion of 22, 26, 28
   invading other countries 19, 151
   magazine printing **Snow, Snow** 164
   performing in Moscow 147
   Soviet novel as source for lyric 166
Sower of Seeds, The 180-4
space program 130
Spain, visiting 162
Spanish Civil War 19, 22, 43
Spanish language songs
   Esta Es Mi Tierra 145
   Estadio Chile 102
   Everybody Loves Saturday Night 126
   Feria de Las Flores, La 66
   Guantanamera 128
   Jacob's Ladder (Sp. tr.) 199
   learning songs in 117
   Martillito, El 39
   Paso a Paso (tr. Step by Step) 35
Span, Norman 216
speaking truth to power 170
Spence, Joseph 289
Spider dropping down from twig, The 74
Spider's Web, The 74
spirituals, African-American 123, 206, 287
   I'll Be All Right 32
   Jacob's Ladder 198
   Old Time Religion 136
spiritual, "White"
   Lonesome Valley 134
Spong Jr., William (Virginia senator) 82
Spring Fever 234
Springsteen, Bruce 149
staccato 288
Staines, Bill 213
Stalin, Joseph 19, 22, 121
"Stardust" 230
Starlight, Starbright 75
"Star Spangled Banner, The" 161
"Steal Away" 123
steel drum music 161, 275
Steele, Bill 140
Steendam, Jacob 206
Steinem, Gloria (quote) 237
Stenka Razin (tune) 120
Step by Step 35
Stern, Arthur 29 – see also Almanac Singers
Stewart, Slam 221-3
Still I choke on the smoke of Treblinka 237
Stookey, Noel Paul – see Peter, Paul & Mary
stories
   Abiyoyo 60
   Beethoven Phenomenon 197

Foolish Frog, The 46
miscellaneous brief 248
Seek & Ye Shall Find 184-6
This Old Car 69
Strange Death of John Doe 21
Subway Circuit, The (singing group) 19
Suchow, Paul 248, verse by 75
Suhl, Yuri (Yiddish poet) 191
suicide, song about 104
Sullivan, Mrs. Clara 110-1
"Swanee River" 245
Swan Lake (ballet) 108
Sweepy, Sweepy, Sweepy 48
Sweet-a-Little Baby 53
"Sweet Roseanne" 08
Sweney, John R. 176
swimming 66, 210, 214, 217
"Swimming to the Other Side" 213
swing music 221
"Sylvie" 8
syncopation 59, 77, 287

T
tablature 288-9
Take a Seat Everybody 220
Take It from Dr. King 264
"Take Me Out to the Ball Game" 46
talent, natural 283
talking blues
Dear Mr President 27
Robert Land's original verses 24
Talking Union 23 (ref. 27)
"Taps" 286
Taubb, Rutthy 159
taxes for military purposes 152, 159, 267
Taylor, Bruce (maker of author's guitar) 79
Taylor, Marcia 251
Tchaikovsky, Pyotr 108-9
teachers – see schools
Teacher Uncle Ho 160
Tehanetorens 87
television – see also news media
commercial use of songs 8, 143
destroying tapes of peace rally 157
Dick Cavett Show 130
music video, idea for 253-5
references (lyrics, story) 141, 148, 159, 198
script by author for 75
Smothers Brothers Show 149
source for songs, as 61
Swedish 159
Tell Me That You Love Me, Junie Moon (film) 230
Tell me what were their names 26
Tempest, The (play) 101
tempo 33, 186, 221, 223, see also rhythm
Tennyson, Alfred 74
Terry, Sonny 58, 137
"T for Texas" 12
Theme from "The Goofing-Off Suite" 10
There is a highway from coast to coast 18
There'll Come a Day (excerpt) 213
There's a Hole in the Bucket 127
There's a RR station here at New... 212

There's a shanty in the town 221
There's lots more to marriage 116
These Bones You See (poem) 228
This Broad Old River 214
This Is a Land 206
This Is War (CBS radio broadcast) 28
This Land Is Your Land 142-6 (refs. 85, 89)
"This Machine Kills Fascists" (slogan on Guthrie guitar case) 271
This 'n' That, A Little a' 256
This Old Car 69-70
This song was written some time ago 134
Thomas, Dylan 98
Thoreau, Henry David 174, 227
Three City Four, The (singing group) 67
Throw Away That Shad Net 210
Time and Rivers Flowing, Of 223
Times A-Getting Hard, Boys 76
Times They Are A-Changin' (new v.) 155
"Todos Venceremos" 34
To Everyone in All the World 50
To everything there is a season 173
Tokens, The 91
To Know Good Will (poem) 94
Tomorrow Is a Highway 37
Tomorrow's Children 228
To My Old Brown Earth 247
Top 40 (hit parade) 107
topical songs 110-3
Torn Flag, The (poem) 153
To the storms to come 116
towns, young people leaving small 164
traditional music, royalties for – see public domain reform
traditions, value of 85
trailer trip, Seeger family's 282
Trainer, Ralph 67
translations of songs Ch. 6 (117-46) 178, 187
He Lies in the American Land 118
Everybody Loves Saturday Night 126
This Is a Land 206
Tzena, Tzena 272
When I Was Most Beautiful 96
see also French, German, Hebrew, Spanish, Yiddish
traveling 18, 56, 138, 203, 248, 282
Travers, Mary – see Peter, Paul & Mary
Travis, Helen Levi 22
Treasury of Jewish Folk Song (book) 120
Treblinka (death camp) 191-2, 237
tremolo 122
Trillin, Calvin 258
triplets, musical 288
TRO (The Richmond Organization) 64, 146, 188
Trotsky, Leon 153
Trouble at the Bottom 275
Truman, Harry 19
truth 237
"Tumbalalaika" 120, 236
Turkey 105
Turner, Jeanette 105
Turner, Nat 236
"Turn the World Around" 274
Turn! Turn! Turn! 173 (refs. 13, 282)

"Twinkle, Twinkle, Little Star" 99, 119, 173, 286
Two Against Three: A Rhythm Skill 156
Two million bushels of North African... 95
Tzena, Tzena 268-70 (ref. 43)

U
Ukraine 122
Uncle Ho, Teacher 160
unemployment 20, 68
unions Ch. 2: Politics, Unions (17-44)
author's membership in 12
Ballad of Harry Bridges 25
British General Strike of 1926 98
Coal Miners Strike of 1932 13, 18, 282
Communist Party USA's role in 12, 25, 27
Deliver the Goods 28
Hays, Lee's teaching at labor school 94
Lonesome Valley (Guthrie v.) 134
Mrs. Clara Sullivan's Letter 110
Reynolds, Bud, as UAW organizer 107
Rockin' Solidarity 250
role re We Shall Overcome 32, 34
singing for 8, 17, 43, 147, 227
songs about (other) 63, 236
Step by Step 35
Talking Union 23
"Union Maid" 8, 85, 123
union printer for this book 72
Unitarian Universalist Church 12
United Mineworkers Union 32
United Nations 32
unity 33-7, 144, 214, 238, 261
see also peace, unions
Unorthodoxology, The (**Old Hundred**) 194
Up and away like the dew of the... 176
USSR – see Soviet Union
utopian communities 119, 238

V
Vallee, Rudy 17
Vann, John Paul (general) 166
Van Ronk, Dave 138
Variety (magazine) 82
Versos Sencillos (**Guantanamera**) 128-9
vibrato 192
Vietnam Ch. 7 (147-66) 8, 130
Village Vanguard, The (club) 43
Village Voice (newspaper) 146
violence 82, 162, 261, 264
Visions of Children 123
"Volga Boatmen" 285
Voltaire 248
vowel sounds in songs 89, 186
see also consonants

W
Wade, Marion 230
Waist Deep in the Big Muddy 150
Walden, Eleanor 246
Wales 98, 187
Walkabout Chorus 191, 223-4, 267
Walking Down Death Row 238
Walkman revolution 84
Wallace, George 151

Wallace, Henry 35
Wallach, Kim 152
Wall Street Crash of 1929 278, 282
war – see also peace, Revolutionary War,
    World War I & II, Vietnam
    crimes 158-9
    deaths in 21-2, 106, 152-3, 166
    taxes 152, 159
Warner, Frank 45
Washington DC 144
Watergate scandal 254
"Water" 62
Water Is Wide, The 134
Waters, James 105-6
Waters, Muddy 76
Way down south in the yankety yank 46
We are climbing Jacob's Ladder 199
We are five thousand 102
Weatherford, Jack 88
Weavers, The 27, 35-43, 45, 128, 188, 218
    author's main role in 37
    commercial success of (1950) 64
    Everybody Loves Sat. Night 125-6
    Here We Are in Madison Square
        Garden 43
    If I Had a Hammer 38-42
    Kisses Sweeter than Wine 64
    Mbube (Wimoweh) 90-2
    photos 37, 125
    Tzena, Tzena 269
    We Wish You a Merry Christmas 189
    Whole Wide World Around 192
    see also Lee Hays, Fred Hellerman
Weber, Sol 276
website (www.peteseeger.net) 7-8
weddings 120, 123, see also love, marriage
    author's 32, 68, 226
    Here's to the Couple 124
Wein, George 76, 90
Weir, R. Stanley 131
Weiss, Cora (peace activist) 156
Weiss, George 91
We'll All Be A-Doubling 207 (ref. 5)
Well it rained all night & I'm feelin'... 222
Well it's C for conscription 12
Well it's hey! Clearwater! 218
Well May the World Go 248
Wells, H.G. 8, 184
Well they got old Reuben down 235
We'll work together 123
Well you know it was 216
Welsh, Dave 250
We say he's innocent 262
We Shall Overcome 32-5
Wesley, John 194
West Africa 125, 180, 180-3
West, Don 123
Western Pacific islanders 214
We will love or we will perish 191
"We Will Overcome Someday" 32
We Wish You a Merry Christmas 189
"Wheels on the Bus, The" 56
When I think of the ways that I've grown 280
When I was a young man & never... 64
When I Was Most Beautiful 96-8

When my songs turn to ashes 151
When something in my history is... 258
When the fun, the fun is all over 137
When the union's inspiration 250
Where Have All the Flowers Gone 166-69
    (refs. 13, 117, 176)
Where Lagan stream sings lullaby 87
Where's My Pajamas? 54
whistling 46, 98, 161, 253, 286
    Living in the Country 79
    Whistling Past a Graveyard 253
"White Christmas" 284
White, E.B. & Katherine 74
Whitehead, Alfred North 130 (quote), 184
White, Josh, Sr. 22
White, Josh, Jr. 266
White House, The 19
Whitman, Walt 95
Who'd Believe I'd Feel So Good 81
Who Fears to Speak of '98 (tune) 81
Who Killed Norma Jean? 104
Whole Wide World Around, The 192
Why Do You Stand There in the Rain 19-20
Wilcox, Jean 144
"Wildwood Flower" 86
Williams, Dar 67
Williams, Earl Jr. 153
Williamson, Cris 172
Williams, Rev. H.C.N. 124
Wingerter, Linda 52
Wimoweh **(Mbube)** 90-2
Wind on the Water (excerpt) 213
Winston, George 77
Winter, Paul 123, 180-3, 220
Wizard of Oz (film) 277
"Woman Tawry Lang" 15
women's movement – see gender issues
Wonderful Friends 280
Woodstock (film) 166
Woody Guthrie Trust Fund 144
"Woody's Rag" 249
Words, Words, Words 174
World International Property Organization
    (WIPO) 61
World War I 19, 153 (poem re), 160, 245,
    282
World War II Ch. 2 (19-32)
    Aircraft Mechanic Song 31
    author's military service in 18, 31-2
    Ballad of October 16th 19
    C for Conscription 12
    Communist Party's position on 22, 26
    Dear Mr. President 27
    Deliver the Goods 28
    Franklin D 22
    I Come and Stand at Every Door 106
    Last Train to Nuremburg 159
    Lisa Kalvelage 158
    Plow Under 22
    Reuben James 26
    "Shtille Di Nacht" 236
    Strange Death of John Doe 19
    When I Was Most Beautiful 96
    Guthrie, Woody and 226, 271
    see also Hitler, Holocaust

WPA Music Project 84
Wreck of the John B. (tune) 56, ref. 287
writing books 238
Wyatt, Lorre 132-3, 213, 255, 280

Y
Yankee Doodle (excerpt) 284, ref. 68
Yankety Yank, The **(The Foolish Frog)** 46
Yarrow, Peter – see Peter, Paul & Mary
Yes this is me, old stick-in-the-mud 155
Yiddish 43, 126 (verse), 185, 236, 278
    Djankoye 121
    Embers of the Martyrs (tr. from) 237
yodeling 252
Yoruba 126
You can't keep this world from... 236
You'd Be So Nice to Come Home To (tune)
    130
You have been directed to look... 175
You have heard of the pilot so daring 31
You know it was 20 years ago 216
You know this language that we speak 14
You'll Sing to Me Too 55
You might be rich as cream 236
Young, Joe 221
Young Communist League 18
"Young Man Who Wouldn't Hoe Corn, The"
    21
You're one of us now, Johann 191

Z
Zeina, Zeina (Arabic tr. Tzena) 270
Zhankoye **(Djankoye)** 121
zipper songs 54, 62
Zulu, song in 90

Cover Illustration Key:

BACK COVER   SPINE   FRONT COVER

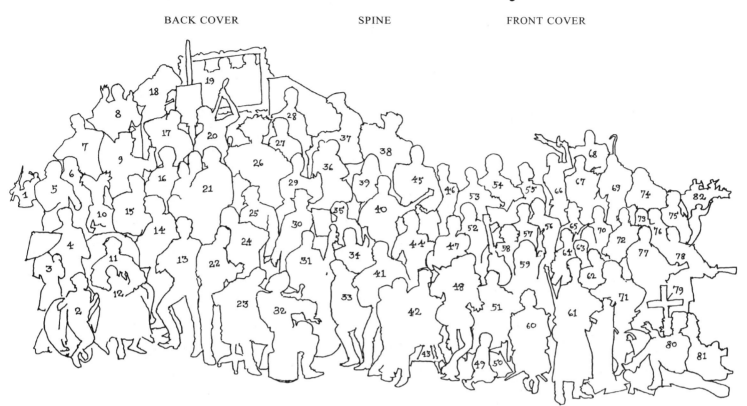

1. Waist Deep In The Big Muddy
2. Skip-a-Rope
3. Vietnamese Woman & Baby
4. José Marti
5. Paul Winter
6. Keita Fodeba
7. Oscar Brand
8. Calixa Lavallée
9. Solomon Linda
10. African Dancer
11. Old Granny
12. Grandbaby
13. Mike Seeger
14. Bob Killian
15. Charlie King
16. Lorre Wyatt
17. Ewan MacColl
18. Joni Mitchell
19. The Byrds
20. Peggy Seeger
21. Victor Jara & Family
22. Joe Hickerson
23. Moses Asch
24. Johannes Brahms
25. Bartolemeo Vanzetti
26. Lord Invader
27. Lisa Kalvelage
28. Cole Porter
29. Ruth Rubin
30. Nicola Sacco
31. "Slam" Stewart
32. "Slim" Gaillard
33. Irving Berlin
34. Sonny Terry
35. Noriko Ibaragi
36. John Jacob Niles
37. LeRoy Carr
38. John Fogerty
39. Buffy Sainte-Marie
40. Ernie Marrs
41. Brownie McGhee
42. E.B. White & Friends
43. Charlotte & her Web
44. Zilphia Horton
45. Paul Robeson
46. Ho Chi Minh
47. Malvina Reynolds
48. William Shakespeare
49. Tinya Seeger
50. Model of the "Clearwater"
51. Toshi Seeger
52. Bernice Johnson Reagon
53. Jewish Prisoners at Treblinka
54. Johann Sebastian Bach
55. Marlene Dietrich
56. Alan Lomax
57. Charles Seeger
58. John Lennon
59. Yoko Ono
60. Rachel Carson
61. Pete Seeger
62. Lee Hays
63. Ronnie Gilbert
64. Fred Hellerman
65. John A. Lomax
66. Blacksmith
67. Slave
68. Rev. Charles Tindley
69. Ecclesiastes
70. Henry Crowdog
71. Ludwig van Beethoven
72. Noel "Paul" Stookey
73. Mary Travers
74. Welsh Coal Miner
75. Aunt Molly Jackson
76. Peter Yarrow
77. Blind Lemon Jefferson
78. Huddie Ledbetter
79. A.N. Onymous
80. Woody Guthrie
81. Arlo Guthrie
82. Cossack Soldiers singing "Where Have All The Flowers Gone"

Notes

A few words about the accompanying Data CD:

On the attached CD, you'll find CD-quality audio files (MP3s) with excerpts for most of the songs and music in the book. Each is coded with a number that coincides with a letter/number combination that matches up with the links included throughout the book. These files can be easily loaded into any computer audio program (like iTunes), and then played from your computer or loaded on a portable MP3 player. (Each of the files includes metadata for the song title, artist and source for the original recording where applicable that will display when the track is playing.) We have also coded the files so that you can easily create three standard audio CDs (A, B & C), and then use any standard CD player to access and play the excerpts. The data disc itself is also compatible with any CD player that is MP3 compatible.

All this is should be very straightforward, but if you have any questions or problems, don't hesitate to contact us at: editor@singout.org or 610-865-5366. Enjoy!